WHAT WENT RIGHT IN THE 1980s

Richard B. McKenzie

Pacific Research Institute for Public Policy
San Francisco, California

Printed in the United States of America
10   9   8   7   6   5   4   3   2   1

Library of Congress Cataloging-in-Publication Data
McKenzie, Richard B.
What went right in the 1980s / Richard B. McKenzie.
p. cm.
Includes index.
ISBN 0-936488-71-9
1. United States—Economic conditions—1981 2. Economic indicators—United States. I. Title.
HC106.8.M364 199393-7236
330.973'0927—dc20CIP

Director of Publications *Kay Mikel*
Cover Design *Irene Imfeld Graphic Design*
Index *Shirley Kessel*
Cover Illustration *Jim Pearson Illustrations*
Interior Illustrations *Chris Lippert*
Printing and Binding *Data Reproductions Corporation*

WHAT WENT RIGHT IN THE 1980s

CONTENTS

PREFACE

William Jefferson Clinton rode into the White House on the back of the 1980s. All through 1992, he had, at practically every campaign stop, replayed his favorite theme: The 1980s was a dismal decade, one of economic decline and decay if not downright economic despair.[1]

In Clinton's view and the view of many of his economic advisers, the 1980s was a lost decade, one in which class warfare ruled the land. They decry the rich, practically all of whom they characterize as having the moral fiber of common criminals, for having become richer by preying on the incomes of the middle and lower classes.

Of course, they lay the wanton economic destruction of the decade—however described and whether revealed by measures of growth, trade, debt, taxes, or income distribution—in the lap of one man, Ronald Reagan. His policies, they claim, were organized for the sole purpose of aiding and abetting the unchecked economic powers of the rich, a group that, supposedly, was becoming ever more privileged and isolated from the masses. In summary, the 1980s were a decade of Big Ds—Decline, Decay, busted Dreams, Debt, Destitution, re-Distribution, and Despair. The economic decline was all being fueled by one Big G—unchecked Greed. The mindless economic funeral march was being led by the very Big R—Reagan.

Since taking office, Clinton has not let the decade die. In the 1993 description of his *Vision for Change*, he writes, "For more than a decade, our government has been caught in the grip of the failed policy of trickle-down economics. While the rich get richer, middle-class Americans pay more taxes to their government and get less in return.[2] His first major economic policy report charges,

In recent years, our leaders...embraced trickle-down policies that benefited the wealthy at the expense of the middle class and the working poor.... While the privileged few have prospered, millions of Americans who worked hard and played by the rules have been

left behind.... Greed and financial scheming have eclipsed the virtues of hard work and sacrifice for the common good. Debt has soared as individuals, businesses, and governments have lived beyond their means. Our commitment to invest in the future and to bequeath a promising future to our children has somehow fallen by the wayside.[3]

Later, his report adds, "Twelve years of neglect have left America's economy suffering from stagnant growth and declining incomes.[4]

Never mind that the national economy expanded during the 1980s by close to a third and that industrial production expanded by even more. Never mind that the incomes of many low-income Americans rose more rapidly than did the incomes of many rich Americans. Never mind that at the end of the decade Americans remained the wealthiest nation on earth. Never mind that the stock market more than tripled during the decade and that charity soared at unprecedented rates. Never mind the facts. The facts have never troubled those who began dumping on the decade in the early 1980s and never stopped their dumping when their dismal forecasts failed to come true.

Having badly caricatured the 1980s as practically the worst—if not the worst—decade in the country's history, Clinton now proclaims a need for dramatic change in government policies; mainly, he advocates more spending and higher taxes (a policy course that actually appears to be more of the same). Moreover, he maintains that his election was a mandate for him to orchestrate whatever change he declares is suitable and that he and his small band of advisers, given enough time and resources, can solve the problems of every one of the 250 million Americans.

If I were to swallow—hook, line, and sinker (as many have)—the full scope of the critics' dismal economic assessment of the 1980s, I might quickly concur with Clinton and other critics (in and out of government and academia) that changes—even dramatic changes—were needed in government policies. Almost any change then would have been likely to improve economic circumstances for many

Americans. However, the decade of the 1980s, as it is scrutinized in this book, did not live down to its widely reported dreadful billing.

The decade of the 1980s was not the best of times in America, but neither was it the worst. Certainly, some things went wrong, but many other unheralded things went right. The country had problems that varied in scope, many social and some economic in nature. To be sure, the country could have done better economically. The federal government—meaning the combined efforts of Congress, the presidency, and the bureaucracy—could have been more helpful and less destructive in the pursuit of the "common good." But, the same could be said of the powers that be in practically every decade.

Critics of the 1980s do have some of their facts correct, but, by the same token, they have grossly exaggerated the country's problems during the era. In many cases, their assessments of economic facts are downright wrong, though perhaps well intended. Their errant assessments may have been concocted to support their view of how the world should work if their policy agendas were not adopted (which they were not). In retrospect, many critics of the 1980s clearly appear to have been more interested in scoring political points on op-ed pages of the country's major newspapers and in voting booths than in accurately describing, in an even-handed manner, what actually happened during the decade, that is, significant economic renewal.

Given that this book does take an even-handed, albeit atypical, viewpoint regarding the U.S. economy during the 1980s, many may still presume that I intended, in writing it, to defend Ronald Reagan and his Republican administration. Nothing could be further from the truth. I refuse to be a political partisan. I am much more concerned with policies than with party labels. It is my intent to set much of the economic record straight by describing, in considerable detail, what actually happened in the 1980s, not so much why it happened nor how policies could have been better designed. My emphasis is, I am quick to admit, on what went right—or on what did not go wrong. I do that for the simple purpose of balancing the debate.

If the reader begins to see the record of the eight years that Ronald Reagan was in office in a more positive light, so be it. I neither credit nor blame Ronald Reagan for the country's economic successes and failures during the decade as much as others do.

To date, no president has ever been as powerful as the critics of the 1980s charge that Reagan was. If the critics are to be believed, Reagan not only altered the course of government policies but fundamentally warped human nature and led 250 million Americans to their economic ruin (solely by his skills as the Great Communicator, which, for many critics, became a none-too-subtle form of damnation with very faint and superficial praise). A little thought on the matter would correct that presumption. The presidency has significant political and economic power—but so does Congress and the bureaucracy. In addition, I am a firm believer in the view that most good things that happen in the country are the consequence of the well-intended and imaginative, largely uncoordinated efforts of hard-working Americans, rich and poor alike, who seek to improve their own lot in life and the lots of their families and fellow Americans.

That is not to say that government policies are inconsequential but that their importance has been grossly overstated by those who ply their trades in Washington. In my view, the tax rate cuts and other market-based policies adopted in the 1980s were the direct result of the combined efforts of Democrats and Republicans, of the White House and of Capitol Hill. Those policies had far less beneficial effects than Reagan's supporters have been willing to acknowledge, and they had far more beneficial effects than Reagan's critics have been willing to concede. [The economy would have realized even more positive effects if Americans could had felt confident that they would not be taxed more heavily at some future point in time (1993?) simply because they responded in the 1980s to the then lower tax rates.] Finally, I am inclined to believe that the federal policies pursued in the 1980s were imposed on American politics by global economic, competitive forces. In my view, it is far more accurate to say that policies adopted during the Reagan era were more the product of the times than the times were a product of the Reagan policies.

In short, contrary to what is argued or just implied by critics, the economic record of the 1980s should not be used as a rationale for reclaiming the failed policy courses of the past.

Furthermore, despite the recession in the early 1990s and the subsequent slow recovery, I remain optimistic about the future of the American (and world) economy. My optimism is grounded in what I believe is a realistic assessment of the 1980s: On balance, things were pretty good—in spite of (partly because of) the global technological and structural revolution under way during the decade. The country now has substantially more wealth—embodied in both physical and human capital—than it had at the start of the 1980s, partly because of the economic successes of the 1980s. Most Americans learned—at times, grudgingly—an extraordinarily important lesson during that decade: We all have to compete on a global scale, and we all must work very hard and "work smart" to do that. Those Americans who resisted the lesson will, simply put, have to play catch-up. The opening up and integration of world markets in the 1980s will surely yield new and exciting opportunities in the 1990s and will, at the same time, impose abiding constraints on the fiscal and regulatory powers of governments. Governments must now understand that much capital—human and physical—is fluid and footloose and that it will flow away from countries where it is mistreated.[6] In spite of their professed preferences, domestic politicians are no longer free to respond to domestic redistributive political forces without serious economic consequences; as never before, they must heed global economic forces.

The Cold War was won in the 1980s—and not by foes of American capitalism (a patently obvious fact that escapes the attention of critics). The country is poised to accomplish, for the first time in more than half a century, what remained, even in the mid-1980s, a pipe dream: to literally turn swords into plows (or, more likely, to computer chips and software). That process will not be without economic hardship, but it will, in the end, yield the long-awaited "peace dividends" for Americans.

A lot of good ideas were translated into new products and services and made their way into world markets during the 1980s. My optimism is fueled, however, by the knowledge that not all the good ideas were discovered, exploited, and exhausted back then. Indeed, the good ideas of the 1980s have spawned and will continue to spawn their successors. What's more, practically all of these good ideas will emanate from the American hinterlands, not from Washington.

I remain convinced that historians of the future will treat the 1980s far more generously than the critics who lived it have treated the decade.

Preface Notes

1. See Bill Clinton and Al Gore, *Putting People First: How We Can All Change America* (New York: Times Books, 1992).

2. William J. Clinton, *A Vision of Change for America* (Washington, DC: U.S. Government Printing Office, February 17, 1993).

3. Ibid., p. 1.

4. Ibid., p. 5.

5. See Richard B. McKenzie and Dwight R. Lee, *Quicksilver Capital: How the Rapid Movement of Wealth Has Changed the World* (New York: Free Press, 1991).

6. For more details on this theme, see McKenzie and Lee, *Quicksilver Capital.*

ACKNOWLEDGMENTS

This book developed over the course of five years. It began as a series of individual policy studies undertaken mainly for the Center for the Study of American Business at Washington University in St. Louis. When I started, it was my impression that many of the policy claims made by critics throughout the 1980s did not describe the America I knew. I wanted to test the impressions I had honed while living and working in South Carolina, Missouri, Mississippi, and California, far removed from Washington and the elite academic centers of the Northeast (where the dismal assessments appear to have their origins). What I found was that almost all the major claims made during the 1980s that economic calamity was pending were, if I put it generously, off base. That is, they were totally out of step with the data at hand. Accordingly, I leave few critics and criticisms unchallenged. I do so in the spirit of lending much-needed balance to the debate, not with the intentions of saying that all debates about the decade can be, or have been, settled here.

I had a great deal of help in developing the book. My colleagues at the Center for the Study of American Business—Murray Weidenbaum, Kenneth Chilton, Melinda Warren, and Ronald Cook—provided an immeasurable amount of help, both in content and style of the studies that form the basis of this book. My best friend and coauthor on other projects, Dwight Lee, read most of the manuscript carefully and was a continuing critic of everything that was written. I was able to refine many points because of good natured and fruitful discussions with my colleague Judy Rosener, who remains skeptical of my positions. I benefited from the insights of Steve Hayward at the Pacific Research Institute, who read the final draft and offered many suggestions for improvement. William Shughart, my colleague while I was at the University of Mississippi, and I coauthored a paper on the federal debt on which chapter 9 is based; I want to fully acknowledge his contribution to that chapter and to extend my appreciation to him for allowing me to draw on our joint work.

Greta Brooks, Karen McKenzie, and Kay Mikel provided editorial guidance on the individual studies and the final book manuscript. My research assistants, Christina Klein, Aliue Mack, and Lynda Ly, were a big help. I am deeply indebted to everyone mentioned, plus many others who offered comments and criticisms on individual papers and at speeches and conferences. These have greatly improved the final manuscript.

Finally, the John M. Olin Foundation and the Lynde and Harry Bradley Foundation provided grants that covered my summer work on the book. Their continuing support has been extraordinarily important to completion of this project.

Richard B. McKenzie
Irvine, California
July 1993

DEDICATION

To Larry Keeter

Although he may not know it, Larry Keeter, a former colleague and
abiding friend (who will take issue with much that is written here)
has helped me understand the minds of those who find fault with
the 1980s at every statistical turn. For more than twenty years he and
I have disagreed, but always in the best of spirits and with the best
of intentions. For that reason, I am pleased to dedicate this book to
him.

1

REALITY IS TRICKY

The reality of the American economy during the 1980s stands in sharp contrast to the rhetoric. While the 1980s failed to match the fondest dreams and hopes of most Americans for economic gain, it was still the most prosperous decade in American history. That means that the vast majority of Americans lived at a higher standard of living than they, or anyone else, ever had before, anywhere on the globe. The 1980s gave birth to the second longest peacetime economic recovery in the United States since World War II, yet in the minds of many Americans, the 1980s were the antithesis of economic renewal. Like the 1920s, the decade of the 1980s was one of decadence. Like the 1930s, it was a period of pervasive economic retreat, of widespread retrogression for the country and the vast majority of its citizens—or so we have been told and then reminded repeatedly.

Unlike the 1960s, many policy commentators have claimed that in the 1980s the competitive position of both U.S. firms and U.S. workers was beaten back everywhere, at home and abroad. The decade gave birth to a new form of robber baron—Wall Street financiers, dubbed "paper entrepreneurs," whose newfound wealth detracted from national production and, at the same time, gave rise to impoverishment of the poor and (more importantly in the rhetoric of politicians) to impoverishment of practically all of the middle class. In the minds of many policy commentators, the economic reality of the 1980s was one of pervasive and deep-seated rot, aided and abetted by a government tax policy designed to pad the pockets of the rich.

At the turn of the 1990s, many of these same critics could be heard breathing a sigh of relief in the fondest hope that the 1990s would be radically different. Their hopes appeared to be greatly buoyed by the fact that Ronald Reagan, whom they blamed for almost everything that went wrong in the 1980s, would no longer be in command. With anyone else in the White House, the country could, just possibly, become a "kinder, gentler America," as well as a more productive and aggressive competitor.

The Rhetoric of Economic Decay

But still, pessimism about the future persisted. After surveying the wanton destruction of property values and other social and economic problems existing in late 1991, Robert Kuttner, a nationally syndicated columnist and ardent opponent of the Reagan/Bush administrations observed, "The supply-side turkey has finally come home to roost."[1] *Washington Post* columnist Hobart Rowen added in early 1992, "American citizens have been battered by almost daily evidence that good jobs are disappearing in manufacturing industries—jobs that are likely to be lost forever as companies that once were the pacesetters in their fields hunker down for an indefinite period."[2]

John Kenneth Galbraith, the venerable Harvard economics professor (emeritus), could not resist laying the blame for the recession that began in 1990 on the perverse behavior of many Americans, especially business and finance leaders, and on the policies followed by the Republicans in the White House during the decade. In "The Economic Hangover from a Binge of Greed," a title that by itself crystallizes the central premise of the underlying theory, Galbraith wrote that it is time to cut through the excuses: "The present recession is not an autonomous, self-correcting economic drama. It is the wholly predictable response to the speculative extravagances and insanities—and specific government policies—of the 1980s."[3] Never mind that the recovery had already begun as his words appeared in print, the country's continuing problems could be blamed, or so Galbraith and many other commentators surmised, on a simple five-letter word—Greed—which supposedly flourished as never before during the 1980s.

Political commentator Kevin Phillips, whose book *The Politics of Rich and Poor* was published as the decade came to a close and sold millions, condemned the decade for the wanton accumulation of wealth that was explicitly and intentionally aided and abetted by partisan politics: "The 1980s were the triumph of upper America—an ostentatious celebration of wealth, the political ascendancy of the richest third of the population, and the glorification of capitalism, free markets and finance. But while the money, greed and luxury had become the stuff of popular culture, hardly anyone asked why such great wealth had concentrated at the top, and whether this was the result of public policy."[4] Phillips' answer was direct: It was the fault of Republican policy that had historically sought to fortify the wealth of the wealthy whenever they gained the reins of power.

When Senator Lloyd Bentsen accepted the Democratic nomination for vice president in 1988, he parroted a favored political stance of the year, perhaps reflecting the mood of many Americans, partisans and independents alike: "My friends, America has just passed through the ultimate epoch of illusion: An eight-year coma in which slogans were confused with solutions, and rhetoric passed for reality; a time when America tried to borrow its way to prosperity and became the largest debtor nation in the history of mankind." And then he added, "At long last, the epoch of illusion is drawing to a close."[5] President Bill Clinton, of course, rode into office on the claim that everything that went wrong in the 1980s was the fault of the Republicans and of "trickle-down economics," which he defined as seeking to help lower- and middle-income Americans by making federal policy work for the rich, a policy Ronald Reagan and George Bush both pursued.

Senator Bentsen's and President Clinton's sentiments might be dismissed as political puffery, designed more to stir emotion and arouse the partisan troops for the political fracas that would shortly be enjoined rather than as an accurate portrayal of the facts and events of the 1980s. However, in an expanding library of books released in the late 1980s and early 1990s, a number of highly respected and widely read university scholars and public policy commentators took no less charitable views of the 1980s than did the political operatives. Although the critics did not always agree on the nature of the problem—the key one being whether America's living standard had been artificially depressed or propped up by past policies—they were nevertheless in accord on the fact that a very serious problem existed. Indeed, the country was beset with an array of problems. Deindustrialization, an excessive federal deficit, an unrealistic private debt load, an aging population, mounting trade deficits, diversion of resources from manufacturing to services (or from high- to low-wage jobs), shrinking union representation, declining wages and family incomes, growing inequality among households and families, deteriorating infrastructure, fading travel bargains and safety (especially in airlines, which were deregulated in 1978), vanishing educational opportunities, and international trade imbalances—all were on most people's short lists of the country's mounting difficulties.

Reflecting the best wisdom of many intellectuals, in 1988 Harvard Professor Benjamin Friedman maintained that there would soon be a "day of reckoning." Why? "Since 1980 we have broken with that tradition [that our children would inherit a better world] by pursuing a policy that amounts to living not just in, but for, the present. We are living well by running up our debt and selling off our assets. America had thrown itself a party and billed the tab to the future."[6] The source of the problem? The quick answer given is easy: The tax and spending policies of the Reagan years that have "rendered every citizen a borrower and every industry a liquidator of assets."[7] Even conservative policy proponent James Dale Davidson, who headed the National Taxpayers Union, agreed but was less optimistic. During the 1990s there would be a "great reckoning," an economic debacle possibly on par with the Great Depression that could be traced to public policies pursued in the 1980s and before.[8]

Friedman's Harvard colleague Robert Reich, one of Clinton's top economic advisers, agreed that Reagan followed the wrong policies but disagreed that all Americans had progressed to higher and higher life-styles during the 1980s: "Between 1978 and 1987, the poorest fifth of American families became eight percent poorer, and the richest fifth became 13 percent richer. That leaves the poorest fifth with less than five percent of the nation's income, and the richest fifth with more than 40 percent."[9] The problem was not the accumulating federal debt; it was the failure of the government to spend more on social programs, especially job training and infrastructure.

Boston-based economists Bennett Harrison and Barry Bluestone remained convinced throughout the 1980s that the country was rapidly "deindustrializing," a fate that was undermining worker bargaining power and giving rise to a "great U-turn" in worker wages.[10] They were concerned that good American jobs were being exported to low-wage countries through "capital flight," aided and abetted by the Reagan administration's free trade policies. By firing tens of thousands of controllers who went on strike in 1981, Ronald Reagan unleashed powerful business opposition to unions, the source of what Harrison and Bluestone consider to have been the disturbing loss of union power in the economy.

M.I.T. Professor Paul Krugman argued in his book that the country had entered an "age of diminished expectations." "The 1980s was the first decade since the 1930s in which large numbers of Americans actually suffered a serious decline in living standards."[11] He attributed the growing income inequality to a major source, finance. "The 1980s," Krugman wrote, "was a golden age for financial wheeling and dealing, and the explosion of profits in financial operations has helped swell the ranks of the really rich—those earning hundreds of thousands or even millions a year."[12]

The Reality of Economic Renewal

The vision many people now harbor of the "go-go" yet dreadful 1980s emerged from a continuing flow of economic pronouncements almost all of which described the sorry state of the American economy that would, regrettably, only get worse—unless its domestic policy course were redirected, if not reversed. Such an overhaul, its advocates maintained, would necessitate greater government expenditures on social programs and more aid and protection for industries and their workers as they sought to cope with changing world circumstances. The policy cry became one of "tit for tat," with the industrial policies of "Japan, Inc." and "Germany, Inc." being confronted with a similarly aggressive agenda of reforms in this country under the banner of "U.S.A., Inc."

In spite of the foreboding prophecies, the recommended policy agenda was, for the most part, spurned throughout the 1980s by Democrats in Congress and Republicans in the White House. Nevertheless, the policy chant continues in the 1990s with even more threatening assessments of the country's economic state and its likely dismal future. Before the recommended reform agenda, articulated under the rubric of a "new industrial policy" (and now discussed under the banner of a "new technology policy"), is seriously considered again as a remedy for the presumed "American disease," the rhetoric of economic destruction, decadence, and decline must be evaluated in the dim light of the claims made during the decade *and* in the bright light of the realities of the evolving economic conditions in the country.

The 1980s was hardly a decade of wanton destruction, decadence, and decline. On the contrary, sober consideration of the details of what actually happened shows that the 1980s was "none of the above." More accurately, the decade of the 1980s was, generally speaking, one of renewed industrial competitiveness. The evidence indicates that the country did not "deindustrialize"; it "re-industrialized." As opposed to going through a great U-turn in incomes, the data reveal that the vast majority of Americans encountered modest, albeit somewhat disappointing, growth in incomes. And many rich people as well as many poor people made substantial economic gains, while others faced significant economic hardship, reflecting conflicting income forces that have been at work through the millennium. By the end of the decade, the rich were assuming a greater share of the country's tax burden than they had at the start of the decade, meaning that the poor were assuming a lesser share of the burden.

As opposed to production declining relative to the rest of the world, which much of the public has been convinced was the case, the U.S. held its own. As opposed to becoming self-indulgent and obsessed with the so-called social theology of "me-ism" on a broad scale, the evidence reveals that Americans increased their charitable giving at an unprecedented rate. As opposed to flying higher-priced, more risky flights, Americans were doing just the opposite, flocking to airports to take advantage of discount fares on flights that were significantly less likely to have accidents.

In general, the U.S. did not fare too badly during the decade, thank you.

Political Rhetoric and Stock Market Gains

During the 1980s, the stock market marched relentlessly upward during the economic expansion, with market indexes tripling between 1980 and 1990—a feat unmatched in the previous three decades. Yet in the 1980s, the Chickens Little of policy circles continued their unrelenting chant: The economic skies are falling; the economic skies are falling. Now, with the onset of the 1990s, they continue to warn that unless the country eschews the free market economic policies of the Reagan era, the economic downfall of America will continue unchecked.

Something is amiss. Either Chicken Little was wrong, or the millions of people operating in the stock market had indeed gone bonkers. As we have seen, Chicken Little chose the latter: Americans had suffered through an era of self-delusion; the market reflected nothing more than unchecked speculation fueled by greed and the accumulation of debt. But could the millions of market operatives be aware of an underlying economic reality that the Chickens Little of the country refused to acknowledge?

In retrospect, the facts undercut the critics' claims. As opposed to stagnating, the country's gross domestic product rose by close to a third. The increase in output had the effect of taking the 1980 output of all states and then adding again the output of sixteen large and small states in the Northeast and Midwest: Maine, New Hampshire, Vermont, Massachusetts, Rhode Island, Connecticut, New York, New Jersey, Pennsylvania, Minnesota, Iowa, Missouri, North Dakota, South Dakota, Nebraska, and Kansas. Granted, economic growth in the 1980s did not set post-World War II records, but the substantial increase stands in stark contrast to the claims of decline. Moreover, the observed growth in the 1980s would probably have been substantially greater if the economy had not had to be throttled at the start of the decade by drastic anti-inflation policies that had to be pursued, given the double-digit inflation and interest rates common in the late 1970s.

The Chickens Little have harped relentlessly on the country's lost competitiveness vis-à-vis Japan and Germany. They don't seem to realize that the growth in U.S. output during the 1980s was the equivalent of adding the entire economy of Germany (East and West) or two-thirds of the Japanese economy to the U.S. economy.

As I will show, the country's growth in output was not all in services and at the expense of manufacturing. Industrial production rose more rapidly than the economy as a whole. Manufacturing output represented a slightly higher percentage of the country's total output at the start of the 1990s than it did at the start of the 1980s or, for that matter, at the start of any other post-war decade. More than a million manufacturing jobs were lost during the decade, but only because productivity in many manufacturing industries grew at record rates, reflecting the growing competitiveness of many U.S. firms. If American manufacturing firms had not trimmed their work forces, it is almost certain that the gloomy predictions of the critics would have come true, and manufacturing would surely have declined as a share of total domestic production.

Ah, but it was all motivated by "greed." Maybe so for small bands of stockbrokers and S & L bankers, but along the way many Americans became substantially more charitable during the 1980s. The growth rate of charitable giving roared past the rates of previous decades.

Surely the rich got richer, and the poor, poorer. Well, the rich did get richer during the 1980s. The poverty count (especially among children) did rise for a time during the decade at the same time that the number of millionaires, decimillionaires, and billionaires in the country jumped skyward. But those widely reported statistics do not tell the whole story. Contrary to conventional wisdom, there were slightly fewer poor people in 1989 (the last year of Ronald Reagan's presidency and prior to the advent of the recession) than there were in 1981 (the first year of the Reagan presidency). The poor as a group also got richer, some actually became millionaires. Indeed, according to one study that tracked the success of the rich and the poor during much of the 1980s, the poor may have, on average, increased their incomes by far more than the rich did. Certainly, the poor as a group were never as poor as the critics made them out to be, or they would not have been able to continue throughout the 1980s to spend two to three times their incomes.

The critics did have some of the facts right. The 1980s was a decade of debt for the federal government. The folks in Washington nearly tripled the amount owed by the federal government despite the fact that real tax revenues continued to rise almost year-to-year. And the critics may be right that the accumulation of debt was intended to choke off Congressional discretion. However, as you will see, they failed to recognize many of the benefits of the accumulating debt, not the least of which is that government expenditures as a share of the economy stagnated during the decade.

Moreover, the critics were wrong to conclude that the marked rise of private debt reflected wanton ways of a whole generation of Americans intent on doing nothing more constructive than consuming now at the expense of a more profitable and secure future. If it is assumed (as the critics did implicitly if not explicitly) that the country's wealth is decaying, then any additional debt might be viewed as an added burden. However, the facts reveal that (measurable) real wealth rose by as much as a fifth. Hence, much of the rise in the country's debt could be justified by the rising wealth. A lot of people went bankrupt during the decade, as has always been the case, but a lot of people took out loans to do a lot of productive things. Indeed, it's probable that the growth in output, wealth, and net worth would not have been so great if Americans had not gone on what has been glibly and mistakenly characterized as a "debt binge." Much of the debt growth during the 1980s can be attributed to inflation and to the significant drop in the U.S. aggregate debt-to-asset ratio in the 1970s.

The predictions of gloom and doom repeated in various forms throughout the 1980s can now be evaluated in light of the economic record of the decade. Fortunately, the events of the 1980s have proven the Chickens Little wrong—again.

The Politics of Recession

Regrettably, the decade of the 1980s ended the way it began, with a recession. That recession, which at this writing had been transformed into a viable but weak recovery, was not particularly important from an economic perspective but was very important from a political perspective. Ominously, it gave new life to the Chickens Little—who continue to be taken seriously by many of our Washington leaders, and who continue to distort the economic record of the 1980s, and who continue to predict that in the 1990s the country will follow its long-charted path of decline.

Fortunately, the millions of investors in the stock market continued to look at the economic record, dismissing much of the rhetoric. The stock market has continued to march upward, albeit irregularly. In mid-1993, the Dow Jones average was reaching new peaks above 3500, more than four times the average at the start of 1980.

The 1980s were not the best of times; they could have been better. But neither were they the worst of times, as we have too often wrongfully been told. On the other hand, it was a decade when the policy critics invariably followed their grossly distorted warnings of economic calamity with a preconceived prescription for relief that seems to direct, rather than to be derived from, their analysis: greater federal involvement in the economic affairs of Americans, more federal regulations and management of internal and external trade, and expanded federal planning.

With the reality of the 1980s failing to match the dismal predictions and with the whole of Eastern Europe and the former Soviet Union seeking to escape as much as possible from the clutches of government controls, the social agenda of the Chickens Little remains a vision in search of empirical justification.

Concluding Comments

Hoover Institution economist Thomas Sowell is reported to have once quipped: "Reality is tricky." Indeed it is. A host of critics of the 1980s have played tricks on their audiences by pretending that reality is as simple as they say it is. Most of these critics have had some of the facts correct, otherwise they would never have been taken seriously. The mistakes they made all too often were not getting all the facts and pretending that their limited arsenal of facts told the whole story of the 1980s. They managed, however, to distort the impression many Americans have of the recent history they have lived. Correcting distorted impressions is crucial; the course of public policy hinges on it.

A far more reasoned view is that the economy continued to expand during the 1980s, reaching a peak in 1990. In the 1980s the stock market tended to pay little heed to the claims of gloom and doom heard so often during the decade (see figure 1-1). Perhaps part of the rise in the market was fueled by speculation. But only perhaps. A careful reading of what went on during the 1980s indicates there was far more substance to the charted stock market gains than many critics may like to believe.

Figure 1-1 Dow Jones Industrial Average, Monthly, 1980–1991, Juxtaposed with Dismal Predictions

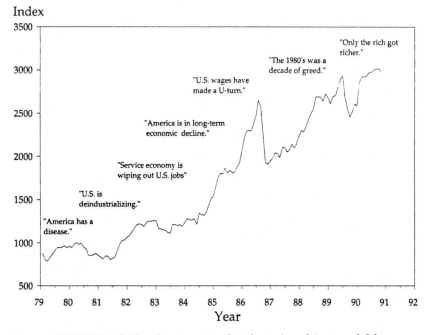

Source: CITIBASE, Citibank economic data base (machine-readable magnetic tape file), 1946–present (New York: Citibank, N.A., 1991).

Notes

1. Robert Kuttner, "Supply-Side Turkey Comes Home to Roost," *Los Angeles Times,* October 14, 1991.

2. Hobart Rowen, "Abdication of the Democrats," *Washington Post National Weekly,* March 2–8, 1992, p. 5.

3. John Kenneth Galbraith, "The Economic Hangover from a Binge of Greed," *Business and Society Review* (Spring 1992), p. 6.

4. Kevin Phillips, *The Politics of Rich and Poor: Wealth and the American Electorate in the Reagan Aftermath* (New York: Random House, 1990), p. xvii.

5. Lloyd Bentsen, Acceptance speech, *Washington Post,* July 22, 1988, as quoted by Robert L. Bartley in *The Seven Fat Years and How to Do It Again* (New York: Free Press, 1992), p. 12.

6. Benjamin M. Friedman, *Day of Reckoning: The Consequences of American Economic Policy under Reagan and After* (New York: Random House, 1988), p. 4.

7. Ibid., p. 6.

8. James Dale Davidson and Lord William Rees-Mogg, *The Great Reckoning: How the World Will Change in the Depression of the 1990s* (New York: Summit Books, 1991).

9. Robert B. Reich, "As the World Turns: U.S. Income Inequality Keeps on Rising," *New Republic* (May 1, 1989), p. 23.

10. Barry Bluestone and Bennett Harrison, *The Deindustrialization of America: Plant Closing, Community Abandonment, and the Dismantling of Basic Industry* (New York: Basic Books, 1982); Bennett Harrison and Barry Bluestone, *The Great U-Turn: Corporate Restructuring and the Polarizing of America* (New York: Basic Books, 1988).

11. Paul Krugman, *The Age of Diminished Expectations: U.S. Economic Policy in the 1990s* (Cambridge, MA: MIT Press, 1990), p. 22.

12. Ibid., p. 23.

2

THE MISUNDERSTOOD "DECLINE OF AMERICA"[1]

For practically the entire decade of the 1980s, the American economy continued to expand. Nonetheless, despair abounded. A growing chorus of scholars, policymakers, and Washington commentators began to worry that the continuing rebound in economic activity amounted to nothing more than temporary relief from a longer term downward trek in America's standing in the world economy.

Critics argued that a plethora of economic data indicated that the so-called American Empire is in decline, not simply militarily and politically but, more importantly, economically, because the country's military and political powers rest on its economic health.[2] Additionally, observers continue to maintain that further decline is inevitable unless remedial actions in public policies are undertaken, and undertaken relatively soon. In general, the economy needs to be managed more carefully from Washington, or so we continue to be told.

Needless to say, the facts and theories of decline must be scrutinized carefully before policy recommendations are adopted. Unfortunately, data series that may test the decline thesis are not always in agreement. However, if nothing more, a careful review of the facts reveals that the absolute decline of economic activity never materialized and that the *relative* decline of the United States in the world economy actually appears to have been truncated in the mid- to late-1970s. By the early to mid-1980s, the global status of the U.S. was clearly on the mend from the "stagflation" of the 1970s.

This conclusion stands in such sharp contrast to contemporary views expressed in a growing body of policy statements that some reconciliation of these interpretations of data is needed. The differences may be explained in part by the fact that proponents of the decline thesis often ended their research efforts in the early to mid-1980s but continued to believe (and to find statistical support for) their foreboding conclusions. If nothing else, updated data draw into question the presumed direction of the observed trends.

The Harbingers of Decline

Daniel Sharp, president of the American Assembly, said flatly, "America can't compete."[3] The chief evidence marshalled is the huge balance of trade deficits and the failure of the falling dollar to materially reduce the deficits. Joel Kurtzman warned that the United States needs to alter its economic course, principally through national planning, to "end the steep decline of our nation so that we can once again assume our position at the helm of the world's economy."[4] He argued that if the country had remained on the path of economic dominance established in the 1950s, "the world of today would be considerably different, with poverty perhaps eradicated from the planet and the American engine of global growth pulling the world to ever higher levels of wealth."[5] "The saddest outcome of all," wrote Harvard University economist Benjamin Friedman, "would be for America's decline to go on, but to go on so gradually that by the time the members of the next generation are old enough to begin asking who was responsible for their diminished circumstances, they will not even know what they have lost."[6]

Former Colorado governor Richard Lamm advised that "the

United States is not structured for long-term success. It is structured for long-term decline."[7] This is true, he asserted, because "the United States is not on the cutting edge of competition anymore, and while the problem has many roots, to a large extent the United States is a victim of its own institutions."[8] The institutional factors Governor Lamm considered to be major drags on growth span virtually the entire American economy: the country's overly generous health care system, excessively complicated and inefficient legal and tax codes, ineffective education system, low saving rate and resulting high cost of capital, and the government and consumer "debt bomb"—just to mention half of Governor Lamm's list.[9]

Former Secretary of the Treasury Michael Blumenthal worried that "on economic matters, we seem to be governing ourselves less adequately than at any time since World War II; sometimes we seem to be confronted by factors and forces that we cannot quite understand, let alone predict or correct. We find ourselves more and more in an environment of unaccustomed economic uncertainty and instability, both at home and abroad, and with no real consensus on what is happening, what is causing it, or what should be done next."[10]

The stock market crash of October 19, 1987, reminded us all that "the system appears no longer to be working as it should."[11] Mr. Blumenthal believed our problems stem from federal deficits of unprecedented proportions, huge trade deficits, excessive indebtedness to the rest of the world, dependence on foreign oil, low savings rate, tolerance of poverty and distress "amid a national binge of borrowing and consumption," and "unprecedented securities market uncertainties, with excessive, sometimes violent, up and down swings that threaten the stability of the system."[12]

Other worried critics warned with equal conviction that the global economy is in deep trouble, mainly because of U.S. excesses: excessive budget deficits, excessive trade deficits, excessive inattentiveness to domestic social ills, and excessive reliance on military strength.[13] "American policy in recent years," these authors told us, "has been more and more addicted to wishful thinking. Economically... the era of comfortable self-indulgence appears near its close.

Today the United States is on a collision course with history. The American fiscal dilemma must be resolved, and the perpetual instability of the dollar that is the consequence must cease."[14] Why is this so? We are forewarned that a breakdown of international monetary and trading arrangements is "so grave a danger that no responsible American government can ignore our own heavy responsibility for the present disarray."[15]

Prominent university scholars charted the inevitability of long-term decline, although their reasoning varied. In the 1980s, University of Maryland economist Mancur Olson was one of the first academics to remind us that history teaches an important principle: Long periods of political stability invariably lead to the decline of nations.[16] This is because political stability means that interest groups will gradually, but persistently, seek to use the powers of their governments for their own private ends. Government regulatory powers will be used to monopolize markets. Government fiscal powers will be exploited not for the "general good" but for subsidies and tax benefits that only serve private interests.

Olson reasoned that the net effect of private efforts to exploit government powers will be an expansion of inefficient government intrusions in the private sector and containment of competitive pressures. Economic growth will be checked, inevitably, by growing private disincentives to innovate and produce. Sluggish economic growth in national production will be foreshadowed by sluggish productivity improvements, and scholars warn that the United States now faces a productivity crisis.[17]

The United States faces the threat of decline, somewhat paradoxically, according to Olson, because it has been blessed (or damned?) with relative political stability for the past 200 years and the absence of natural disasters or all-consuming military conquests for the past four decades. Understandably, natural and military calamities may never be sought for their own sake, but these disasters have the saving grace of loosening the privately engineered economic constraints imposed on economic growth. According to Olson, Germany and Japan were able to orchestrate their respective post-war economic miracles precisely because their defeats included breaking the hammerlocks imposed by interest groups on their respective economies.[18]

Through his widely read book, Yale historian Paul Kennedy has probably done more than anyone else to substantiate growing despair over the country's fate. In spite of modern signs to the contrary, Kennedy argued that America is following a well-worn, historically validated road to economic decline, if not ruin.[19] According to Kennedy, history is replete with records of countries rising to the status of world powers, measured by economic and military might, only to overextend themselves and fall relatively, if not absolutely, to their world neighbors. Kennedy told his readers that relative economic standing among nations is important only because relative economic performance largely determines relative political and military might in the world.[20]

During the nineteenth and early twentieth centuries, the United States rose through the ranks of world powers partly because of a favored resource base but also partly because of extensive reliance on market institutions and the absence of world military responsibilities. However, in the 1980s the United States confronted the prospects of decline partly, if not principally, by seeking to police the world, something that cannot be done without escalating military expenditures. Kennedy wrote,

> *This test of American abilities [to fend off relative decline among Great Powers] will be the greater because it, like Imperial Spain around 1600 or the British Empire around 1900, is the inheritor of a vast array of strategic commitments which had been made decades earlier, when the nation's political, economic, and military capacity to influence world affairs seemed so much more assured. In consequence, the United States now runs the risk, so familiar to historians of the rise and fall of previous Great Powers, of what might be called "imperial overstretch": that is to say, decision-makers in Washington must face the awkward and enduring fact that the sum total of the United States' global interests and obligations is nowadays far larger than the country's power to defend them all simultaneously.[21]*

Through growing tax demands on the citizenry, the demands of any escalating military build-up inevitably sap private investment expenditures, which in turn retard a country's economic development and growth.[22] Expanding defense budgets and lagging saving and investment rates in the United States (as well as in the former Soviet Union and Western Europe) suggest that in the 1980s the country was following the established historical pattern. Indeed, the ascendancy of Japan, China, and other Pacific Rim countries made the *relative* decline of America altogether certain. Post-World War II Japan, in particular, was blessed with the absence of world military responsibilities, imposed partly by the United States.

According to Kennedy, the relative decline of the United States was apparent in its declining share of world gross domestic product (especially the manufactured goods component), lost industrial jobs, growing trade balance, and in the shrinking share of world trade dominated by United States producers.[23] For example, in 1945, the United States accounted for approximately half of the world's aggregate production. By 1953, the expected economic recovery of war-torn countries had lowered the United States' share to 44.7 percent. However, by 1980, production had fallen to 31.5 percent, "and it was still falling" when Kennedy completed his survey of the available empirical literature in the early 1980s.[24]

According to Kennedy, future decline is practically assured unless the United States dramatically reforms its ways. At the same time, Kennedy doubted the capacity of the United States to buck historical trends. In fact, he was so sure of his gloomy prognosis that he maintained that the main "task facing American statesmen over the next decades, therefore, is to recognize that broad trends are under way, and that there is a need to 'manage' affairs so that the *relative* erosion of the United States' position takes place slowly and smoothly, and is not accelerated by policies which bring merely short-term advantage but longer-term disadvantage."[25]

No matter who the author is, modern scenarios of U.S. decline point to one overriding conclusion: The United States must reverse its dwindling saving and investment rates to remain a world class economic, political, and military power. Much disagreement exists over exactly what policies should be implemented,[26] but most proponents of the decline thesis maintain that the United States must first pay attention to reviving its economy. While it is not always true that economic prosperity and world military and political power go hand-in-hand, "the fact remains that all of the major shifts in the world's *military-power* balances have followed alterations in the *productive* balances; and further, that the rising and falling of various empires and states in the international system has been confirmed by the outcomes of the major Great Power wars, where victory has always gone to the side with the greatest material resources."[27]

According to Kennedy, the required shift in emphasis in government policy demands that the country rescind, if not renege on, many of its military and political commitments and demand that other countries—most notably Japan and members of the European Economic Community—take on a greater defense burden. It may also require a reorganization of the fiscal priorities to ensure that the country's "consequent decline in our capacity to add value to the world economy"[28] does not continue unabated.

The general presumption is that "America's first problem may be that it spends too little on civilian benefits rather than too much."[29] The only recourse, or so we are told by virtually every advocate of the decline thesis, is that government must increase its incentives for investment and its spending on job training, nutrition, education, research and development, and infrastructure.[30]

Sources of the Decline Thesis

The controversy over the disarray of the American economy is nothing particularly new to the late 1980s. The growing perception that the United States is beset with long-term decline is built on a continuing flow of policy commentaries that highlight persistent problems in the economy. During the immediate post-World War II years, the late 1940s and 1950s, the *relative* decline of the U.S. economy was widely predicted—even hoped for, so long as relative decline implied Allied recovery. Many world economies had been left in ruin by the war. The U.S. economy achieved prominence mainly because "in 1945 Europe and Japan were starving and in ruins. The merchant marine of every country on earth had been sunk, militarized, or confiscated; the United States alone possessed food, industrial capacity, and the means of transportation. With a stable political system, a huge internal market, and a rich endowment of resources, America was in a position to assume the leadership of the world."[31]

A relative fall of the U.S. hegemony was expected, if for no other reason, because even though the devastated European countries had few undamaged factories they still had an ample reserve of "human capital." In short, they knew how to rebuild. It was only a matter of time until the rebuilding process would erode the market power of U.S. firms.

During the 1960s, commentators and scholars projected further decline caused by the explosion of a "population bomb," which assumed that Thomas Robert Malthus (the nineteenth century clergyman/economist) would be right: the world would indeed no longer be able to feed itself. The rate of growth in the world's population would increase worldwide demand for all resources, and growth of countries would then be checked by the scarcity of cheap resources to fuel further growth. Growth in the United States, especially, would be contained because it was so extravagant in the use of the world's scarce resources.

During the 1970s, a popular consensus emerged that the world was running out of energy, especially in the form of carbon-based fuel. If the supplies of oil did not dwindle naturally through over consumption and escalating costs of discovering new reserves, then the relatively small number of oil-producing countries would artificially curtail use through monopolistic production and pricing controls. Activation of the Organization of Petroleum Exporting Countries (OPEC) as a working cartel in the mid-1970s became the precursor of constrained growth. Again, the growth of oil-dependent, energy-extravagant countries like the United States would be choked, if not reversed, by limitations on critical resources that literally energize growth for advanced countries.

The early 1980s witnessed emergence of a new source of economic decline, captured in a phrase that eventually became integrated into the country's political vernacular, "the deindustrialization of America."[32] The whole of the Washington-based so-called industrial policy debate (which was mainly a debate over whether the federal government should assist industrial markets in "picking winners" and "easing the pain of losers") was founded to a considerable extent on the view that the United States was in economic decline. The loss of "good" industrial jobs and plants and the recent decline of industrial production were cited as evidence.[33] We were told by Robert Reich, then a principal advocate of a coherent national industrial policy, just before the 1984 election that:

> *America confronts a choice. We can continue to endure a painful and slow economic transition in which industrial assets and managers are endlessly rearranged through paper entrepreneurialism, political coalitions seek and obtain shelter from foreign competitors, and a growing share of American labor become locked into dead-end employment. This kind of transition can lead only to a lower standard of living for many Americans. It will be coupled with political rancor and divisiveness as the steadily shrinking economic pie is divided into even smaller slices.*[34]

Deindustrialization was, according to the proponents of this perspective, caused by many divergent forces, not the least of which were growing energy dependence, the decline of union power, the monopolization of American markets, the loss of managerial skills, the openness of U.S. markets to foreign goods, the appreciation of the dollar, and the ascendancy of Reaganomics. In general, however, the view emerged that capitalism was—by the standards of social justice—faltering badly, being driven to ruin by "greed and fear."[35]

The central problem with the decline thesis embedded in the industrial policy debate is that, on close examination, the country did not appear to be deindustrializing, at least not to the extent and in the ways advertised by the proponents of industrial policy reforms. The industrial policy movement lost much of its steam when it was pointed out that U.S. aggregate industrial production was on an upward trend, that manufactured output had remained at a constant (more or less) percentage of gross national product since at least the 1950s, and that the relationship between manufacturing employment and overall economic activity had remained relatively stable over the decades.[36] Proposals for industrial policy reforms generally emanated from the Democratic party, but even economic scholars among Democrats were unwilling to accept the industrial policy thesis. One prominent Democratic economist actually condemned the whole idea as industrial folly.[37]

Undaunted, all the arguments concerning decline have more recently been reintroduced to the policy debates of the late 1980s under the political banner of "competitiveness," wherein we were told repeatedly that the country had lost its ability to compete in world markets. The primary evidence of uncompetitiveness is conversion of the trade surplus of $69 billion in 1981 to a deficit of $87 billion in 1982, which must be considered modest by the standards of the 1987 peak deficit of $161 billion (all in 1982 prices). The annual trade deficit with Japan, which exceeded $50 billion for most years in the 1980s, is especially indicative of the nation's inability to holds its own in world markets.

Statistics can help settle many policy debates. Nonetheless, they often misguide them because of an inappropriate selection of dates on which numbers are compared or because of the interpretation given to the numbers at hand. Proponents of the decline thesis have many of the numbers correct, as far as they are reported. However, as I will show, changes in the dates covered by data series often unsettle what are believed to be settled conclusions.

The Reindustrialization of America

Policy debates during the late 1970s were often filled with mournful discussions of "economic malaise" or stagnation, or even more descriptively, "stagflation," meaning high inflation with slow or no economic growth. Indeed, during the late 1970s, inflation was high by historical standards, reaching higher and higher peaks year after year. Economic growth was slowed as productivity growth fell close to zero in several years, attributable in part to the OPEC embargoes and U.S. energy policies that held down the rise in the price of energy and thereby further restrained the growth in energy supplies. The Dow Jones industrial average index stood at 860 at the start of 1980, less than 80 points (or 10 percent) above the start of 1970.

Public commentaries concerning the fate of the U.S. economy began to take on a more foreboding tone after the turn of the decade, especially after the advent of the 1981–1982 recession, which was itself caused, to a considerable extent, by the harsh anti-inflation policies the Federal Reserve adopted in late 1979. Harvard Business School Professor George Lodge warned that the country was beset with a peculiarly "American disease" (a phrase obviously intended to equate American problems with Great Britain and its "British disease"), opening his 1984 book on the subject with a dreadful assessment:

> The cold winter of 1982 brought home to America the realization that our economy, once the wonder of the world, was failing. The power and efficiency of the industrial system, which since World War II had been taken for granted, was eroding. The United States was aware, for the first time, of losing ground in the competitive race with other developed nations.[38]

The symptoms of the American disease were everywhere to be found—slow economic growth, rising economic interest rates, plunging profits, lagging business investment, and stagnating wealth. "In fact," Lodge adds, "every indicator, social as well as economic, revealed sickness,"[39] indicating that the sickness was not solely a product of the recession and would not likely be cured by normal recovery forces.

Boston economist Barry Bluestone agreed, proclaiming with every stroke of his pen that the pace of job destruction, especially in the industrial sector, was alarming and was accelerating. He recounted that 31 million jobs had been destroyed between 1978 and 1982, noting that meant that "fully one-third of all private sector jobs in 1978 had disappeared by 1982."[40] In 1984, Harrison and Bluestone developed their empirical case of job losses sufficiently to declare flatly that America was rapidly deindustrializing, meaning the country was losing its manufacturing base, the supposed heart of the economy. The primary causes: decline of unions, growing competitiveness of world markets, invasion of domestic markets by imports, and failure of the government to adopt explicit industrial policies to guide the industrial redevelopment of the country. Harvard's Robert Reich, as well as other academics in northeastern universities, seconded the call for a national industrial policy with a more solemn pronouncement: the country was unraveling, slowly but surely.[41] This theme struck a responsive chord with the public who flocked to buy his book on *The Next American Frontier*, perhaps because the Dow Jones average had fallen from just over 1000 in April 1981 to 804 in June 1982.

Now that the decade is behind us, what did happen? We know that proposals for a national industrial policy went down in flaming defeat in the 1984 election, with Walter Mondale, who had made such policies the hallmark of his campaign. Moreover, the economy did not continue on the economic skids, as had been forcefully predicted. Instead, economic growth rebounded. Total employment went up by 19 million between 1980 and 1990, despite all the talk about jobs being destroyed.

Industrial production continued upward. Figure 2-1 shows the continuing rise in inflation-adjusted or real gross national product (GNP). Indeed, between 1980 and 1990, real GNP expanded by over 30 percent. As noted in chapter 1, this increase in real production amounts to more than $1 trillion and is the equivalent of taking the U.S. economy in 1980 and then re-adding the production of sixteen states. The increase in national output was accomplished, however, by increasing the country's labor force by the population of just Maine and New York.

Accordingly, real per capita GNP expanded by less than aggregate GNP, but still by a reasonable amount, 18 percent. Notably, economic growth began to accelerate at about the same time

Figure 2-1   Real Gross National Product and Real Gross National Product Per Capita, 1970–1990

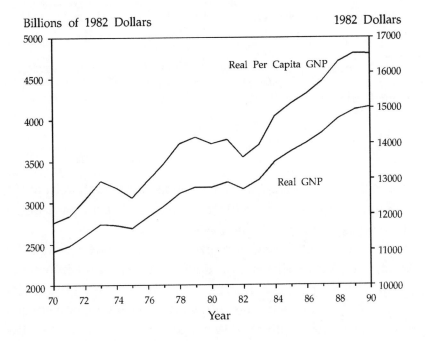

(around 1982) that many of the initial dreadful predictions were reaching print (see figure 2-1).

Granted, as indicated in table 2-1, real growth in GNP was not stellar by post-World War II standards. Indeed, the 1980s recorded the lowest percentage increase in real GNP of all the post-war decades. Real GNP grew by 46 percent in the 1960s, the greatest amount for any decade. However, it must be added quickly that the other post-war decades were not beset at the start with the throttling effects of a severe anti-inflationary policy, which the Federal Reserve began orchestrating in October 1979. The monetary constraints on domestic expansion in the early 1980s no doubt reduced the expansion of GNP during the 1980s by hundreds of billions of dollars. That is to say, growth would likely have been much higher during the

Table 2-1 Percentage Change in Gross National Product by
Decades, 1950–1990

1950–1960	1960–1970	1970–1980	1980–1990
38.3	45.5	31.9	30.4

Source: Executive Office of the President, Council of Economic Advisers, *Economic Report of the President: 1991* (Washington, DC: U.S. Government Printing Office, February 1991).

1980s had not the Fed had to wring double-digit inflation from the economy. Slow growth in the 1980s was part of the price paid for the inflationary spiral begun in the 1960s.

Did the country deindustrialize? Hardly. Figure 2-2 plots the Federal Reserve's industrial production index for all industries and for manufacturing alone. It shows that the overall industrial production index rose in line with GNP—by 29 percent between January 1980 and September 1990 (just prior to the start of the current recession). Contrary to all the predictions of demise in U.S. manufacturing, the manufacturing industrial production index rose absolutely and relatively, by 36 percent, during the same period.

Moreover, comparisons of the industrial production indexes by major industrial classification indicate that the expansion was fairly broad (see table 2-2). Only one of the nine durable goods industries listed, primary metals, did not increase significantly over the 1980–1989 period, and even then primary metals production was at approximately the same level at the end of the decade as it was at the beginning. Only two of the nondurable goods industries listed—tobacco and leather—did not rise. The contraction in the production of tobacco goods is understandable, given the varied efforts of political groups to curb smoking.

Figure 2-2 Total Industrial Production Index and Manufacturing Industrial Production Index, 1970–1990 (1987=100)

Total Index · Manufacturing Index

Manufacturing Industrial Production Index

Total Industrial Production

Year

Furthermore, manufacturing output in real dollar terms rose by 38 percent between 1980 and 1989 (the latest year of available data). This means that in 1989 manufacturing output represented a higher percentage of GNP (23 percent) than it did in 1980 (21 percent). For that matter, as is evident in figure 2-3, manufacturing output as a share of GNP was higher, albeit modestly so, in 1989 than in any other year (aside from 1988) since 1947.

Finally, the increase in manufacturing over the last two decades has not been absorbed extensively by nonconsequential consumer goods. Between 1967 (the source does not give data for 1980) and 1989, capital goods production (excluding defense and automobiles) rose as a share of manufacturing production from 28 percent to 38 percent. During the same period, exports of capital goods rose from

20 percent of total capital goods production to 45 percent, tripling as a share of the country's gross output.[42]

The belief that the country was deindustrializing was aggravated by the view that we were becoming a service economy. This

Table 2-2 Industrial Production Indexes by Industry, 1980 and 1989 (1987=100)

Major Industry Group	1980	1989	% Change
Industrial Production	84.1	108.1	28.5
Manufacturing	78.8	108.9	38.2
Durable Goods	75.7	110.9	46.5
Lumber and products	76.9	103.0	33.9
Furniture and fixtures	78.5	105.3	34.1
Clay, glass, and stone	92.0	108.0	17.4
Primary metals	110.8	109.2	-1.4
Fabricated metal	92.5	107.2	48.3
Transportation equipment	72.3	107.2	48.3
Instruments	78.8	116.4	47.7
Nondurable Goods	83.1	106.4	28.0
Food	84.6	105.5	24.7
Tobacco products	103.6	99.7	-3.8
Textile mill products	92.1	101.9	10.6
Paper and products	83.1	103.2	24.2
Printing and publishing	70.3	108.5	54.3
Chemicals and products	87.8	108.5	23.7
Petroleum products	99.0	106.1	7.2
Rubber and plastics	61.7	108.9	76.5
Leather and products	161.7	103.7	-35.9
Mining	110.0	100.5	-8.6
Utilities	95.9	107.1	11.7

Source: U.S. Department of Commerce, Bureau of the Census, *Statistical Abstract of the United States: 1991* (Washington, DC: U.S. Government Printing Office, 1991), p.750.

was truly worrisome not only because, the country was often reminded that manufacturing matters but also because the survival, not just the health, of the service economy is tied inextricably to the manufacturing sector. "Lose manufacturing and you lose—not develop—those high-wage services."[43] Others warned that we "could not really afford to become a nation of people engaged in selling Egg McMuffins and insurance to one another."[44] "Surely the American people," a national newspaper editorialized, "are not willing to become merely a service economy. The American economy is as much built around the sinews and muscle of the factory line as the white-collar office."[45] Nevertheless, service employment continued to displace manufacturing employment. However, during the 1980s, service employment as a percentage of total employment was very close to its long-term trend established long before the 1980s. At the same time, incomes rose.[46]

Figure 2-3 U.S. Manufacturing Output as a Percentage of Gross National Product, 1947–1990

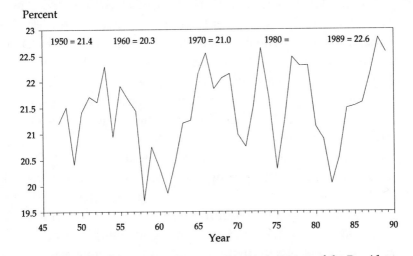

Source: Council of Economic Advisers, *Economic Report of the President: 1991* (Washington, DC: U.S. Government Printing Office, February 1991); and author's calculations.

Admittedly, domestic-based manufacturing employment fell by 6 percent, from 20.3 million in 1980 to 19.1 million in 1990. However, that loss points to the fact that manufacturing productivity in many industries was surging during the 1980s in response to competitive pressures from abroad and at home. If manufacturing employment had risen in line with production, it is a safe bet that manufacturing output would have represented a smaller share of GNP in 1990 than it actually did. This is because manufacturing in the United States would not then have been cost-effective. With improvement in the cost-effectiveness of manufacturing, U.S. exports of manufactured goods grew by a remarkable 90 percent between 1986 and 1992, compared with 25 percent for the rest of the members of the Organization of Economic Cooperation and Development. These relative changes enabled the United States to raise its share of the world's manufacturing exports from 14 percent in 1987 to 18 percent in 1991, regaining its 1980 share of world manufacturing trade.

Just as important, the U.S. manufacturing base is no longer represented by the fifty states in the domestic economy; it is scattered worldwide. While U.S. manufacturing employment fell as a share of total employment from 20 percent in 1980 to 16 percent in 1990, U.S. manufacturing employment worldwide held steady at 30 percent of total world manufacturing employment through at least 1986 (the latest year of available data).[47] This suggests that the decline in manufacturing employment in the United States was part of a world phenomenon, sparked by world competition that U.S. producers had to meet—and most did.

From reading commentaries concerning the country's low saving and investment rates during the 1980s as well as discussions about the evaporation of basic production, you might think that the stock market was totally disconnected from the real world. However, few have recognized that the compound annual rate of growth of real private net worth (including tangible and financial wealth) during the 1960s was 2.69 percent, and in the 1970s, 3.02 percent. During the 1980–1989 period, the compound annual rate of growth was 3.43 percent—14 percent higher than the 1970s and 28 percent higher than the 1960s.[48]

Relative Production Levels

With deindustrialization fears dashed by the continuing expansion and without ever acknowledging the errors in their previous claims, in the mid-1980s critics began to twist, albeit judiciously, their foreboding prophecies. While ignoring the continuing expansion, critics began to profess that the country was in long-term economic decline, not so much absolutely (it clearly was not) but relatively—that is, when compared to the rest of the world. The collapse of communism and the current efforts of former Soviet Union republics and the former Eastern Bloc countries to duplicate the market system of the United States speaks volumes about the misguided predictions of the harbingers of the decline thesis. But U.S. political successes obscured the economic tumble of the country in the world economy, or so it has been argued.

The critics' main claim became that U.S. production relative to the world and major collections of countries was declining and would likely continue to decline. In this regard, it is unfortunate that Paul Kennedy and others truncated their empirical research in the early 1980s and did not look at the data year-to-year for the time period from which they drew their dismal conclusions and prophecies. Extension of his data draws the decline thesis into question.

Real gross national product for the U.S. and for the world (excluding the U.S.) as computed and reported by the Central Intelligence Agency (a principal data source of the studies cited by Paul Kennedy) does indeed show an expansion of world and U.S. real GNP. Between 1960 and 1990, world GNP grew by 203 percent, whereas U.S. GNP grew by 150 percent. A long-term relative decline of sorts is evident in those comparisons.

However, when U.S. GNP is computed as a percentage of GNP in the rest of the world (world GNP minus U.S. GNP), conclusions of long-term economic decline for the United States become far more tenuous, if not totally premature. As is evident in figure 2-4, U.S. GNP as a percentage of GNP for the rest of the world fell from 1960 through the mid-1970s. But, somewhere around 1975, U.S. GNP relative to the rest of the world began to level off, holding close to a 34 percent share in 1975 and 1980, only to fall off to under 32 percent in 1982. What may be startling about the data in figure 2-4 is that in the mid- and late-1980s, U.S. national production relative to the rest of the world began to rise somewhat, reaching a peak of over 34 percent in 1988 (and remaining just under 34 percent in 1990).

Critics might worry that the argument has been distorted by comparing the performance of the United States with the rest of the world, which includes a lot of underdeveloped countries that grew slowly or retrogressed during the 1980s. Well, it is true that U.S. national production declined relative to Japan during the 1980s. In

Figure 2-4 U.S. Gross National Product as a Percentage of the Gross Product of the Rest of the World, Selected Years, 1960–1990

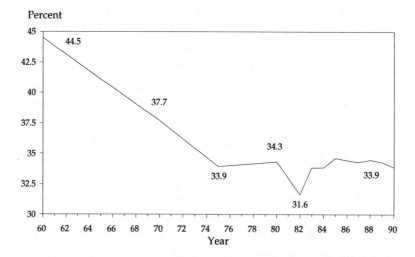

Source: Central Intelligence Agency, *Handbook of Economic Statistics* (Washington, DC: U.S. Department of Commerce, National Technical Information Service, 1987, 1988, 1990, and 1991 editions); and author's calculations.

1990, the U.S. GNP was 2.6 times Japan's GNP, down from 3 times Japan's GNP in 1980. On the other hand, U.S. GNP grew from 5.1 times Germany's GNP in 1980 to 5.4 times Germany's GNP in 1990. With respect to all developed countries, aside for Japan and Germany, U.S. GNP grew relatively but modestly, from 97 percent of the rest of the developed world (excluding Japan and Germany) in 1980 to 101 percent of the rest of the developed world in 1989 (the latest year of available data).[49]

For the most part, real world investors continued to ignore the pundits of gloom and continued to look at what was really happening to the economy. Granted, the Dow Jones index fell by more than 700 points (or 28 percent) in late 1987, a precipitous drop that fortified the confidence of the prophets of gloom in their dismal prediction. Nevertheless, the market had recovered all of the lost ground by late 1988, reaching 2148 in December, two and a half times its level at the start of the decade.

International Trade

According to most proponents of the decline thesis, the mounting international trade deficit of the United States is prima facie evidence of lost competitiveness, lost drive, and a declining standing in the world economy. Paul Kennedy tells us:

> The uncompetitiveness of U.S. industrial products abroad and the declining sales of agricultural exports have together produced staggering deficits in visible trade—$160 billion in the twelve months to May 1986—but what is alarming is that such a gap can no longer be covered by American earnings on "invisibles," which is the traditional recourse of a mature economy. ... On the contrary, the only way the United States can pay its way in the world is by importing ever larger sums of capital, which has transformed it from being the world's largest creditor to the world's largest debtor nation in the space of a few years.[50] (emphasis in original)

Indeed, over the past decade there has been a marked reversal of U.S. international fortunes, at least as measured by the difference between the dollar value of internationally exported and imported goods. As can be seen in figure 2-5, the United States had several years in the 1960s and 1970s when its balance of trade in real goods and services was in surplus (exports exceeded imports); in other years during those decades the deficits were relatively modest (imports exceeded exports). However, as is also evident in the figure, the economic screws began to turn in the early 1980s, with the balance shifting from surplus in 1980 to relatively large deficits after the middle of the 1980s. The deficit on goods and services reached a peak of $130 billion in 1986, after which it began to fall. In 1990, the deficit on goods and services was back down to $38 billion.

It is equally evident in figure 2-6 that a portion of the deficit in the early 1980s was due to declining real exports of goods and services, which may explain why the decline of America thesis began to be accepted in the early 1980s. Constant (1982) exports of goods and services reached $393 billion in 1981, a level not regained again until 1986. All the while, constant (1982) dollar imports of goods and

Figure 2-5 The Balance of Trade on Merchandise and Services (1982 Dollars)

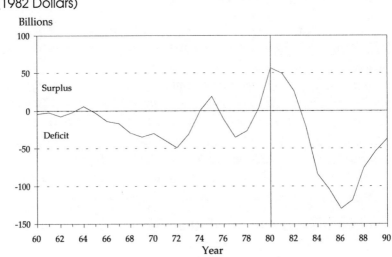

Figure 2-6 Exports and Imports of Goods and Services (1982 Dollars)

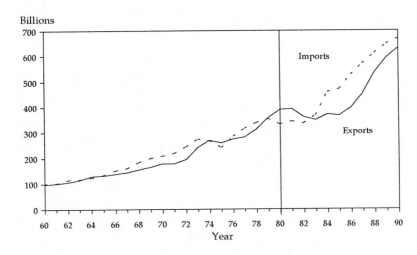

services stayed close to their 1979 peak of $353 billion or rose. By 1986, real imports exceeded $527 billion. The trade deficit was then, as noted, $130 billion.

The decline of the United States is also evident in the relationship between exports and imports of goods and services as a percentage of GNP. Figure 2-7 shows that exports expanded as a percentage of GNP in the U.S. for most of the years in the 1960–1980 period, reaching 12.2 percent of GNP in 1980. However, by 1985, exports were down to 10.1 percent of GNP. On the other hand, imports continued to rise as a percentage of GNP throughout most of the 1960–1985 period, although dipping during recessions. However, figure 2-7 shows that concern over the decline of America, as measured by the role of exports in national production, was premature. After 1985, exports began to rise as a percentage of gross national product, reaching 15.2 percent in 1990. In the late 1980s, exports were rising as a percentage of national production more rapidly than were imports.

Figure 2-7 U.S. Exports and Imports of Goods and Services as a Percentage of Gross National Product, 1960–1990

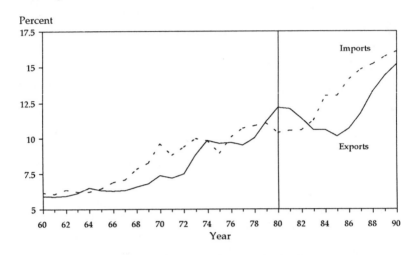

Source: Economic Report: 1991; and author's calculations.

Figure 2-8 U.S. Exports of Goods and Services as a Percentage of the Rest of the World's Gross National Product, 1960–1990

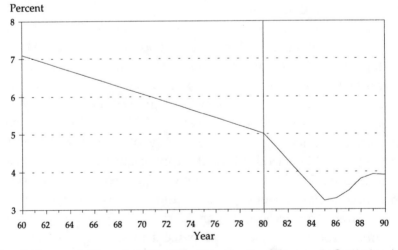

Source: Economic Report: 1991; CIA, Handbook of Economic Statistics, 1991; and author's calculations.

What about U.S. exports relative to production in the rest of the world? Is there not evidence of some decline? The evidence is a bit mixed. Figure 2-8 lends some support to the claim that U.S. exports became a smaller percentage of the economy of the rest of the world during the 1980s. U.S. exports fell from 5 percent of GNP of the rest of the world in 1980 to 3.9 percent in 1990, but figure 2-8 also shows some expansion of U.S. exports relative to production in the rest of the world in the late 1980s.

Implications for Trade Balances

Does the rise in the trade deficit, however measured, support the more general claim that America is in decline because of a growing inability on the part of its businesses to compete in world markets? I have sought to answer that question in substantial detail in another publication.[51] However, two lines of argument are summarized here.

First, one reason for the rise in the U.S. trade deficit in the 1980s is the faster pace of economic growth in the United States compared to that of many other countries around the world.[52] With a more rapid rate of growth, producers need more resources, many of which must be drawn from abroad in the form of imports. Fewer domestic resources are available for the production of goods for export (this is especially true when other countries are not growing as rapidly). The decline in real U.S. exports in the 1980s probably reflects, at least in part, the significant rise in domestic production.

Clearly, imports do not always measure the decline in economic strength of a country. On the contrary, they may retard decline or even contribute to the relative growth of a country. On domestic and world markets, many imported products can make U.S. firms more competitive, not less so, directly increasing the productivity of domestic firms.

For example, in the 1980s American textile firms imported a substantial share of their new machinery from abroad (50 percent in 1987), but they did so to increase productivity by more than they could have otherwise. The rise in imported textile machinery, spurred by efforts to reduce domestic production costs, may have itself been spurred marginally by the rise in textile imports. Without much question, the substantial rise in textile productivity over the past decade and a half has contributed to a reduction in the number of workers in the domestic textile industry.[53] This meant that the imported machinery in textiles made more workers available for an expansion of domestic industries, and the same can be said for many other industries. It also meant that domestic textile firms could then better fend off foreign competition and extend their penetration of foreign markets. Both imports of textiles and textile machinery very likely contributed to the long-run competitive health of the domestic textile industry.

Second, the balance on the capital account necessarily mirrors the balance on the trade account (with adjustments for other elements in the overall balance of payments). This means that exports are not the only U.S. products that foreigners want. As was evident in the growing balance of the capital account surplus in the 1980s, foreigners also wanted capital goods that could be put to work in this country. The demand for (competitively produced) capital goods in this country could have been a cause for the appreciation of the dollar during the first half of the 1980s. American exporters of goods stand at all times in competition with American producers of investment opportunities for the dollars held by foreigners.

In other words, the trade deficits could have (and did to an extent) reflected the fact that American exporters of goods were simply out-competed, not by foreign producers but by domestic producers of investment opportunities in the United States. Seen from this perspective, the growing balance of trade deficits in the 1980s reflects not so much some overall demise of American competitive drive but a shift in competitiveness among producers in the United States, not between U.S. and foreign producers.

As indicated, proponents of the decline thesis suggest that U.S. competitiveness can be assessed by U.S. sales of "things" produced domestically as a percentage of aggregate world production. When it is recognized that domestic investment opportunities are also things sold to foreigners, it does not follow that the aggregate of sales of all things (exports and investment opportunities) are on the decline.[54] Indeed, these have been on the rise over the decades.

In short, analyzing trade deficit statistics by themselves is not a very good means of assessing the decline thesis or the lack of international competitiveness on the part of U.S. firms.[55] So long as international trade for goods, services, and assets is voluntary, it seems reasonable to assume that it is, generally speaking, beneficial to the parties involved.[56]

Whether the parties in the United States gain more or less than the parties in other countries with whom they trade is impossible to say. All we do know is that U.S. domestic production held its own relative to the world economy after the mid-1970s *at the very time trade deficits began to emerge.* The deficits of the early 1980s were also accompanied by relatively rapid rates of growth in the domestic economy. That fact can be discerned by looking once again at figures 2-7 and 2-8. U.S. exports and imports rose less rapidly with respect to world output than with respect to domestic output. That is about all that can be concluded from the data. Of course, it would have been great had the U.S. economy performed even better than it did during the 1980s. World and American citizens would have been even better off if the U.S. economy had grown faster—and both proponents and opponents of the decline thesis might have been able to agree on some policy proposals to spur growth. However, contemplating proposals to spur greater growth is a grossly different policy perspective than the one grounded in the presumption that American firms and workers are being beaten back by competition from all world ports. If that were the case, real U.S. exports would not have risen as much as they did.

Proponents of the decline thesis might quickly object to the foregoing analysis, arguing forcefully that data on trade deficits were accompanied by an enormous expansion in the U.S. federal budget deficit to levels above $200 billion. These proponents might argue that those deficits increased upward pressures on real interest rates and caused capital to flow into this country. The resulting larger capital inflow (and lower capital outflow) caused the U.S. dollar to appreciate on the international money markets. The budget deficits thereby reduced (artificially) the competitiveness of U.S. goods' producers in foreign markets.

Although appealing and widely believed to be true (even by opponents of the decline thesis), the so-called twin-deficit problem loses much of its force when it is recognized that federal budget deficits do not appear to influence real interest rates very much (if at all), and real interest rates do not appear to be highly correlated with exchange rate movements.[57] Indeed, in the mid-1980s, real interest rates in the United States appeared to be falling as budget deficits were rising most rapidly and the international value of the dollar was falling.[58]

Besides, the claimed linkages between the budget and trade deficits presume that if the budget deficit is eliminated (say, by a tax hike), interest rates will fall and the dollar will depreciate.[59] However, elimination of the deficit through tax increases would be accompanied by largely offsetting forces on the nation's money markets. The tax hike (especially when focused on the rich) might reduce the federal government's demand for loanable funds, but it would also reduce the supply of loanable funds. The net effect on real interest rates would probably be little or nothing.

This line of argument does not lead to the conclusion that the federal government has no influence on the country's competitiveness and future economic, political, and military capabilities in the world, however. But the focus of government policymakers should be on the size of government expenditures. Because government expenditures draw resources away from private sector activities, they are the ultimate form of taxation on the economy. Government expenditures may very well have contributed to a reduction in the capacity of U.S. businesses to expand exports and fend off imports. Proponents of a more active government role in fostering competitiveness are likely to have a difficult time with this assessment.[60]

Discussions of decline probably never became more confused and misleading than when the specter of the "debtor nation" was raised. We have noted Paul Kennedy's concern that the United States has "in the space of a few years" switched from being the largest creditor to being the largest debtor nation. Robert Reich seems to share this view, stating, "Our failure to invest in future productivity is now reflected in ... the steady sale to foreigners of shares in our companies and of our prime real estate. ... Trying to offset our trade imbalance by selling off our assets makes as much sense as selling the house to help pay future rent."[61]

Such comments suggest that wealth in the United States was actually falling during the decade. This was clearly not the case given that growth in U.S. wealth is measured directly by adding up tangible properties and indirectly by expansion in national production.

Granted, capital inflows can imply "selling off assets," but they can also contribute to a net increase in the nation's assets held by Americans as well as by foreigners. So long as they are invested productively, capital inflows increase the future flow of income to both Americans and foreigners. Surely foreign investment in U.S. railroads in the 1800s could not be considered "selling off assets."

Finally, it must be realized that American resources, assets, are used up or sold off to produce exports, and those resources could have been used to produce capital goods in the United States. It simply does not follow that had the trade deficit been offset by exports, as opposed to capital inflows, the country's economic future would be any brighter than it is.

Kennedy (as well as others) insists that his factual and conceptual review of the history of the past five centuries leads inexorably to one overriding conclusion: America is in decline, relatively. The decline is more or less natural, dictated by the natural proclivities of great powers to overextend themselves. Furthermore, he suggests that the decline is not relative to just one or to a few countries but encompasses most of the developed and developing world. If nothing else, this review of available data should cast a healthy measure of doubt over the validity of the professor's conclusions.

A more reasonable conclusion may be that the United States did experience a relative decline, as measured by various economic data sources, from the end of World War II to the mid-1970s, and the United States remains in relative decline with respect to Japan and maybe a handful of other countries. However, sometime after the mid-1970s, the U.S. decline relative to the "rest of the world" was slowed, if not altogether abated. This conclusion is founded on updated data from several of the same data sources employed by Kennedy (or the research on which he relies).[62]

Concluding Comments

Predictions of impending economic calamities are the mainstay of American politics. They attract a great deal of attention, sell a lot of books, and give life to political movements for dramatic change in policies. Much of the doom and gloom simply exploits our fear of the future and of the unknown.[63] However, a number of contemporary treatises that chart the past and future decline of America are scholarly and sophisticated, as well as ingenious in their development of arguments, and are worthy of serious consideration by policymakers. These treatises are also reflective, outlining a gradual erosion of the substantial post-World War II position of the United States in the world body politic.

At the same time, a close examination of the empirical and conceptual case made in support of the decline thesis suggests that pessimistic predictions appear to be premature, and perhaps misdirected. To a degree, the predictions represent an overly aggressive extrapolation of the natural, anticipated decline of American prominence after World War II. To a degree, they are also founded on data sources that, after updating to the end of the 1980s, no longer confirm popular and scholarly visions of relative decline.

There are good reasons for believing that the facts of American decline have been misinterpreted. What appears to be the case is that an absolute decline in the power and influence of America on the world stage has been interpreted as a relative decline. The political powers of all governments to influence world events are being suppressed by international economic forces. These forces are driven extensively by technological changes that are dramatically increasing the mobility of capital (human and physical) across national and regional boundaries. The power of the U.S. government to influence events may be declining absolutely, along with declines in the power of all other governments, but the relative power of the U.S. government may not be declining as much as supposed.

Of course, nothing that has been written should be construed as saying that the United States does not have any serious economic problems, that economic conditions could not be improved, or that policymakers should not be attuned to changes in inappropriate policies (for example, tax, regulatory, and redistributive policies). On the contrary, the growing competitiveness around the globe will necessitate that U.S. policymakers be more attentive to ineffective and inefficient policies that obstruct the capacity of the United States to retain its current and its prospective capital and income bases.

Notes

1. This chapter is drawn from Richard B. McKenzie, *The Decline of America: Myth or Fate?* (St. Louis: Center for the Study of American Business, Washington University, 1988).

2. Walter Russell Mead observes,

    That great empires should fall as well as rise seems perfectly natural when we consider the land of the pharaohs or ancient Babylon. That the American Empire should suffer such a fate is more disturbing. And that the decline, and ultimately the fall, of the American Empire is the basic political fact of the present period in world history is more disturbing still. We cannot sit back and observe the fall of the American Empire with the detachment with which we view Rome; our hope and fears are too closely bound up in the fate of the American Empire [Mortal Splendor: The American Empire in Transition (Boston: Houghton Mifflin, 1987), p. 10].

    See also, Paul Kennedy's *The Rise and Fall of Great Powers: Economic Change and Military Conflict from 1500 to 2000* (New York: Random House, 1987), a book that guided much of the debate over the decline of the country and that will be considered in some depth in the course of the chapter.

3. Daniel A. Sharp, "America is Running Out of Time," *New York Times* (February 7, 1988), as reprinted in *The World Trade Imbalance: When Profit Motives Collide* (Washington: Executive Council on Foreign Diplomats, U.S. Department of State, 1988), p. 25.

4. Joel Kurtzman, *The Decline and Crash of the American Economy* (New York: W.W. Norton, 1988), p. 212.

5. Ibid., pp. 25–34.

6. Benjamin M. Friedman, *Day of Reckoning: The Consequences of American Economic Policy Under Reagan and After* (New York: Random House, 1988) p. 300.

7. Richard D. Lamm, "Crisis: The Uncompetitive Society," In *Global Competitiveness: Getting the U.S. Back on Track*, Martin K. Starr, ed. (New York: W. W. Norton, 1988), p. 13.

8. Ibid.

9. Ibid., pp. 17–39.

10. W. Michael Blumenthal, "The World Economy and Technological Change," *Foreign Affairs*, vol. 66, no. 3 (1987/1988), p. 528.

11. Ibid.

12. Ibid., pp. 529–531.

13. David P. Calleo, Harold van B. Cleveland, and Leonard Silk, "The Dollar and the Defense of the West," *Foreign Affairs*, vol. 66, no. 4 (Spring 1988), p. 845.

14. Ibid.

15. Ibid.

16. Mancur Olson, *The Rise and Decline of Nations* (New Haven, CN: Yale University Press, 1982).

17. Brookings Institution researchers Martin Baily and Alok Chakrabarti found that the productivity crisis is evident in statistics on growth of GDP per hour and growth of manufacturing output per hour. In the United States in the 1950–1973 period, GDP per hour increased at an average annual rate of 2.44 percent, while manufacturing output per hour grew at an average annual rate of slightly more, 2.62 percent. However, GDP per hour in the 1979–1984 period grew at one-half its earlier rate, 1.09 percent per year. Manufacturing output per hour grew more rapidly in the more recent period, 3.10 percent per year [Martin Neil Baily and Alok K. Chakrabarti, *Innovation and the Productivity Crisis* (Washington, DC: Brookings Institution, 1988), p. 5 (see also p. 9 for alternative measures of productivity growth relative to other countries)].

18. Professor Olson argues effectively that "The everyday use of the word *miracle* to describe the rapid economic growth in these countries [Japan and West Germany] testifies that this growth was not only unexpected, but also outside the range of known laws and experience. in Japan and West Germany, totalitarian governments were followed by Allied occupiers determined to promote institutional change and to ensure that institutional life would start almost anew. In Germany, Hitler had done away with independent unions as well as all other dissenting groups, whereas the Allies, through measures such as the decartelization decrees of 1947 and denazification programs, had emasculated cartels and organizations with right-wing backgrounds. In Japan, the militaristic regime had kept down left-wing organizations, and the Supreme Commander of the Allied Powers imposed the antimonopoly law of 1947 and purged many hundreds of officers of Zaibatsu and other organizations for their war-time activities." (In Italy, the institutional destruction from totalitarianism, war, and Allied occupation was less severe and the postwar growth "miracle" correspondingly shorter.) [Ibid., pp. 75–76]

19. Paul Kennedy, *The Rise and Decline of Great Powers: Economic Change and Military Conflict from 1500 to 2000* (New York: Random House, 1987).

20. Kennedy admits that he is not arguing that economics is the sole

cause of the rise and decline of great powers: "There simply is too much evidence pointing to other things: geography, military organization, national morale, the alliance system, and many other factors can all affect the relative power of members of the states system. ... What does seem incontestable, however, is that in a long-run-drawn-out Great Power (and usually coalition) war, victory has repeatedly gone to the side with the more flourishing productive base—or, as the Spanish captains used to say, to him who has the last escudo" (Ibid., p. xxiv.).

21. Ibid., p. 515.

22. This theme is also fundamental to the analysis of David P. Calleo, *Beyond American Hegemony: The Future of the Western Alliance* (New York: Basic Books, 1987), especially chap. 7.

23. Kennedy, *The Rise and Decline of Great Powers*, pp. 413–437.

24. Ibid., p. 432. As his primary source for data on world production shares, Kennedy cites P. Bairoch, "International Industrialization Levels from 1750 to 1980," Journal of European Economic History 11 (1980), pp. 304. Kennedy also points out that Central Intelligence Agency figures show that the United States' share of world output dropped from 25.9 percent in 1960 to 21.5 percent in 1980 [Central Intelligence Agency, Handbook of Economic Statistics (Washington, DC: 1984), p. 4]. However, he acknowledges that CIA figures may be influenced by exchange-rate considerations [Kennedy, *The Rise and Decline of Great Powers*, p. 608 (footnote 248)].

25. Ibid., p. 534.

26. Consider, for example, the conflicting protectionist positions of Senator Lloyd Bentsen (D-Tex) and Harvard economist Robert Reich, both of whom worry that the U.S. economy is, at the very least, not working very well and may be in long-term decline without remedial policies [Lloyd Bentsen, "National Press Club Speech," *Congressional Record* (May 20, 1987); and Robert B. Reich, "The Economics of Illusion and the Illusion of Economics," *Foreign Affairs,* vol. 66, no. 3 (Winter 1987/1988), pp. 516–528].

27. Ibid., p. 439.

28. Ibid., p. 523.

29. Calleo, et al., "The Dollar and the Defense of the West," p. 852. The authors continue, "Equally unrealistic, in our view, is the strategy that would eliminate the deficit by heavy cuts in our country's comparatively undeveloped welfare spending, as the Reagan Administration has always advocated rhetorically, or by large cuts in America's comparatively low level of 'middle-class entitlements,' as advocated by many of the Administration's critics" [Ibid.].

30. Ibid., pp. 526–528. See also Sharp, "America is Running Out of Time" and Martin K. Starr, *Global Competitiveness: Getting the U.S. Back on Track* (New York: W. W. Norton, 1988) pp. 299–310.

31. Mead, *Mortal Splendor*, p. 16.

32. Kennedy appears to accept as fact the major tenants of the industrial policy proponents [Kennedy, *The Rise and Decline of Great Powers*, pp. 514–535]. For an opposing outlook to the industrial policy issues raised, see Richard B. McKenzie, *Competing Visions: The Economics and Politics of America's Economic Future* (Washington, DC: Cato Institute, 1985).

33. This view was most effectively promoted among politicians and policymakers by Robert Reich in *The Next American Frontier* (New York: Times Books, 1983). He reinforced the more specialized themes of Barry Bluestone and Bennett Harrison, *The Deindustrialization of America: Plant Closings, Community Abandonment, and the Dismantling of Basic Industry* (New York: Basic Books, 1982). A series of books and monographs on the deindustrialization theme, picked up by scholars and interest groups and the Catholic bishops, began to appear in the mid-1980s. These works are critically evaluated in three books by the author: *Fugitive Industries: The Economics and Politics of Deindustrialization* (San Francisco: Ballenger Books and the Pacific Institute for Public Policy Research, 1984); *Competing Visions: the Political Conflict and America's Economic Future* (Washington: Cato Institute, 1985); and *The American Job Machine* (New York: Universe Books, 1988).

34. Reich, *The Next American Frontier*, p. 255.

35. Ibid., p. 20. The perceived flaws of capitalism are evaluated by the Catholic bishops in "Pastoral Letter on the Social Economy," third draft (duplicated, 1986). A contrary view of capitalism is expressed in *Toward the Future: Catholic Social Thought and the U.S. Economy* (New York: Lay Commission on Catholic Social Teaching, 1984).

36. One of the first, if not the first, economists to point out the stable relationship between production of manufactured goods and real gross national product was Thomas J. DiLorenzo, "The Myth of America's Declining Manufacturing Sector," *Backgrounder* (Washington, DC: Heritage Foundation, January 13, 1984). Professor Dilorenzo's original analysis has been fortified in a more recent examination of the issue, Randall W. Elberts and John R. Swinton, "Has Manufacturing's Presence in the Economy Diminished?" *Economic Commentary* (Federal Reserve Bank of Cleveland, January 1, 1988). At about the same time, the argument has again been made that the U.S. manufacturing base is indeed eroding relative to gross national product. According to this more complicated line of inquiry,

the erosion is hidden behind faulty statistics [Lawrence Mishel, *Manufacturing Numbers: How Inaccurate Statistics Conceal U.S. Industrial Decline* (Washington, DC: Economic Policy Institute, 1988)].

37. See Charles Schultze, "Industrial Policy: A Dissent," *Brookings Review* (October 1983), pp. 3–12.

38. George C. Lodge, *The American Disease* (New York: Alfred A. Knopf, 1984), p. 3.

39. Ibid., p. 5.

40. Barry Bluestone, "Industrial Dislocation and the Implications for Public Policy," paper prepared for the third annual policy forum on employability development, Displaced Workers: Implications for Educational and Training Institutions, National Center for Research in Vocational Education, Ohio State University (Washington, DC, September 12–13, 1983), p. 3.

41. Reich, *The Next American Frontier*, p. 3.

42. Andrew M. Warner, "Does World Investment Determine American Exports?" (Washington, DC: Federal Reserve Board of Governors, January 1992, working paper), pp. 18–19.

43. Stephen S. Cohen and John Zysman, *Manufacturing Matters: The Myth of the Post-Industrial Economy* (New York: Basic Books, 1987), p. 3.

44. John F. McGillicuddy, "The Corporate Pulpit," *The Corporate Board: The Journal of Corporate Governance* (July/August 1987), p. 1.

45. "Getting America Moving Again" (editorial), *Christian Science Monitor*, January 20, 1987.

46. See Mack Ott, "The Growing Share of Services in the U.S. Economy—Degeneration or Evolution?" *Review*, Federal Reserve Bank of St. Louis (June/July 1987), p. 15.

47. Kenichi Ohmae, "No Manufacturing Exodus, No Great Comeback," *Wall Street Journal*, April 25, 1988, p. 26.

48. The rate of growth is computed for the 1980–1989 period because of a precipitous $700 billion decline in real private net worth between 1989 and 1990 that may prove temporary and be a reflection of the recession. Similarly, the rate of growth for the 1960s may be somewhat distorted by the fall-off in net worth after 1968. The compound rate of growth is 4.03 percent in the 1960–1968 period and 3.06 percent in the 1960–1972 period.

The compound rates of growth in net worth per capita are, of course, lower for all decades, but the rate of growth for the 1980–1989 period is higher than the previous two decades: 2.42 percent for 1980–1989, 1.95 percent for the 1970s, and 1.4 percent for the 1960s. The data on private net worth is from the Federal Reserve's *Balance*

Sheet, as reported in the Council of Economic Advisers' *Economic Report of the President: 1992* (Washington, DC: U.S. Government Printing Office, February 1992), p. 423.

49. U.S. production relative to other groupings of countries, including major industrial countries and what were at the time major communist countries, follows much the same pattern for most of the 1980s that is indicated here. For more details, see Richard B. McKenzie, *The Decline of America: Myth or Fate?* (St. Louis: Center for the Study of American Business, Washington University, November 1988).

50. Kennedy, *The Rise and Decline of Great Powers,* p. 526.

51. Richard B. McKenzie, "American Competitiveness: Do We Really Need to Worry?", *Public Interest* (Winter 1988), pp. 66–80.

52. For an elaboration of this line of argument, see Council of Economic Advisers, *Economic Report of the President* (Washington, DC: U.S. Government Printing Office, 1987), pp. 101–107.

53. See Baily and Chakrabarti, *Innovation and the Productivity Crisis,* chap. 3; McKenzie, *The American Job Machine,* chap. 7.

54. It must be recognized that domestic investment opportunities sold to foreigners represent things not shipped out of the country. They are, however, no less goods that are produced. For example, if a foreigner buys a Mack truck for use in construction in a foreign country, the sale will be classified in the U.S. balance of payments as an export and will reduce the trade deficit. If the Mack truck is, on the other hand, retained in the United States for use in construction in the United States, it is no less a capital good produced domestically. At the same time, the truck sale will be classified as a capital inflow, and will not reduce the trade deficit. The classification system in this and many other cases is largely arbitrary.

55. See the extended discussion of Allen J. Lenz, "U.S. International Competitiveness: Conceptual and Measurement Problems," in International Trade Administration, U.S. Department of Commerce, *United States Trade: Performance in 1985 and Outlook* (Washington, DC: U.S. Government Printing Office, 1986), pp. 97–101.

56. For additional points on this line of argument, see Herbert Stein, "A Primer on the Other Deficit," *AEI Economist* (Washington, DC: American Enterprise Institute, March 1987), from which Stein drew an incisive column, "Leave the Trade Deficit Alone," *Wall Street Journal* (March 11, 1987), p. 36.

57. For studies that report an uncertain connection between government deficit, interest rates, and trade deficits, see John Tatom, "Domestic vs. International Explanations for Recent U.S. Manufacturing

Developments," *Review* (St. Louis Federal Reserve Bank, April 1986), pp. 5–18; William Anderson, Myles S. Wallace, and John T. Warner, "Government Spending and Taxation: What Causes What," *Southern Economic Journal*, January 1986, pp. 630–639; and David Bowles, Holley Ulbrich, and Myles Wallace, "Default Risk, Interest Differentials, and Fiscal Policy: A New Look at Crowding Out," Clemson, SC: Economics Department, Clemson University, 1986; and Nathan Childs, *International Trade Explanations for Farm Troubles in the 1980s,* Clemson, SC: Agriculture Economics and Rural Sociology Department, Clemson University, Ph.D. dissertation, 1987. A statistically significant correlation between the budget deficit and the trade deficit may eventually be found. However, it is unlikely that the computed effect will explain a substantial share of the variation of the trade deficit.

58. See the discussion on this point with accompanying charts in McKenzie, *The American Job Machine*, chap. 6.

59. Professor Reich recommends a tax increase to partially solve the deficit problem ("The Economics of Illusion and the Illusion of Economics," p. 527). Almost everyone recommends scaling back defense expenditures (Calleo, et al., "The Dollar and the Defense of the West," pp. 853–856).

60. See Calleo, et al., "The Dollar and the Defense of the West." Proponents of the decline thesis often look to reduction in defense expenditures to finance their proposed expansion of domestic programs.

61. Reich, "The Economics of Illusion and the Illusion of Economics," p. 524.

62. This does not mean that the power and influence of America, as a country or as a political entity, has not declined, absolutely. Much factual and anecdotal evidence can be marshalled to demonstrate that the United States government continues to lose influence—economically, politically, and militarily. The inability of the United States to thwart the military efforts of small countries like North Vietnam and Iran speaks eloquently of absolute decline. The ability of American producers to transfer their production facilities abroad speaks to a growing inability of U.S. government to tax and regulate its own production and, thereby, to control production on a worldwide scale. The growing dependence of the U.S. economy on imports, exports, and capital flows—and the overall growing interdependence of the U.S. economy with the rest of the world—says much about the waning capacity of U.S. governments to control, manipulate, or influence political and economic events around the world. Clearly, the U.S. government retains a great deal

of influence around the globe; but just as clearly, its influence is slipping—absolutely.

The reason for the emphasis on the absolute slippage of power and influence is that the power and influence of other countries is slipping as well. The power of any country to control events in the world is simply on the wane, absolutely. One explanation for the slippage in the absolute power of governments is capital mobility inspired by technological advances that force governments to compete for the capital bases from which they draw revenues. Hence, contrary to what Professor Kennedy and others maintain, American power and influence is probably not slipping as badly on a relative basis as it is on an absolute basis. This slippage may be insignificant in relationship to that of most other countries.

For an extended discussion of the relationship between capital mobility and the power of government to tax and regulate, see Richard B. McKenzie, "The Twilight of Government Growth in a Competitive World Economy," *Policy Analysis* (Washington, DC: Cato Institute, August 1988); and Dwight R. Lee and Richard B. McKenzie, "The International Political Economy of Declining Tax Rates," *National Tax Journal* (March 1989), pp. 79–83.

63. Southern Methodist University economist Ravi Batra, in *The Great Depression of 1990* (New York: Simon and Schuster, 1987), blatantly feeds on the public's fear of future calamity. He argues that because economic activity follows predetermined 30- and 60-year cycles, the United States will experience a depression in the 1990s as severe as the one in the 1930s. His views achieved more-than-usual credibility, coming out before the stock market crash of October 19, 1987.

3

THE DECADE OF
GREED THAT WASN'T

G reed has been a problem since at least biblical times. Nevertheless, policy critics have maintained that greed was unabashedly fostered during the 1980s by the Reagan administration,
intent on lowering tax rates to encourage excessive and ostentatious
consumption among the administration's principal supporters. Presumably, the Reagan supporters included the rich, famous, and
powerful, most notably from Hollywood; members of the "me-gen-
eration"; and the "Yuppies" (young urban professionals) and
"Whoppies" (well-heeled older professionals)—all of whom supposedly had a substantial influence on public attitudes and spending
and saving patterns, as well as charitable intentions.

Worrying that the 1990s would be the decade in which the bills
of the 1980s would come due, *Time* magazine reporter Otto Friedrich
declared, "The past decade brought growth, avarice and an anything
goes attitude," and then later glibly summarized the 1980s with five
words, "Get rich, borrow, spend, enjoy," suggesting that the dealings of Ivan Boesky, "the diaper king of arbitrage," epitomized the
wanton ways of a whole decade.[1] In his book *The Hunger for More*,
Laurence Shames added that "the 1980s raised the clamor for more

to new heights of shrillness, insistence, and general obnoxiousness, but this, it can be argued, was in the nature of the final binge, the storm before the calm."[2]

Supposedly, during the 1980s, Americans went on a consumption binge, casting aside their historic concern for the welfare of others. As opposed to helping others, American workers, managers, and owners became more concerned than ever with themselves; that is, with what they could take in pay from their work and what they could buy to promote what liberal political pundit Kevin Phillips dubbed "conspicuous opulence." American university students supposedly began mimicking their parents and their parents' friends by harboring a "single ambition—*doing something that would make money.*"[3]

The evidence offered in support of the contention that the 1980s was a decade of greed includes casual references to the jump in sales of luxury automobiles, the increase in the number of MBAs (most of whom, presumably, set their sights on making money on Wall Street), growth in the number of self-help books, and the number of Wall Street brokers who went to prison. At best, myopic focus on spectacular examples of errant behavior does not offer a complete picture of America in the 1980s. At worst, it paints a warped picture of the way Americans lived during a decade of renewed growth.[4]

The presumption that greed reigned supreme in the American economy during the 1980s is crucial to the critics' efforts to damn the entire decade on an array of other counts. If people were in fact excessively motivated by unbridled greed, then it might be plausible that the economic policies chosen were intellectually and morally bankrupt and that actual economic activity was driven out of its historical mooring and set adrift. It might then be reasonable to conclude that the income gains of some, the greedy rich, were at the expense of others, those still interested in fair and reasonable dealings with one another. Of course, the presumption of widespread greed gives plausibility to the charge that the American society was following the well-worn path of other morally decadent civilizations, most notably the Romans, into long-term decay. The charge of pervasive greed does raise the specter of the 1990s being a decade of decline.

I have already shown that the presumption of long-term decay was premature at best and ill-conceived at worst. Interestingly, while all critics suggest Americans were less charitable, none have actually looked at the most direct means of assessing greed—the pattern of charitable giving. If they had, they would have quickly discovered that they had misrepresented the 1980s by telling only half the story, leaving out the most positive and striking parts.

Measured by giving, the 1980s was not the highly touted decade of greed. On the contrary, giving by individuals and corporations jumped dramatically in the 1980s. This finding holds for giving measured not just in absolute current dollar terms but also in total real dollars contributed, real charitable contributions per capita, and charitable contributions relative to national income.

Indeed, giving in the 1980s was above the level that would have been predicted from the upward trend established in the twenty-five years prior to the advent of the 1980s. This conclusion holds even after adjusting for several economic and policy changes that might reasonably be expected to have boosted charitable contributions. Given the evidence assembled here, it appears that the editors of the *Wall Street Journal* were on target when they observed, "A 'Decade of Greed' was really never much more than a rhetorical device, a hammer in someone's argument. The argument was fundamentally political and philosophical."[5]

Nonetheless, from Kevin Phillips' perspective, the imagery of widespread and unchecked greed justified higher taxes on the (supposedly) undeserving and squandering rich. *Washington Post* columnist Robert Samuelson pointed out, however, that "it's now fashionable to attack the 1980s' glitz and greed. But this is a lazy and ultimately ineffective argument for better or bigger government."[6]

Regardless of the motivation for labeling the 1980s the decade of greed, the facts just do not support the charge. The decade of the 1980s was actually a decade of unusual generosity on the part of Americans. This point is self-evident in the review of the total level of giving in constant dollars from 1955 to 1989. The point is reinforced when giving by individuals and corporations are considered separately. The analysis of giving on a per capita basis and relative to national income further fortifies the view that, relatively speaking, the 1980s was a decade of renewed charity, a conclusion that remains undisturbed when the actual levels of charity in the 1980s are compared with the predicted levels of charity computed from an econometric model of giving using data for 1955 through 1980. Accordingly, the 1990s will not likely be anywhere near as dreadful as many critics warn.

Aggregate Giving

Total giving is composed of gifts from living individuals, corporations, foundations, and bequests. The focus of this section will be on total real giving, with giving by individuals and corporations considered separately.[7]

Total Giving

Figure 3-1 reveals the pattern of total giving and giving by individuals and by corporations in constant (1990) dollars from 1955 through 1990.[8] In the twenty-five-year period prior to the decade of greed, total charitable giving, in real terms, more than doubled, increasing from $34.5 billion in 1955 to $77.5 billion in 1980—or at a compounded annual growth rate of 3.3 percent. Between 1980 and 1989, total giving in real dollars expanded by 56 percent to $121 billion, or by a compound growth rate of 5.1 percent. The annual rate of growth in total real giving in the 1980s was nearly 55 percent higher than in the previous twenty-five years.[9]

Figure 3-1 Total, Individual, and Corporate Giving in Constant (1990) Dollars

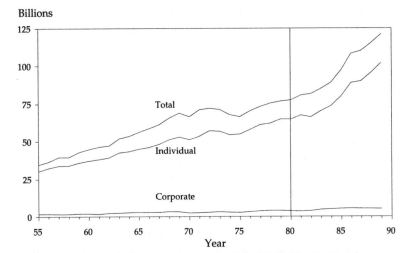

Billions

Year

Source: Giving USA: 1990 (New York: AAFRC Trust for Philanthropy, 1990); and author's calculations.

Individual Giving

Because giving by living individuals accounts for over 80 percent of all giving, it is not surprising that the category also more than doubled from $30.2 billion to $64.7 billion between 1955 and 1980—at a compounded growth rate of 3.1 percent a year. Individual giving reached $102 billion in 1989, after expanding at a compounded rate of 5.2 percent between 1980 and 1989.[10]

Individual giving as a percentage of total giving declined gradually during the 1955–1989 period, from almost 88 percent in 1955 to 84 percent of giving in 1989. Nevertheless, the data reveal that giving by individuals in constant dollars was rising faster in the 1980s than in previous decades. In fact, the compound rate of growth in individual giving in the 1980s was more than two-thirds higher than in the prior two and a half decades.

Giving has also been widespread in America, especially considering the apparent concentration of discretionary income over and above expenditures on necessities like food, clothing, and shelter. A 1989 survey of 60,000 households by the U.S. Bureau of the Census and the Conference Board found that only 29 percent of American households have discretionary earnings.[11] However, another 1987 survey of 3,000 households by the Independent Sector found that 71 percent of American households made charitable contributions.[12]

Moreover, it is important to note that in the 1980s the growth in private giving exceeded the growth of expenditures on a variety of goods and services that might be considered extravagances—for example, jewelry and watches (41 percent), alcoholic beverages (less than 1 percent), meals eaten outside the home (21.9 percent), tobacco products (-12.1 percent), and personal services (that is, barbershops, beauty parlors, and health clubs; 37.9 percent). Expenditures on new automobiles increased by 59.8 percent, by more than the increase in charitable contributions, but part of the increase may be attributed to the suppressed demand for automobiles in the 1970s due to the repeated energy crises during that decade. Between 1980 and 1989, real total giving by individuals increased by 57.7 percent, exceeding the growth in real total consumer expenditures (32.8 percent) by a wide margin. The increase in total giving by individuals (57.7 percent) exceeded the increase in total consumer credit outstanding (47.7 percent).[13]

Corporate Giving

Corporate giving is far more erratic than individual giving, very likely because corporate giving depends heavily on corporation profits, which fluctuate greatly with the business cycle—far more over time than worker wages and salaries, to which individual giving is tied. Corporate profits (measured both before and after taxes) as a percentage of national income were also on a downward trend during the 1955–1990 period (see figure 3-2). Before-tax corporate profits represented nearly 15 percent of national income in 1955 and only a little more than 7 percent of national income in 1989. After-tax corporate profits represented 8 percent of national income

Figure 3-2 Corporate Profits, Before and After Taxes, as a
Percentage of National Income

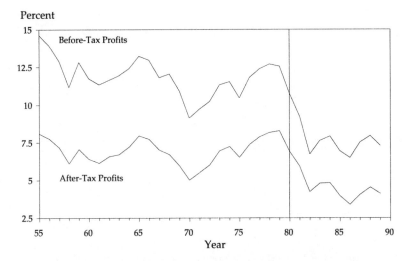

Percent

Source: CITIBASE, Citibank economic data base, 1946–present (New
York: Citibank, N.A., 1991); and author's calculations.

in 1955, falling to half that share in 1989.[14] These downward trends
likely suppressed corporate giving relative to individual giving.

Nevertheless, figure 3-1 shows an increase in corporate giving
over the 1955–1989 period. Corporate giving in real terms rose from
under $1.9 billion in 1955 to over $3.7 billion in 1980, a compound
annual rate of increase of 2.7 percent. By 1989, real corporate giving
had reached almost $5.3 billion, increasing in the 1980s at a com-
pound rate of 4.1 percent. The growth rate in corporate giving was
52 percent higher in the 1980s than in the earlier decades covered by
this study.[15]

Corporate giving both as a percentage of before-tax profits and
as a percentage of after-tax profits was significantly higher in the
1980s than in the 1955–1980 period (see figure 3-3). Corporate giving
as a percentage of profits before and after taxes slumped after 1986.
This slump can be explained in large part by the changes in corporate
tax laws that were passed in 1986.[16] In spite of the drop-off in
corporate giving after 1986, corporate giving as a percentage of

Figure 3-3   Corporate Giving as a Percentage of Before-Tax and
After-Tax Profits

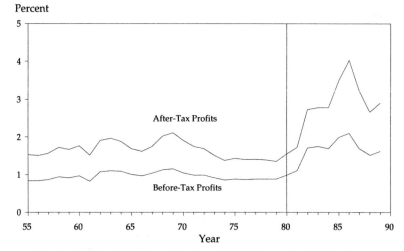

Percent

Source: Giving USA: 1990 (New York: AAFRC Trust for Philanthropy,
1990), and author's calculations.

profits before and after taxes remained higher in the late 1980s than
in the decades prior to the 1980s.

Per Capita Giving

When measured on a per capita basis, individual giving and corporate giving both followed the same pattern as was observed in the
analysis of the total giving numbers (compare figure 3-1 and figure
3-4). Total per capita giving in real dollars expanded relatively
rapidly in the late 1950s and 1960s, rising from $208 per person in
1955 to $324 per person in 1970. The per capita giving moved down
as a result of the economic slump brought on by the OPEC oil supply
shocks in the first half of the 1970s, but giving remained within the
range of $308 to $343 for the rest of the decade. Total per capita giving
then began rising markedly in the 1980s, from $340 in 1980 to $486
in 1989. The annual compound growth rate over the nine years 1980

Figure 3-4 Total, Individual, and Corporate Giving Per Capita in Constant (1990) Dollars

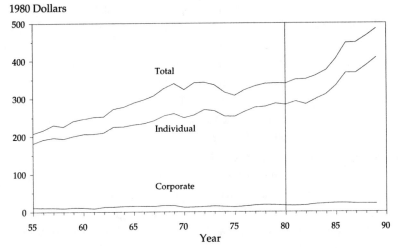

Source: Giving USA: 1990 (New York: AAFRC Trust for Philanthropy, 1990); and author's calculations.

through 1989, 4 percent a year, is robust when compared with the 2 percent average annual increase in the twenty-five years prior to the 1980s.

Individual giving on a per capita basis (and in constant 1990 dollars) rose irregularly from 1955 to 1980, increasing from $182 in 1955 to $284 in 1980. It then spurted upwards once the recession of 1980/81 was over, reaching $409 in 1989. The compound annual rate of growth in individual giving per capita was 4.1 percent in the 1980s compared to 1.8 percent for the previous twenty-five-year period.

Real corporate giving on a per capita basis rose modestly during the entire 1955-1989 period, from $11 in 1955 to $16 in 1980 and then to $21 in 1989. The compound rate of growth for per capita corporate giving in the 1980s, 3.1 percent a year, was more than twice the compound rate of growth in the earlier decades, 1.5 percent a year.

Giving Relative to National Income

Giving in the United States has never absorbed more than a very small fraction of national income. Figure 3-5 reveals that total giving never reached 3 percent of national income between 1955 and 1989. However, what is also obvious is that total giving as a percentage of national income began a marked decline in the 1970s as a result of a downward trend in individual giving as a percentage of national income. Both total and individual giving relative to national income made an obvious turnaround in the late 1970s and continued generally upward throughout the 1980s.

Specifically, total giving as a percentage of national income rose irregularly from 2.3 percent in 1955 to 2.5 percent in 1970, only to fall to a low of 2.1 percent in 1979. By 1986, total giving as a percentage of national income had surpassed its former high and reached 2.7

Figure 3-5 Total, Individual, and Corporate Giving as a Percentage of National Income

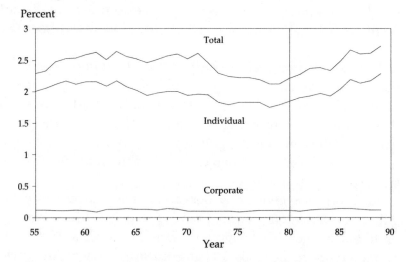

Source: Giving USA: 1990 (New York: AAFRC Trust for Philanthropy, 1990); and author's calculations.

percent in 1989. Corporate giving as a percentage of national income varied within a narrow range of .09 and .14 percent during the 1955–1989 period, with no apparent upward or downward trend.

Actual and Predicted Giving

The unusual surge in giving in the 1980s could possibly be explained by favorable changes in economic conditions during the decade. As a consequence, it might be said that greed was still rampant during the 1980s. Americans were giving more in the 1980s, not because they were more charitable but because they had higher incomes and confronted varying tax rates or because of a long-term upward trend in giving (attributable to many difficult-to-quantify factors, such as changes in religious convictions) that was established prior to the 1980s. Put another way, it might be argued that the growth in giving in the 1980s was merely an extension of past economic relationships and historical trends.

To assess the validity of this argument, statistical analysis (involving regression equations) of the economic determinants of total, individual, and corporate giving in real dollar terms was undertaken for the 1955–1980 period. With the computed equations, predictions for giving during the 1980s can be made, and the actual giving levels can be compared with the predicted levels to determine if giving was unusually high or low given the economic conditions of the 1980s.

Total Giving

The analysis for total giving in real dollars determined that giving is directly related (to a statistically significant degree) to real gross national product (GNP) per capita, the average tax rate (defined as total government receipts divided by national income), and the population.

The higher real GNP is per capita, the higher total giving is in real dollars. This is understandable since people have more to give with higher incomes. The higher the average tax rate, the higher the total giving in real dollars, a relationship that may be explained by the fact that giving does not "cost" as much when tax rates are high as when they are low.[17] The larger the population, the greater the total giving in real dollars, possibly because there are more people to share both the burden and the benefits of the gifts.

The analysis also found a statistically significant downward trend in total real dollar giving during the 1955–1980 period. This suggests that during the 1955–1980 period people were gradually giving a smaller amount after adjusting for the growth in income, tax rates, and population.[18]

Using the regression formulas developed from 1955–1980 data, the levels of total real dollar giving by year were computed for the 1980s and the predicted total giving is shown by the dashed line in figure 3-6. The actual real level of total giving was higher in every year in the 1980s than would have been predicted from the statistical relationships established in the 1955–1980 period. Indeed, a close comparison of the actual and predicted total giving levels reveals that during the decade of the 1980s actual total giving exceeded predicted total giving by an annual average of $14 billion, or by 16 percent. (In 1989, actual total giving exceeded predicted total giving by more than $28 billion, or by 30 percent.) This means that during the so-called decade of greed Americans increased their aggregate giving by the equivalent of one and one-half years over what would have been predicted for the 1980s.

Individual Giving

Statistical procedures similar to those used for total giving were employed for individual giving. The major differences are that individual giving was made a function of real per capita personal income (not real GNP per capita) and average tax rates were computed using personal taxes (not total taxes) as a percentage of personal income (not national income).[19] Figure 3-7 shows the actual and predicted individual giving in real dollars. A comparison of the actual and predicted figures reveals that during the 1980s real individual giving

Figure 3-6 Actual and Predicted Total Giving in Constant (1990) Dollars

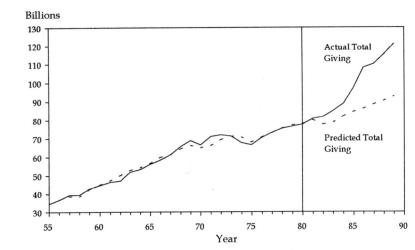

Source: Author's calculations.

Figure 3-7 Actual and Predicted Individual Giving in Constant (1990) Dollars

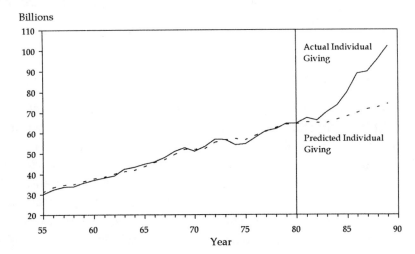

Source: Author's calculations.

Figure 3-8   Actual and Predicted Corporate Giving in Constant (1990) Dollars

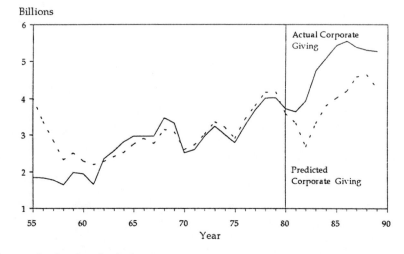

Source: Author's calculations.

exceeded predicted real individual giving by an annual average of $13 billion, or by 18 percent. (In 1989, actual individual giving exceeded predicted individual giving by more that $27 billion, or by nearly 37 percent.)

Corporate Giving

Figure 3-8 reveals the highly erratic movements in corporate charity that, considering the statistical procedures employed, were assumed to be related to real before-tax profits plus the corporate capital accumulation allowances, the average corporate tax rate (corporate taxes divided by before-tax profits), and a long-term trend.[20] A comparison of actual and predicted corporate giving reveals that during the 1980s actual corporate giving in real dollars exceeded predicted giving by an annual average of $1.1 billion, which amounts to a substantial 28 percent greater annual level of giving than would have been predicted from the corporate giving patterns established in the 1955–1980 period. (In 1989, actual corporate giving exceeded predicted corporate giving by slightly less than $1 billion, or by 23.2 percent.)

Tax Payments

People can express their charitable inclinations through adopted tax policies as well as through private donations. Many of these tax payments (but hardly all) are intended to serve humanitarian and societal goals that might otherwise be served by private charities. Figure 3-9 shows that total taxes as a percentage of national income were on the rise throughout the period, increasing from 30 percent in 1955 to 40 percent in 1989. Total taxes plus total giving as a percentage of national income followed much the same path but, of course, at higher percentages.

Figure 3-9 Total Taxes and Total Taxes Plus Total Giving as a Percentage of National Income

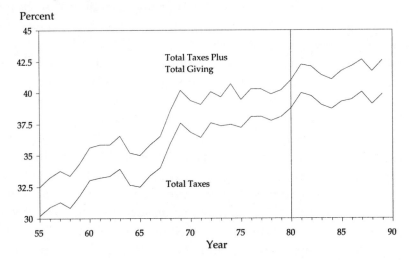

Source: CITIBASE: Citibank economic data base (machine-readable magnetic data file), 1946–present (New York: Citibank, N.A., 1991); and author's calculations.

Why Greater Giving?

While the facts of increased giving are self-evident, the causes of increased giving are not so easily discerned. Hence, identifying the causes is necessarily a somewhat speculative endeavor. Nevertheless, it is worth noting that casual observation and econometric analysis of the charitable data reveal that the level of giving is clearly related to people's incomes and to tax rates. Higher incomes lead to increased giving. One highly plausible explanation for the increased giving in the 1980s was that virtually the whole decade was a period of economic expansion, and incomes rose faster in the 1980s than in the 1970s.

Accordingly, when incomes fell with the recession that began in 1990, total giving in real dollars barely grew (less than 1 percent) between 1989 and 1990.[21] However, when the economy began a weak turnaround in 1991, total giving bounded upward by 6.5 percent.[22]

High tax rates can also lead to more giving. This is the case because many charitable contributions are tax deductible. The higher the tax rates, the lower the after-tax costs of any given gift. The Reagan administration did institute a much lower tax rate structure, which, taken by itself, might imply less giving. Every dollar that is given to a charity is a dollar that can be deducted from taxable income, which means that the giver actually loses the contribution minus the saving on taxes. The lower the tax rate, the higher the after-tax cost of the contribution. The highest marginal tax rate did fall from 70 percent in 1980 to 28 percent in 1990. The marginal tax rate applied to the median income fell from 24 percent in 1980 to 15 percent in 1990. Accordingly, the after-tax cost of a $1,000 contribution for a top-income earner rose from $300 in 1980 to $720 in 1990. The after-tax cost of the same contribution for a median-income earner rose from $760 in 1980 to $850 in 1990.[23] Such after-tax cost changes, by themselves, should have reduced giving (or tempered any increases).

However, the lower rates could have stimulated economic activity, and the resulting greater income could have stimulated greater giving in two ways. First, the higher earnings enabled people to give more. Second, the higher incomes could have driven some taxpayers into higher brackets, lowering the after-tax cost of some giving for them. The net effect of all changes in tax policies is that the "average tax rate" (total taxes paid divided by national income) went up slightly during the decade, rising from 38.8 percent in 1980 to 39.9 percent in 1989 (after increasing from 30.2 percent in 1955).

The greater economic activity along with the prospects of even greater future rewards, in part stimulated by the lower marginal rates and other policy developments, could have been capitalized into greater values for people's wealth holdings, giving rise to a charitable "wealth effect"—more giving because people felt wealthier. As I will show in a later chapter, the country's wealth did rise rapidly during the 1980s. The stock market tripled during the decade, a feat unmatched in post-World War II decades. In all these regards, the growth in giving may be one of the most important overlooked supply-side consequence of the cuts in federal tax rates passed in 1981.

Giving probably went up for a number of other reasons, the most notable of which may be changes in religious attitudes and activities. While the number of Americans who were church members stayed close to 60 percent throughout the 1980s (down from 64 percent in 1960), giving to religious causes escalated. In 1980, religious contributions represented 46 percent of total giving. During the 1980s, the increase in religious contributions accounted for 74 percent of the increase in total giving, which means that by 1989 giving to religious causes had increased to 54 percent of total giving.

During the 1980s, contributions to education, human services, and health causes grew in real dollar terms but fell or stayed more or less the same as a percentage of total giving, probably reflecting greater government expenditures on those areas of social needs. On the other hand, giving in other major categories—arts and cultural, public/society benefits, and environment and wildlife—rose in real dollars and as a percentage of total giving. For example, between 1980 and 1989, real giving to the arts and culture expanded by 42 percent; real giving to education, by 31 percent; real giving to public and societal causes expanded by 56 percent; real giving to environmental and wildlife causes expanded dramatically in the late 1980s, by 22 percent between 1987 (the earliest year for which data is available) and 1989—and rose another 25 percent in 1990 alone.

Still, such descriptive statistics do not reveal why people gave more to the various causes. It may be that changes in the country's income distribution explain a portion of the greater giving. However, it is not clear whether those changes raised or lowered giving. People earning less than $10,000 and over $75,000 in 1989 gave between 2.4 and 2.9 percent of their incomes to charitable causes. However, the vast middle class with incomes between $10,000 and $75,000 generally gave less than 2 percent of their incomes.[24]

Maybe, given that the electorate turned to conservative political agendas and that governments were confronted by the fiscal constraints of rising deficits, many people recognized in the 1980s that government agencies were not able to meet—and would not meet—all social needs, and they responded accordingly, especially when prodded by nightly news reports concerning the plight of the homeless and environmental damage. It may also be that the technology of fund-raising improved, and charitable organizations and fundraisers discovered the usefulness of the new technology, especially cable television which began to be used extensively in the 1980s for religious broadcasts and other forms of fund-raising. Evangelical religious organizations did expand relative to many other churches during the 1980s. It may also be that giving rose because more resources were devoted to fund-raising. This prospect suggests that the actual funds available to charitable causes may not have risen as much as giving did.

The full range of causes of the charitable explosion during the 1980s awaits further research, a fact that should at least temper the enthusiasm of the 1980s critics for sweeping, ready-made, shorthand explanations for how a quarter-billion Americans behaved on balance during an entire decade. All we really know at this juncture is that the 1980s did not live down to its billing; it was not the well-advertised decade of greed, at least not as measured by the giving of Americans.

Concluding Comments

Economic claims, which may have been based solely on isolated cases of obvious abuse of economic power, have a way of being repeated so frequently that they are believed without hesitation and with conviction. The 1980s may have been, by some measures not considered here, a decade of greed. There were, no doubt, individual instances of outlandish efforts to achieve "conspicuous opulence" with total disregard for the welfare of other people. However, as the *Wall Street Journal* editors noted, "The greedy are undoubtedly always with us," but then asked prophetically the question that others should have asked, "Were the 1980s really the Greed Decade?"[25]

The charity data reveal that claims about wanton and rampant greed in the 1980s have been far too sweeping, bordering on reckless. In terms of charitable contributions, the American public and the corporate sector out-paced by a wide margin their giving patterns established in earlier decades. In addition, it should be noted that individuals and corporations increased their rate of giving at a time when their real tax payments, part of which were intended to serve charitable goals, were on the rise.

Notes

1. Otto Friedrich, "Freed from Greed?" *Time*, January 1, 1990, pp. 76–77.

2. Laurence Shames, *The Hunger for More: Searching for Values in an Age of Greed* (New York: Vantage Books, 1991), p. 27.

3. Kevin Phillips, *The Politics of the Rich and Poor: Wealth and the American Electorate in the Reagan Aftermath* (New York: Random House, 1990), p. 43, emphasis in the original.

4. This report uses data from *Giving USA: 1990* (New York: American Association of Fund Raising Council Trust for Philanthropy, 1990). Other data sources for charitable contributions (namely, the Independent Sector and the U.S. Bureau of Labor Statistics) provide similar but slightly different pictures of giving during the 1980s. For a graphical summary of several sources, see "The Demographics of Giving," *The American Enterprise*, September/October 1991, pp. 101–104.

5. "The Greed Decade Reversed," *Wall Street Journal*, July 12, 1991.

6. Robert J. Samuelson, "Kevin Phillips' America," *Washington Post*, June 29, 1990.

7. The data are collected and reported by the AAFRC Trust for Philanthropy, *Giving USA: 1990* (New York: AAFRC Trust for Philanthropy, 1990). Total giving also includes gifts by foundations, bequests, and "others." Aside from gross national product, inflation (real or constant-dollar) values for data series were obtained by using the experimental consumer price index, not the standard consumer price index, with 1990 as the base year. The method for accounting for changes in housing prices was abruptly changed in 1983 in the standard consumer price index, which means the methodology is inconsistent. Furthermore, the method for computing price levels prior to 1983 overstates inflation. Therefore, use of the standard consumer price index would overstate the downward adjustments in the data series and understate the growth in giving in the 1970s as compared to the growth of giving in the 1980s.

8. Giving through bequests and foundations are not considered here in detail because of their complicated linkages with tax laws. Nevertheless, constant-dollar bequests and foundation giving followed much the same pattern during the 1955–1989 period. The total of bequests and foundation giving rose in terms of 1990 dollars from $2.4 billion in 1955 to $14.9 billion in 1971, only to fall to under $8 billion in 1979. The total of bequests and foundation giving then began to rise once again, reaching $14 billion again in 1989.

9. Because of the advent of the recession, total giving in real dollars grew by slightly less than 1 percent in 1990.

10. Real giving by individuals in 1990 grew by only .4 percent, very likely so low because of the recession that began in 1990.

11. As reported in AAFRC Trust for Philanthropy, *Giving USA: 1990*, p. 34.

12. Ibid.

13. The percentage rise in total giving between 1980 and 1989 exceeded the percentage increase in consumer expenditures on all of the selected goods and services, save new automobiles, which was 59.8 percent. And the increased purchases of new cars is distorted by the 18 percent drop in real new car sales between 1978 and 1980 and the 8 percent drop in new car sales between 1986 and 1989. The increase in American's expenditures on new cars between the average sales for 1977–1980 and 1986–1989 is 42.9 percent.

14. Corporate profits with inventory and capital accumulation adjustments, which is a much broader measure of corporate profitability, also trended downward, dropping from 14 percent of national income in 1955 to 7.4 percent of national income in 1989. The decline in the relative share of income going into profits helps explain why corporate taxes as a percentage of national income also trended downward throughout the 1955–1989 period, falling from 6.6 percent of national income in 1955 to 3.2 percent in 1989. Of course, annual corporate earnings are sensitive to changes in the tax system, especially with regard to depreciation allowances.

15. Corporate giving varies somewhat with the business cycles. About half of the relatively greater growth rate can be explained by the drop in corporate giving from slightly more than $4 billion in 1979 to $3.7 billion in 1980. Using the annual average level of corporate giving for the 1978–1982 period of $3.9 billion as the base, corporate giving escalated in the 1980s by a compound growth rate of 3.5 percent, which still makes the growth rate in corporate giving in the 1980s 30 percent higher than in the prior period.

16. The AAFRC Trust for Philanthropy reports actual giving by corporations for 1986 at $5.179 billion but in a footnote indicates this reported figure "most likely includes significant portions of grants made in 1987, but reported on 1986 corporate returns for tax purposes. Realistic estimate is $4.65 billion for a 3.98% change" (AAFRC, *Giving USA*, p. 11). To remain on the conservative side, all computations for this study were done using the AAFRC's estimated lower corporate giving level of $4.65 billion for 1986.

17. At a tax rate of 25 percent, a tax-deductible gift of $100 costs the

taxpayer $75 after taxes. When the tax rate is 40 percent, the gift costs the taxpayer only $60.

18. The regression equation used to predict real total giving is as follows:

Total Giving = -3.70 + 476271.6 GNP Per Capita + 979807353 Tax Rate + 2021.7 Population - 4.55 Trend + .609 AR(1).

All coefficients are significant at the .05 confidence level. The adjusted R-square is .986, and the Durbin-Watson statistic is 1.744.

19. The regression equation used to predict constant dollar giving by individuals is as follows:

Real Individual Giving = - 1.44 + 2350609 Real Personal Income Per Capita + 9.13 Personal Tax Rate + 876.49 Population - 1.62 Trend + .282 AR(1)

All coefficients are significant at the .05 confidence level, and the adjusted R-square is .99. The Durbin-Watson statistic is 1.784.

20. The regression equation used to predict constant-dollar corporate giving is as follows:

Real Corporate Giving = -2.55 + .0088 Profits + 4.88 Corporate Tax Rate - 45699525 Trend + .652 AR(1)

The corporate tax rate is not significant at the .10 confidence level. The coefficients for Profits and Trend are significant at the .05 confidence level. The adjusted R-square is .94, and the Durbin-Watson statistic is 2.01.

21. AAFRC Trust for Philanthropy, *Giving USA: 1991* (New York: AAFRC Trust for Philanthropy, 1991).

22. AAFRC Trust for Philanthropy, *Giving USA: 1992* (New York: AAFRC Trust for Philanthropy, 1992).

23. See Gerald E. Auten, James M. Cilke, and William C. Randolph, "The Effects of Tax Reform on Charitable Contributions," (Washington, DC: Office of Tax Analysis, U.S. Department of the Treasury, draft May 1992).

24. As reported in "The Demographics of Giving," *The American Enterprise,* September/October 1991, p. 104.

25. "The Greed Decade Reversed," *Wall Street Journal,* July 12, 1991.

4

POLITICS OF THE RICH
AND THE POOR: INCOMES

The welfare of the vast majority of Americans is not good, and the future offers little hope of correction without government initiatives. That was the stark reality of American economic life during the 1980s, which will continue into the 1990s—according to a growing number of social commentators.

The modern prophets of gloom worry that at some time during the 1980s the "American dream" began to erode for upwards of 80 percent of Americans because of intensifying global competition and the presumed ethical bankruptcy of the Reagan administration's economic and social policies. The convulsive economic changes of the 1980s caused a "seismic" shift in the income distribution with, as commonly argued, the rich getting richer and the rest, poorer.[1] Moreover, many critics stress that the gains of the rich are directly responsible for the losses of the nonrich. The economic game played during the 1980s was rigged, and it was effectively a negative-sum game. What the rich got was taken from the poor—the critical ingredient in what many see as renewed class warfare that will ultimately be fought in the Halls of Congress over a new tax policy designed to right the wrongs of the income distribution. Of course,

Bill Clinton became president partly because he argued that the changes in the nation's income distribution clearly indicated that "trickle-down economics," as he caricatured the policies of the Reagan administration, had failed.

While this disconcerting perspective on the income distribution is widely held with a continuing flow of supporting data and commentaries, careful study reveals that the perspective is founded on a partial and misleading statistical analysis. Accordingly, many of the conclusions deduced from the surveyed statistics are misguided exaggerations of what really happened to the income distribution during the 1970s and 1980s.

By historical standards economic growth during the past two decades was continuous but sluggish, distinguished especially in the late 1970s and early 1980s by a disappointing rebound in productivity and real wage increases. Without question, some Americans ended the 1980s with much lower standards of living than they had at the start of the decade. However, the economy has always been beset with people moving down the income scale. The vast majority of Americans were much better off at the start of the 1990s than they were a decade earlier. Furthermore, it is inaccurate to claim, as argued by Harvard Professor Robert Reich, that only the "most fortunate fifth" of the income distribution—those 20 percent of American households with the highest incomes—gained by the changes in the 1980s, and that they gained solely, or mainly, at the expense of Americans with lower incomes.[2] Contrary to popular wisdom, the real (inflation-adjusted) incomes of people in the lowest quintile on average were higher in 1990 than they were two decades earlier. Furthermore, their incomes began climbing in the 1980s, after the 1981–1982 recession.

Many of the apparent changes in the income distribution can be attributed to demographic forces that had little or nothing to do with presidential policies and politics, for example, the rising divorce rate, the declining size of families in lower income groups, the changing age distribution within the population, the growing number of two-income earners in higher income groups, the declining work experience of many family units, and the inability or refusal of some people to stay in school or to take advantage of educational opportunities. A portion of the apparent perverse changes in the income distribution can also be chalked up to a flawed measure of the cost of living used by some researchers to adjust for inflation and to the growing importance of fringe benefits in compensation packages that caused many workers' money wages to fall, giving the impression that their total compensation likewise fell.

Finally, the evidence indicates that convenient classifications like the "poorest fifth" (or lowest 20 percent of the income distribution, also known as the lowest quintile) and the "richest fifth"—or even the "fortunate fifth"—of income earners do not cover fixed groups of workers. Indeed, myopic focus on fifths of the income distribution, as if they were immutable clubs, obscures a tremendous movement of people up and down the income distribution. A significant number of Americans in the lowest quintile at the start of the decade were in the highest quintile at the end of the decade, meaning that many in the top quintile at the start of the decade must have moved down the income distribution. Of course, many Americans in the middle three-fifths of the income distribution moved within their income class too, while others moved to the polar ends of the distribution.

Such facts make fallacious the simplistic claim that only the fortunate fifth gained during the 1980s. Nevertheless, such claims have been repeated in various forums by reputable commentators of virtually all political persuasions.

Political Posturing on Incomes

Commentators from many points on the political spectrum have articulated and purveyed a bleak picture of the country's economic and social structure. In their defense of "America's misunderstood welfare state," Yale Professors Theodore Marmor and Jerry Mashaw and New York Attorney Philip Harvey announced that the country's "economic story is easily told."[3] Their story is told with what have come to be standard charts of the median family income—first rising more or less steadily from 1947 to the early 1970s, then flattening out, and thereafter turning downward. Marmor, Mashaw, and Harvey also make confident claims regarding the "increasing gap between the wealthiest and the poorer segments of society" that, along with a host of other problems, "continue to undermine the public's sense of well-being."[4] In the more descriptive words of Greg Duncan, Timothy Smeeding, and Willard Rodgers in a study for the Levy Institute on Income Inequality, "the rising tide of economic growth in the 1980s appears to have lifted the yachts, but neither the tugboats nor the rowboats."[5]

Reich gives the details on this growing inequality,

Controlling for family size, geography, and other changes, the best estimate... is that between 1977 and 1990 the average income of the poorest fifth of Americans declined by about 5 percent, while the richest fifth became about 9 percent wealthier. During these years, the average incomes of American families declined by about 7 percent, while the average income of the richest fifth of American families *increased about 15 percent. That left the poorest fifth of Americans with 3.7 percent of the nation's total income, down from 5.5 percent twenty years before—the lowest portion they have received since 1954.*[6] (emphasis in the original)

Reich suggests that the "routine production workers," who constitute about a fourth of all workers, and "routine personal service" providers, who constitute approximately 30 percent of the work force, have skills that can be relatively easily duplicated by lower paid workers abroad. Hence, their real wages have suffered with the advent of the global economy.[7] Many government workers and defense contractors, who Reich estimates constitute another quarter of the labor force, may not face global competition, but their hopes for wage increases have been dashed by tightening government budgets.

Only the "most fortunate fifth" of workers, composed principally of "symbolic analysts" (who are involved in data and word manipulation) have been sheltered from foreign competition and have been in sufficiently high demand to exact higher real wages, or so Reich maintains.[8] This fortunate fifth of workers—all of whom have, presumably, "princely incomes"—has been able to produce 40 percent of the country's output and to receive comparable incomes. These workers, Reich concludes, are the ones who must shoulder the burden of helping the less fortunate workers with greater government-provided education and health care and more expenditures on the nation's infrastructure.

The perception of growing income disparity has not, however, been the exclusive concern of the political left. More moderate, if not conservative, commentators have accepted the left's basic premises and facts on the nation's income distribution. *New York Times* business columnist Leonard Silk has declared that "there is a widespread awareness that living standards for most people have been stagnating and that life is harder for the young than it was for their parents."[9] *Wall Street Journal* reporter Alan Murray mused, "From 1978 to 1990, those fortunate American households in the top 5% of the income scale saw their average incomes increase 16%, after adjusting for inflation. But the people in the middle of the income scale watched their incomes fall slightly," a problem he attributes partially to huge tax cuts for the wealthy and Social Security tax increases on the middle and lower income classes.[10]

On economic equality, *Washington Post* and *Newsweek* economics columnist Robert Samuelson has stated flatly, "There's less of it. We are more a society of haves and have nots."[11] A *Business Week* reporter has echoed these sentiments, stressing that the "underlying shifts in income over the past 15 years have been seismic" and that the growing income disparity threatens long-term economic growth.[12] "What's more," said Pennar, "there don't seem to have been any economic benefits from the rich having gotten richer, as some economists argued in the early 1980s, when the Reagan administration first slashed taxes,"[13] a presumed major cause of the growing inequality. Similarly, a *Los Angeles Times* labor columnist placed the blame for current economic problems on the failing "Reagan-Bush 'trickle-down,' supply-side economic policies" that have helped the rich get richer: "Already generally known is that the real income of middle-income workers continues to drop and that of the poor is plummeting, while the income of those at the top of the economic pile soars."[14]

Evidence of Decay: A Matter of How Data Are Viewed

The economic history of the 1960s, 1970s, and 1980s is a confused statistical picture. Complaints of growing income stagnation and inequality emerged as gross national product (GNP) and disposable income per American continued their historical upward trek, albeit at a slower rate of growth. Real per capita GNP rose by 28 percent from 1960 to 1970, by 19 percent between 1970 and 1980, and by 18 percent between 1980 and 1990. If the economic well-being of most income groups was eroding, critics have understandably charged it must have been because the expanding income pie was gradually being divided differently.

The picture of economic stagnation and decline for the vast majority of American workers is often painted with reference to average worker wages and median family income. The "Gini index" (a measure of income inequality) and income shares by quintiles of the population are also commonly used to measure changes in income distribution. Each claim and data series used to indicate growing inequality needs to be carefully and separately evaluated.[15]

The Great U-Turn Revisited

One of the first lines of assault on the income distribution was on what was happening to the "average" earnings of Americans. In *The Great U-Turn*, Harrison and Bluestone explained how the American economy had, beginning in the early 1970s, begun to make a U-turn on the road of economic progress.[16] Professors Harrison and Bluestone open their book with a foreboding claim: "The standard of living of American workers—and a growing number of their families—is in serious trouble. For every affluent 'yuppie' in an expensive big-city condominium... there are many more people whose wages have fallen and whose families are finding it more and more difficult to make ends meet."[17] The evidence, Harrison and Bluestone argued, demands that the country "turn back toward greater planning and away from the treacherous path of laissez-faire."[18]

A key statistic used to support their conclusion is the reversal in the real (inflation-adjusted) average wage of production and nonsupervisory workers.[19] Everyone knows that the average worker wage in current dollars has continued to rise. However, Harrison and Bluestone rightfully argued that the change in the number of dollars earned per hour can be misleading, mainly because each dollar of wage cannot buy as much as it once could. After adjusting for changes in prices, the higher worker wage might even buy less, in which case one could argue that workers have suffered a "U-turn" in their standard of living.

Professors Harrison and Bluestone plotted average real wages of workers. The real (inflation-adjusted to 1990 prices) average worker wage did rise by 28 percent from 1959 ($9.07) to 1973 ($11.60), after which it fell irregularly by 14 percent, or to $10.02, over the following seventeen-year span. There is something of an inverted "U" in the data. However, the consumer price index (CPI) that Harrison and Bluestone use is inconsistent, since the method used for computing it was abruptly changed in 1983. Until 1983, the method used to compute the index overstated the rate of inflation by estimating the change in the cost of housing by considering the change in the purchase price of housing, not the more realistic change in the imputed rental cost of housing used since 1983 in computing the consumer price index. Hence, use of the standard CPI in adjusting wages for the effects of inflation understates the growth in real wages (or overstates their fall).[20]

The Harrison and Bluestone analysis is defective because it relies on the standard CPI, with its inconsistent methods of controlling for changes in the cost of housing. Fortunately, although not widely known, statisticians at the BLS have developed the "experimental" consumer price index (dubbed the CPI-X or, more properly, the CPI-X-U1), which is founded on the new method of computing the cost of housing throughout all years. The BLS has recomputed the CPI-X back to 1967, and the Council of Economic Advisers has extended it back to 1959.

If workers' average real wages are computed using this experimental price index, the "U" in the U-turn is not so great. Still, there remains some decline in worker real wages, from $11.02 in 1978 to $10.02 in 1990—a decline of about 9 percent.

Does this mean that American workers were, on average, worse off at the end of the 1980s, albeit slightly? This data would certainly suggest the obvious answer is an unqualified, "Yes." However, there are good reasons for doubt. The most important reason is that per capita disposable income in the U.S. grew in real dollar terms by 21 percent between 1978 and 1990. It would appear odd that real wages declined at the same time real disposable income per capita grew.

This income paradox can be partially explained by another form of income redistribution, a shift in the form in which earnings are received—from worker money wages to worker nonmoney benefits (employer contributions to social insurance, health and life insurance, retirement, vacation days, as well as many other identified worker fringe benefits). Nonwage compensation as a percentage of wages and salaries rose dramatically in the 1960s and 1970s, from just under 9 percent in 1960 to nearly 21 percent in 1990. The fact of the matter is that workers were gradually taking a larger share of their earnings in nonmoney forms, understandably so. Fringe benefits are often nontaxable forms of income.

Moreover, by persistently raising Social Security and other payroll taxes imposed on employers, Congress has forced workers to accept lower wages. In terms of 1990 dollars, employer real dollar contributions to social insurance more than tripled between 1960 and 1988, from 4.6 percent of wages and salaries in 1960 to 7.8 percent of wages and salaries in 1973, and then to 10.4 percent of wages and salaries in 1988. These are wages employers would just as soon have passed on to their workers, but could not.

Figure 4-1 includes the Harrison and Bluestone U-turn in real worker wages, but with a difference: The real wage for each year is computed relative to the 1959 level. This index (represented by the bottom line in figure 4-1), rises from 1.0 in 1959, to 1.28 in 1973, and then falls off to 1.10 in 1990. When fringe benefits are added to worker real hourly wages and the total real compensation per hour is recomputed with the CPI-X, the total real hourly compensation (shown by the middle line in figure 4-1) rises from 1.0 in 1959, to 1.45 in 1978, and then falls to 1.33 in 1990, a drop of 8 percent. This produces a "U" that looks more like an upside-down "L."

Even with these adjustments, the "average hourly wage" remains defective as a measure of incomes, mainly because the wages of 20 percent or so of American workers is not included. In addition, the rise in the labor force participation of women and minorities and the growing use of part-time workers during the 1970s and 1980s

Figure 4-1 Different Measures of Workers' Hourly Wage, 1959–1990

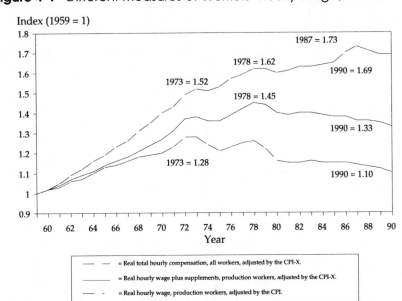

Source: Council of Economic Advisers, *Economic Report of the President: 1991* (Washington, DC: U.S. Government Printing Office, February 1991); unpublished data from the Council of Economic Advisers; and author's calculations.

pulled the average wage down, despite the fact that the greater employment of women and minorities meant income gains for many families. Women, minorities, and part-time workers tend to earn less than average wages, so their increased participation lowers the overall average hourly wage rate. In 1973, women represented 38 percent of the civilian labor force; by 1990, they represented 45 percent of the labor force. In 1973, nonwhite workers represented 11 percent of the civilian labor force; they represented 14 percent in 1990.

Moreover, during the 1980s hourly wages gradually gave way to other forms of compensation, namely salaries and year-end and production bonuses.[21] In 1973 total hourly wages represented 57 percent of total wages and salaries, and in 1989 they represented 49 percent.

If total worker compensation (including all money and non-money benefits) in all forms for all workers is computed on an average hourly basis and adjusted for inflation via the CPI-X, the widely advertised "Great U-turn" evaporates totally (see the top line of figure 4-1). Total compensation per hour was $9.61 in 1959, $14.58 in 1973, $15.53 in 1978, and (after peaking at $16.60 in 1987) $16.25 in 1990. Average worker welfare has continued to march upward throughout the 1980s.

Even this higher measure of income does not account for the fact that "quality" improvements in the goods and services Americans buy often result in higher prices. If the consumer price index does not properly adjust for quality changes, which cannot always be done, then the computed real wages will understate the true rise in living standard. For many American industries in the 1980s, "quality" was greatly elevated as a goal, partially because of the growing importance of international trade. The fact that quality has become "Job 1" for many firms probably means that computed real wages understate the improvement in America's living standard.

Nevertheless, it is evident that this more optimistic reformulation of American real wages indicates that the growth in average real compensation slowed significantly after 1973. From 1959 to 1973, real compensation grew at a compound annual rate of slightly more than

3 percent. From 1973 to 1990, real compensation rose at a rate of less than two-thirds of 1 percent. This, then, is the core of the real economic problem of the 1970s and 1980s—a slowdown instead of a U-turn in worker wages. No one has been able to fully explain this phenomenon, but most analysts link it to a slowdown in the growth of worker productivity from growth rates achieved prior to the early 1980s. This slowdown in worker productivity growth has been attributed to a host of factors, not the least of which are:

➤ the low private saving and investment rates,

➤ declines in the academic performance of American students in public schools,

➤ the oil crises of the 1970s (which, in turn, may be attributed to freeing the dollar on international money markets in August 1971),[22]

➤ growth in government regulations (especially environmental regulation),

➤ the decline of unions with the growing competitiveness of the domestic and international economies, and

➤ growth in social problems since the early 1970s.

The only consolation in the productivity data over the past two decades is that during the 1980s productivity growth did indeed revive from the close-to-zero rates endured in the late 1970s. Moreover, in the 1980s manufacturing productivity increased in many industries at record rates. Finally, some of the productivity increase (and resulting increase in real earnings) might be obscured behind difficulties in measuring productivity increases in services—especially services like health care, which were taking a greater share of gross domestic product—and behind increases in the quality of products.

To deny a great U-turn and to acknowledge that there was a slowdown in the growth of real workers wages is not to dismiss the problems confronting the American economy. It is, however, a way to put the country's problems in perspective so unnecessary policy solutions will be avoided. Dramatic policies organized to reverse a great U-turn may not be appropriate for bolstering the already rising income level. Furthermore, averages are just that, averages, and even when the average is falling, the real hourly compensation of many American workers (including many low-income workers) could be rising, as was the case in the 1980s.

Median Household Income

Critics of the economic plight of most Americans almost always cite the most readily available measure of income, median household income adjusted for inflation.[23] Using the conventional means of adjusting for inflation—the standard CPI rather than the CPI-X—this measure of the fate of households is disconcerting, as was true of the average hourly wage.

As evident in the top panel of figure 4-2, real median family income moved up and down strongly during the 1970s and 1980s with the trend virtually flat.[24] Real median household income in 1990 (and in 1990 prices) of $29,943 was $1,001 below the 1973 peak (again in 1990 prices) of $30,944. However, contrary to widely reported claims, real median income hardly stagnated during the 1980s. In fact, it plunged by 10 percent from 1978 ($30,197) to 1982 ($27,320), due in no small way to the Federal Reserve's severe anti-inflation policies initiated in 1979. After the recession, this measure of real median income rose by 11.5 percent from the low in 1982 to the high in 1989 ($30,468), revealing that an important boost for household income is the combined effects of increasing worker productivity and an expanding economy, which characterized the 1982–1989 period.

Moreover, this measure of household income understates the actual total real earnings of households during the 1970s and 1980s in three key ways. First, it uses an inflation index (the CPI) that is inconsistent and progressively overstates the increase in the cost of living during the 1970s and early 1980s, when the inflation rate was rising. Hence, growth in real median incomes during the 1970s and early 1980s is progressively understated.

Figure 4-2   Real Median Household Income with Trend, in 1990 Dollars, Using the CPI and the CPI-X, 1967–1990

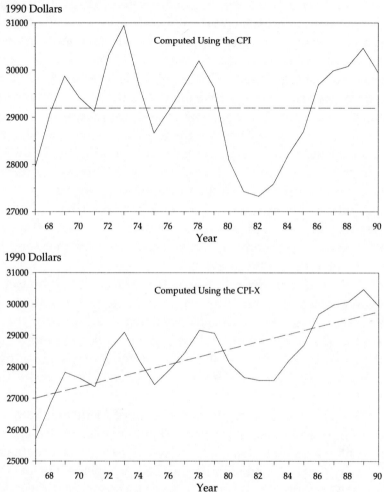

When the median household income is adjusted for inflation with the CPI-X, a decidedly different picture of real median household income can be observed (see bottom panel in figure 4-2). This recomputed real median household income still falls and rises with recessions and recoveries during the 1970s and 1980s, but the trend is clearly upward.

Second, as is true of hourly wages, the standard measure of

median income does not include compensation received in kind by
the poor (for example, subsidized housing, Medicaid, and food
stamps) and in fringe benefits (popularly referred to as "fringes") by
higher income families (such as health and life insurance).[25] Both the
in-kind and wage and salary supplements in nonmoney forms were
rising as a proportion of total income during the two decades. We
have already noted the rise in fringes in the 1970s and 1980s, indeed,
a 64 percent greater share in 1990 than in 1970; and for many worker
groups the value of fringes approximated twice the average percentage.[26] According to the Census Bureau, including only health insurance supplements to wage and salary income would have boosted
the median household income by $1,342, or by about 4.5 percent.[27]

Many worker groups explicitly traded away wages and salaries
for added benefits and greater job security.[28] Those trades, or "givebacks" as they are often labeled, actually lowered the average median, even though many of the workers believed that they had
improved their economic positions.

The top line in figure 4-3 adjusts the real median household
income for the increases in the wages and salary supplements that
have been measured.[29] As can be seen, with that adjustment, the real
median is decidedly more upward sloping, indicating more rapid
real income growth. Indeed, the real household median rises by 20
percent between 1967 and 1990 and by 13 percent between 1973 and
1990.

In 1970, in-kind benefits in the form of Medicare, Medicaid,
food stamps, and housing assistance represented slightly more than
3 percent of aggregate personal income. By 1984, these benefits had
practically doubled and stood at just under 6 percent of personal
income. Again, the Census Bureau estimates that in 1990, the in-kind
benefits added 4 percent ($1,227) to the median income for all
households.[30]

Third, the real median household income charted in figure 4-2
is not adjusted for the declining size of households and families
throughout the period covered. Between 1970 and 1986, the average
family size fell by 17 percent, from 3 to 2.5 people, partially because
couples had fewer children, single-parent families doubled as a

Figure 4-3   Real Median Household Income with Adjustments for
Supplements and Family Size

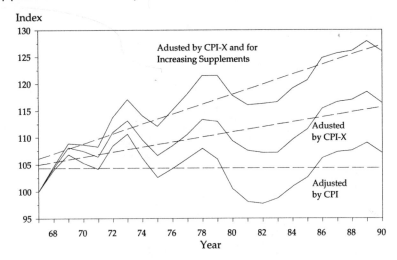

share of all families (from 10 to 20 percent), and households with
nonelderly heads not living with relatives expanded as a share of
families by nearly two-thirds (from 14 to 23 percent).[31] As evident in
figure 4-4, the real median family income, computed with the CPI
and unadjusted for changing family size, fell by 4 percent between
1970 and 1986 (the last year the adjusted family data are available).
However, after adjusting for the economies associated with smaller
families and using the CPI-X, researchers at the Congressional
Budget Office found the median rose by slightly more than 20
percent between 1970 and 1986.[32] After further adjusting real median
family income for increases in supplements, the trend has a steeper
slope and the increase is 28 percent between 1970 and 1986.

Of course, the adjusted real family income for all families
represented in figure 4-4 could hide growing economic distress
among many subgroups of families. Figure 4-5 reports the adjusted
family income of six categories of families: (1) nonelderly childless
families, (2) married couples with children, (3) elderly childless
families, (4) nonelderly unrelated individuals, (5) elderly unrelated
individuals, and (6) single parents with children. In all categories,

Figure 4-4 Real Median Family Income with Adjustments for Supplements and Family Size

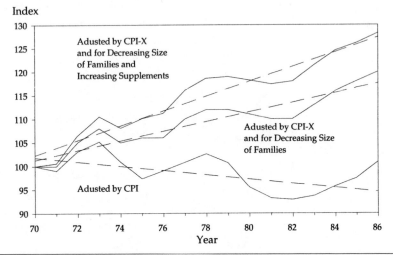

Figure 4-5 Trends in Real Median Adjusted Family Income (using the CPI-X) by Family Type, 1970–1986

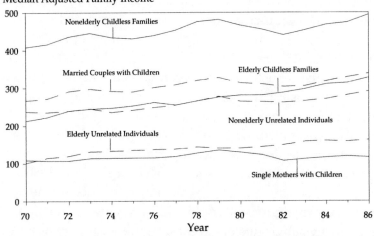

Note: Unrelated individuals are considered to be one-person families.

Source: Congressional Budget Office, U.S. Congress, *Trends in Family Income: 1970–1986* (Washington, DC: U.S. Government Printing Office, February 1988), p. xviii.

the adjusted family income was higher in 1986 than in 1970, with single parents with children receiving only slightly more in 1986 than in 1970. However, it needs to be reiterated that "adjusted family income" does not include the value of in-kind transfers and fringe benefits.

Moreover, as a reminder, no adjustment is included for many improvements in the quality of the products purchased, for income earned illegally, or for the value of the goods and services produced for personal use, all of which would likely increase "family income." Most researchers agree that the hidden (underground or illegal) economy grew significantly as a percentage of the national economy during the 1970–1990 period. According to one recent study, by the early 1980s the hidden economy in the United States very possibly represented at least 10 percent and quite possibly more than a quarter of the official gross national product (or more than $1 trillion in 1990 dollars).[33] These black and grey markets were, of course, boosting the incomes and wealth of many American households.[34]

Still, there may be identifiable age groups that have suffered, and these age groups might be sizable, but do they represent anywhere close to 80 percent of the population? Did only the "most fortunate fifth" gain? Figure 4-6 reports the adjusted real income for families classified according to the age of the head, under age 25, 25–34, 35–54, 55–64, and 65 and over. This picture of changing real income by age of family head reveals at least some income growth for four out of the five age groups.

Only the families with heads under 25 had a median adjusted income in 1986 lower than in 1970. This group, however, represented only 8 percent of all families in 1986. While those families with heads age 25–34 had a higher adjusted median income in 1986 than in 1970, they had a slightly lower adjusted median income than in 1979. These families represented 24 percent of all families in 1986. These two groups of families in total represented nearly a third of families. The data still do not support the exorbitant claim that four-fifths of families became worse off. No more than 32 percent of families (the sum of the under 25 and 25–34 age groups) could possibly have been made worse off. In addition, it must be emphasized that these figures

Figure 4-6 Trends in Real Median Adjusted Family Income (using the CPI-X) by Age of Family Head, 1970–1986

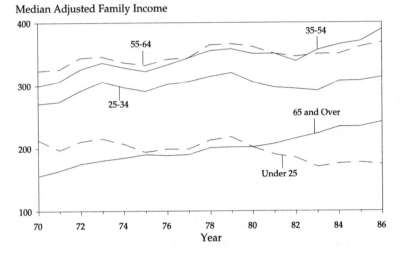

Note: Unrelated individuals are considered to be one-person families.
Source: Congressional Budget Office, U.S. Congress, *Trends in Family Income: 1970–1986* (Washington, DC: U.S. Government Printing Office, February 1988), p. 37.

represent averages, which no doubt hide the rising real incomes of many (perhaps as many as half or more) in those age groups. Such data may be of little comfort to families whose economic well-being eroded, but they do help clarify the true dimensions of the social problems associated with the evolving income distribution.

The Income Distribution

One of the most widely cited measures of income inequality is the Gini index, which ranges from zero (perfect equality, with individuals having equal shares of income) to 1 (perfect inequality, with one person having all the income). As indicated in figure 4-7, the Gini indexes in 1967 for households and families were .399 and .358, respectively. By 1990, the indexes had risen to .428 and .396, again respectively. The increase in the Gini index for households was 7.3

Figure 4-7 The Gini Index for Households and Families, 1967–1990

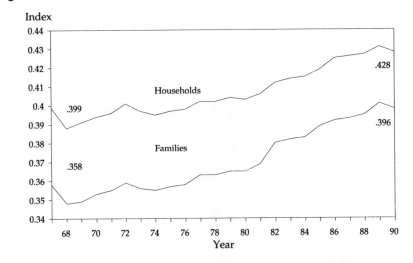

percent, while the increase in the Gini index for families was 10.6 percent, indicating growing inequality in both cases.[35] But does this mean the country became more a country of haves and have nots, with growing inequality emerging supposedly only after free-marketeers took over the White House in the 1980s? Were the have nots getting progressively less on average during the 1980s? Was the growth in inequality the result of the incomes of the haves rising more rapidly than the incomes of the have nots? Or was the Gini rising because many have nots were rapidly moving up the income scale?

The rising Gini has persuaded many people to believe that American society is not only more unequal but also more inequitable than in the past. Moreover, the perception of growing inequality is reinforced by the shares of aggregate income going to the five quintiles of the income distribution. Figure 4-8 shows the percentage of household income going to the quintile of households having the lowest incomes, the middle three quintiles with the next highest incomes, and then the quintile of households with the highest incomes. The figures reveal that the share of total household incomes received by the middle 60 percent consistently fell, from 52.7 percent

Figure 4-8 Share of Aggregate Household Income by Quintile:
1970, 1980, and 1990

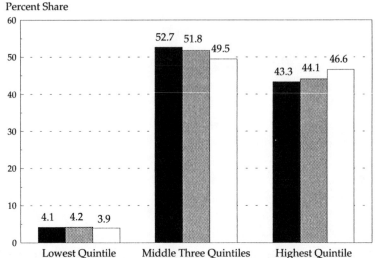

Source: U.S. Census Bureau, *Money Income of Households, Families, and
Persons in the U.S.* (Washington, DC: U.S. Government Printing Office), p. 7.

in 1970 to 51.8 percent in 1980, and then to 49.5 percent in 1990. The
lowest quintile moved up marginally between 1970, 4.1 percent, and
1980, 4.2 percent, and then fell back to 3.9 percent in 1990.

On the other hand, the quintile of households with the highest
income gained gradually throughout the period, from 43.3 percent
in 1970, to 44.1 percent in 1980, to 46.6 percent in 1990. As often
stressed by critics of the country's income structure, these statistics
mean that the 20 percent of households with the highest incomes—
the so-called fortunate fifth—had practically as much total income
in 1990 as all the rest of the households in the country combined. The
extent of income inequality is further revealed by the fact that the
average income of households in the top quintile in 1990 was nearly
twelve times the average income of households in the bottom quintile. Moreover, income of the top quintile was highly concentrated
in the 5 percent of households with the very highest incomes. This
top 5 percent (not shown in the figure) received 18.6 percent of total

household income in 1990 (with an average income nineteen times the average income of the lowest quintile), up from 16.6 percent in 1970 (when the average income of the top 5 percent of households was seventeen times the average of the lowest quintile).

From this evidence, growing inequality appears to be indisputable. And the data have been used to declare that the problem was the 1980s—to be more exact, Ronald Reagan. You can believe what you want about Reagan and his policies. This book is not about him, or a defense of him; it is about the facts of the matter as they relate to the 1980s. Casual observation of figure 4-7 indicates that the upward trend in the Gini index began long before the 1980s. Nevertheless, the fortunate fifth do appear to have been the only gainers from the long upward trek of the Gini. However, appearances, especially as represented in figure 4-8, can be misleading. These statistics are concerned with shares of income received by the various quintiles. The shares of the lower quintiles can fall at the same time that the real incomes of most people within the quintile are on the rise. This would be the case if the incomes of higher quintiles rise faster than the incomes of the lower quintiles. Figure 4-9 plots the real dollar values of the mean (or average) incomes for all quintiles from 1967 to 1990. The reported shares of incomes might suggest that the welfare of the people in the lower quintiles deteriorated during the 1970s and 1980s. Figure 4-9, which shows data on real income levels year by year, reveals that that was not the case. The top three quintiles clearly had strong real income increases. Indeed, because of the tight scale required in figure 4-9 to accommodate the higher income groups (and such graphical techniques have been used often by critics of the 1980s), the appearance of a totally flat slope for the lowest and second quintiles might suggest that there was no growth in their respective average incomes, which is also not the case.

Consider figure 4-10, which plots the real mean income for each quintile along with its trend. The panels for the bottom four quintiles include the upper income limits for the quintile along with their trends. There is no upper limit in the panel for the highest quintile and the top 5 percent of households with the highest incomes. There is, however, a lower limit to the incomes of the top 5 percent.

Figure 4-9   Real Mean Income of Households by Quintiles in 1990
Dollars (using the CPI-X), 1967–1990

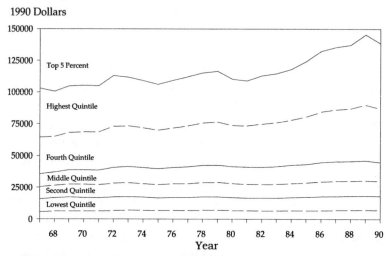

Source: U.S. Bureau of the Census, Department of Commerce, Current
Population Reports: Consumer Income, Series P–60, no. 174, *Money
Income of Households, Families, and Persons in the United States: 1990*
(Washington, DC: U.S. Government Printing Office, August 1991), p. 216.

Several important observations can be made from this income
data. First, as was evident in earlier charts of the real median income
level, the economic fortunes of all quintiles are strongly influenced
by business cycles, rising and falling with employment and national
production. The mean incomes of all quintiles fell significantly with
the recession of the early 1980s.

Second, the means for the lower quintiles stagnated (along with
worker productivity) during the 1970s and early 1980s but not
during the last two-thirds of the 1980s.

Third, as opposed to trending downward, as has been frequently suggested, the mean of the lowest quintile moved upward,
albeit at a much slower pace than the higher income groups. The
mean of the lowest quintile rose (in constant 1990 dollars) from
$5,761 in 1967 to $7,039 in 1973 and then, more slowly, to $7,372 in
1989 (before the advent of the recession, which forced the mean

Figure 4-10 The Mean Income and Upper-Limit Income Levels of Quintiles of Households, Actual and Trend, 1967–1990

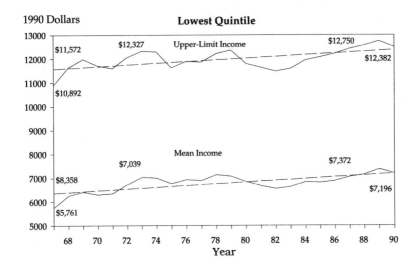

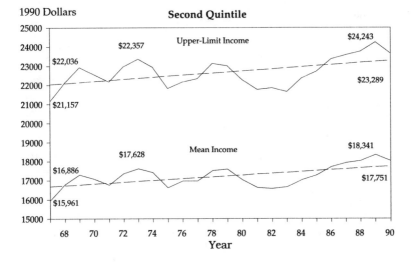

Figure 4-10 The Mean Income and Upper-Limit Income Levels of Quintiles of Households, Actual and Trend, 1967–1990 *(continued)*

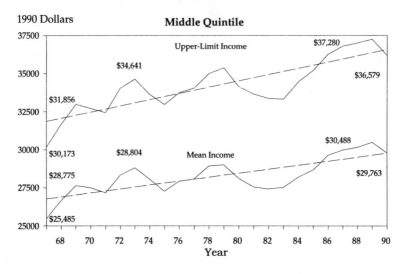

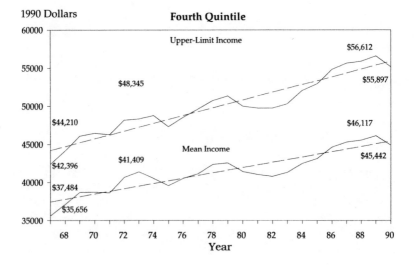

Figure 4-10 The Mean Income and Upper-Limit Income Levels of Quintiles of Households, Actual and Trend, 1967–1990 *(continued)*

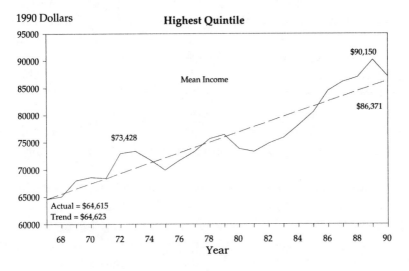

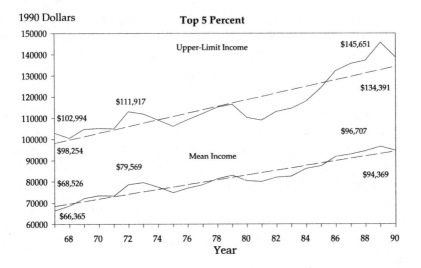

down to $7,195). The trend covering the 1967-1990 period was upward sloping, albeit slightly so.

Fourth, the upper limit of the mean for the lowest quintile was trending upward (as was also the case for all other quintiles), which means that the lowest quintile was gradually including households with progressively higher real incomes. The actual real value of the upper limit increased from $10,892 in 1967 to $12,750 in 1989 (the trend value increased from $11,572 in 1967 to $12,382 in 1990). The upper limit went from 105 percent of the 1990 poverty threshold level (the income level below which people are considered poor) for a family of three in 1967 to 119 percent of the 1990 poverty threshold in 1990.[36]

Fifth, contrary to what has been claimed, the means of the lower quintiles did not "plummet" or even "stagnate" throughout the decade of the 1980s. The means fell precipitously during the recession of 1981–1982. After the recovery began in earnest, the means for the various quintiles actually began to rise almost as rapidly as they had fallen during the recession. The mean for the lowest quintile rose by 11.1 percent from 1983 to 1989, while the average income of the second quintile rose by 10.1 percent. The average income of the middle and fourth quintiles expanded by 10.7 percent and 11.6 percent, respectively, in the 1983–1989 period.

Granted, the average real income of the top 20 percent rose by much more, 18.8 percent—a figure that, when compared with the percentage growth of the other quintiles, goes a long way toward explaining the rising income dispersion as measured by the Gini index.[37] Nevertheless, it is naive to assume that the top quintile is an exclusive club. It is in fact comprised of changing collections of households with changing collections of household members operating on continually changing conditions.[38] Students who were in school in the early 1980s, for example, had jumped several quintiles by the end of the decade simply by taking their first job or by marrying someone with an income.

Moreover, the nature of the quintiles of households is biased toward greater income growth for the top quintile. People in the top quintile who increase their productivity and hours of work, marry (or stay married), or decide to have a nonworking spouse or family member go to work automatically raise their quintile's mean household income. These people cannot move to a higher category. People in any of the lower quintiles who do the same can easily move up one or more quintiles, increasing their own welfare but, in the process, possibly reducing the mean income of their former quintile.

Sixth, the data in figure 4-9 and 4-10 do in fact suggest that the economic fate of the various quintiles is inextricably linked in that they certainly moved more or less together. However, the positive effects are not likely to be in one direction, as implied by the so-called trickle-down theories. The welfare gains very likely trickle in both directions, with the prosperity of each end of the distribution depending on the welfare of the other and with people moving up and down the income scale (a point that will be considered in greater detail later). However, the evidence in figure 4-10 indicates that after 1982 the mean of the highest quintile was moving strongly with the mean income of the lowest quintile. Such data contradict eloquent claims that the economic tide in the 1980s raised the yachts but not the tugboats and rowboats. Clearly, all the quintile "boats" were being raised by the continuing recovery in the 1980s.

Seventh, the households in the two top quintiles do not all have the princely incomes that have been attributed to them. To be in the second-to-the-top quintile in 1990, a household only had to have an annual income of $36,200 ($37,260 in 1989). To be in the top 20 percent in 1990, the household had to have a minimum annual income of only $55,205 ($56,612 in 1989). To reach the top 5 percent, the household needed an annual income of $94,748 in 1990. In short, being in the fortunate fifth does not require the earnings of a professional baseball player or rock star or Wall Street financier as many critics appear to think. The fortunate fifth, obviously, includes a lot of pretty ordinary industrious Americans who put in many hours on their jobs.

Overall, these statistics prove that critics of the income distribution do have some of the facts correct. The real incomes of the high income quintiles did tend to rise relative to the other quintiles, and, generally, the higher the quintile, the greater the percentage rise in real income.[39] As a consequence, there was a growing gap in the income levels between the low and high quintiles, as measured by their means taken year-to-year for ever-changing collections of households and families (a qualification the importance of which will become fully apparent after the data on income mobility are considered).[40]

On the other hand, the data just as clearly undercuts a major claim of the critics that only the people in the fortunate fifth of the income distribution were better off at the end of the 1980s than they were at the beginning of the 1980s, or even the 1970s. There was a growing gap alright, but the gap was emerging because of the differing rates of growth in income among the quintiles, with the "rich's" incomes growing relatively more rapidly than the "poor's." It was not emerging because the income of the highest quintile was rising at the same time that the income of the lowest quintile was falling.

Evaluating Income Distribution Data

The distribution of income, as developed in fifths of the population, cannot be taken at face value. Several social, economic, and demographic considerations, mainly relating to the definition of quintiles and earnings, must be kept in mind.[41] The data presented above, which is at the heart of the fortunate-fifth controversy, refers to quintiles of households measured by their reported real money wages and salaries. As noted earlier, the sizes of households declined steadily during the 1967–1990 period. With the growing number of elderly and single-parent households, the decline in the sizes of low-income households was more pronounced than that of higher income households. Less than 45 percent of the households in the lowest quintile were families, with only 21 percent of the households in the lowest quintile married. The proportion of households in the lowest 20 percent with married heads fell dramatically throughout the 1970s and 1980s. Moreover, 22 percent of the households in the lowest quintile were 65 and older, while slightly more than 9.2 percent of the households in the highest quintile were elderly. The high concentration of elderly in the lowest quintile helps explain why more than 37 percent of the people in the lowest quintile lived alone.[42] Nearly 90 percent of the households in the highest quintiles were families, and almost 94 percent of these families were married couples.

An important consideration in evaluating the relative welfare of people in the various quintiles is that in 1990 the mean family size rose from 2.98 in the lowest quintile to 3.19 in the middle quintile to 3.41 in the highest quintile. This means that there were over 14 percent (or 6 million) more people in the highest quintile of families than in the lowest quintile of families, as estimated by the Census Bureau. In short, the share of the income received by the lowest quintile of households does not fairly represent the distribution of income among people (as distinguished from the somewhat artificial measures of "families" and "households").

Second, the growth in wage and salary supplements was probably concentrated on the higher quintiles, but the growth in in-kind transfers was probably concentrated on the lower quintiles. This means that the actual share of income going to people in the lowest quintile is much larger than the measured income (according to one study undertaken in the 1970s, perhaps close to 12 percent of aggregate family income[43]). It also means the welfare of the lower quintiles probably rose more rapidly than the figures indicate.

Third, because of the growing importance of the hidden economy and the service sector, both of which are dominated by workers who do not report their illegal incomes and who under-report their legal incomes for tax purposes, the income gains of the lower quintile are probably greater than those reported. (In the next chapter, I will show that this must be the case, since the expenditures of the people in the lowest quintile are always significantly greater than their reported incomes.)

In addition, the marginal tax rates of the higher income groups were lowered in the 1980s by more than for other income groups, which means that the higher income groups had fewer tax incentives to under-report their incomes during the decade. Therefore, the absolute and relative income growth of the higher income groups is probably significantly, if not substantially, overstated. In other words, the actual increase in incomes of the top group of American income earners may not be nearly as great as the reported increase in their incomes. Indeed, a 1992 study from Daniel Feenberg and James Poterba, economists with the National Bureau of Economic Research, strongly supports the supply-side theory behind the 1981 and 1986 reductions in marginal tax rates. [44] These researchers found that much of the increase in the incomes of the top fifth of taxpayers was actually captured by the top one-quarter of 1 percent of taxpayers. However, the income increase of that elite group can be largely attributed to changes in tax laws:

> Our results also suggest that the increase in reported income inequality is not simply an artifact of capital gains realizations in the 1980s, but reflects changes in the distribution of most other income sources as well. The share of income reported by top income taxpayers rose throughout the 1980s, but we find the sharpest increase in 1987 and 1989, the years following a significant decline in marginal tax rates. We therefore conclude... that changes in decisions about how much taxable income to report contributed to the observed increase in the reported incomes of high-income households. [45]

The tax-rate reforms, which reduced the top marginal rates from 70 percent in 1980 to 28 percent in 1986, appear to have substantially reduced the incentives high-income taxpayers had to take their income in the nontaxable form of fringe benefits (including health insurance, vacations, and company cars), to defer receipt of their currently earned income, to hold their wealth in municipal bonds the interest on which is nontaxable, to hide their taxable income in various forms of corporations designed to reduce their tax burdens, and to reduce their earnings through less work and the assumption of less risky investments. As evidence of the impact of tax reform in 1986, the researchers point to several charts, the most notable of which shows a dramatic increase in the reported wages of the top 2 percent of taxpayers. Three-quarters of their wage gains during the decade occurred between 1986 and 1988, an observation that caused the authors to conclude, "The sharp break in the trend growth rate in 1986 is strongly suggestive of a link between the Tax Reform Act of 1986 and this pattern of reported income."[46] While this study does not settle the debate, and much more research is needed, such studies must force critics of the income distribution to rethink their claims that the reported income statistics on which they rely accurately tell the story they have woven.

Fourth, there were more people doing more work in the higher quintiles than in the lower ones. In 1990, 55 percent of the families in the lowest quintile had no income earners while only 2.5 percent of the families in the highest quintile had no income earners. Just under 20 percent of the families in the lowest quintile had two or more earners, while over 83 percent of the families in the highest quintile had two or more earners. Indeed, 11 percent of the families in the highest quintile had four or more earners. On average, the families in the highest quintile had nearly three times the (full- and part-time) income earners as did the lowest quintile, taking into account the fact that there were more people to earn incomes in the highest quintile. Moreover, the 20 percent of families with the highest incomes had, on average, seven times the number of full-time income earners.[47]

Critics of the nation's income distribution often talk about the incomes of the highest income earners as if they are totally undeserved, perhaps the result of collecting interest on stored wealth that may have been passed down to them. There are, without a doubt, people in the top fifth who fit that stereotype, but the overwhelming majority have members who work full time. Indeed, in 88 percent of the households in the highest quintile at least one person works full time. In contrast, only 24 percent of the workers in the lowest quintile works full time. Many of the workers in the lowest quintile do not work, no doubt, partly because they were involuntarily unemployed, but also partly because many chose to be out of work to attend school or to reorient their lives in other ways for work in the future.[48]

Fifth, more than 27 percent of the households in the highest quintile had a member in the prime earning age of 45 to 54. Less than 9 percent of the heads of households in the lowest quintile were in the 45 to 54 age category. In other words, the share of the income going to the lowest quintile is distorted by the relative youth of many of the workers and the disproportionate number of elderly householders.

Sixth, critics of the economy have argued that many families were not able to maintain their standards of living without both spouses going to work. Figure 4-11 suggests they have a point, given that the trend in real income for the one-earner family angled slightly downward during the 1967–1988 period (see the top panel of figure 4-11). While real 1988 median income for these families was 4.6 percent above the 1967 level, the 1988 median was 7 percent below the 1973 peak (see the bottom panel of figure 4-11).

However, to keep the problem in perspective, the caveats regarding the growing importance of nonmoney income and the declining size of families must be kept in mind. Furthermore, the one-earner families represented slightly more than a quarter of all families. The top panel of figure 4-11 also shows that the real median income of two-income earner families trended upward, rising from $29,236 to $34,583 in 1973, and then on to $38,702, an increase of 32 percent over the 1967–1988 period.[49] Obviously, by sending another family member back to work, families were trying to do more than just compensate for lost hourly wages; they were improving their economic positions.

Interestingly, the real median income of families with no earners, 79 percent of whom are in the lowest two quintiles, also trended upward. Their real increase was an amazing 72 percent from 1967 ($7,991) to 1988 ($13,729). The relatively greater increase of the families with no earners is clearly evident in the bottom panel of figure 4-11. A part of the explanation for the unusual rate of income increase for families with no earners is the growth in Social Security and other government transfer payments and pensions going to the expanding elderly population. A disproportionate percentage of elderly people live in no-earner families and fall in the lowest two quintiles. Between 1967 and the end of 1990, real government transfers per capita nearly tripled, rising from $1,009 in 1967 to $2,879 in 1990.[50]

Figure 4-11   Median Incomes of Families, by Income Earners, in Real (1988) Dollars and Percentage Increase from 1967

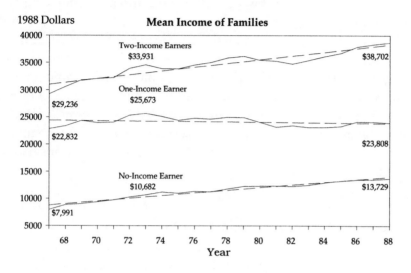

1988 Dollars   **Mean Income of Families**

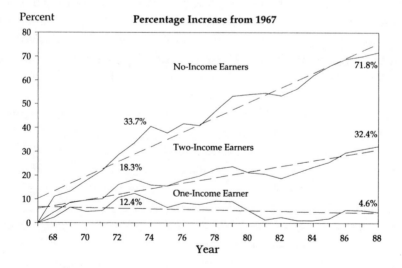

Percent   **Percentage Increase from 1967**

Of course, we should not forget that the 1980s began with a severe anti-inflationary policy orchestrated by the Federal Reserve, which clearly crimped the income growth of many Americans for the decade. Had inflation not spiraled upward in the 1960s and 1970s, the income growth of many Americans would probably have been higher in the 1980s. In addition, the world experienced something of a minor industrial, electronic, globalized economic revolution. American firms and workers had to adjust to the global forces at work, and the required adjustments probably temporarily diminished the income gains of many Americans. Some of the resulting suppressed income growth could not be avoided; Americans had to meet the competitive challenges.

Mobility Among the Quintiles

Discussion of the economic fate of "quintiles" of households is usually conducted as if each of the fifths of the population represent fixed and exclusive clubs with few people able to move up or down through them. Robert Reich's pejorative use of the "fortunate fifth" suggests that there is a fifth of the population as identifiable individuals who were blessed at the start of the 1980s and who rapidly became more blessed as the decade progressed. Everyone else was not so fortunate. Their incomes declined in lockstep with everyone else's, or just stagnated, or so Reich maintains. The analysis reported here clearly reveals that far more people than those in the fortunate fifth prospered during the 1980s. Even when in-kind benefits are not counted, and without adjustments for changes in the sizes of households, the mean incomes of all quintiles rose, albeit at times slowly, during much of the 1967–1990 period, and especially after 1982.

However, during the 1980s many people rose rapidly through the quintiles while others fell from their lofty perches at the upper end with almost equal rapidity. Many undergraduate students moved up one or more quintiles in the 1980s when they took their first jobs. University of North Carolina basketball star Michael Jordan was catapulted from the lowest quintile to one of the country's top income earners when he gave up his nonpaying, amateur college basketball status for his rewarding career with the Chicago Bulls professional basketball team. Many, if not most, students who took graduate degrees in finance and medicine in the 1980s jumped immediately from, at times, the lowest quintile to the highest. Many couples married and joined households and incomes—often moving one or more quintiles in the process.

These upward movements invariably raised the means of the quintiles and, at the same time, sent other people down the income distribution, simply because there can be no more than 20 percent of households in any one quintile. But many other high-income earners lost their businesses or were laid off and, accordingly, went tumbling down the income scale, often experiencing undeniable hardship. But that does not mean that the lifetime incomes of everyone who experienced hardship were reduced. This is because many, if not most, people can expect setbacks from time to time. Some people's income reductions were normal, expected setbacks.

Furthermore, economic hardship was not always the consequence of reduced income. Some harried executives and even production workers gave up relatively high paying positions in urban centers for quieter and lower paying jobs in suburban or rural areas closer to home. And many elderly people simply decided to call it quits. They all moved down the income distribution.

Assessing the movement of people among the quintiles is far more difficult than assessing the movement of the means of the quintiles, which probably explains why so little attention has been given it. Nevertheless, there are now several studies from different sources that shed light on income mobility and on the actual income changes during the 1980s of people who started the decade in the different income quintiles.

Table 4-1 reveals the extent of the movement among quintiles on a year-to-year basis.[51] For example, almost 82 percent of the people in the lowest quintile of families in 1984 were in the same quintile in 1985. Nevertheless, that means that in one year 18 percent of the people in the lowest quintile moved up one or more quintiles (the data do not permit specifying how far up the people moved).

The table also reveals that 19.5 percent of the people in the highest quintile in 1984 moved down one or more quintiles by 1985. Slightly more than 44 percent of the people in the middle quintile moved quintiles between 1984 and 1985, with approximately half moving up and half moving down. Much the same pattern of quintile shifts was observed for 1985–1986 and 1987–1988.

Table 4-1 Percentage Mobility Among the Quintiles, Year to Year, During the 1980s

Income Level	Declined One or More Quintiles	Stayed in Same Quintile	Moved Up One or More Quintiles
1984–1985			
Lowest Quintile	N/A	81.8	18.2
Second Quintile	14.5	60.9	24.6
Middle Quintile	21.0	55.8	23.2
Fourth Quintile	23.8	60.5	15.8
Highest Quintile	19.5	80.5	N/A
1985–1986			
Lowest Quintile	N/A	81.6	18.4
Second Quintile	15.2	62.1	22.7
Middle Quintile	22.8	55.3	21.9
Fourth Quintile	26.2	57.0	16.8
Highest Quintile	20.5	76.3	N/A
1987–1988			
Lowest Quintile	N/A	83.0	17.0
Second Quintile	17.5	63.3	19.2
Middle Quintile	25.7	55.9	18.4
Fourth Quintile	26.8	59.9	13.3
Highest Quintile	24.3	75.7	N/A

Source: As reported by Bruce Bartlett, "A Class Struggle that Won't Stay Put," *Wall Street Journal*, November 20, 1991.

Unfortunately, these Census Bureau data do not permit assessment of the cumulative effects of the shifts over time. Without doubt, many low-income people moved up one year only to fall back the following year, and many rich people recovered from their falls from grace in 1984 in following years.

A study undertaken several years ago by the Institute for Social Research at the University of Michigan indicates that the cumulative effects of the year-to-year shifts are, on balance, very likely substantial.[52] Table 4-2 provides the detailed findings. That study indicates that 55.5 percent of the families in the lowest quintile in 1971 were also in the lowest quintile in 1978. But that means that 44.5 percent of the families had moved up at least one quintile by the end of the seven-year period. Slightly more than 22 percent moved from the lowest to the second quintile. Another 9.4 percent moved to the middle quintile, and 7 percent moved to the fourth quintile. Somewhat remarkably, 6 percent of the families in the lowest quintile in 1971 had jumped to the highest quintile by 1978.

Table 4-2 Estimated Percentage Shifts of People Among the Family Income Quintiles Between 1971 and 1978

Family Income Quintile in 1971	Family Income Quintile in 1978				
	Lowest	Second	Middle	Fourth	Highest
Lowest	55.5	22.0	9.5	7.0	6.0
Second	21.5	34.5	21.5	13.5	9.0
Middle	13.5	23.5	30.5	18.5	14.0
Fourth	6.0	15.0	25.5	29.5	22.0
Highest	3.5	4.5	14.0	29.5	48.5

Note: The table reads as follows: 20 percent of families had incomes that placed them in the lowest quintile in 1971. In 1978, 55.5 percent of those families remained in the lowest quintile. However, 22 percent had moved up one quintile; 9.5 percent had moved up to the middle quintile; 7 percent had moved up to the fourth quintile; and 6 percent had moved up to the highest quintile.

Source: Greg J. Duncan, *Years of Poverty, Years of Plenty (Ann Arbor, MI: Survey Research Center, Institute for Social Research, University of Michigan, 1984), p. 10.*

On the other end of the income distribution, close to half of the families who were in the highest quintile in 1971 were able to retain their relatively high incomes for 1978, but that means that more than half were not. Nearly 30 percent moved down one quintile. Just under 14 percent moved to the middle quintile. And 8 percent moved to the bottom two quintiles.

Only 31.5 percent of the people in the middle quintile stayed put between 1971 and 1978. About half of the rest of the families moved up one or more quintiles, and about half moved down one or more quintiles.

Of course, this categorization of the income data into quintiles hides many other movements. Using another approach, researchers at the Labor Department concluded that between 1969 and 1986 a "majority of the decline in the middle is offset by an increase in the upper class,"[53] not so much by an increase in the lower class. Bruce Bartlett, former assistant secretary of the Treasury, summed up these findings when he observed that "many of the poor do lift themselves out of poverty every year and many of the rich find their wealth is fleeting."[54]

That conclusion is fortified by two recent studies, one from the U.S. Treasury and one from the Urban Institute.[55] The Treasury study involved a stratified sample of the tax returns of more than 14,000 Americans who filed tax returns from 1979 through 1988. Because many low-income Americans do not file tax returns, the findings (necessarily but regrettably) do not represent the full range of experience by the entire population during the 1980s. Nevertheless, the study did find substantial mobility between the rich and poor, and every other income division, as delimited by their tax returns.[56] Indeed, this study found that "in no quintile of the income distribution defined in 1979 are more than two-thirds of the taxpayers in that same quintile in 1988."[57]

Moreover, there was more income movement up the income ladder than down it. Of the taxpayers who were in the lowest quintile in 1979, nearly 40 percent had moved up at least one income bracket by 1980. Only 14 percent of the taxpayers in the lowest quintile in 1979 were still there in 1988. Almost 15 percent had moved all the way to the top quintile by 1988. Of the taxpayers who were in the top quintile in 1979, a third were in a lower income bracket in 1988.[58] The Treasury researchers further conceded a point that is rarely acknowledged: The incomes people make in any one year are poorly correlated with their lifetime incomes, "suggesting that income observed in a given year is not a very good measure of whether the taxpayer is on average 'high income,' 'middle income,' or 'low income.'"[59]

By tracking the income growth of 5,000 families from 1967 to 1986, Isabel Sawhill and Mark Condon, researchers at the Urban Institute, were able to get around the central problem with the Treasury study, which was reliance on the reported incomes of those who filed tax returns. Nevertheless, they confirmed the Treasury's central finding of considerable income mobility during the 1980s. Indeed, they found that "the rich got a little richer and the poor got much richer" during the 1980s as well as during the 1970s.[60]

Table 4-3 Change in Average Family Incomes of Individuals by Their Quintile from 1977 to 1986 (1991 Dollars)

	Average Family Income		
Quintile	1977 Quintile Members in 1977	1977 Quintile Members in 1986	Percentage Change
Lowest	$15,853	$27,998	77
Second	31,340	43,041	37
Middle	43,297	51,796	20
Fourth	57,486	63,314	10
Highest	92,531	97,140	5
All	48,101	56,658	18

Note: Sample limited to adults, ages 25 to 54 for starting year.

Source: Isabel V. Sawhill and Mark Condon, "Is U.S. Income Inequality Really Growing? Sorting Out the Fairness Question," *Policy Bites* (Washington, DC: Urban Institute, June 1992), p. 3.

As can be seen in table 4-3, while the average increase for all families between 1977 and 1986 (the latest year of available data) was 18 percent, the average income of those families in the bottom quintile in 1977 rose 77 percent by 1986 as many of the families moved up through the income ladder. The average income of those families in the top quintile rose by only 5 percent, as some families remained in the top bracket with income increases and others descended the income ladder. The average increase of those families in the middle quintile in 1977 was 20 percent.[61] The average increases for the quintiles during the 1967–1977 period was much the same as the average increase for the 1977–1986 period.

The only notable difference is that the increase for those in the lowest quintile in the 1977–1986 period (77 percent) was slightly higher than the increase for the 1967–1977 period (72 percent).

The Educated Fifth

Did the economic fortunes of all identifiable groups of workers, households, and families move in lockstep during the 1967–1990 period? It would truly be surprising if they did, given the myriad changes in the domestic and international economy during the period. Clearly, the pace of income improvement slowed noticeably in the 1970s, very likely due to a host of forces, not the least of which were the oil-price shocks (and resulting energy policies adopted in the United States) and the slowdown in domestic saving and investment rates. Furthermore, the data reveal that the reported money incomes of the top and bottom quintiles spread further apart, albeit to a more limited extent than may have been suggested by political partisans.

Moreover, education became a more prominent determinant of relative economic success in the 1970s and 1980s. In general, households whose members had a high school diploma or less stood witness to a reversal of their incomes, switching from rising real incomes before 1973 to declining real incomes thereafter. Households whose heads had a four-year college degree or more education saw their real incomes stagnate during the 1970s and then surge upward after 1982.

Figure 4-12 indicates that college graduates were indeed a fortunate fifth—the only group with rising incomes. Households with less education had median incomes that varied around what appears to be a level or falling trend. Because of the scale used, the figure does not reveal the true magnitude of the changes in the groups' median incomes. Figure 4-13 includes separate panels for each level of education and provides a more revealing picture of what was happening to each group.

Figure 4-12 Educational Attainment of Householders—Median Income of Households with Householder Twenty-Five Years Old and Over, 1967–1989

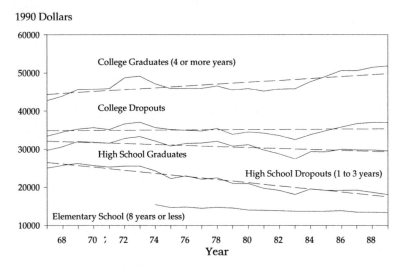

Source: U.S. Department of Commerce, Bureau of the Census, Population Reports, Consumer Income, Series P-60, no. 167, *Trends in Income, by Selected Characteristics: 1947–1988* (Washington, DC: U.S. Government Printing Office, April 1990); and U.S. Department of Commerce, Bureau of the Census, Current Population Reports, Consumer Income, Series P-60, no. 174, *Money Income of Households, Families, and Persons in the United States: 1990* (Washington, DC: U.S. Government Printing Office, August 1991).

Figure 4-13 Educational Attainment of Householders—Median Income of Households with Householder Twenty-Five Years Old and Over, 1967–1989

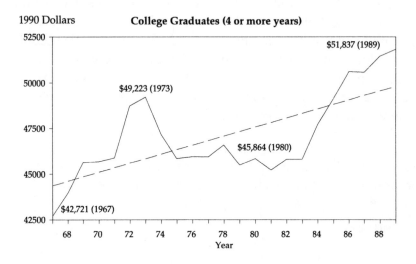

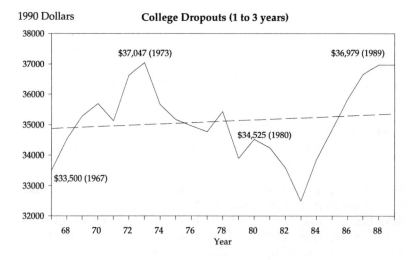

Figure 4-13 Educational Attainment of Householders—Median Income of Households with Householder Twenty-Five Years Old and Over, 1967–1989 *(continued)*

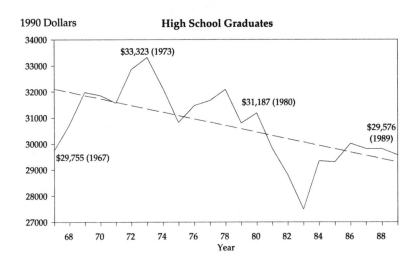

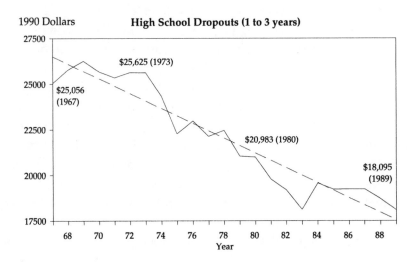

Figure 4-13   Educational Attainment of Householders—Median Income of Households with Householder Twenty-Five Years Old and Over, 1967–1989 *(continued)*

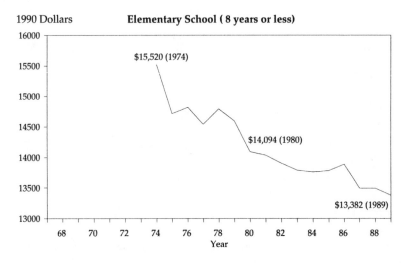

The real median incomes of households (in 1990 dollars) with only an elementary school education or less fell by nearly 14 percent from 1974 ($15,520) to 1989 ($13,382). Their median incomes obviously continued on a relentless downward course throughout the period.

The median income of households with high school dropouts as heads fell even more, by slightly more than 29 percent from 1973 ($26,625) to 1989 ($18,095). High school graduates experienced a more modest decrease of a little more than 11 percent between 1973 ($33,323) and 1989 ($29,576). These households' median incomes obviously fell during the recession of the early 1980s, then recovered somewhat between 1983 and 1986, only to continue on a slow decline.

On the other hand, the real average incomes of households with some college trended upward during the 1967–1989 period. After falling precipitously throughout the 1973–1983 period, this group had by 1989 almost reclaimed its 1973 income perch of $37,047.

The median income of households with college graduates as heads trended decidedly upward during the period in spite of the 7 percent decline in their real median from $49,223 in 1973 to $45,864 in 1975. Overall, this group's median rose by 5.3 percent, from $45,820 in 1973 to $51,837 in 1989, and by 13 percent between 1980 ($45,864) and 1989.

As widely recognized, these divergent changes in the fortunes of high school and college graduates caused a dramatic jump in their relative average incomes. The average income of college graduates climbed modestly from 144 percent of high school graduates' earnings in 1967 to 147 percent in 1980. However, two years later college graduates earned on average 167 percent of high school graduates' earnings. In 1989, college graduates earned 175 percent of high school graduates' earnings. The change in the spread between the median incomes of college graduates and high school dropouts was even more dramatic, with the median of college graduates rising from 171 percent of the high school dropouts' median in 1967 to 286 percent in 1989.

The data in figures 4-12 and 4-13 do seem to suggest that a significant proportion of households suffered a loss of real income or received no increase during the 1970s and 1980s. Those households with heads with one or more college degrees constituted the only group that had a significant net increase in real median income from 1973 to 1989, and they constituted 23 percent of householders with heads who are twenty-five years old or older.

Does this data mean that only a fifth—approximately speaking, Robert Reich's fortunate fifth—of Americans gained during the 1980s? Not really, for several reasons. Foremost, the data in figures 4-12 and 4-13 describe what happened to the median incomes for the various groups. While the medians were falling, there were households within each educational grouping that experienced real income increases. This fact alone indicates that more than a fifth—indeed, far more than a fifth—of households experienced gains during the 1970s and 1980s. This is especially true when fringe benefits, in-kind transfers, and unreported incomes are considered and when the data are adjusted for changes in household sizes.

Furthermore, as recognized in the foregoing section, the categories do not represent fixed groups, or exclusive clubs, of households. For example, the households headed by college graduates in 1989, with a median of $51,837, were not the same collection of households in 1973, with a median of $49,223, or in 1980, with a median of $45,864. Some of the households in the top bracket completed their undergraduate and graduate degrees during the 1970s and 1980s, thus moving up the income scale. The same can be said of the group with high school graduates as heads. Some unidentifiable number of these households were, in earlier periods, high school or even elementary school dropouts. They moved up because they completed their degrees.

As others have argued, there clearly were global competitive market forces at work depressing the wages of American workers with limited education. Some repetitive manufacturing jobs did migrate abroad during the 1970s and 1980s as American firms sought to meet foreign competition with cheaper foreign labor and as foreign firms began to produce manufactured goods with cheap domestic labor and export goods to the United States. Many American workers with limited educations who were unable or not inclined to add to their education had to seek employment in the expanding domestic service industry where wages have been historically low. However, many have learned from their experience and have, no doubt, taken remedial action on their own.

Granted, those changes cannot be the whole story of income losses among groups with limited education. Many workers with limited education benefited from the lower priced imports and the improvements in domestic products induced by foreign competition. Much has been made of the decline in the educational performance of American students during the 1970s and 1980s. An undetermined portion of the decline in the median incomes of the lower groups is that the educational attainment of each group was not held constant. Indeed, the educational attainment for any given number of years was generally in decline, which implies that for a given level of education the median incomes of the lower groups did not deteriorate quite as much as indicated in the figures. Again, one of the reasons the median of the highest group very likely rose relative to the other educational groupings is that there is no upper educational bound to the households included in the highest income group. In short, the higher income group was increasing its real income because it was increasing the educational level of its members.

Also, part of the decline in the incomes of the lower educational groups occurred because some of their members, perhaps many with the relatively higher incomes within the groups, sought more education and moved up the income scale, thereby depressing the median for the people left behind in the lower educational groups by more than would have been the case in the absence of the mobility. The percentage of Americans twenty-five years old and over who were not high school graduates was cut in half between 1970 and 1989. It is not unreasonable to speculate that the people who were left behind had relatively low salaries for their educational groupings, possibly because of relatively low motivation.

These observations are not meant to deny that real economic hardship was experienced by a number of people with limited education. The data clearly reveal that education had far greater value in the 1980s than in earlier decades. Again, the value of additional years of schooling was probably rising faster than the value of education per se simply because the value of any given number of years of education was falling. Many people chose to continue their education to compensate for the deterioration in the quality and economic value of each year. Due to the demands of the global economy, those who did not continue their schooling suffered greater competitive disadvantages and had to compete with more educated Americans and even with automated machines and robots that could supplant low-skilled laborers.

Finally, it must be noted that it is wrong to presume that all members of this educated fortunate fifth, defined as those with four or more years of college education, had princely incomes that should be subjected to greater taxation and redistributed to segments of the unfortunate four-fifths of the less-educated population. The median income of the most educated group would have placed the group's median not in the top 5 percent or even the top 20 percent of all income earners, but in the fourth quintile. Obviously, many people with college degrees—public school teachers, nurses, social workers, artists, musicians, and loan officers—had very modest incomes. Indeed, while their group's median income was relatively high throughout the decades in question, many college graduates were in the lower fifths of the income distribution. Some were there by hard luck, but that fact should not obscure the fact that some were there by choice.

The Potential for Reconciliation on the Numbers

Statistical debates can be numbing, especially when researchers use different data series, manipulate the data in different ways, and emphasize their differences. However, the various claims and counterclaims in a growing number of studies appear to be yielding something of a compromise view of what did happen to incomes during the 1980s. There are three elements in this potential compromise. First, it now appears that claims that *only* the rich got richer are a gross distortion of the facts. There were just too many poor and not-so-poor people who moved up the income ladder during the decade for that claim to hold much water.

Second, the vast majority of American's incomes (when all forms of compensation are included and the data are properly adjusted for inflation) did rise during the decade, although the rise was at lower rates than was experienced during the 1950s and 1960s.

Third, some Americans—perhaps a larger number than was the case in earlier decades—suffered real income losses. No one has actually tabulated the number or percentages of people who fell behind in the 1980s and earlier decades.

Fourth, most Americans have a lifetime income profile that is characterized by growing real income during the working years; their income profiles have a positive slope. As a person moves through his or her career, his or her real income tends to grow with age and the accumulation of experience, skills, and education. While

University of Michigan researchers have validated the positive slopes of most groups' income profiles, they have deduced that the income profiles for identified groups—especially males with a high school education or less—may have, on average, fallen between 1979 and 1988.[62] At the same time, the income profiles of males with some college and with a college degree and all females except those without a high school diploma either stayed the same or increased. These researchers attribute the shifts in the income profiles to technological developments that require workers to have more sophisticated skills.

These calculated shifts can be reconciled with studies that indicate relatively low increases for the vast majority of Americans during the 1980s in the following way. At the same time that some workers' income profiles were falling, the workers (say, high school dropouts) were gaining experience, the net effect of which is that their incomes continued to grow, albeit at a tempered pace. This result is described in panel A of figure 4-14. Others (say, college graduates) progressed during the 1980s not only because they gained experience but also because their income profiles rose (see panel B). Finally, no doubt there were some people whose income profiles fell so rapidly that their growing experience was not enough to stop their incomes from falling (see panel C). How many were in the last category is, at this point, anyone's guess. It seems clear that panel C does not represent the income records of more than a minor fraction of the population. Only additional research can actually give an answer.

Was there a great U-turn? Certainly not in the way it has been described, which is that a large percentage of the population actually saw their economic fortunes reverse course during the 1980s. However, there may have been something of a not-so-great U-turn when the available studies are reconsidered from another perspective, in terms of the present value of people's lifetime income streams. Given the fall in the income profiles, some workers (especially young workers) who witnessed the fall could have seen a drop in the present value of their projected future incomes. They may have continued to expect to earn more over their lives, but the present

Figure 4-14 The Real Income Profiles of Workers in 1970 and 1990

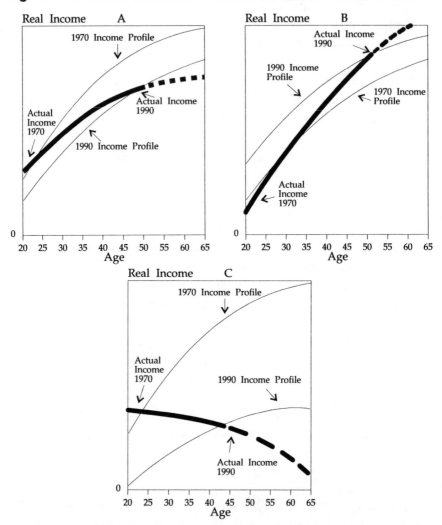

value dropped with their lifetime profiles. In this sense, but only in this sense, they suffered a reversal of their fortunes. To them, the U-turn was real.

This may be the perspective that has led so many Americans to conclude that they are "worse off" despite rising incomes. It may also be the perspective from which others have begun to wonder if the American dream has begun to fade. During any period of transition—and the 1980s was definitely a period of major reorientation for the world in both economic and political terms—we should not be surprised that many Americans see themselves living a nightmare at the same time that others are living the dream they had always imagined. It is also not surprising that those who confront the nightmare are more vocal than those who confront their fondest dreams.

Constructive Dimensions of Price and Income Signals

Critics of the changing income distribution have understandably focused on the hardship that is inevitably present when the economy adjusts to major economic changes, especially when these changes are global in scope. Many of these forces are beyond the control of individual workers.

Nevertheless, there is a positive side to the changes in the relative prices of American and foreign products and relative wages of various groups of workers that is rarely stressed. The decline in the "mean" or "median" incomes for some groups was in part a consequence of some Americans choosing to improve their economic positions. Many American workers purposefully moved from urban to rural areas and from East to West and from North to South (and in every other direction), fully aware that their money incomes would be lower, but fully expecting their welfare, as they measured it (adjusting for the cost of living and amenities), would rise. Many political commentators seem to think that the only "good" jobs are traditional manufacturing jobs and that the ongoing shift from manufacturing employment to service employment (which has been following, more or less the path charted before 1940[63]) represents a grave loss in welfare for Americans.[64] However, many Americans (including hundreds of thousands of college graduates in education and the arts) made the choices they did in the 1980s because they preferred the service jobs to the manufacturing jobs. This is not to say that none of the changes that took place were involuntary. Rather, it is to emphasize a positive dimension of income change that critics rarely, if ever, mention, possibly because the overall impact of worker choices is so hard to measure.

Furthermore, the ongoing changes in prices and wages have been necessary market signals to the 250 million Americans to adjust their ways, their products, their work habits, and their education to meet prevailing world standards. Those market signals have redirected the efforts of most Americans. Those signals have forced many firms to intensify their efforts to improve the quality and competitive standings of their products and services. They have also forced many workers to redouble their efforts to increase their efficiency, to change their lines of work, and to acquire more education even at a higher cost.

These changing market signals have forced policymakers to reconsider how government policies and institutions can reform the social environment within which American firms and workers must compete. One of the most notable positive consequences of the changing income distribution has been a growing awareness by American managers and workers that domestic quality and cost standards are not "good enough"; world standards must be met to maintain real incomes in the global economy. Another notable consequence has been heightened concern over the efficiency and effectiveness of American education.

Critics of the income distribution tend to look almost exclusively to government programs for solutions for income declines. While there are definite opportunities for government to better organize its efforts to relieve the hardship of truly unfortunate citizens, it is equally important to remember that the pricing system from which the income distribution must emerge is a feedback system with tremendous opportunity for self-correction. And much of the data reviewed here indicate that self-correction was obviously under way during most of the 1980s.

Perhaps more important, we should remember that the most enduring solutions will come, as they have in the past, from people acting privately and as members of small groups (firms, households, and families). These individuals possess the necessary information from which productive and constructive change can be made because they can tailor their adjustments to fit their circumstances and the information close at hand, and because they have the incentive to make sure that their expenditures of time and money are profitable.

Concluding Comments

Exorbitant claims about the changing income distribution have a way of being repeated so often that they are widely believed, often with unflinching dedication. They were the types of claims that Bill Clinton ran so successfully on, primarily because George Bush would not or could not rebut them. No one disputes the fact that during the 1970s and 1980s the incomes of many Americans floundered, even declined, nor that the rise in people's incomes was significantly slowed by historic standards (in line with changes in worker productivity, first slowing to virtually zero in the late 1970s and then rising again in the 1980s). Single parents and people with very limited education were especially hard hit. Union workers, many of whom were and remain "routine production workers," frequently lost their protected bargaining positions due to growing domestic and international competition.[65] As a consequence, many workers' real incomes sank, forcing their spouses to enter the labor force to maintain or improve their families' economic status.

At the same time, the American economy has always been beset with a great deal of churning in people's economic fortunes. The question is not whether there have been misfortunes but whether the data support the charges that the changes in the income distribution were, even cumulatively speaking, "seismic," or that the incomes of the vast majority of Americans "plummeted," or that only the "most fortunate fifth" of the population, whose incomes supposedly soared, realized gains; or that the "American dream" was shattered for practically everyone.

The facts do square with the impression that competition became more intense and that real wages began to slow markedly, but the facts simply do not square with the widely propagated dreadful vision of what happened during the 1980s. The oil shocks and recessions of the 1970s and early 1980s undercut the real incomes of American households. The incomes of some groups dropped rapidly in the late 1970s and early 1980s, but the incomes of most groups recovered about as rapidly as they fell. The data reveal that the real mean incomes of all quintiles rose, albeit modestly, from the early 1970s to the late 1980s, and during the 1980s the real means rose together and, compared with the previous decade, relatively rapidly.

Even though the incomes of the "rich," defined as a quintile, climbed absolutely and relatively, it simply does not follow that everyone in the lower income or educational groups was not gaining in the process. The standard assessment of median or average income is far too simplistic. Repeated references to "means" and "medians" of groups grossly exaggerate the various experiences of the people in the groups. Furthermore, given the nature of the various groupings of households and families, it should not be surprising that the top income groups rose more rapidly than the lower groups. When people in the bottom groupings substantially improve their economic positions, they often move to higher groupings. People in the top grouping cannot do the same.

Carnegie Mellon University economist Allan Meltzer noted the standard explanation for the relative rise in the incomes of people in the top brackets: "[T]he greedy grabbed from the needy," but then added an observation that is hard to deny, "If before-tax income of the highest group increased relative to others, it must be because they reported more income. Either they worked more and earned more, or they took less income as non-taxable benefits and perquisites. None of these would hurt the middle class."[66] When individuals (as distinct from quintiles), were tracked during the 1980s, the best evidence available indicates a far more positive picture of income growth. In fact, it looks as though the poor may have, on average and in percentage terms, gained more than the rich during the 1980s.

The late Sam Walton's wealth soared during the 1980s with the expansion of his Walmart discount store chain, but his wealth expanded because he was providing his customers with what they considered to be better products at more favorable prices than they could get from other vendors. The owners of Nucor Steel also experienced wealth increases, but only because the market was working, that is, was passing out rewards for more competitive products. Similarly, at the same time American automobile and textile workers were laid off, the real purchasing power of American consumers, many of whom were in the lower income quintiles, rose with their purchases of what they considered to be superior (albeit often, foreign) products.

Reality is far brighter than the critics have surmised. While the dream of a brighter economic future obviously dimmed for many Americans, especially those with little education and without the skill or inclination to meet the intensifying competition, the American dream was, just as obviously, being lived by a substantial majority of Americans—especially those who stayed in school, went on for extended education, withstood the temptation to have children at early ages, and met the competition. In short, policy commentators and policymakers can and should acknowledge those experiencing hardship and seek solutions for their problems—but without making the problem far bigger than it is.

If there is a fifth of the population that is worthy of concern, it is far more correct and productive to talk about the "unfortunate fifth." People in this category had relatively low incomes at the start of the 1980s and, often through no fault of their own, saw their incomes fall during the following decade. Discussing the misfortunes of a fifth of the population also reduces the issue of relief to a manageable proportion, with fewer people who must be helped and more of those who can do the helping. This is especially true since many in the "unfortunate fifth" have learned from their experience and have begun to take corrective action—without directives from Washington.

Notes

1. See Karen Pennar, "The Rich Are Richer—And America May Be the Poorer," *Business Week*, November 18, 1991, pp. 85–86.

2. Robert B. Reich, *The Work of Nations: Preparing Ourselves for the 21st-Century Capitalism* (New York: Alfred A. Knopf, 1991).

3. Theodore R. Marmor, Jerry L. Mashaw, and Philip L. Harvey, *America's Misunderstood Welfare State: Persistent Myths, Enduring Realities* (New York: Basic Books, 1991), p. 8.

4. Ibid.

5. Greg J. Duncan, Timothy M. Smeeding, and Willard Rodgers, "W(h)ither the Middle Class? A Dynamic View," a paper presented at the Levy Institute Conference on Income Inequality, Bard College, June 18–20, 1991, p. 7.

6. Reich, *The Work of Nations*, p. 197, cites U.S. Bureau of the Census work on the Current Population Survey and the Bureau of Labor statistics work on the Consumer Expenditure Survey.

    More specifically, he cites the Congressional Budget Office, U.S. House of Representatives, Ways and Means Committee, *The Changing Distribution of Federal Taxes, 1977–1990* (Washington, DC: U.S. Government Printing Office, February 1987); and U.S. House of Representatives, Ways and Means Committee, *Tax Progressivity and Income Distribution* (Washington, DC: U.S. Government Printing Office, October 1988).

7. Robert B. Reich, "U.S. Income Inequality Keeps on Rising: As the World Turns," *The New Republic*, May 1, 1989, pp. 23–28.

8. Ibid., p. 28.

9. Leonard Silk, "Economic Scene: Why Fiscal Policy Has to Have Soul," *New York Times*, December 6, 1991.

10. Alan Murray, "Tax Cuts the Answer? What's the Question?", *Wall Street Journal*, October 28, 1991.

11. Robert J. Samuelson, "The Fragmenting of America," *Washington Post National Weekly*, August 12–18, 1991, p. 29.

12. Pennar, "The Rich Are Richer," p. 86.

13. Ibid., p. 85.

14. Harry Bernstein, "Surge in Part-Time Workers Ominous," *Los Angeles Times*, December 10, 1991.

15. Claims about a "great U-turn" in average real worker wages have been considered in detail elsewhere. See Richard B. McKenzie,

"Workers and Wages: No U-Turn," *The Margin*, September/October 1990, pp. 36–37.

16. Bennett Harrison and Barry Bluestone, *The Great U-Turn: Corporate Restructuring and the Polarizing of America* (New York: Basic Books, 1988).

17. Ibid, p. 3.

18. Ibid., p. 20.

19. Ibid., p. 6 (see figure 1.1). These authors actually cite "real average weekly earnings," which has a more pronounced "U" than real average worker wages, primarily because of the downward trend in the number of hours worked per week. However, it needs to be stressed that this downward trend has been under way for most of this century, if not much longer.

20. Prior to 1983, the consumer price index incorrectly assessed the change in the cost of living because changes in the asset prices of houses, per se, were included. If the price of new homes went up by 10 percent, then the CPI would include that information (after properly weighing housing for its importance in people's budgets). However, most people who own their own homes do not experience an increase in their "cost of living" in line with the increase in the market prices of houses. As a consequence, many economists reasoned that the CPI overstated the rise in the cost of living, and this defect was getting worse as inflation accelerated in the 1960s and 1970s. This means that use of the CPI, especially in times of relative rapid inflation, like the 1970s, understates the rise (or overstates the decline) in real worker wages. Officials at the Bureau of Labor Statistics concluded that a "better" way to measure changes in the cost of living from changes in housing costs was to measure changes in the monthly *rental payments* for housing (not in the prices of the houses themselves). The published CPI represents this new method—since 1983. However, the widely published CPI before 1983 remains wedded to the old "defective" method of assessing housing costs.

21. For discussions of how the "average wage" (and many other statistics) is measured by the BLS, see Bureau of Labor Statistics, U.S. Department of Commerce, *BLS Handbook of Methods* (Washington, DC: U.S. Government Printing Office, April 1988), Bulletin No. 2285.

22. See Robert L. Bartley, *The Seven Fat Years and How to Do It Again* (New York: Free Press, 1992), pp. 31–33.

23. The median household income is the income level at which half of all households earn more and half earn less. It can be distinguished from the average household income, which is total income of all households divided by the number of households.

24. The trend value for the top panel of figure 4-2 increased from $29,201
    in 1967 to $29,231 in 1990. Many of the statistics in this section were
    obtained from the U.S. Bureau of the Census, Department of
    Commerce, Current Population Reports: Consumer Income, Series
    P-60, no. 174, *Money Income of Households, Families, and Persons in the
    United States: 1990* (Washington, DC: U.S. Government Printing
    Office, August 1991); and Congressional Budget Office, U.S.
    Congress, *Trends in Family Incomes: 1970–1986* (Washington, DC: U.S.
    Government Printing Office, February 1988).

25. The measure of money also does not include noncash benefits in the
    form of the use of business transportation and facilities, full or
    partial payments by business for retirement programs, and
    educational expenses (Bureau of the Census, *Money Income*, 1990, p.
    226).

26. Executive Office of the President, Council of Economic Advisers, *The
    Economic Report of the President* (Washington, DC: U.S. Government
    Printing Office, February 1991), p. 312.

27. U.S. Department of Commerce, Bureau of the Census, *Measuring the
    Effects of Benefits and Taxes on Income and Poverty: 1990*, Current
    Population Reports: Consumer Income, Series P-60, no. 176-RD
    (1991), p. 8.

28. Job security should be viewed as a fringe benefit just like health
    insurance because it is a form of insurance, which carries a cost.
    Companies must make plans to cover the costs associated with not
    closing plants and not laying off workers when economic conditions
    might otherwise warrant closing plants or laying off workers. The
    automobile industry is a good example of such trade-offs.

29. The index for adjusted family income is computed from
    supplements as a percentage of wage and salary income as reported
    in the national income statistics [Executive Office of the President,
    Council of Economic Advisers, *The Economic Report of the President:
    1991* (Washington, DC: U.S. Government Printing Office, 1991), p.
    312]. For example, when supplements represented 12 percent of
    wages and salaries in 1970, the median household income was
    increased by 12 percent; 1967 real median income was then made the
    base year (=100).

30. Ibid., and author's computations. The in-kind benefits added a much
    higher, but undetermined, percentage to the total incomes of the
    lowest quintile, the mean income of which was less than one-fourth
    of the median income for all households. On the other hand, the
    standard computation of median income does not account for the
    rising tax bite from worker incomes during the 1970s and 1980s. To
    that extent, the median income overstates families' resources. Total

Social Security, federal income taxes, and state income taxes totaled $4,832 in 1990, and represented 16.1 percent of median income.

31. Ibid., p. 53.

32. Income of various families is adjusted for size using the "family equivalence scale" implicit in official poverty thresholds. This scale assumes that family needs rise with size but that the additional needs caused by the addition of one member to a family of, say, four is not as great as the additional needs created for a family of, say, two. For the exact "equivalence scale" used to make the adjustment, see U.S. Congress, Congressional Budget Office, *Trends in Family Income: 1970–1986* (Washington, DC: U.S. Government Printing Office, February 1988), p. 6.

33. See Dennis J. Aigner, Friedrich Schneider, and Damayanti Ghosh, "Me and My Shadow: Estimating the Size of the U.S. Hidden Economy from Time Series Data," *Dynamic Econometric Modeling: Proceedings of the Third International Symposium in Economic Theory and Econometrics*, edited by William A. Barnett, Ernst R. Berndt, and Halbert White (New York: Cambridge University Press, 1988), pp. 297–334.

34. Two studies found that the net worth of families increased in percentage terms by substantially more than the mean and median income. Researchers at the Federal Reserve Board of Governors found that the net worth (assets minus liabilities) for all families increased by 23.2 percent between 1983 and 1989, whereas their median increased by 10.5 percent (indicating, they suggest, growing concentration of wealth among the wealthy). The real mean net worth for all income groups, aside from families with less than $10,000 in annual income, increased significantly. The mean for those families with less than $10,000 moved up but only very slightly. The mean net worth of families with $10,000 to $19,999 in annual income and with $50,000 or more increased by 19 percent and by 6.6 percent, respectively. For more details, see Arthur Kennickell and Janice Shack-Marquez, "Changes in Family Finances from 1983 to 1989: Evidence from the Survey of Consumer Finance," *Federal Reserve Bulletin*, January 1992, p. 3.

Duncan, Smeeding, and Rodgers found that between 1984 and 1989 the real net worth of households in the lowest quintile rose by 55 percent, while the net worth of the top quintile rose by less, 49 percent [Duncan, Smeeding, and Rodgers, "W(h)ither the Middle Class?" table 4]. However, these researchers concluded there was growing inequality in net worth, but only in absolute terms since the absolute real dollar increase in the net worth of the lowest quintile was much smaller than the absolute real dollar increase of the top quintile. However, they could have deduced growing inequality in net worth on absolute grounds so long as the real net worth of the bottom quintile increased by less than 22 times, which is obviously a totally unreasonable basis for drawing inferences about growing inequality.

35. Bureau of Census, *Money Income of Households, Families, and Persons in the United States: 1990*, pp. 5–8.

36. The poverty threshold for a family of three was $10,419 in 1990. This threshold for the calculations is used because in 1990 the average family in the lowest quintile was 2.98 persons. Nevertheless, the upper limit for the lowest quintile was 81 percent of the 1990 threshold for a family of four in 1967 and 93 percent of that threshold in 1990.

37. Obviously, the mean income of the highest quintile rose by a much greater percentage than all others in the 1980s, but it is noteworthy that, on balance, the percentage increase of the lowest quintile was generally higher than the percentage increase of the second and middle quintiles. During the 1980s, the percentage increase of the lowest quintile closely tracked the percentage increase of the next-to-highest quintile.

38. See Edgar K. Browning, "Inequality and Poverty," *Southern Economic Journal*, April 1989, p. 820; and Mark Lilla, "Why the 'Income Distribution' Is So Misleading," *Public Interest*, Fall 1984, pp. 62–76.

39. Figures 4-9 and 4-10 show that the second, third, and fourth quintiles also exhibited some increase in their real mean incomes with, generally speaking, the rates of increase rising with the quintile. The mean of the second quintile rose from $15,961 in 1967 to $18,341 in 1989, or 115 percent of its 1967 level. The mean of the third quintile rose from $25,485 in 1967 to $30,488 in 1989, reaching 120 percent of its 1967 mean. The mean of the fourth quintile rose from $35,656 in 1967 to $46,117 in 1989, reaching 129 percent of its 1967 level. These figures clearly disclose the relatively more rapid increase in the mean incomes of the higher income categories. The mean of the highest 20 percent of households rose from $64,615 in 1967 to $90,150 in 1989, reaching almost 140 percent of its 1967 mean. The 5 percent of households with the highest income saw their mean income rise from $102,994 in 1967 to $145,651 in 1990, rising to 141 percent of the 1967 mean.

40. University of Maryland economist Frank Levy and Urban Institute researcher Richard Michel considered the changes in the percentage distribution of families by level of real income between two years, 1973 and 1986. Using the CPI to adjust for inflation, they argue that there was a partial erosion of the percentage size of the middle class

at the same time that the percentage sizes of the lower and upper income groups rose. [Frank Levy and Richard C. Michel, *The Economic Future of American Families: Income and Wealth Trends,* (Washington, DC: Urban Institute, 1991), chap 4 (especially Fig. 4.1)]. A similar conclusion can be drawn with more recent Census data using the CPI-X to adjust for inflation. However, the picture of income changes is not as bleak as Levy and Michel suggest. The percentage of families with less than $10,000 rises very slightly, from 10.1 percent in 1973 (the absolute low point for the 1967–1988 period) to 10.8 percent in 1988. Furthermore, all of the increase is attributable to increase in those families with less than $5,000 of income. The percentage of families in the $5,000–$10,000 range generally fell, albeit slightly, from 1973 to 1988. And the percentage of families in the under $10,000 category in 1988 was down from 13.4 percent in 1967 and 12.7 percent in 1983. The percentage of families with incomes between $10,000 and $25,000 also trended decidedly downward in the 1970s and 1980s, falling from 34.6 percent of all families in 1967, to 28.9 percent in 1973, to 26.6 percent in 1988 [see U.S. Bureau of the Census, *Trends in Income by Selected Characteristics: 1947 to 1988,* p. 55]. These data suggest that many families in the lower incomes groups were experiencing some economic improvement, as measured by the Levy/Michel standard. Admittedly, some families moved down the income scale, a point that Levy/Michel and others emphasize. However, other families obviously moved up the scale. The 2.3 percentage point decrease in the families in the $10,000 to $25,000 of real income range was more than three times the .7 percentage point increase in the families with less than $10,000 of real income.

41. The relative importance of these social, economic, and demographic considerations are "decomposited" by Gordon Green, Paul Ryscavage, and Edward Welniak, "Factors Affecting Growing Income Inequality: A Decomposition" (Washington, DC: Housing and Household Economic Statistics Division, U.S. Bureau of the Census, July 2, 1991), draft.

42. Bureau of the Census researchers have evaluated the relative importance of these and other social, demographic, and economic factors. They found that the aging population and the growing percentage of blacks in the population had a small but consequential negative effect on the real median income. On balance, these two demographic factors together depressed the median income in 1989 by almost 2 percent. The growth in the prevalence of single-parent and single households depressed incomes by 10 percent below what they would have been in 1989, while the increase in education increased the median income by nearly 12 percent. Finally, changing economic conditions—specifically, the decline in the work

experience of householders, the growth in the number of working spouses with little work experience, and the shifts in employment from industrial to service employment—had negative effects on the median income. If these shifts had not occurred, the median income would have been 8.3 percent higher in 1989 than it was. The effect of education was to suppress the Gini index to reduce the poverty rate, while the effect of all other variables was to increase the Gini index and increase the poverty rate. However, all economic, social, and demographic considerations together depressed the median by a scant .8 percent, mainly because the positive effects of added education offset the negative effects of the social, demographic, and economic effects (Green, Ryscavage, and Welniak, "Factors Affecting Growing Income Inequality: A Decomposition," pp. 16–21).

43. This is true after adjusting for receipt of in-kind benefits and for taxes. Browning figures that if additional adjustments are made for the economic value of time not on the job, the lowest quintile has an even greater share of family income (Edgar K. Browning, "How Much More Equality Can We Afford?" *Public Interest*, Spring 1976, pp. 90–100).

44. Daniel R. Feenberg and James M. Poterba, *Income Inequality and the Incomes of Very High Income Taxpayers: Evidence from Tax Returns*, working paper no. 4229 (Cambridge, MA: National Bureau of Economic Research, December 1992).

45. Ibid., p. 4.

46. Ibid., p. 17.

47. One researcher estimates that a major share of household income differences can be explained by the amount of work, with the rich working far more than people in lower income groups [see Lawrence M. Mead, *The New Politics of Poverty: The Nonworking Poor in America* (New York: Basic Books, 1992)].

48. Along these lines, the rise in the percentage of the population going on to higher education from 4.2 percent in 1970 to 5.3 percent in 1988 probably contributed, albeit marginally, to the decline in the share of current income going to the lowest quintile, even though most of the students could anticipate higher future incomes.

49. A portion of the increase in the fortunes of the two-earner families may be explained by spouses switching from part-time to full-time work. On the other hand, the growing number of part-time workers could have been pulling down the growth in the average. The growing use of part-time workers could also have been affecting the median income of the one-earner families, although the directional effect cannot be specified.

50. Government transfers include Social Security payments,

unemployment payments, veterans benefits, government employee retirement benefits, aid to families with dependent children, and "others" (Council of Economic Advisers, *The Economic Report of the President: 1991*, p. 315).

51. As reported by Bruce Bartlett, "A Class Struggle that Won't Stay Put," *Wall Street Journal*, November 20, 1991. Very similar, but not identical, statistical shifts have been reported by the staff of the Joint Economic Committee [prepared for Representative Richard K. Armey, "Income Mobility and the U.S. Economy: Open Society or Caste System?" (Washington, DC: Joint Economic Committee, U.S. Congress, December 30, 1991). The JEC staff used Bureau of Census data [as reported in U.S. Department of Commerce, Bureau of the Census, Current Population Reports, series P-70, no. 18, *Transition in Income and Poverty: 1985–1986* (Washington, DC: U.S. Government Printing Office, 1990); and U.S. Department of Commerce, Bureau of the Census, Current Population Reports, series P-70, no. 24, *Transition in Income and Poverty: 1987–1988* (Washington, DC: U.S. Government Printing Office, 1990)].

52. See Greg J. Duncan, *Years of Poverty, Years of Plenty* (Ann Arbor, MI: Survey Research Center, Institute for Social Research, University of Michigan, 1984), p. 13.

53. Michael W. Horrigan and Steven E. Haugen, "The Declining Middle-Class Thesis: A Sensitivity Analysis," *Monthly Labor Review*, May 1988, p. 3.

54. Bartlett, "A Class Struggle that Won't Stay Put."

55. U.S. Department of the Treasury, Office of Tax Analysis, "Household Income Mobility during the 1980's: A Statistical Assessment Based on Tax Return Data" (Washington, DC: U.S. Government Printing Office, June 1, 1992); and Isabel V. Sawhill and Mark Condon, "Is U.S. Income Inequality Really Growing? Sorting Out the Fairness Question," *Policy Bites*, no. 13 (Washington, DC: Urban Institute, June 1992).

56. U.S. Department of the Treasury, "Household Income Mobility during the 1980's: A Statistical Assessment Based on Tax Return Data." One of the problems with this study is that it covers only Americans with sufficient income to warrant filing an income tax return. Many of the poorest of American families are, therefore, not covered by the data. The mobility of those who do not file income tax returns may not be as great as the Treasury reports for those who do.

57. Ibid., p. 1. The taxpayers' incomes were adjusted to account for changes in the tax law, and the conclusions are based on what the

Treasury economists call "real constant-law adjusted gross income," a measure of income that does not change when the tax law changes.

58. Ibid., p. 5. Of the taxpayers in the top 1 percent of income earners, more than half (53 percent) had dropped out of the top 1 percent by 1988.

59. Ibid., p. 2. In short, the data for given years are what they are—merely reports on the people who happened to be classified within the group at the time of the survey. Over time, people can move up and down the income distribution and can be classified in different quintiles in different years. Their movements among the quintiles can be attributed to many considerations, some of which have nothing to do with hourly or weekly earnings. Of course, people who are successful can move up the income distribution, raising the average income of the group into which they move (and only indirectly and to a minor extent raising the average income of the group they left). Two single people with incomes just below the cut-off income level for the bottom quintile can marry and move to the middle quintile, raising the average income of the middle quintile by more than they raise the average income of the lowest quintile. Similarly, when a couple in the middle of the distribution divorces, each person may become a single household in the lowest quintile, potentially lowering the average incomes for both quintiles.

60. Sawhill and Condon, "Is U.S. Income Mobility Really Growing?", p. 1.

61. Ibid., p. 3 (table 2).

62. John Bound and George Johnson, "Changes in the Structure of Wages in the 1980's: An Evaluation of Alternative Explanations," *American Economic Review*, June 1992, pp. 371–392.

63. Service employment as a percentage of total employment is very close to the upward linear trend plotted from 1880 to 1930. See Mack Ott, "The Growing Share of Services in the U.S. Economy—Degeneration or Evolution?" *Review* [Federal Reserve Bank of St. Louis], June/July 1987, p. 15.

64. See Stephen S. Cohen and John Zysman, *Manufacturing Matters: The Myth of the Post-Industrial Economy* (New York: Basic Books, 1987).

65. For a discussion of the relative importance of the shifts in labor market demands and aggregate economic expansion on incomes, see David M. Cutler and Lawrence F. Katz, "Untouched by the Rising Tide," *Brookings Review*, Winter 1992, pp. 41–45.

66. Allan H. Meltzer, "If the Middle Class Is Falling Behind, Solution Lies in Higher Productivity," *Los Angeles Times*, December 8, 1991.

5

POLITICS OF THE RICH AND THE POOR: EXPENDITURES

The theme of the last chapter was straightforward: Much political oratory is based on a widely repeated but misguided social belief: During the 1980s, only the rich got richer, and the poor and the middle class got poorer. The data on the income distribution among households reviewed in that chapter support the claim that the rich got richer during the decade. These same data, however, undercut the claim that the poor and the middle class became poorer during the last decade. Many in the lower income groups became quite rich, even by the standards of the decade's harshest critics.

Similarly, data on the distribution of consumer expenditures confirm the view that all income groups—rich, poor, and middle class alike—got richer during the 1980s. The poor and middle income groups increased their consumption expenditures in constant (inflation-adjusted) dollars, although the rich, defined as changing collections of people in the top quintile, did increase their expenditures at a significantly faster pace. In addition, the expenditure data reveal that the poor and the not-so-poor income groups are not, on average, nearly as poor as is commonly believed (or as their reported incomes suggest).

A detailed investigation of the before-tax incomes and expenditures of consumer "units"—compiled by the Bureau of Labor Statistics' Consumer Expenditure Survey—reveals several points that have been overlooked in the current political debate over the nation's income distribution. First, the real or inflation-adjusted before-tax income of the lowest fifth, or quintile, of consumer units (or households) jumped dramatically between 1984 and 1989 (the earliest and latest years of consistent data). In fact, it increased by a far greater percentage than the before-tax income of the other fifths of the income distribution. Second, in 1984, on a per capita basis the lowest income group spent more than three times its reported income. In 1989, per capita expenditures of the lowest quintile were higher than they had been five years earlier but declined relative to the group's before-tax income. Nevertheless, this group still spent more than twice its per capita income that year.

Third, of course, a widely recognized reason higher income groups spend more than the lower income groups is that they have more income. However, another major reason is that there are far more people in the higher income groups to earn incomes and to do the spending—three times as many income earners and more than 66 percent more consumers in the top quintile than in the bottom quintile.

Fourth, in 1984 and 1989, the total income of the top income group was more than twelve times the aggregate income of the lowest group. However, spending by those in the top group was less than two and a half times the amount spent per capita by the lowest income group. Fifth, the considerable income mobility within the American economy enables the lower income groups to spend far more than they earn. And sixth, Americans' expenditures are less unequal than their incomes. Indeed, evidence is beginning to emerge that suggests that the distribution of expenditures between upper and lower income classes did not become less equal during the 1980s (nor, for that matter, during the 1970s).

In general, the income and expenditure data reported here for the 1980s suggest that the rich, poor, and middle classes got richer in real dollars and that their gains showed up in the amount of goods and services they bought.[1]

Vital Statistics on Quintiles

The distribution of before-tax income and expenditures can be understood only by knowing some of the details of how the distributions are determined. Major explanations for observed changes in the expenditure distribution lie in the nature of each quintile. This is especially true for the data at the heart of the analysis in this chapter.

In 1984 and 1989, the Bureau of Labor Statistics (BLS) in the Department of Labor surveyed a representative sample of "consuming units" among the country's noninstitutional population. A unit can be a single person living alone, a household of unrelated people, or a family related by blood or law. The results of the survey enabled the BLS to divide the distribution of households into quintiles by their reported before-tax income. In 1984 (the earliest year of integrated data for the 1980s), the BLS estimated that there were approximately 16.2 to 16.3 million units in each quintile.[2] By 1989 (the latest year of available data), the number of units in each quintile had increased to 16.6 million.

While the number of consuming units in each quintile is approximately equal, the average number of people in each unit varies substantially across the quintiles. Table 5-1 gives the details of average unit sizes by quintiles. The quintile of units with the lowest before-tax incomes on average contained 2.0 people in 1984 and 1.8 people in 1989, a decline of 10 percent. As can be seen, the average size of units rises with each higher quintile. In 1984, the average size of the top quintile was 3.3 people, 66 percent larger than the average size of the lowest quintile for the year. Like all quintiles, other than the middle, the average size of the top quintile declined slightly, reaching 3.1 members in 1989 (but was still 72 percent higher than the average size of the lowest quintile).

Table 5-1 Characteristics of Quintiles of Consuming Units, Divided by Before-Tax Earnings, 1984 and 1989

	Lowest Quintile	Second Quintile	Middle Quintile	Fourth Quintile	Highest Quintile
Number of Consuming Units (millions)					
1984	16.2	16.3	16.2	16.2	16.3
1989	16.6	16.6	16.6	16.6	16.6
Average Number of People in Consuming Units					
1984	2.0	2.3	2.6	3.0	3.3
1989	1.8	2.2	2.6	2.9	3.1
Total Estimated Population (millions)					
1984	32.4	37.4	42.2	48.7	53.7
1989	29.8	36.5	43.2	48.2	51.5
Percent of Population					
1984	15.1	17.4	19.7	22.7	25.1
1989	14.3	17.4	20.6	23.0	24.6

Note: Data for both 1984 and 1989 are from the integrated survey, which means the data are the combined findings from the interview survey and diaries kept by units and that they cover only complete reporting units.

Source: U.S. Department of Labor, Bureau of Labor Statistics, *Consumer Expenditure Survey: Integrated Survey Data, 1984–86,* Bulletin 2333 (Washington, DC: U.S. Government Printing Office, August 1989), pp. 86–89; and U.S. Department of Labor, Bureau of Labor Statistics, *Consumer Expenditure Survey, 1988–89,* Bulletin 2383 (Washington, DC: U.S. Government Printing Office, August 1991), pp. 11–141; and author's calculations.

This difference in average sizes of consuming units means that the actual population in each quintile varies substantially. Table 5-1 also shows that in 1989 the lowest quintile accounted for only 14 percent (not 20 percent as might be supposed) of the total estimated population,[3] while the top group accounted for 52 million people, or 25 percent of the estimated population.

Differences in the size of population for the quintiles help explain differences in the earnings and consumption expenditures of the groups. The 1989 data in table 5-1 reveal 22 million, or 73 percent, more people in the top group than in the bottom group. The BLS estimated that the highest quintile had three times the income earners of the bottom quintile. According to another survey by the Bureau of Census, in 1990 there were three times as many full- and part-time workers and seven times as many full-time workers in the top group as in the bottom group.[4]

The BLS survey data have the peculiar result of covering fewer people in all quintiles, other than the middle quintile, in 1989 than in 1984 (when, in fact, the Census Bureau showed growth in the country's population). For this reason, greater emphasis will be placed on per capita and unit estimates of income and expenditures and relative income shares than on total income and expenditures.

One of the more obvious explanations for the relatively small size of the lower groups is the high concentration in these groups of elderly couples without children, single people, and single parents with children. In 1989, people sixty-five years of age and older represented 28 percent of the lowest group and only 3 percent of the top group. The number of children under 18 in the top group was 61 percent greater than the number in the bottom group, meaning there was a disproportionate number of two-parent families in the top group and a disproportionate number of singles and childless couples in the bottom group.[5]

Another explanation for the greater expenditures of the top group is the greater education levels attained, which increased both the group's earning and consumption ability. The percentage of the top units in which at least one person had a college degree rose from 69 percent in 1984 to 73 percent in 1989. In the bottom group, units in which someone held a college degree was a surprisingly high 31 percent in 1984 and was down one percentage point in 1989.

Finally, an important point from chapter four must be kept in mind: Commentaries on the income distribution are often written as though "the rich" and "the poor," as defined by the highest and lowest quintiles, are unchanging groups of people.[6] However, recent studies indicate substantial movement of people, families, and households up and down the income ladder.[7]

Distribution of Before-Tax Income

As can be seen in both table 5-2 and figure 5-1, the findings from income surveys done by the Census Bureau (covered in chapter four) do not always correspond with the results of surveys done by the BLS (covered in this chapter). Recall that Census Bureau surveys determined that the real incomes of the bottom four quintiles increased by 10 to 12 percent between 1983 and 1989. As can be seen in both table 5-2 and figure 5-1, for people in the lowest quintile, real before-tax incomes, adjusted to constant (1990) dollars by the experimental consumer price index (CPI-X), jumped dramatically between 1984 and 1989, much more than for any other group.[8] The real total before-tax income of the lowest group expanded 53.8 percent, from $65 billion in 1984 to $100 billion in 1989. During that period, real per unit income of the lowest quintile increased 51 percent, rising from $3,986 to $6,029. The real per capita income increased even more, by 68 percent, from $1,993 to $3,349.[9]

The top quintile's total before-tax income rose only 6 percent, from less than $1.2 trillion to more than $1.2 trillion. Its per unit income increased 12 percent, from $70,981 in 1984 to $79,480 in 1989, and its per capita income rose 19 percent, from $21,509 to $25,639.

Distribution of Expenditures

The distribution of out-of-pocket expenditures by quintiles can, with all the caveats mentioned, provide useful though limited insights into the changing welfare of American households.[10] The total expenditures of the lowest quintile fell between 1984 and 1989, while expenditures of the other quintiles rose. The decline can be associated largely with the decline in the estimated population of the lowest group (probably attributable to expected variations resulting

Table 5-2 Annual Before-Tax Income of Consumer Units, by
Quintiles, 1984 and 1989, in Constant (1990) Dollars

	Lowest Quintile	Second Quintile	Middle Quintile	Fourth Quintile	Highest Quintile
Total Before-Tax Income (billions of dollars)					
1984	65	210	374	593	1,160
1989	100	243	418	657	1,230
% Change	53.8	15.7	11.8	10.8	6.0
Before-Tax Income Per Unit					
1984	3,986	12,893	23,071	36,490	70,981
1989	6,029	14,645	25,145	39,552	79,480
% Change	51.3	13.6	9.0	8.4	12.0
Before-Tax Income Per Capita					
1984	1,993	5,606	8,873	12,163	21,509
1989	3,349	6,657	9,671	13,638	25,639
% Change	68.0	18.7	9.0	12.1	19.2

Note: Data for both 1984 and 1989 are from the integrated survey, which means
the data are the combined findings from the interview survey and diaries kept by
units and that they cover only complete reporting units.

Source: U.S. Department of Labor, Bureau of Labor Statistics, *Consumer
Expenditure Survey: Integrated Survey Data, 1984–86*, Bulletin 2333
(Washington, DC: U.S. Government Printing Office, August 1989), pp.
86–89; and U.S. Department of Labor, Bureau of Labor Statistics,
Consumer Expenditure Survey, 1988–89, Bulletin 2383 (Washington, DC:
U.S. Government Printing Office, August 1991), pp. 11–14; and author's
calculations.

Figure 5-1 Income Per Capita of Complete Reporting Units, by
Quintiles, 1984 and 1989, in Constant (1990) Dollars

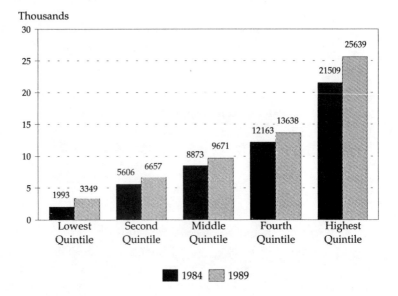

Source: U.S. Department of Labor, Consumer Expenditure Survey,
1984–86 and 1988–89.

from sampling estimation techniques). When the data are computed
on a per unit or per capita basis, one conclusion stands out: The
consumption expenditures of all income groups expanded in constant dollars during the 1980s.

Expenditure Data

Table 5-3 summarizes the main findings of the BLS Consumer Expenditure Survey for 1984 and 1989. Raw survey data reported in
the table have, again, been adjusted by the CPI-X to constant (1990)
dollars. As is evident in that table, in 1984 the top group spent in total
3.9 times ($856 billion) the amount spent by the lowest group ($222
billion). The highest quintile had a reported total income for that year
(just under to $1.2 trillion) close to 18 times that of the lowest quintile
($60 billion). However, between 1984 and 1989, *per unit* spending in

Table 5-3 Annual Expenditures of Consumer Units, by Quintiles, of Income Before Taxes, 1984 and 1989, in Constant (1990) Dollars

	Lowest Quintile	Second Quintile	Middle Quintile	Fourth Quintile	Highest Quintile
Total Expenditures (billions of dollars)					
1984	222	293	397	534	856
1989	212	308	428	599	930
% Change	-4.5	5.1	7.8	12.2	8.6
Expenditures Per Unit					
1984	13,704	18,035	24,491	32,880	52,613
1989	12,774	18,568	25,798	36,081	55,962
% Change	-6.8	3.0	5.3	9.7	6.4
Expenditures Per Capita					
1984	6,852	7,841	9,420	10,703	15,943
1989	7,097	8,440	9,922	12,442	18,052
% Change	3.6	7.6	5.3	16.2	13.3

Note: Data for both 1984 and 1989 are from the integrated survey, which means the data are the combined findings from the interview survey and diaries kept by units and that they cover only complete reporting units.

Source: U.S. Department of Labor, Bureau of Labor Statistics, *Consumer Expenditure Survey: Integrated Survey Data, 1984–86*, Bulletin 2333 (Washington, DC: U.S. Government Printing Office, August 1989), pp. 86–89; and U.S. Department of Labor, Bureau of Labor Statistics, *Consumer Expenditure Survey, 1988–89*, Bulletin 2383 (Washington, DC: U.S. Government Printing Office, August 1991), pp. 11–141; and author's calculations.

the highest group increased by less than 9 percent while in the poorest group spending declined by about 5 percent. Apparently, the computed increase in total spending of all groups was held down by the lower estimated population. The per unit expenditures of all quintiles except the lowest one rose, with the percentage increasing with each higher quintile. Per unit expenditures for units within the bottom quintile fell from $13,704 in 1984 to $12,774 in 1989, that is, by 6.8 percent. Per unit expenditures for units within the middle quintile rose from $24,491 to $25,798 (5.3 percent), and the per unit expenditures of the top quintile rose from $52,613 to $55,962 (6.4 percent).

Given the problems with the population estimates, the real expenditures per person provide the critical numbers, and real expenditures per capita within all quintiles rose from 1984 to 1989. However, the increase tended to be higher for the higher income groups: 3.6 percent for the bottom quintile, 7.6 percent for the second quintile, 5.3 percent for the middle quintile, 16.2 percent for the fourth quintile, and 13.3 percent for the top quintile. As can be seen in figure 5-2, the relatively greater rise in per capita expenditures for the higher groups can be explained, in part, by the relatively greater income gains of the higher groups.

The expenditure data, especially the per capita data, unequivocally indicate that all income groups got richer during the 1980s. Moreover, the expansion in consumption was not financed solely by increased use of credit; in the main, financing came from each group's greater earnings. Why the poorest group's income increased so much faster than its consumption remains something of a mystery.

Relative Income and Expenditures

Table 5-4 compares the reported real incomes per capita and the real expenditures per capita by quintiles for 1984 and 1989. That table reveals that the real income per capita rose substantially for the lowest income group, while the group's expenditures rose modestly (see figure 5-3). Its per capita income grew 68 percent while its per capita expenditures grew less than 4 percent.

Figure 5-2   Expenditures Per Capita of Complete Reporting Units, by Quintiles, 1984 and 1989, in Constant (1990) Dollars

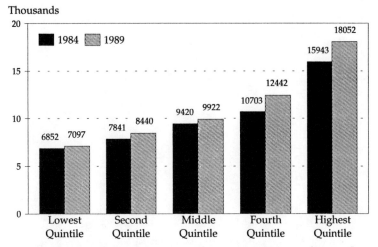

Source: U.S. Department of Labor, Consumer Expenditure Survey, 1984–86 and 1988–89.

Figure 5-3   Percentage Change in Per Capita Income and Per Capita Expenditures Between 1984 and 1989

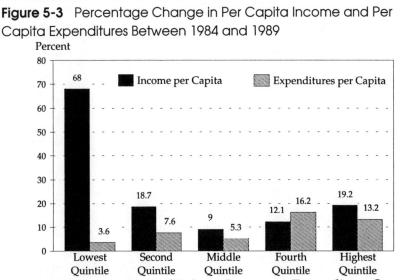

Source: U.S. Department of Labor, Consumer Expenditure Survey, 1984–86 and 1988–89.

Table 5-4 Real Average Annual Before-Tax Incomes and Real Average Annual Expenditures Compared, 1984 and 1989, in 1990 Dollars

	Lowest Quintile		Second Quintile		Middle Quintile		Fourth Quintile		Highest Quintile	
	Income	Expenditure	Income	Expenditure	Income	Expenditure	Income	Expenditure	Income	Expenditure
Real Incomes and Expenditures Per Capita										
1984	1,993	6,852	5,606	7,841	8,873	9,420	12,163	10,703	21,509	15,943
1989	3,349	7,097	6,657	8,440	9,671	9,922	13,638	12,442	25,639	18,052
Real Per Capita Expenditures as a Percentage of Real Per Capita Before-Tax Income										
1984	344		140		106		88		74	
1989	212		127		103		91		70	
Percentage of Total Before-Tax Income and Total Expenditures										
1984	2.7	9.6	8.7	12.7	15.6	17.3	23.2	24.7	48.2	37.2
1989	3.6	8.5	8.9	12.4	15.3	17.3	24.2	24.0	48.2	37.5

Note: Data for both 1984 and 1989 are from the integrated survey, which means the data are the combined findings from the interview survey and diaries kept by units and that they cover only complete reporting units.

Source: U.S. Department of Labor, Bureau of Labor Statistics, *Consumer Expenditure Survey: Integrated Survey Data, 1984–86,* Bulletin 2333 (Washington, DC: U.S. Government Printing Office, August 1989), pp. 86–89; and U.S. Department of Labor, Bureau of Labor Statistics, *Consumer Expenditure Survey, 1988–89,* Bulletin 2383 (Washington, DC: U.S. Government Printing Office, August 1991), pp. 11–141; and author's calculations.

Notice also that in both 1984 and 1989, consumers in the two lowest income groups spent on average substantially more each year than they received in before-tax income (see figure 5-4). For the middle income group, expenditures and incomes were approximately equal in both 1984 and 1989. The two top groups spent significantly less than they earned before taxes. In 1984, the average for the lowest quintile's real before-tax per capita income was $1,993, while its real expenditures per capita totaled $6,852, nearly three and a half times per capita income. In 1989, its per capita expenditures were up slightly in real dollar terms but, in relative terms, down to slightly more than twice per capita income: $3,349 per capita income versus $7,097 per capita expenditures. The second quintile spent, on average, 40 percent more than it earned before taxes in 1984. In 1989, it spent 27 percent more than it earned. The middle quintile, on average, spent slightly more than it earned in both years, 6 percent more in 1984 and 3 percent more in 1989.

Figure 5-4 Real Per Capita Expenditures as a Percentage of Real Per Capita Income, by Quintiles, 1984 and 1989

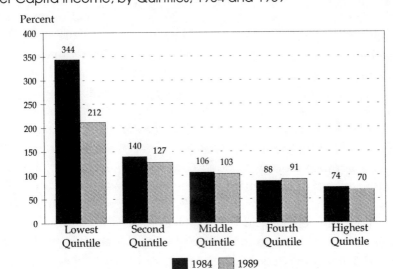

Source: U.S. Department of Labor, Consumer Expenditure Survey, 1984–86 and 1988–89.

Table 5-4 also shows that the two highest income groups spent, on average, less than they earned before taxes in 1984 and 1989. In 1984, the fourth quintile received $12,163 per capita and spent $10,703 per capita. By 1989, the group's per capita income was 12 percent greater, or $13,638, and its per capita expenditures were up by 16 percent, meaning it spent, on average, a greater share of its per capita income in 1989 (91 percent) than in 1984 (88 percent). In 1984, the top income group earned $21,509 per capita and spent $15,943 per capita. By 1989, its per capita income was up 19 percent, to $25,639, while its per capita expenditures rose by 13 percent to $18,052. The top group spent a lower portion of its income in 1989 (70 percent) than in 1984 (74 percent).

The income gap between the highest and lowest income earners is substantial. The total income of the top quintile for 1989 was more than twelve times the total income of the lowest quintile that year. However, what is important to remember is that per capita expenditures of the highest quintile were just two and a half times the per capita expenditures of the lowest quintile.

The data in the bottom two lines of table 5-4 indicate changes in the shares of incomes and expenditures of the quintiles, points often stressed by critics of the 1980s. However, it is also important to remember that the three bottom quintiles spent more than their total income. Interestingly, in 1984, the expenditure share of the lowest quintile, close to 10 percent, was three and a half times its share of income that year, 2.7 percent. By 1989, the lowest quintile's expenditure share had fallen slightly, to 8.5 percent, at the same time its income share rose to 3.6 percent, which still left the expenditure share close to two and a half times its income share. Cutler and Katz found a significant deterioration in the capacity of the lowest fifth to make purchases per "equivalent person" between 1980 and 1988. They found that "average real per equivalent consumption of the lowest quintile fell from $6,162 in 1980 to $5,873 in 1988, a 4.5 percent decline."[11] They also found a slightly smaller decline in the consumption share per "equivalent person" between 1984 and 1988; the drop was from 7.8 percent to 7.5 percent. Cutler and Katz's statistical base is different from the one used here in that Cutler and Katz make several adjustments to the expenditure totals reported in the consumer expenditure survey data. First, they deduct pension contributions and Social Security payments, arguing that those expenditures are more akin to saving than consumption expenditures. Second, they also deduct contributions. Third, they deduct expenditures on new cars and homes and replace them with estimated annualized expenditures. These adjustments have the effect of making expenditures come closer to measuring income flows than out-of-pocket expenditures.

The income share of the second quintile rose slightly at the same time that its expenditure share fell somewhat. The income share of the middle quintile, on the other hand, fell slightly, while its expenditure share stayed the same. For the fourth quintile, the income share fell slightly while its expenditure share rose slightly.

Most notably, the income share of the top quintile remained unchanged at slightly above 48 percent, while its expenditure share rose ever so slightly (from 37.2 percent to 37.5 percent).

Still, it must be kept in mind that focusing excessively on the shares can obscure the fact that per capita real incomes and expenditures of all quintiles rose from 1984 to 1989.

How can it be that the lower income groups were able to spend substantially more each year than they earned? There could be as many answers to this question as there are households in these groups. However, several explanations indicate the vast range of factors which may account for this phenomenon:

1. Many people make a lifetime plan for income and consumption cycles. In many cases this involves spending less than they earn and saving the difference during some parts of their lives and reducing their earnings and spending more than they earn (dissaving) at other times, especially after retirement. During the 1980s, many elderly people in all income groups, but especially those in lower income groups, were in the dissaving phase of their life cycles.

2. Many lower income people are students receiving in-

come support from their higher income parents, and others are elderly being supported by their children and friends.

3. Income that may go unreported for fear of tax and legal repercussions can show up as consumer expenditures. This is especially true of income earned illegally (for example, payments for prostitution and drugs) or that earned legally but on which no taxes are paid (the tips of restaurant servers). As noted in the last chapter, the underground economy in the United States in the 1980s was at least 10 percent that of the above-ground economy and may have reached above 25 percent.[12] This means that in 1989 between $400 billion and $1 trillion may have been earned illegally (and not reported) and then spent (and reported).

4. Some earnings are simply overlooked when people report their incomes. A 1989 study found that people in all quintiles underreport their incomes, but people in the lowest quintile may understate their incomes by as much as 20 percent.[13]

5. Poverty is often temporary.[14] Many people overcome occasional loss of jobs and income (which may have caused them to fall into a lower income group) by dipping into their savings, part of which was set aside for such episodes of misfortune and by drawing on credit. According to the Treasury study cited earlier, close to 40 percent of the people who are officially defined as "poor" are not poor one year later.[15]

6. People often spend more than they earn when they expect their earnings to rise. Therefore, the ability of the poor to consume more than they earn does not always indicate misfortune or bleak economic circumstances; it can indicate expectations of future prosperity. In a true economic sense, many people are really not spending more than they earn. They are, in fact, organizing their expenditures and earnings to accommodate what may occur at different points in their lives.

The fact that the rich spent only 70 percent of their income in 1989 does not mean they saved the other 30 percent. Fifteen percent—half of that which was not spent—went to taxes (whereas the taxes of the poor averaged less than 4 percent of their before-tax incomes). Another (undetermined) portion of the rich's income was set aside so the rich can, at some future point in time, do just what the poor have done: Spend more than they earn.[16]

To avoid misunderstanding, note that the data presented indicate that the rich were not the only ones who saved. Many people in the lower income groups saved, which helps explain why so many of them moved up the income ladder. However, their savings were more than offset by the substantial dissavings of others within their group.

Distribution of the Increase in Expenditures

Much discussion has centered on what portion of the increase in the nation's income during the 1980s went to the top quintile. One study claims that the top 1 percent of income earners of the 1980s garnered 60 percent (or more) of the total increase in before-tax income.[17]

The distribution of expenditures indicates that such estimates are probably wide of the mark. If the rich were garnering practically all income gains, they certainly were not spending their increase, at least not in the year the income was earned. In addition, as is obvious in the data presented, the middle classes and the poor significantly increased their expenditures. Aggregate shares of income and expenditures are heavily influenced by the population estimates for the quintiles, which fell between 1984 and 1989. The shares of before-tax income and of expenditures for 1984 and 1989 and the share of the increase are computed as a percentage of the sum of the per capita before-tax incomes of all quintiles (see table 5-5). That is to say, in 1984, the per capita income of the lowest quintile ($1,993) represented 4 percent of the sum of all per capita incomes for the year ($1,993+$5,606+$8,873+$12,163+21,509=$50,144). The lowest quintile's share of the increase in per capita income between 1984 and 1989 was substantially higher than its 1984 share, over 15 percent, leaving the group with a significantly higher share of the summed per capita income in 1989, close to 6 percent. Notably, the top income

Table 5-5 Share of Per Capita Before-Tax Income, 1984 and 1989, and Share of the Increase in Per Capita Income, 1984 to 1989

Lowest Quintile	Second Quintile	Middle Quintile	Fourth Quintile	Highest Quintile
Share of Per Capita Before-Tax Income in 1984				
4.0	11.2	17.7	24.3	42.9
Share of Change in Per Capita Before-Tax Income				
15.4	11.9	9.0	16.7	46.9
Share of Per Capita Before-Tax Income in 1989				
5.7	11.3	16.4	23.1	43.5

Note: Data for both 1984 and 1989 are from the integrated survey, which means the data are the combined findings from the interview survey and diaries kept by units and that they cover only complete reporting units. Share of per capita before-tax income in 1984 and 1989 was computed by dividing each quintile's per capita before-tax income by the sum of all five per capita before-tax incomes.

Source: U.S. Department of Labor, Bureau of Labor Statistics, *Consumer Expenditure Survey: Integrated Survey Data, 1984–86*, Bulletin 2333 (Washington, DC: U.S. Government Printing Office, August 1989), pp. 86–89; and U.S. Department of Labor, Bureau of Labor Statistics, *Consumer Expenditure Survey, 1988–89*, Bulletin 2383 (Washington, DC: U.S. Government Printing Office, August 1991), pp. 11–14; and author's calculations.

group's share of the increase in per capita income was 46.9 percent, but it must be noted that share enabled the top group to increase its share of the sum from just under 43 to only 43.5 percent.

Looking at expenditure share this way (see table 5-6), we see that approximately 14 percent of the summed per capita expenditures in 1984 were by the lowest group. This means its share of the summed per capita expenditures were five times its share of total before-tax income. This group's share of the increase was close to 5 percent, leaving the group with under 13 percent of the summed per capita expenditures in 1989. The top group, on the other hand, had 31.4 percent of the summed per capita expenditures in 1984, took 40.6 percent of the increase in summed per capita expenditures, and

Table 5-6 Percentage Share of Per Capita Expenditures, 1984 and 1989, and Percentage Share of the Increase in Per Capita Expenditures, 1984 to 1989

Lowest Quintile	Second Quintile	Middle Quintile	Fourth Quintile	Highest Quintile
Share of Per Capita Expenditures in 1984				
13.5	15.4	18.6	21.1	31.4
Share of Increase in Per Capita Expenditures 1984 to 1989				
4.7	11.5	9.7	33.5	40.6
Share of Per Capita Expenditures in 1989				
12.7	15.1	17.7	22.2	32.3

Note: Data for both 1984 and 1989 are from the integrated survey, which means the data are the combined findings from the interview survey and diaries kept by units and that they cover only complete reporting units. Share of per capita before-tax income in 1984 and 1989 was computed by dividing each quintile's per capita before-tax income by the sum of all five per capita before-tax incomes.

Source: U.S. Department of Labor, Bureau of Labor Statistics, *Consumer Expenditure Survey: Integrated Survey Data, 1984–86,* Bulletin 2333 (Washington, DC: U.S. Government Printing Office, August 1989), pp. 86–89; and U.S. Department of Labor, Bureau of Labor Statistics, *Consumer Expenditure Survey, 1988–89,* Bulletin 2383 (Washington, DC: U.S. Government Printing Office, August 1991), pp. 11–141; and author's calculations.

had a slightly higher share, 32.3 percent, of the summed per capita expenditures in 1989.[18]

Virtually everyone now agrees that the distribution of (current) income—as measured, for example, by the Gini coefficient—became less equal during the 1970s and 1980s. However, we have argued that current income may not be the best measure for determining the extent of inequality in the country. Income can change radically from year to year or over the course of a few years. People may understandably plot their expenditures not on the basis of their annual income but on the basis of their "permanent" income trend. A person who has a "bad" year may continue to consume at his or her past levels because of the recognition that current income is a poor reflection of expenditure capacity. Indeed, people who expect their incomes to rise can be expected to consume at levels beyond their current incomes, and many low-income people appear to be doing just that.

Hence, it is not unreasonable to argue that year-to-year expenditures are a far better measure of equality or inequality of true "incomes" than year-to-year incomes. Indeed, Harvard economist Dale Jorgenson has taken what may appear to the critics of the 1980s as a startling position: "The corrected statistics show that the standard of living is rising, inequality is falling and poverty disappearing."[19] Moreover, University of Texas economist Daniel Slesnick found that after adjusting consumption data for changes in such factors as household size the "level of inequality" was 23 percent lower in 1989 than in 1947. Reductions in inequality slowed during the 1980s, but there was also no U-turn in the data.[20] Christopher Jencks and Susan Meyer, sociologists from the University of Chicago, found that the ratio of expenditures by the top and bottom income groups barely changed between 1972–73 (4.78) and 1988–89 (4.81), even though the ratio of incomes changed significantly (from 7.95 to 9.79).[21]

In short, it appears that current incomes (hashed and rehashed in media and policy circles) varied a great deal more during the 1970s and 1980s than did "permanent incomes" (which have been almost totally ignored in media and policy circles).

Concluding Comments

Public policy discussions of changes in income distribution have been fueled, regrettably, by misinformation and by what the late great Friedrich Hayek called the "pretense of knowledge." Dividing groups of families and households into quintiles can be misleading when inherent statistical problems are not mentioned, and the categories have often been used with the effect, if not the intent, of suggesting conclusions that data do not substantiate.

Quintiles have two basic defects. First, the people counted in the various income and expenditure quintiles rarely, if ever, represent 20 percent of the population, contrary to what many people assume when they read or hear that the top quintile of families or households got richer during the 1980s. The bottom quintile covered only 14 percent of the population in 1989, while the top quintile covered 25 percent. Such a contrast in shares of the population should lead to the rich receiving a disproportionate share of the income and making a disproportionate share of the expenditures.

Second, because people are constantly moving up and down the income distribution, the quintiles are constantly changing groups. An increase in the average income of the top quintile may be due to the work and good fortune of people who have always been in that quintile. But the increase might also result from people moving up into the top quintile, thus raising the overall average. When this occurs, others are forced down the income distribution—not because they lost economic ground but because others gained ground.

Even when judged by the data for both incomes and expenditures of the various quintiles, the overriding conclusion remains: It is patently unreasonable to claim that only the rich got richer during the 1980s. The per capita incomes of all quintiles rose during the 1980s, albeit often at disappointing rates. The changing distribution of expenditures reported here supports that conclusion. Furthermore, the real before-tax per capita income data for 1984 and 1989 even cast doubt on the conclusion that the incomes of the rich rose more rapidly during the 1980s than the incomes of the poor. Between 1984 and 1989, the opposite occurred: The real per capita income of the lowest income group rose substantially faster than the per capita income of the highest income group. Moreover, recent studies on the changing fortunes of people who were at the low end of the income distribution at the start of the decade may have gained more, on average, than is indicated by the percentage changes in the average incomes and expenditures of the lowest groups. Their increases are simply not added to the gains of the lowest group.

Of course, not all Americans prospered during the 1980s. Some people fell behind, just as some have during every decade with recorded statistics. The data presented here, however, do imply that the case for income redistribution is not as strong as has been thought. While there are poor people in the bottom quintile, the expenditure data indicate many included in the bottom quintile are far richer than their reported incomes suggest. Frankly, some of the so-called poor are rich by any reasonable welfare standard. Moreover, many in the top quintile appear, when one looks solely at their incomes in one or more years, richer than they actually are. Many in the top quintiles have obviously metered their spending and savings with the view that they will not always be among the nation's top income earners.

Furthermore, the distribution of expenditures is far more even than the distribution of incomes and was more or less constant throughout the 1960s, 1970s, *and* 1980s! Nevertheless, in the final analysis, there is nothing inherently wrong with an uneven distribution of income and expenditures. Increases received by the rich need not come at the expense of the poor (or vice versa) and may reflect improvements in the welfare of many poor people. The increases for rich and poor alike may reflect their greater contributions to total production and earnings. Those who propose income redistribution should assume a greater obligation to explain why those who make a greater contribution to society and, hence, earn more, should not be allowed to spend what they have rightfully earned. Glib claims that the incomes of the rich are undeserved or that they are the product of theft are hardly grounds for redistribution. Moreover, basing income redistribution on quintile data could mean redistributing income from some genuinely poor (who happen to have risen, briefly, into the top income bracket) to some who actually are rich (who happen to be, for one reason or another, in the bottom income bracket for a short time).

Notes

1. The findings of the BLS report stand in contrast to the recent work on the distribution of income and consumption expenditures by David M. Cutler and Lawrence F. Katz, "Rising Inequality? Changes in the Distribution of Income and Consumption in the 1980's," *American Economic Review*, May 1992, pp. 546–551. Cutler and Katz emphasized the economic losses of the lowest income group and the economic gains of the highest income group during the 1980s.

2. The number of units in each quintile were not identical. For example, the number of units in the highest quintile exceeded the number in the lowest by 83,000 in 1984 and 62,000 in 1989. The data are characterized as "integrated" because the final income and expenditure data were obtained by combining the information from repeated interviews and diaries kept by the sample units.

3. The population shares were determined by dividing the number of people estimated by the BLS to be in each quintile by the total estimated population for all quintiles. The estimated population covers only about four-fifths of the entire U.S. population.

4. U.S. Department of Commerce, Bureau of the Census, Current Population Reports: Consumer Income, P-60 , no. 174, *Money Income of Households, Families, and Persons in the United States: 1990* (Washington, DC: U.S. Government Printing Office, August 1991), p. 19.

5. In 1989, the average age of people in the bottom group was 51 years, 13 percent higher than the average age (45 years) of the top group.

6. For example, Cutler and Katz write about people in the lowest quintile of the income and consumption distribution without acknowledging that not everyone in the lowest quintile is poor (Cutler and Katz, "Rising Inequality?")

7. U.S. Department of the Treasury, Office of Tax Analysis, "Household Income Mobility During the 1980's: A Statistical Assessment Based on Tax Return Data" (Washington, DC: U.S. Government Printing Office, June 1, 1992); and Isabel V. Sawhill and Mark Condon, "Is U.S. Income Inequality Really Growing? Sorting Out the Fairness Question," *Policy Bites*, no. 13 (Washington, DC: Urban Institute, June 1992).

8. Before-tax income includes wages and salaries, self-employment income, Social Security payments, pensions, interest, dividends, rental and other property income, unemployment and workers' compensation benefits, veterans' benefits, public assistance, supplemental security income, food stamps, regular contributions for support, and "other income."

9. Per capita income was determined by dividing average unit income by average unit size.

10. The survey does not include expenditures paid for indirectly. For consuming units, for example, it does not include fringe benefits paid for by employers. The big expenditures—for example, appliance purchases—were determined by interviews; the smaller expenditures—for example, food and drink—were determined by diaries.

11. Cutler and Katz, "Rising Inequality?", p. 548.

12. See Dennis J. Aigner, Friedrich Schneider, and Damayanti Ghosh, "Me and My Shadow: Estimating the Size of the U.S. Hidden Economy from Time Series Data," *Dynamic Econometric Modeling: Proceedings of the Third International Symposium in Economic Theory and Econometrics*, edited by William A. Barnett, Ernst R. Berndt, and Halbert White (New York: Cambridge University Press, 1988), pp. 297–334.

13. See "The Numbers News," *American Demographics*, January 1990, as reported in Robert L. Bartley, *Seven Fat Years, And How to Do It Again* (New York: Free Press, 1992), p. 273.

14. As reported by Bruce Bartlett, "A Class Struggle that Won't Stay Put," *Wall Street Journal*, November 20, 1991. Very similar, but not identical, statistical shifts have been reported by the staff of the Joint Economic Committee [prepared for Representative Richard K. Armey, "Income Mobility and the U.S. Economy: Open Society or Caste System?" (Washington, DC: Joint Economic Committee, U.S. Congress, December 30, 1991).] The JEC staff used Bureau of Census data [as reported in U.S. Department of Commerce, Bureau of the Census, Current Population Reports, series P-70, no. 18, *Transition in Income and Poverty: 1985–1986* (Washington, DC: U.S. Government Printing Office, 1990); and U.S. Department of Commerce, Bureau of the Census, Current Population Reports, series P-70, no. 24, *Transition in Income and Poverty: 1987–1988* (Washington, DC: U.S. Government Printing Office, 1990).]

15. U.S. Department of the Treasury, "Household Income Mobility During the 1980s."

16. Indeed, one of the reasons the poor were able to spend more than twice their earnings in 1989 was that some people in the top quintile in 1984 spent less than they earned and therefore could spend more than they earned during their retirement years, including 1989, when they had descended down the income ladder—some all the way to the lowest quintile. See Greg J. Duncan, *Years of Poverty, Years of Plenty* (Ann Arbor, MI: Survey Research Center, Institute for Social Research, University of Michigan, 1984), p. 10; U.S. Department of

the Treasury, "Household Income Mobility during the 1980s"; and Sawhill and Condon, "Is U.S. Income Inequality Really Growing?"

17. See "The 1980s: A Very Good Time for the Very Rich," *New York Times*, March 5, 1992; and Sylvia Nasar, "However You Slice the Data the Richest Did Get Richer," *New York Times*, May 11, 1992.

18. If the conventional wisdom of retrogression for most families were valid, we would have expected Americans to be less able to buy and maintain housing and household appliances. However, the affordability of housing increased substantially in the 1980s. Americans' payments for principal interest on their mortgages for the median priced house dropped from a high of 36 percent of median income in 1981 to 22 percent in 1988 (the only data available at this writing), a decrease of nearly 40 percent. The National Association of Realtors' housing "affordability index" rose by 77 percent, from 68.9 in 1981 to 122 in 1988. This increase in the index indicates a significant gain in housing affordability in spite of the fact that the average size of new homes rose by 13 percent between 1980 (1,595 square feet) and 1988 (1,810 square feet) [as reported by Ed Rubenstein, "The Fading American Dream?" *National Review*, August 31, 1992, p. 50]. The National Association of Realtors' "affordability index" equals 100 when the median family income equals the income necessary to qualify for the median priced house. This means that between 1981 and 1988 median family income went from 32 percent of the qualifying income in 1981 to 22 percent above the qualifying income in 1988.

19. As quoted in Jonathan Marshall, "Inconspicuous Consumption," *Reason* (July 1993), p. 42.

20. Ibid.

21. Ibid.

6

THE DANCE WITH THE DEBT DEVIL THAT WAS SOMETHING OF A WALTZ[1]

Was the decade of the 1980s a "decade of debt"? The axiomatic answer among many policy observers is an emphatic "Yes!" The decade represented (supposedly) the worst in overindulgence. Public debt did indeed ratchet upward each year during the 1980s by progressively greater increments, with the annual increase exceeding $200 billion in fiscal year 1990. The reasons usually given for the rising public debt burden depend largely on political persuasion—federal income tax rates on the rich were dramatically lowered after 1981 (the Democrats' favored explanation) or federal expenditures continued to rise with abandon (the Republicans' favored explanation). A more politically neutral explanation is that public debt soared because the Federal Reserve did not (or could not) inflate it away as it had done during the previous three decades (especially during the late 1970s). For whatever reason, total public debt for all levels of government nearly tripled during the decade of the 1980s.

Many policy observers maintain that private citizens collectively followed the lead of the public sector. Personal debt also mounted as people went on unchecked consumption sprees driven by the worst of human motives: greed, self-indulgence, "me-ism," and reckless disregard for the future. Business debt surged as deregulated banks lowered their credit standards, as enterprising "paper entrepreneurs" started pushing junk bonds, as firms of all sizes went on a buyout binge or tried to protect themselves from being bought out.

These same critics posit that the growth in debt reflects something of a change in basic human nature in every sphere of life: personal, business, and political. The Reagan administration was blamed for the mounting debt. The direct effects of its budget policies on the expanding federal debt and the indirect effects of its free-market ideology presumably encouraged unbridled behavior with regard to assuming private debt or, as the critics of debt might put it: Americans got caught up in the mindless pursuit of "more."

As a consequence, critics maintain that the 1990s will be a time of long-term retrenchment, of protracted abstinence—of paying down the excessive debt burden. The debt-induced retrenchment began in the late 1980s and, purportedly, inspired the recession that started in 1990. Accordingly, the recovery now under way will be restrained by the unredeemed debt carried forward from the eighties.

According to these dismal prophets, the decade of the 1990s will be lean years. Many people have reached the limits of their borrowing capacities and will suffer personal budget constraints as they struggle to pay the interest that accompanies their debt. Thus, consumer and business expenditures cannot now be counted on to spur growth as they did in the 1980s. In 1992, interest payments on the mounting federal debt accounted for 20 percent of the federal budget, leaving the federal government strapped for discretionary funds to expand social programs.

During the 1980s, public and private debt did rise at post-World War II record rates. The federal debt, especially, grew by leaps and bounds. Studying this debt record reveals that growth in public (non-interest) expenditures on social programs and the nation's infrastructure probably was constrained, at least somewhat, by the growing public debt burden.[2]

On the other hand, many widely read reports and analyses of the growth in private debt have been incomplete and unbalanced. Those who lament the 1980s as some of the worst of times fail to notice, or they under-report, the growth in private assets, a necessary counterweight to private debt. This oversight is crucial to a proper reassessment of the debt burden because private assets enable individuals, nonprofit organizations, and businesses to take on more debt. Just as important, greater leveraging of existing assets can give rise to even greater assets. It must be stressed that the growth of real (inflation-adjusted) private assets also bounded upward during the 1980s.

As will be seen, inflation explains a significant share of the rise in private debt in the 1980s. Much of the rest of the dollar rise can be accounted for by noting the surge in real assets during the 1980s.

An additional portion of the growing debt burden can be attributed to the significant slowdown of private debt growth relative to private asset growth during the last half of the 1970s and the early years of the 1980s. That is to say, between the end of World War II and the early 1970s, private debt as a percentage of private assets was on a steady, almost straight-line upward trend. That upward trend was abruptly truncated in the early 1970s, partly because of the oil crises and partly because of rapidly escalating inflation rates. The upswing in private debt beginning after the recession in the early 1980s can be explained, in part, as an attempt by the private sectors of the economy to respond to moderating inflation rates and lower nominal interest rates and to move back toward the upward trend experienced before 1973.

In 1990, contrary to general belief, private debt as a percentage of private assets was slightly below the estimate of what it would have been if the upward trend established in the 1947–1973 period had continued without abrupt interruption. Granted, extrapolations from a trend have limits that must be kept in mind. At the same time, there are reasons for believing (to be covered later in the chapter) that the trend could and would have continued into the 1990s. Critics

•

of private debt growth have implicitly assumed that the relatively low debt-to-asset ratios of the 1970s must be maintained. This is a dubious position at best, given much higher debt-to-asset ratios in other countries and continuing technological and institutional developments within firms and credit markets that would allow for greater assumption of debt.

In short, criticisms of the 1980s have been founded on an incomplete picture of what really happened during the decade. A balanced analysis of the private economy's historical balance sheets that weighs assets against liabilities reveals that human nature did not change in the 1980s as radically as supposed, if at all, nor were the American people and firms as irrational or irresponsible as they have been described.

Certainly, there were many instances of debt abuse in the 1980s and, as a consequence, people and businesses went bankrupt at record rates. However, the debts of those involved in bankruptcies account for only a minor share of the rise in debt. It appears that the overwhelming majority of Americans and American enterprises expanded their debts in a strategic manner because they had the assets to back them up or because they could use their newfound credit to expand their asset base.

Indeed, during the 1980s, Americans' real or inflation-adjusted private net worth (real assets minus real liabilities) expanded at a record post-war average annual rate. Private American citizens, who have been liberally lambasted by critics, knew a great deal about their own financial circumstances that their critics did not know and, because of their limited capacities to appraise the multitude of individual circumstances, could not have known.

Accordingly, the 1990s are not likely to live down to the dire predictions (just as the 1990–1991 recession did not match the dismal projections of the debt cavils), and the decade of the 1990s may even be dynamic—activated, in part, by the private debt accumulated during the 1980s.

The Rhetoric of Debt

In the 1980s, media attention to problems surrounding private and public debt grew far more rapidly than did debt itself. In 1980, "debt" was used in 8,600 media reports, an admittedly rough gauge.[3] Nevertheless, it is useful to note that media reports on debt were up to 50,000 in 1985. In 1991, more than 120,000 media reports cited debt, a fourteen-fold increase in citations in eleven years. This provides a rough but graphic image of the media's growing concern with the profligate ways of its citizens. At the same time, media attention to debt probably fortified policymakers' and pundits' convictions that expanding private debt (quite apart from its even more rapidly expanding public counterpart) represented a growing burden.

In his caustic attack on economic and social policies adopted during Ronald Reagan's presidency, political commentator Kevin Phillips noted that household debt reached more than $3 trillion during the same period nonfinancial corporate debt doubled to $2 trillion, partly because new debt instruments became an "art form": "The financial community pioneered hundreds, from OIDS (original issue discount securities) to PIKS (payment in kind securities—bonds that pay additional bonds as interest). Led by Merrill Lynch and First Boston, Wall Street even turned car loans, boat loans, and credit-card bills and recreational vehicle loans into 'asset-backed securities,' prompting one investment banker to joke that the only type of consumer credit untouched by this trend was 'watches and jewelry at pawnshops.'"[4] Phillips attributed the growing debt burden to the Reagan administration. He argued that most Republican administrations are driven by the "praiseworthy desire to promote commerce," designed to redistribute the nation's wealth from the poor (mainly Democrats) to the rich (mainly Republicans).[5] At the same time, the whole process of debt expansion had "degenerated into speculation and worse, promoting a serious misallocation of national income and resources."[6] This speculative experience validated a dictum Phillips approvingly attributes to British economist John Maynard Keynes: "Speculators may do no more harm as bubbles on a steady stream of enterprise. But the position is serious when enterprise becomes a bubble on a whirlpool of speculation,"[7] which the 1980s surely was, or so Phillips repeatedly assures his readers.

In 1991, *U.S. News and World Report* reporters characterized the 1980s as a "dance with the debt devil."[8]

Newsweek reporters dubbed the 1980s the "Buy Now, Pay Later" decade, noting that household debt rose 50 percent faster than the rate of inflation.[9] One *Business Week* reporter wrote in 1990 about the "debt binge of the 1980s" as if it were an addiction similar to alcoholism that has an eventual and, very likely, unsavory end.[10] Still, another set of reporters at *Business Week* gave the same characterization more punch with a glib lead, "Charge it. That simple slogan was almost a battle cry for a generation that spent its way through most of the 1980s."[11] A *Wall Street Journal* reporter simply repeated what had become in the 1990s a fashionable expression when he cited the 1980s for being the "decade of debt," a phrase used in news articles 578 times from 1980 through the first quarter of 1992.[12]

Why had debt been rising so rapidly? That question has rarely been addressed. When addressed, the answers offered vary widely, from reasonably sophisticated comments about the debt-distorting effects of the tax systems to passing claims about the "go-go eighties."[13]

Even many Wall Street operators agreed that debt had gotten out of hand. In the words of one obviously distraught Wall Street investment broker, "Today's financial age has become a period of unbridled excess with accepted risk soaring out of proportion to possible reward."[14] In the late 1980s, many of these same observers welcomed the slowdown in the growth of debt with equally vivid leads. A *Business Week* reporter led with an exuberant claim, "The debt binge is over," implying that the "binge" was an accepted fact.[15]

Why had the American public fallen off the debt wagon? The response made without elaboration was that a fundamental change had occurred in social philosophy: "A new conservatism is taking hold."[16] Other *Business Week* colleagues started a follow-up report on the debt slowdown with an athletic metaphor: "Call it the Great

American Workout, corporate style. After a decade-long debt binge, companies are finally beginning to ease the burden."[17]

When the economy began to sputter in 1990, the causes were often found, not surprisingly, in the escalating debt burden that previously had been bemoaned. In mid-1990, before a recession had been declared, *Business Week* columnists recounted, "Economists have long said it: There's no free lunch. The massive buildup of debt during the 1980s is finally taking a toll on this 7 1/2-year expansion."[18] In late 1990, *Business Week* reporters concluded, after surveying the rising bankruptcy rate, "As overdue bills mount, consumers may have little choice but to tighten the hold on their wallets. And bankers won't be the only ones to suffer. What would have been a mild recession could end up a lot nastier."[19] In 1991, *U.S. News & World Report* editor-in-chief Mortimer B. Zuckerman determined that the recession was caused by the "reverse-wealth effect" of declining asset prices rather than by standard factors, for example, inventory liquidation:

> *Excess debt is the troubling background here. In the 1980s, we borrowed against our assets as never before. Now, the combination of high debt and lower asset values has substantially reduced the net worth of both individuals and corporations. The result? A decline in consumer expenditures and capital investment.[20]*

All told, in the early 1990s, debt has become public *and* private enemy number one.

The Debt Data

Claims having to do with whole countries—or their people and firms—that span an entire decade need to be rooted in careful attention to the data. Such claims are venturesome at best. Assessments that go beyond reporting the debt data and involve charges of "excess" or "binge" or "irresponsibility" require knowledge not always readily apparent in raw statistics and thereby must be viewed with a healthy skepticism in the absence of strong supporting arguments. As anyone who has made loans knows, an expansion of debt can be either good or bad, depending upon the circumstances of those doing the borrowing.

Reports on individual forms of debt—for example, trade credit or mortgages—are especially troublesome. These debtors can increase one form of debt at the same time they contract some other liability. For this reason, I will consider only the total liabilities of the nonfinancial sectors of the private economy, which represent all claims against total assets as the measure of the country's indebtedness.[21]

Only the private nonfinancial sector of the economy is considered, because extending debt to others is a big part of financial firms' business; the liabilities of the nonfinancial sector show up as assets of the financial sector. Furthermore, claims of a "debt binge" have generally been a commentary on the behavior of individual Americans or nonfinancial firms. I will assess only claims of excessive debt growth in the nonfinancial sector, not the health of the financial sector.

Figure 6-1 Total Private Liabilities, Current and Constant (1990) Dollars, 1980–1990

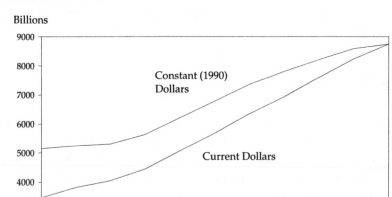

Raw debt statistics that have not been adjusted for inflation can be misleading. For example, as shown in figure 6-1, total private liabilities for all nonfinancial sectors of the country (households, nonprofit organizations, farms, nonfarm and noncorporate businesses, and nonfinancial and nonfarm corporations) expanded from $3.5 trillion in 1980 to $8.8 trillion in 1990, an increase of 152 percent. After adjusting for the price increase, total liabilities expanded by only 70 percent. More than 60 percent of the rise in unadjusted debt is explained by inflation. Because unadjusted debt figures radically distort inferences about the debt burden, only real debt figures are reported for individual private sectors and the private economy taken as a whole.[22]

Households, Personal Trusts, and Nonprofit Organizations

The records of real or inflation-adjusted total liabilities—or just debt—of four major nonfinancial sectors of the private economy are reported in figure 6-2 for 1947 through 1990. The total liabilities of households, personal trusts, and nonprofit organizations—or just personal debt23—corroborates a major claim of the debt critics that real personal debt, which rose throughout the post-war period, increased especially rapidly in the 1980s. Personal debt does appear to have risen at unequaled rates during the 1980s. However, appearances can be deceiving, as revealed by the compound annual growth rates for the various decades reported in table 6-1.

The compound rate of growth in personal debt for the 1980s, slightly more than 6 percent, was substantially higher than for the 1970s. However, the rates of growth in personal debt in the 1950s and 1960s were both significantly higher than the 1980s. If ever there was a "decade of debt" for households, it was the 1950s. The annual growth rate in personal debt in the 1950s at over 9 percent was 50 percent higher than the growth rate in the 1980s.

Figure 6-2   Private Liabilities by Sector, in Constant (1990) Dollars, 1947–1990

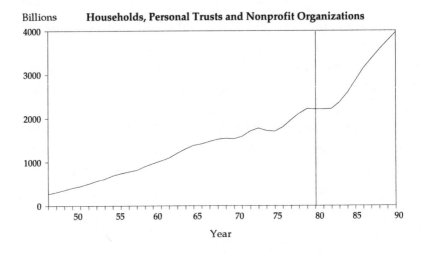

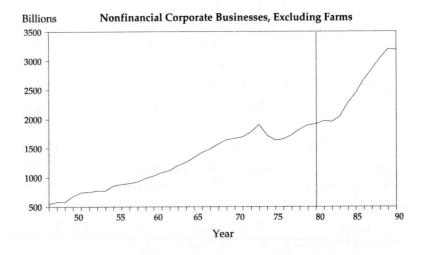

Figure 6-2 Private Liabilities by Sector, in Constant (1990) Dollars, 1947–1990 *(continued)*

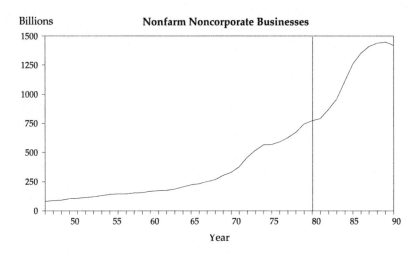

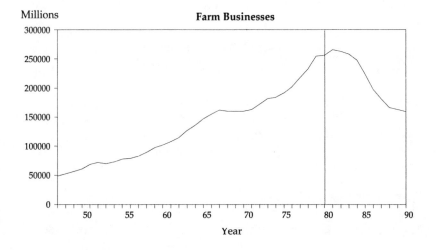

Table 6-1 Compound Annual Rates of Growth (- Decline) in Real Private Liabilities of Nonfinancial Sectors for each Decade between 1950 and 1990

1950–1960	1960–1970	1970–1980	1980–1990	1950–1990
Households, Personal Trusts, and Nonprofit Organizations				
9.05	6.63	3.75	6.03	5.85
Nonfarm, Noncorporate Businesses				
4.89	7.15	8.82	6.30	6.78
Nonfinancial Corporations				
4.25	4.95	1.40	5.21	3.94
Farm Businesses				
5.34	4.60	4.81	-4.65	2.44
Total Liabilities All Sectors Above				
6.15	5.01	3.38	5.42	4.99

Source: Author's calculations from data in Federal Reserve Board of Governors, *Balance Sheets of the U.S. Economy: 1949–90* (Washington, DC: U.S. Government Printing Office, September 1991).

Noncorporate Businesses

The total liabilities of nonfarm, noncorporate businesses also seem to have spurted upward at an unprecedented rate during the 1980s, rising from $771 billion in 1980 to $1.4 trillion in 1990.[24] However, the compound annual rate of increase for noncorporate businesses during the 1980s (6.3 percent) was significantly lower than during the 1960s and 1970s (7.2 percent and 8.8 percent, respectively).

Corporations

The total liabilities of nonfinancial corporations, excluding farms, also appears to have surged upward at a relatively rapid pace, 5.2 percent a year compounded.[25] Indeed, relative to the 1970s, when the compound growth rate was 1.4 percent a year, the impression is correct. However, the 1980s growth rate was not too far removed from the growth rates for the 1960s (4.95 percent) and, to a lesser extent, the 1950s (4.25 percent).

Farm Businesses

The total liabilities of farmers plunged during the 1980s, a complete reversal of the trend for the previous post-war period. That is, the debt of farmers expanded at an annual compound growth rate of 5.2 percent from 1947 to 1980, and then declined by a compound annual rate of 4.65 percent in the 1980s.[26] This rise in farmers' debt was tied to their assets, which rose with inflation prior to 1980 and sank precipitously with deflation in the 1980s. Such an association suggests an important caveat: rising debt, taken by itself, is not necessarily a harbinger of economic distress, just as falling debt is not necessarily a precursor of improved economic health.

The Private, Nonfinancial Economy

The total liabilities of private, nonfinancial sectors covered rose at a compound annual rate of 5.4 percent in the eighties (see figure 6-3 for dollar amounts)—much higher than the rate for the seventies (3.4 percent), not far removed from the rate of the sixties (5 percent), and significantly below the rate for the fifties (6.2 percent). Given such data, and granted that debt underwent renewed growth during the 1980s, claims that the accumulation of debt during the decade was unprecedented are simply inaccurate. Characterizations of debt accumulation as a "binge" or as "excessive" appear, themselves, to be excessive, possibly the result of a failure to put the 1980s in historical context.

Figure 6-3 Total Private and Public Liabilities, in Constant (1990) Dollars, 1947–1990

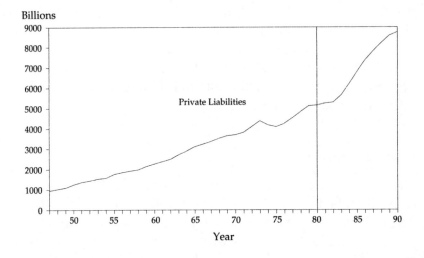

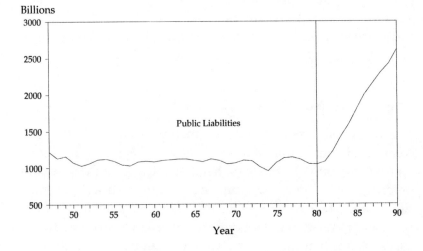

Perhaps the data on particular forms of debt, say, consumer credit, warrant the characterizations used. However, isolating particular forms of debt for study can lead to ill-informed judgments regarding the *overall debt burden* felt by sectors of the economy, because increases in one form of debt can be offset, totally or partially, by decreases in other forms of debt.

In contrast to overstated concern about growth in personal debt, the concern over the rising public debt may *not* have been overstated (see figure 6-3). Total federal, state, and local government debt moved irregularly around a flat trend from 1947 to 1980 at about $1 trillion. In the 1980s, however, public debt experienced a dramatic break with that no-growth trend. Total government debt rose close to 120 percent between 1980 and 1990 (most of which was the increase in federal debt), reaching $2.6 trillion in 1990.

Assets and Net Worth

Debt becomes a burden only when it is used to finance consumption expenditures rather than to increase assets holdings and when the added interest payments are not offset by increases in cash flow or reductions in other fixed payments.[27] Debt, which is merely a claim on assets, is no burden at all when it is used to acquire assets that are at least equal in value to the collateral assets. Indeed, when debt is used to buy or develop assets whose value exceeds the debt, the burden felt by the debtor can actually be reduced. The claims of creditors can be met using the added value of assets, and the value remaining after claims are satisfied (called net worth) will belong to the debtor. However, media reports have paid very little attention to private assets and net worth (or assets minus claims against them) in the public debate over private debt. Compared to the attention given the debt burden, mention of net worth is remarkably sparse, and growth in media awareness has been equally modest.

Casual observers of public reports on private debt, constantly confronted with explosive rhetoric on "the debt binge" and "excessive debt," undoubtedly began to agree with the critics that debt was not being extended based on growing assets and was not being used to build assets. To many Americans, it must have seemed that the country's net worth fell during the decade. However, the facts belie the popular impression. Private assets in constant dollars rose more rapidly (in real dollar terms) during the 1980s than did private debt, yielding an increase in total private net worth. Moreover, as will be seen, real private net worth per capita also rose substantially during the 1980s.

Granted, a growth in private debt relative to assets can be accompanied by an increase in interest payments in absolute real dollars and relative to cash flow, which may then give rise to what experts call "financial distress," a term applied to the multitude of risks ranging from illiquidity to bankruptcy. However, a growth in interest payments, even when faster than the growth in revenues, may not give rise to the feared distress if revenues have become more stable or other firm payments have become less fixed.

Assets and Net Worth of Households, Personal Trusts, and Nonprofit Organizations

The value of total assets of households, personal trusts, and nonprofit organizations is usually expressed as the total of tangible, reproducible assets (minus straight-line depreciation) measured at current cost; land measured at market value; and financial assets, measured, where possible, at market value.[28]

The data on assets probably understate their true value, to the extent that historically the term has been applied only to tangible and financial assets. Resources bought years ago may have become more productive and, therefore, of greater value, but their greater value is not always included in asset estimates. Computer hardware represents an asset that over the years has become progressively more powerful as it has become progressively cheaper, which means that its inclusion at current cost also distorts asset values over time. Hence, the declining prices of computers can give the impression that "total assets" are declining, whereas their power and value is actually increasing. In addition, once an asset has been fully depreciated (for tax purposes), it will add nothing to total assets even though it may continue to be used.

Moreover, many assets are "intangible" and come in the form of knowledge and information, goodwill, working relationships and networks, market position, product recognition, and quality of the items purchased. There is growing awareness of the importance of human capital. However, no dollar value has been assigned to human capital, so it does not show up in the country's measure of assets, and the human capital at the disposal of both firms and households is growing in importance in both sectors. In short, the available measure of assets (and, for that matter, liabilities) in total and by sector is rather crude, probably understating true total assets.

Nevertheless, the available Federal Reserve data on assets (see figure 6-4) show growth in real or inflation-adjusted personal assets. Real personal assets rose by nearly $6 trillion, or by 36 percent, during the 1980s, from $15.5 trillion in 1980 to $21.1 trillion in 1990. By way of contrast, personal debt rose by $1.8 trillion, or by 79 percent. Nevertheless, the growth in real-dollar personal assets was three times the growth in real-dollar personal debt—which means that the net worth of households, personal trusts, and nonprofit organizations rose by $3.8 trillion, or by 29 percent.

Table 6-2 reveals that the growth in personal assets in the 1980s, which continued at a compound annual rate of 3.1 percent, was in line with the compound growth rates for the 1960s and 1970s (2.9 percent and 3.1 percent, respectively). During the 1950s, when debt growth was so high, the annual growth rate of assets was significantly higher, 4.3 percent, again showing that debt growth, per se, is no harbinger of economic decline.

Assets and Net Worth of Nonfarm, Noncorporate Businesses

The climb in the total real assets of nonfarm, noncorporate businesses followed much the same pattern as personal assets.[29] Assets for these businesses climbed $760 billion, or by 29 percent, from $2.58 trillion in 1980 to $3.3 trillion in 1990. The debt of these businesses, on the

Figure 6-4   Private Assets by Nonfinancial Sector, in Constant
(1990) Dollars, 1947–1990

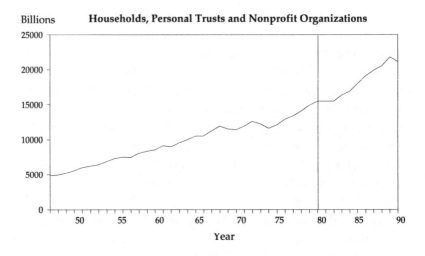

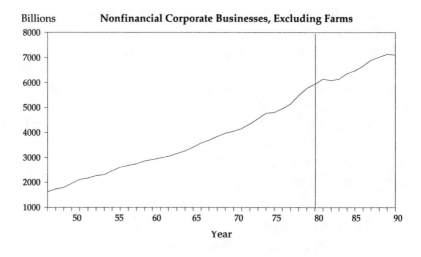

Figure 6-4 Private Assets by Nonfinancial Sector, in Constant (1990) Dollars, 1947–1990 *(continued)*

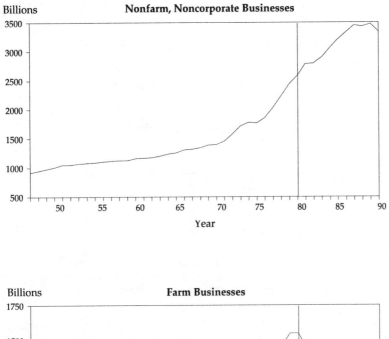

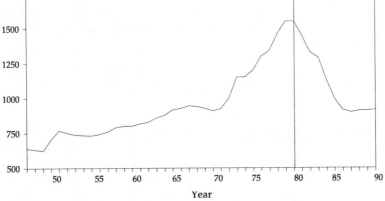

Table 6-2 Compound Annual Rates of Growth in Real Private Assets by Nonfinancial Sector for Decades from 1950–1990

1950–1960	1960–1970	1970–1980	1980–1990	1950–1990
Households, Personal Trusts, and Nonprofit Organizations				
4.34	2.94	3.12	3.13	3.38
Nonfarm, Noncorporate Businesses				
4.89	7.15	8.82	6.30	6.78
Nonfarm Corporations				
4.12	3.35	3.88	1.83	3.29
Farm Businesses				
1.29	1.24	5.48	-5.11	.65
Total Assets All Sectors Above				
3.78	2.88	3.70	2.42	3.19

Source: Author's calculations from data in Federal Reserve Board of Governors, *Balance Sheets of the U.S. Economy: 1949–90* (Washington, DC: U.S. Government Printing Office, September 1991).

other hand, expanded by $649 billion, or by 84 percent, during the decade. Nevertheless, the real-dollar increase in their real assets exceeded the increase in debt, resulting in an $11 billion rise in their net worth, a 6 percent rise from 1980 to 1990 (in spite of a more than 5 percent fall between 1989 and 1990).

Assets and Net Worth of Corporations

The real assets of the nation's nonfinancial and nonfarm corporations rose by $1.2 trillion, or by 20 percent, during the eighties, from $5.9 trillion in 1980 to $7.1 trillion in 1990.[30] Their debts increased by $1.3 trillion, or by 66 percent, with the increase in debt being slightly greater than the increase in assets. The compound annual rate of growth in real assets of corporations during the 1980s (1.8 percent) was substantially lower than in previous decades (4.1 percent in the 1950s, 3.4 percent in the 1960s, and 3.9 percent in the 1970s).

However, the deterioration in corporations' overall economic health was exceedingly modest (given all the rhetoric of excessive debt growth) and may be more apparent than real. Again, the data include only tangible assets, and the importance of intangible assets in production was very likely experiencing a relative rise during the 1980s, when indeed, reports abounded concerning the growing importance to the success of firms of knowledge and information, goodwill, and product market position in the global economy. At the very least, the stock markets recognized the rising value of the listed firms, because the Dow-Jones index more than tripled from the start of 1980 to the end of 1990, a rise unprecedented in previous post-war decades. For nonfinancial corporations, the ratio of corporate debt to total assets, measured at market value, rose dramatically from less than .4 in 1969 to .6 in 1974, only to decline, albeit irregularly, through the rest of the 1970s and all of the 1980s, returning to .4 in 1989.[31]

Assets and Net Worth of Farm Businesses

The real assets of farmers dropped precipitously during the 1980s, as did their liabilities.[32] Farm assets declined $633 billion (41 percent) from the historic high of $1.6 trillion in 1980 to $917 billion in 1990. (Much of the decline in assets was in the value of real estate/land holdings.) By contrast, farm debts declined by $97 billion, worsening farmers' net worth by more than a half trillion dollars. Interestingly, the greatest downturn in net worth occurred in that sector of the economy where debt was actually falling.

Total (Consolidated) Net Worth

Reports on private debt growth have rarely mentioned that the total assets of the private nonfinancial sector expanded by $6.9 trillion during the 1980s, as shown in figure 6-5. Furthermore, the consolidated net worth (after the problem of double-counting is eliminated) of the private nonfinancial American economy increased by $2.1 trillion, or by 14 percent, from $14.5 trillion in 1980 to $16.6 trillion in 1990 (see figure 6-6). And per capita net worth also expanded, by

Figure 6-5 Total Assets of the Nonfinancial Private Sector, in
Constant (1990) Dollars, 1947–1990

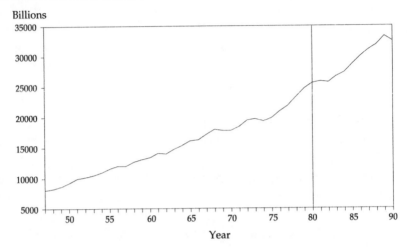

4 percent, from $63,583 in 1980 to $65,907 in 1990 (after falling 4
percent between 1989 and 1990). Again, many intangible assets are
not included in these figures.

While many of the claims regarding the debt binge of the 1980s
were out of line with reality, it is also clear that growth in real private
net worth slowed markedly in the 1980s. The compound annual rate
of increase in total net worth was 1.4 percent, quite low by historical
standards. The compound annual growth rate of net worth for the
1950s was 2.9 percent. For the 1960s, the growth rate was 2.4 percent;
and for the 1970s, 4.3 percent. But then, we must be careful because
the value of the nation's human capital stock (not included in the
data) bounded upward during the 1980s with the rise in the wage
premiums for education.

Private Debt Relative to Private Assets

Between the end of World War II and the early 1970s, total private
debt of all nonfinancial sectors grew steadily relative to total private
assets, a fact made obvious in figure 6-7. Indeed, the actual data fit
closely along the straight-line trend. Figure 6-8 reveals that the

Figure 6-6 Private (Consolidated) Net Worth, Total and Per Capita, in Constant (1990) Dollars, 1947–1990

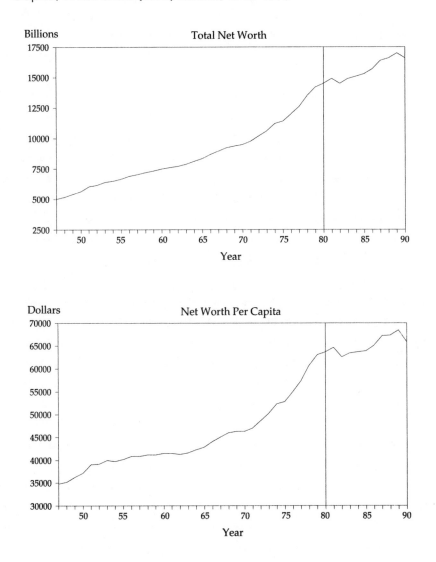

Figure 6-7 Total Private Liabilities as a Percentage of Total Private Assets, Nonfinancial Sector, Actual and Predicted, 1947–1990

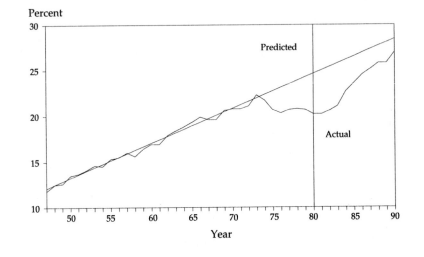

Figure 6-8 Nonfinancial Corporations Liabilities as a Percentage of Assets, Actual and Predicted, 1947–1990

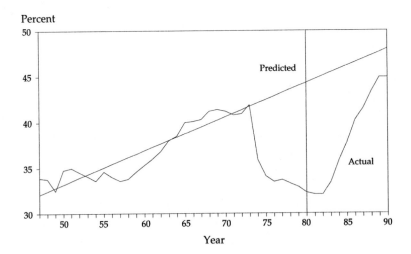

liabilities of the nonfinancial corporate sector grew dramatically relative to corporate assets in the 1947 to 1973 period.

No doubt, the relative rise in debt during the 1947 to 1973 period has many disparate causes, some of the more important ones are:

➤ Growing assets and incomes enabled firms to become more highly leveraged.

➤ The variety of debt instruments was expanding, along with the efficiency of credit and financial markets. Credit-card use is an obvious institutional change that spurred debt expansion.

➤ In the decades prior to the 1980s, higher tax rates and progressively higher inflation rates combined to provide a growing tax subsidy for debt financing. The demand for mortgages to finance the purchase of houses and land was especially boosted. The cut in tax rates and the inflation rate in the first half of the 1980s undercut the demand for real estate, but the investment tax credit and accelerated depreciation allowances included in the 1981 tax bill boosted the demand for debt by raising the demand for plant and equipment.[33]

However, the upward trend in all sectors taken together and in the corporate sector taken separately was abruptly broken in 1973, with the drop in the corporate sector relatively more severe than in all sectors togethers. The reasons are not entirely clear, however, the OPEC-induced energy crisis of 1973 and the acceleration in the inflation rates in the late 1970s probably played major roles. The OPEC crisis destabilized the economy, increasing default risk. The stock and bond markets also dropped substantially in 1974, further increasing risk and uncertainty over future events. To complicate matters even more, federal energy policies, which were intended to control energy prices and centrally allocate the nation's energy supplies, actually exacerbated energy shortfalls, giving rise to abrupt shutdowns in factories and curbs in the return on capital. Inflation rates broached 13 percent in 1979 and stayed over 12 percent in 1980, further distorting credit markets as bond prices fell and interest rates rose to accommodate the escalating inflation rates. Of course, all of Richard Nixon's efforts to control the prices of everything (aside from gold) after 1971 did nothing to help matters. Naturally, matters were not helped by the recession of the early 1980s that resulted from the Federal Reserve's 1979 clamp-down on the growth in the money stock (and the reversal in the term structure of interest rates, which had short-term rates exceeding long-term rates).

In 1980, with the encouragement of the Carter administration, the Federal Reserve also imposed credit controls on banks (under the authority granted by the Credit Control Act of 1969). Although the credit controls were in effect for a matter of only several months, banks were confused by the new regulations and responded by cutting down on the number of loans made. Banks were required to hold additional reserves at the Fed and to abide by an array of complicated credit regulations:

> The new reserves were due if banks made frowned-upon loans such as increases in outstanding credits on credit cards, bank overdrafts and money market funds. Nicer loans, for mortgages, autos and furniture, needed no special reserves. But banks were expected to hold the growth of all loans during the year to 6 percent to 9 percent.[34]

By late 1982, the economy was on its way to recovery.

In December 1982, Congress repealed the Credit Control Act, thus eliminating a bureaucratic threat to bank credit expansion and giving rise to an explosion of credit-card use. From 1980 to 1989 (the latest year of available data), the total number of cardholders rose by 27 percent (from 86 million in 1980 to 110 million in 1989); the total number of cards in circulation rose by 82 percent (from 526 million in 1980 to 957 million in 1989); and the total credit card debt increased by 157 percent (from $80 billion in 1980 to $207 billion in 1989). However, during the 1980s, the delinquency rate on bank cards (with past-due balances of 30 or more days) dropped by 18 percent, from 2.7 percent of all cards in 1980 to 2.2 percent in 1989 (after falling to a low of 1.9 percent in 1983).[35]

In short, events of the 1970s forced Americans and American corporations to accept lower levels of leverage than they probably would have accepted otherwise. After inflation was stopped suddenly in the early 1980s and markets had had time to adjust and credit controls were relaxed, the attractiveness of credit financing returned. As is evident in figures 6-7 and 6-8, debt as a percentage of assets began to rise again in the early 1980s toward the long-run upward trend established prior to 1973. Nonetheless, as shown in both figures, ratios of debts to assets remained below the values predicted by the long-term 1947 to 1973 trend.

Seen from this perspective, debt growth in the 1980s may appear more out of line than it actually was, an illusion caused by the fact that the growth in debt during the 1970s was out of line—indeed, below what would have been expected from the past relationship of debts to assets.[36] In troubled times, which the 1970s surely were, it is understandable that people and firms will restrain their use of credit and permit their net worth to rise for purposes of self-insurance against adverse outcomes.

Clearly, continuance of the upward trend of the debt-to-asset ratio in a straight line (see figures 6-7 and 6-8), more or less, through the 1970s and 1980s is oversimplified. Just as clearly, one could extend the trend until a debt-to-asset ratio of greater than one is projected, which would be unreasonable. At the same time, plotting the trend as a straight line provides a visually dramatic way to demonstrate the point at which the data break from the trend and to show that a significant portion of the increase in the debt-to-asset ratio was merely a return to the level achieved in 1973.[37] With debt-to-asset ratios in the range of 20 to 25 percent for all nonfinancial sectors (and in the range of 40 to 45 percent for nonfinancial corporations) in the early 1970s, there was also some room for growth in the ratio. This is even likely to be the case, if the higher ratios of other industrialized countries are considered. According to reports, the ratio of total public and private debt to national production in most Western nations is twice what it is in the United States.[38] Furthermore, ongoing institutional changes within the private sector throughout the 1970s and 1980s permitted higher debt-to-asset ratios.

The often overlooked but over-arching point of the analysis that remains worthy of consideration is that the debt-to-asset ratio in 1990 probably was not far out of line with what it would have been had the disruptions of the 1970s not occurred, and it may actually have been lower.

Debt, Per Se, Is Not a Problem

Data on increasing debt, unaccompanied by an explanation for the rise, are not, in and of themselves, particularly interesting. The numbers remain nothing more than an array of facts strung together. Their appeal may be that they correspond to the public's association of debt with readily apparent negative consequences: Debt requires interest payments that are fixed by contract and ultimately requires repayment or refinancing at a future date, also specified by contract. It should be noted that interest payments—even when they are increasing in absolute dollars or as a percentage of revenues (or cash flow or current accounts)—are not necessarily bad for the individual and firm debtors. The interest can be paid from a greater flow of revenues (cash flow or current accounts) attributable to the assumption of greater debt. Similarly, principal can also be repaid by drawing on the debtors' increasing flow of funds. In fact, the interest and principal payments can even be drawn from a decreasing flow of funds, and the additional debt could, at the same time, improve the financial health of the debtors' portfolios. Without the additional debt, the flow of funds may have declined at an even faster pace.

Such basic points of financial analysis are not presented to whitewash or excuse irresponsible behavior. They are, however, stressed to help place debt in its proper perspective—to make a balanced assessment of the growth in the country's debt burden during the 1980s (or any other relatively short period of time). Clearly, greater debt has both costs and benefits. Less obvious, but perhaps more important, the costs and benefits of debt assumption may vary no less than do the people and firms who assume the greater debt. This does not mean that nothing can be deduced about the changing burden of debt. But, at the same time, the varied circumstances of the millions of debtors in a country impose a rarely mentioned limitation on the capacity of outside analysts to judge the reasonableness of any debt growth.

Healthy skepticism should be applied to claims that people and firms went on a debt binge in the 1980s or changed their behavior in some fundamental way. How do the critics really know whether there was a binge, in the sense that the assumption of debt was out of control? Neither the mounting debt nor the various debt ratios is proof, but merely facts to be observed that cannot be used to explain themselves. Can the critics assess the reasonableness of greater debt without knowing all the circumstances of the debtors or how those circumstances are changing? The short answer is, "No." Without more details, whether the rise in debt is a product of a fundamental change in behavior or of the myriad changes in the circumstances of the debtors remains essentially conjecture.

The Minuses and Pluses of Growing Debt

The potential negative consequences of growing debt have been extensively discussed. During a recession, especially, greater debt can lead to financial instability. Given the debt levels assumed by corporations by 1988, one study estimated that as many as 25 percent of nonfinancial corporations would be threatened with bankruptcy if a recession as severe as the 1981–1982 recession were to strike.[39] And, conversely, a recession can be caused by excessive debt accumulation in the same way that past recessions have been caused by excessive inventory accumulation. Once assets have been leveraged fully or almost fully, the expansion of demand may be capped and then reversed as funds are set aside for repayment. Alternately, funds can be rechanneled, say, from purchasing supplies to paying off principal, causing temporary distortions and adjustments in resource use, the effect of which is a period of unemployment.

Having said that, however, it does not follow that the growth in debt was excessive. The growth may have been reasonable, given changing circumstances. Several key changes can be identified that would justify the greater debt (or that made additional debt less of a burden than it would otherwise have been). No one explanation listed explains all of the change in debt, but each was important to a subset of people and firms who sought to increase their indebtedness.[40]

➤ Debt is not the only financial lever open to managerial abuse. As distinguished finance professors Michael Jensen and William Meckling have argued, some of the growth in debt in the 1980s may have been the result of owners' efforts to restrict managerial discretion over their firms' cash flows and, in that way, to solve, somewhat, the so-called principal/agent problem, the difficulties principals (owners) face when seeking to control their agents (managers who have private goals at odds with those of the owners).[41] In the absence of heavy interest payments, managers might squander the earnings on perks or might not pay out the earnings to owners, reinvesting them in projects less profitable than those known to the owners. The recent growth in debt, especially high debt assumed in leverage takeovers or in defending against such takeovers, might have been the result of some owners forcing a financial restructuring of firms and imposing a built-in curb on managerial discretion. The growth in debt for some firms, in other words, was intended to curb, not extend, managerial (nondebt) "excesses."

➤ As is often mentioned, debt growth imposes a corresponding growth in interest payments, which are fixed. However, as is rarely conceded, interest payments are not the only fixed expense faced by firms. Firms may have been able to assume more debt during the 1980s because other payments may have become less fixed or reduced, meaning the fixity of many firms' total financial obligations may not have grown in proportion to their interest payments, and in some instances may have fallen. As widely reported, worker groups—in particular, unions—lost bargaining power during the decade, resulting in concessions, givebacks, and tempered growth in wages in many labor markets. Given that the firms acquired more flexibility on wages, they may have felt that they could take on more fixed interest payments without an undue financial burden.

➤ Some of the growth in debt was in forms that, because they restricted managerial discretion or gave the bondholders decision-rights on the issuance of additional debt, were more like equity, but with deductible interest payments. Junk bonds are the most widely discussed example, expanding from $5.4 billion in 1980 to a peak of $46 billion in 1986, only to fall to $35 billion in 1989 (after which high-risk securities virtually dried up until 1992 when they once again became attractive, primarily because their rates of return were above the rates achievable on other securities). Even then, this form of debt has been greatly maligned by commentators who have mistakenly assumed that such debt was more widely used, more irresponsible, and more destructive than it actually was. Less than a third of the funds raised were used to finance acquisitions (the rest was used to finance internal firm expansions).[42] Moreover, only 10 percent of required financing for tender offers in the 1980s was acquired through junk bonds; 73 percent of the financing was acquired from banks. In hostile takeovers (and all takeovers were not hostile), banks provided 78 percent of the financing.[43] Even then, the industrial restructuring that occurred from mergers and takeovers, however financed, accounted for 4.4 percent of the mass layoffs, and 6.6 percent of total job losses in plant shutdowns was attributable to ownership changes.[44]

Yago, who developed the foregoing data, also found that only 10 of the plants studied were involved in management buyouts, and those "plants involved in management buyouts were substantially less likely to close than other plants."[45] Nonetheless, the annual yield on junk bonds averaged 14.1 percent for the 1981–1991 period, substantially higher than the average for Treasury Bills (10.4 percent) and the Dow Jones Industrial Average (12.9 percent).[46]

Still, perhaps junk bond debt should not be included in the growth of debt, because it is a radically different instrument, closer to preferred stock than to debt.[47] For that matter, financial markets have developed means of hedging interest rate risks (through interest rate swaps, caps, and swap options) to reduce the overall risk of debt. Admittedly, these changes have not proven to be statistically important in reducing financial difficulty,[48] but such a finding understandably caused one reviewer to wonder, "If interest rate hedging does not prevent financial distress, why do so many companies engage in it?"[49]

➤ The deregulation of the banking industry permitted banks to take on riskier loans that paid higher interest rates without increasing their insurance premiums, thus broadening the availability of credit through an increase in this implicit government subsidy. Banks may not have gotten any greedier; they merely faced fewer constraints and were responding to government subsidies embedded in the depositors' insurance system.

➤ The globalization of financial markets enabled Americans to draw on world savings, not just American savings, thereby increasing their debts relative to assets with a lower risk premium than would have been required from domestic sources.[50]

➤ The globalization of all other economic activity expanded many firms' sources of supplies and market outlets in the 1980s, thereby reducing their dependence on the U.S. market. The prospects of shifting their purchases and sales from market to market probably somewhat stabilized expected expenses and earnings of many firms, permitting them to take on more debt.

➤ The technology of computerized machinery allowed a growing number of firms to achieve greater flexibility in production, meaning they could adjust their input and output mixes more readily to move with shifts in market demands and supplies. This growing flexibility could have increased the capacity of affected firms to accept more indebtedness without increasing the overall risk to their operations.

➤ Firms also increased the extent of outsourcing of supplies, so much so that media policy analysts began worrying about the development of "hollow corporations," firms that outsource practically everything. Outsourcing is a means of spreading the risk of production among a larger number of producers, thus enabling some firms to take on more debt.

➤ Many firms were under immense competitive pressures from domestic and foreign sources (but especially from foreign sources) during the first half of the 1980s when the dollar appreciated against the yen and other currencies, making imports less expensive. To meet the pressures, firms rushed to adopt new technologies that harbored the prospects of improved productivity, and many of these projects had to be funded. Firms had to reinvent themselves, paying more attention to structuring incentives within their organizations. For example, they made stronger linkages between pay and performance, and they set up departments as profit centers. Some firms developed new organizational forms for partnerships and strategic alliances with cross-country ties. Others developed stronger relationships with banks and other lenders, closer to the models observed in Japan. Critics of growing debt often implicitly assume the nature of the firm has remained static, which was hardly the case in the 1980s. The growing flexibility in payment schemes, which provided improved incentives for employees, may also have improved the firms' capacity to handle debt.[51]

➤ The substantial decline in inflation rates in the early 1980s led to a drop in nominal interest rates (but not real interest rates).[52] Believing that the rates were a much better deal than they were (because they had not had time to adjust their expectations of inflation), many debtors may have been induced to borrow more than they would have if inflation had been more constant in the 1970s. Other potential borrowers may have viewed the mounting public debt and concluded that the Fed sooner or later would have to inflate it away, as it had done in the past, which means that their debts may have become more of a burden than the borrowers had expected.

➤ The service economy continued to grow in importance during the 1980s.[53] Since the service economy had been historically more stable than the goods economy, the growing importance of services could have led to more debt. While the evidence of the influence of economic stability on debt assumption is mixed, it is still possible that the growth in stability of some (although not the large majority of) firms may have contributed to the growth in debt.[54]

➤ One of the obvious reasons consumers took on more debt in the form of consumer credit is that credit cards became more widespread, available to a wider range of income earners and accepted by more stores.[55] They became a ready and convenient substitute for cash and checks.

➤ Incomes went up during the 1980s, enabling people to handle more debt and still have more discretionary income after the interest and debt payments.[56]

➤ The demographics of the country changed significantly during the 1980s, with the elderly population growing relative to younger components. The "graying of America" could have contributed to greater indebtedness, simply because elderly people often look for the steady returns in interest payments that bonds provide.[57] The greater use of bonds may have resulted, in part, from managers seeking to provide more investors with what they wanted in the way of securities. Moreover, many "baby boomers," those 78 million people born from 1946 through 1964, reached their spending peaks at the beginning of the 1980s. Their expenditures may have fueled the growth of debt in the economy for much of the 1980s.

➤ The decline in debt financing relative to assets during the 1970s was noted earlier. Once the country's energy policies and inflation record stabilized, households and firms found themselves under-leveraged. A part of the growth in debt in the 1980s could be construed as a return to the upward trend of the debt-to-asset ratio after the disruptions in the first half of the 1970s. In an article for *Forbes*, a money manager may have expressed the sentiments of many Americans in the 1980s: "No, overall we don't have too much debt. We have too little and have had too little ever since first becoming a modern society. Which is why for 60 years we have been adding debt relative to our economy's size. And will for maybe 30 more years."[58]

➤ There were significant changes in the tax structure in the 1980s. In 1981, the Reagan administration successfully pressed for passage of a new tax bill that cut income tax rates and created incentives to stimulate the real estate industry. This bill accelerated depreciation of property and equipment. The 1986 tax law was passed, which reversed the depreciation rules. Nevertheless, the tax law changes probably contributed to an expansion in the use of credit over much of the decade.

Yet, no one should be too impressed with the chart that plots a progressively higher debt-to-asset ratio. As noted, assets include only tangible assets, not intangible ones that may have grown with time, implying that the upward bent of the true ratio on trend may not be as steep as the one pictured and may not even be upward sloping. Nevertheless, just because outside observers cannot know the true trend, it does not follow that the hands-on-managers/owners do not know, at least in a rough manner, what the trend is. They are in the best position to judge their capacity, or their firm's capacity, to take on more debt.

The purpose in listing explanations for the rise in private debt is not to explain away the growth in debt. It is, rather, to suggest the tremendous variety of legitimate reasons people may have had to take on more debt. Clearly, some debt is irresponsibly assumed. Without much question, unchecked greed motivated some people to buy out other firms in highly leveraged deals. But irresponsible behavior and behavior motivated strictly by greed have always been driving forces in the economy, regardless of how they have been organized, privately or collectively. Growth in debt, on balance, does not necessarily imply greater irresponsibility and greediness. Indeed, it may imply the exact opposite.

The Proper Role for Policy

Those concerned about growing debt seem to think the case for government involvement is relatively straightforward, the application of common arguments in the theory of government. One group of researchers maintains,

> In the abstract, the case for overruling the free market's capital structure decisions is not difficult to make. Firms' leverage decisions create externalities at both the microeconomic and macroeconomic levels. At the microeconomic level, the risk of financial distress is borne not only by the firms' managers and owners, but by their workers, suppliers, and customers, among others. Managers have little incentive to take the costs imposed on

*third parties into account when deciding how much debt to issue.
At the macroeconomic level, both traditional Keynesian models and
more recent theories of aggregate demand externalities and multiple
equilibria ascribe great importance to how firms respond to changes
in current activity (that is, firms' decisions create an externality).*[59]

If only the real world conformed with such abstractions and the
analysis were carried no further, government involvement need not
be disputed. However, making the case for government involvement
in the above way is like listening to the first of two opera singers and
then awarding the prize to the second.

To assume that an improvement in economic affairs will be
forthcoming as a result of a shift of decision-making authority from
the private to the public domain is a leap of faith. The decisions of
public officials will have just as many external effects, and those
decisions can be just as destabilizing. Indeed, public officials, far
removed from the day-to-day operations faced by debtors and creditors, will likely incur none of the costs of their decisions, right or
wrong. Externality problems are increased, not diminished, by shifting creditor/debtor decisions from the private to the public sector.

The presumption of an improvement from making the shift
certainly flies in the face of the facts on the recent growth in public
debt. The presumption also goes against the prevailing wisdom that
changes in public policies, if made at all, should be slow and incre-
mental "precisely because the profession's understanding of how
capital structure affects the economy is so rudimentary."[60]

Does it follow that government has no role to play in improving
the country's financial statements? Certainly, its role in micro-man-
aging debt accumulation must necessarily be limited by its lack of
information involved in decisions for 250 million Americans. While
it may be very difficult for policymakers to judge the reasonableness
of the debt burden people and firms assume, given their circumstances, it is not out of bounds for policymakers to evaluate the
impact of their policies on debt and to decide whether the policies
encourage or discourage excessive (or, more to the point, inefficient
or counter-productive) debt assumption and whether the effects are

desirable, given whatever goals they harbor. Policymakers can decide, for instance, whether the deductibility of interest from taxable
income on firms' income statements unreasonably encourages debt
financing (given that stock dividends are not deductible). They can
also decide whether government-backed deposit insurance at
banks—made with their insurance premiums determined inde-
pendently of the riskiness of loans banks make—unreasonably encourages debt financing. In short, government has a role in
determining the framework within which people use debt, but not
in determining the details and content of these debts. Such a limited
role for government is a far cry from proposing that government get
into the business of discouraging debt simply because debt is growing or because people are presumed to be on a binge. Again, the latter
role requires policymakers to have detailed knowledge they could
never obtain about the multitude of people's business circumstances. Limiting the role of policymakers to determining the framework reduces the knowledge they must have to manageable
proportions.

Having the government supplant the private sector on debt
decisions appears, in the final analysis, to be what Washington
policy circles might call a "nonstarter." At the same time, cases of
excess—or even periods of excess—are to be expected. What should
concern government is whether the financial market processes are
self-correcting, that is, whether they incorporate appropriate incentives or disincentives to amend errant behavior. Markets do have
built-in self-correcting mechanisms in the form of risk premiums on
loans, bankruptcies, and the ultimate dissolution of firms. Reports
on downgrading corporate financial ratings and the downturn in the
growth of private debt in the late 1980s and early 1990s, as well as
the growing number of bankruptcies, indicate that the self-correcting mechanisms of the market were at work.[61] An appropriate
concern of government is, then, to leave the self-correcting processes
unfettered—to ensure that appropriate penalties remain for those
who use debt excessively. Government policymakers must remember that efforts to reduce the force of market penalties (through, for
example, subsidizing those who fail or have to pay high interest

rates) can encourage the same excesses that are the object of disapproval.

Concluding Comments

Claims that the 1980s was a "decade of debt" have made the head-lines repeatedly. However, on careful reflection, the decade of the 1980s did not live down to claims of an unbridled binge. Granted, debt in all private sectors, aside from farming, rose substantially. In current dollars, total private liabilities of the nonfinancial sector rose from $3.5 trillion in 1980 to $8.8 trillion in 1990. It is no doubt true that many people indiscriminately added to their debt during that time and are now paying for their wanton ways through the pain of bankruptcy. However, such aberrant behavior is not unique to the 1980s.

The fact remains that there were many good, often overlooked, reasons for the rise in debt during the decade of the 1980s. If total private liabilities had only kept pace with inflation, they would have reached $5.5 trillion in 1990.

A major reason for the rise is that peoples' and firms' asset values increased, enabling them to take on more debt and to acquire even more assets. Moreover, I noted that the ratio of private liabilities to assets rose steadily from 1947 to 1973, only to be diverted from the upward trend in part by the energy supply shock after 1973. The ratio of liabilities to assets rose especially rapidly during the 1980s; one explanation is that private sector creditors and debtors were seeking to return to the upward trend they left in 1973. The liabilities-to-assets ratio was actually lower in 1990 than it would have been if the 1947 to 1973 trend had continued uninterrupted through 1990.

If the debt-to-asset ratio had returned only to the 1973 level (22.3 percent), total private liabilities in 1990 would have been $7.2 trillion, 17 percent below the actual level of $8.8 trillion. However, there is every reason to believe that by 1990 a higher debt-to-asset ratio could be tolerated. If the 1947 to 1973 trend had continued until 1990, the debt-to-asset ratio would have been 28.4 percent and total liabilities would have been $9.2 trillion, over $400 billion (or 5 percent) above the actual level.[62]

All in all, the "debt crisis" of the 1980s never materialized. The country did go through a recession, but the downturn did not match the predicted dip, which, according to accounts, should have come close to an outright depression. Even then, a number of forces contributed to the recession, not the least of which were that the expansion had lasted so long, that military spending took a nosedive after the 1989 revolution, and that taxes were increased in 1990. That is obvious food for rethinking claims that Americans went on a "debt binge" in the 1980s.

Notes

1. This chapter is reprinted with revisions from Christina Klein and Richard B. McKenzie, *The 1980s: A "Dance with the Debt Devil"?...Hardly!* (St. Louis: Center for the Study of American Business, Washington University, August 1992).

2. See chapter 9.

3. As identified through a computer search of the Nexis Data Base undertaken April 20, 1992.

4. Kevin Phillips, *The Politics of Rich and Poor: Wealth and the American Electorate in the Reagan Aftermath* (New York: Harper Perennial, 1991), p. 114.

5. Ibid.

6. Ibid., p. 217.

7. Ibid.

8. Robert F. Black, Don L. Boroughs, Sara Collins, and Kenneth Sheets, "Heavy Lifting: How America's Debt Burden Threatens the Economic Recovery," *U.S. News and World Report,* May 6, 1991, p. 53.

9. Larry Reibstein, Rich Thomas, Carolyn Friday, and Doby Tsiantar, "Tapped Out for the Holidays: The Personal Debt Crisis," *Newsweek,* December 10, 1990, p. 54.

10. Christopher Ferrell, "Learning to Kick the Debt Habit," *Business Week,* March 12, 1990, p. 112.

11. John Meehan, Catherine Yang, Geoffrey Smith, and Joan O. C. Hamilton, "Past Due! The Bill for Consumer Debt Arrives," *Business Week,* December 10, 1990, p. 204.

12. Fred R. Bleakley, "A Decade of Debt Is Now Giving Way to the Age of Equity," *Wall Street Journal,* December 16, 1991. The number of times news articles used "decade of debt" was identified on April 20, 1992, by the Nexis Computer Data Base, which covers major media outlets. The phrase "excess debt" was used 1,059 times in media reports in 1980–1992, while the phrase "debt binge" was employed 212 times during the same period.

13. See Martin Feldstein, "Tax Policy for the 1990s: Personal, Business Investment, and Corporate Debt," *American Economic Review,* May 1989, pp. 108–112; and Michael Stone, "Caught in the Eighties: The New Debtors," *New York,* April 24, 1989, pp. 42–46.

14. Theodore J. Forstmann, "Corporate Finance, 'Leveraged to the Hilt': Violating Our Rules of Prudence," *Wall Street Journal,* October 25, 1988.

15. Christopher Farrell, "Learning to Kick the Debt Habit," *Business Week*, March 12, 1990, p. 112.

16. Ibid.

17. Howard Gleckman, Stephanie Anderson Forest, Zochary Schiller, and Walecia Konrad, "The Great American Debt Diet," *Business Week*, October 28, 1991, p. 36.

18. James C. Cooper and Kathleen Madigan, "Hauling a Mountain of Debt Is Finally Starting to Strain the Economy," *Business Week*, June 25, 1990, p. 19.

19. Meechan, Yang, Smith, and Hamilton, "Past Due!" p. 205.

20. Mortimer B. Zuckerman, "The Wages of Debt," *U.S. News & World Report*, April 18, 1991, p. 76.

21. Total liabilities in the country are estimated and reported by the Federal Reserve Board of Governors, *Balance Sheets for the U.S. Economy: 1945–1990* (Washington, DC: U.S. Government Printing Office, September 1991).

22. Prices in this report are consistently deflated by the GNP implicit price deflator. This index is used because it is the broadest measure of price changes available and because the data series on debt and assets cover items purchased not included in other price indexes, for example, the consumer price index. Use of the GNP price deflator follows the lead of the Council of Economic Advisers [*Economic Report of the President: 1992* (Washington, DC: U.S. Government Printing Office, February 1992), p. 423]. The Council reports that it uses the implicit deflator as published prior to the benchmark revision of the national income and product accounts in December 1991 (deflator averaged for fourth quarter of the year shown and first quarter of the following year).

23. Personal debt includes home mortgages, other mortgages, tax-exempt debt installment consumer credit, other consumer credit, bank loans, other loans, security credit, trade credit, and deferred and unpaid life insurance premiums. See Federal Reserve Board of Governors, *Balance Sheets for the U.S. Economy: 1949–90*, pp. 19–24.

24. The debt of nonfarm, noncorporate businesses includes mortgages on residences, multifamily housing units, and commercial property; bank loans; other loans; other taxes payable; trade debt; and a catch-all category called "miscellaneous liabilities." See Federal Reserve Board of Governors, *Balance Sheets for the U.S. Economy: 1949–90*, pp. 25–30.

25. The debt of nonfarm, corporate businesses includes tax-exempt debt and corporate bonds; mortgages on residences, multifamily units, and commercial property; bank loans; loans from foreign sources;

acceptance liabilities to banks; nonbank finance loans; U.S. government loans; profit taxes payable; trade debt; and foreign direct investment in the United states. See Federal Reserve Board of Governors, *Balance Sheets for the U.S. Economy: 1949–90*, pp. 31–36.

26. The debt of farmers includes mortgages, bank loans, U.S. government loans, Federal Intermediate Credit Bank loans, and trade debt. See Federal Reserve Board of Governors, *Balance Sheets for the U.S. Economy: 1949–90*, pp. 25–30.

27. However, you should not conclude that the consumer/investor regards certain purchases as "investments" simply because the Commerce Department classifies the purchases of those goods as "consumption." Hence, the classification scheme does not mean that incurring debt to purchase a particular good will necessarily impose a future burden on the borrower. For example, a VCR is classified as a durable consumer good, but its purchase through credit may be appropriate because the good can, over the course of its life, reduce other household expenditures. For example, a family with a VCR may spend less on movies and other forms of entertainment that are more expensive than the prorated share of the cost of the VCR.

28. Corporate equity and land are measured at market value, whereas bonds are measured at par value. Tangible assets include residential structures, nonprofit plant and equipment, consumer durables, and land. Total financial assets include checkable deposits, small time and saving deposits, money market fund shares, large time deposits, U.S. government securities, tax-exempt obligations, mortgages and foreign bonds, mortgages, open-market paper, corporate equities, life insurance reserves, pension fund reserves, equity in noncorporate businesses, security credit, and miscellaneous assets. Tangible assets represented 25 percent of total assets in 1947 and 34 percent of total assets in 1973 and 1990.

29. The tangible assets of nonfarm, noncorporate businesses include residential structures, nonresidential plant and equipment, inventories, and land. The financial assets include checkable deposits and currency, time deposits, U.S. government securities, consumer credit, mortgages, trade credit, insurance receivables, equity in sponsoring agencies, and "other." In 1947, tangible assets represented 88 percent of total assets. In 1973, they represented 90 percent of total assets; and in 1990, 87 percent of total assets.

30. Tangible assets of corporate businesses include residential structures, nonresidential plant and equipment, inventories, and land. The financial assets include checkable deposits and currency, time deposits, money market fund shares, security RPs, foreign deposits, U.S. government securities, tax-exempt obligations, open-market paper, consumer credit, mutual fund shares, trade

credit, foreign direct investment, insurance receivables, equity in sponsoring agencies, and "other." Tangible assets of corporations accounted for 73 percent of total assets in 1947, 70 percent in 1973, and 71 percent in 1990.

31. Mark Warshawsky, "Comments," *Brookings Papers on Economic Activity*, Spring 1990, p. 282.

32. The tangible assets of farm businesses include residential structures, nonresidential plant and equipment, inventories, and land. The financial assets include checkable deposits and currency, insurance receivables, and equity in sponsoring agencies. Tangible assets represented 92 percent of total farm business assets in 1947, 97 percent in 1973, and 95 percent in 1990.

33. Investment tax credit and accelerated depreciation allowances are advantages that Congress and the Reagan administration began taking away through the Tax Equity and Fiscal Responsibility Act of 1982.

34. Robert L. Bartley, *The Seven Fat Years and How to Do It Again* (New York: Free Press, 1992), p. 110.

35. Statistical Abstract: 1991, p. 510.

36. Even if we accept the fact that the liabilities-to-assets ratio would not have continued along a straight-line trend from 1973 to 1990, it still appears that the actual ratios for 1990 in the separate figures would not have been too far out of line.

37. The straight-line trend is solely a reference line, intended to highlight the break in 1973. A simple least-squares regression equation with the total private debt-to-asset ratio made a function of variables like the real interest rate, inflation rate, and private net worth computed from data from 1947 to 1973 and projected forward indicates that the predicted debt-to-asset ratio would have risen dramatically (above the straight-line trend indicated) after 1973. The gap between the actual and predicted debt-to-asset ratio for 1990 generated from this regression equation is greater than what is indicated. Needless to say, more work is warranted to determine the causes of the abrupt downturn in the debt-to-asset ratio in the 1970s.

38. The household debt-to-gross domestic product ratios for Japan and the United States were close in both 1980 and 1990 (Japan: 54 percent and 76 percent in 1980 and 1990, respectively; and the United States: 55 percent and 72 percent for 1980 and 1990, respectively). The corporate debt-to-gross domestic product ratios in Japan (as well as Germany, France, the United Kingdom, and Canada) were much higher than in the United States in both 1980 and 1990 (Japan: 149 percent and 196 percent in 1980 and 1990, respectively; and the United States: 74 percent and 91 percent in 1980 and 1990,

respectively), as reported by Paul Craig Roberts, "Debt, Lies, and Inflation," *National Review*, August 31, 1992), p. 32. See also Kenneth L. Fisher, "Dumb Bears," *Forbes*, August 5, 1991, p. 118.

39. See Ben S. Bernanke and John Y. Campbell, "Is There a Corporate Debt Crisis?" *Brookings Papers on Economic Activity*, Spring 1988, pp. 83–125; and Ben S. Bernanke, John Y. Campbell, and Toni M. Whited, "U.S. Corporate Leverage: Developments in 1987 and 1988," *Brookings Papers on Economic Activity*, Spring 1990, pp. 225–278.

40. The fact that researchers are unable to show that any given variable does not have a statistically significant effect on debt may indicate that the number of explanatory variables is indeed large, not that the identified variable has had no impact at all on the growth in debt.

41. Michael C. Jensen and William H. Meckling, "Theory of the Firm: Managerial Behavior, Agency Costs and Capital Structure," *Journal of Financial Economics*, October 1976, pp. 305–360.

42. Bartley, *Seven Fat Years*, p. 144 who cites Glenn Yago, *Junk Bonds: How High Yield Securities Restructured Corporate America* (New York: Oxford University Press, 1991), p. 36.

43. Glenn Yago, "High Yield or Junk?" *National Review*, August 31, 1992, p. 43.

44. Ibid.

45. Ibid.

46. Ibid., p. 45.

47. See Gertler and Hubbard (1989) and Baker and Wruck (1990), as cited in Bernanke, Campbell, and Whited, pp. 271, 272.

48. Bernanke, Campbell, and Whited, "U.S. Corporate Leverage: Developments in 1987 and 1988," p. 271.

49. Warshawsky, "Comments," p. 282.

50. Foreign holdings of U.S. corporate bonds rose ninefold, from $22 billion in 1980 to $194 billion in 1990. Foreign loans to U.S. nonbank borrowers rose even more, twenty-one-fold, from $4 billion in 1980 to $83 billion in 1990. Foreign trade credit to U.S. firms expanded more modestly, by 52 percent, from $29 billion in 1980 to $44 billion in 1990 (*Balance Sheets for the U.S. Economy: 1945–1990*, pp. 11, 12.)

51. See Harvey S. James, Jr. and Murray Weidenbaum, *When Businesses Cross International Borders: Strategic Alliances and Their Alternatives* (Westport, CN: Praeger Publishers, 1993).

52. The yield on corporate bonds with a Moody's triple-A rating rose from 7.21 percent in 1972 to 14.17 percent in 1981, only to decline steadily during the 1980s and to reach 9.32 percent in 1990 (Economic Report of the President: 1992, p. 378).

53. Service expenditures represented 29 percent of gross domestic product in 1970, 31 percent in 1980, and 37 percent in 1990 (*Economic Report of the President: 1992*, p. 298; and author's calculations).

54. See Bernanke, Campbell, and Whited, "U.S. Corporate Leverage: Developments in 1987 and 1988," pp. 261–269; and a report on a study by Stephen S. Roach from Morgan Stanley & Co. by Kathleen Madigan, "O.K., So the Debt Spree Wasn't All that Risky," *Business Week*, November 26, 1990, p. 22.

55. The number of credit cards in use rose from 526 million in 1980 to 957 million in 1989, or by 82 percent (*Statistical Abstract: 1991*, p. 510).

56. Granted, per capita real disposable incomes rose by 18 percent between 1980 and 1990, at the same time that real per capita interest payments made by persons rose 131 percent. However, the actual real dollar increase in per capita disposable incomes was twenty-eight times the increase in the real dollar increase of per capita interest payments. The improvement in the average credit worthiness of people is indicated in the low, and somewhat declining, loan delinquency rates. The delinquency rate on closed-end installment loans dropped from 2.8 percent of all loans in 1980 to 2.6 percent in 1989 (after reaching a low of 1.9 percent in 1983, which could have been attributed to the Credit Control Act of 1969 being in effect until December 1982) [*Statistical Abstract: 1991*, p. 510].

57. The percentage of Americans 65 years of age and older rose from 11.3 percent of the population in 1980 to 12.5 percent in 1990 (*Statistical Abstract: 1991*, p. 13).

58. Fisher, "Dumb Bears," p. 118.

59. Bernanke, Campbell, and Whited, "U.S. Corporate Leverage: Developments in 1987 and 1988," p. 275.

60. Ibid.

61. See Cooper and Madigan, "Hauling a Mountain of Debt," p. 19; Farrell, "Learning to Kick the Debt Habit," pp. 112, 114; Gleckman, Forest, Schiller, and Konrad, "The Great American Debt Diet," pp. 36, 38; Gene Koretz, "America Is Kicking the Debt Habit—But Is that Good?" *Business Week*, February 19, 1990, p. 22; Bleakley, "A Decade of Debt Is Now Giving Way to the Age of Equity."

62. Alternately, the $8.8 trillion in debt in 1990 could have been achieved with a debt-to-asset ratio of 26.9 percent, the level actually achieved in 1986.

7

RETREAT OF THE
PART-TIME ECONOMY

Part-time workers have always sought economic improvement for themselves and their families. They have, serendipitously, become an invaluable economic resource to employers and to the country. Part-time workers provide more than dedicated work; they also offer employers much needed production flexibility in an increasingly competitive global economy. Part-time jobs offer American families flexibility in planning for major foreseeable expenditures such as those that accompany college education, and to accommodate sudden, unforeseen increases in expenditures due to sickness or accidents.

The prospects as well as the actuality of part-time work buttress economic activity by providing a form of privately funded social insurance for individuals, families, and businesses. The incomes of part-time workers bolster community economic welfare in another important but indirect way—additional tax revenues for all levels of government. Government revenues are increased still further as the earnings of part-time workers are added to the incomes of their spouses (or parents) and then are taxed at a higher rate than for single American workers. Nevertheless, in the late 1980s, the critics began to worry that all the employment growth was in part-time jobs and that the economy was suffering because millions of Americans were either choosing to take part-time jobs or were being forced to take part-time jobs.

Clearly, over the past three decades, the importance of part-time workers to the economy has grown, both in terms of absolute numbers and relative to the work force. Thus far into the 1990s, part-time employment has remained a higher share of total jobs than in the early 1960s; but during the 1980s the part-time share of total jobs actually declined.

A well-intended political movement is afoot that would undercut, albeit unintentionally, the many actual and potential contributions of part-time workers. While it is easy to identify the economic and social contributions of part-time workers to the economy and the economic gains of part-time workers, a number of policy commentators and key political leaders in Washington have observed that many part-time workers are paid less than their full-time counterparts and receive fewer fringe benefits. Proponents of this new political movement reason that employers should not be permitted to discriminate in the pay and fringe benefits provided full- and part-time workers. They maintain that employers should be forced, under threat of penalty, to pay part-time workers in wages and fringe benefits comparable to those of full-time workers. Government mandates, they contend, have been made all the more necessary by economic conditions that have forced a growing percentage of workers to take part-time work, sometimes in lieu of full-time employment.

The motivation of the proponents of these new mandated benefits cannot be imputed. No one is interested in seeing the welfare of workers reduced—especially by government policies. At the same time, the facts on which these reforms are based and the assessed effects of reform can be subjected to serious dispute. For instance, note that for the decade of the 1980s, the number of workers who took part-time jobs out of economic necessity declined as a percentage of total part-time workers and as a percentage of total employed (part-time and full-time workers).

Much of the competitive advantage of using part-time workers would be reduced—perhaps dramatically—by the proposed mandates. A substantial body of scholarly literature forcefully indicates that increasing the relative cost of any resource—especially of a part-time labor resource—will increase unemployment by decreasing employment opportunities.

Moreover, the reduced demand for part-time workers would probably have the perverse effect of undercutting the real wages and net welfare gains not only of part-time workers but of many (but not all) full-time workers. To the extent that fringe benefits are substituted for wages in the compensation packages of part-time workers, the incentive of these workers to maintain job performance and quality standards will be impaired because less of worker pay is dependent on performance and quality.

Finally, as a direct consequence of the mandates and as an indirect consequence of American production being less flexible, less productive, and more costly (and, hence, less competitive), part-time and full-time jobs will be driven overseas and underground as employment costs rise. These perverse economic effects will be compounded by the fact that the proposed remedies do not apply to all workers, namely, to full-time workers in this country and full-time and part-time workers around the world. Also, they do not apply to "mechanical workers," that is, to robots or other mechanical substitutes for labor. And it should be stressed that human workers can be replaced by mechanical substitutes that are either available or are in the development stage. Employers will be forced by the standards of world competition to continue to speed up development of such labor substitutes when confronted with expensive mandates for part-time American workers, thus undermining the economic welfare of the part-time workers and their families.

The proponents of mandated benefits for part-time workers may believe they are doing the right thing, but more objective analysis indicates that the reforms will have effects precisely opposite the ones intended. If the reformists succeed in getting mandates, the targeted workers will suffer even more pressing hardship.

The Reform Agenda

Critics of part-time work force policies usually ground their case for federally mandated benefits in the form of higher wages and greater fringe benefits in an array of facts that show that part-time wages and fringe benefits are, on average, lower than those paid full-time workers. In 1989, Bureau of Labor Statistics shows that the average hourly wage of part-time workers (including only those paid by the hour) was $4.83. The average wage of full-time workers was 62 percent higher, $7.83.[1] However, it must be quickly added that a major portion of the wage difference can be explained by the fact that many jobs held by part-time workers have wages significantly below the average. A high percentage of the part-time work force is women and young workers who have limited skills (many of whom earn the minimum wage), and most part-time workers are in the service sector. A disproportionate number are nonwhite.[2] At the same time, critics should also acknowledge the benefits, to employers and employees alike, of part-time work. For example, in opening congressional hearings on "The Rising Use of Part-Time and Temporary Workers: Who Benefits and Who Loses?," Representative Tom Lantos recognized that part-time work helps American firms meet foreign competition, but he quickly stressed the negative aspects of the growing use of part-time workers, especially for those who would prefer full-time work. He noted that females constitute most of the part-time labor force that, he maintained, has continued to grow as a share of the nation's entire labor force and that part-time employees usually receive lower wages and fewer benefits than their full-time counterparts, suggesting exploitation.[3] Similarly, Representative Joseph DioGuardi indicated that, while more than 80 percent of all "contingent workers" are pleased with their jobs, part-time employment raises many opportunities for exploitation.[4]

In testimony supporting her recently introduced legislation, Representative Pat Schroeder disregarded Representative DioGuardi's data on the extent to which most part-time workers are content with their work status and stated flatly, "The problem is that part-time workers are being exploited, and that's the real issue and that's what we are looking at."[5] She decried the creation of a "bifur-cated type of employment system" with "two classes of employees," an invention she tagged as very "dangerous."[6] She noted that before 1986 the growth of part-time work may have out-paced the growth of full-time work by as much as 10 percent and that 35 percent of part-time working mothers surveyed by the National Association of Working Women prefer more hours of work but are unable to find adequate day-care.[7] Furthermore, she argued, only 16 percent of part-time workers have health insurance: "Now, we know they aren't healthier. So, that means that an awful lot of them aren't covered, and they still get sick. That has a real effect on their family and themselves."[8] Finally, she notes that only 27 percent of part-time workers are covered by their employers' pension plans. The problems part-time workers face will continue to grow as still more women enter the labor force.[9]

Schroeder's proposed solution, The Part-Time and Temporary Workers Protection Act of 1991 (H.R. 2575), will, if passed, require employers to provide their part-time workers with the same fringe benefits they give their full-time workers. Schroeder explains how her proposed mandated benefits for part-time employees would work: "All employees working less than full time would receive a prorated share of health benefits under an employer-sponsored health plan based on the amount of time they work. Part-time employees would be those, for the purposes of determining health benefits, who work less than 30 hours per week. If a part-time employee worked the equivalent of 40 percent time, the employer would be required to pay 40 percent of the employer contribution made for a full-time worker to participate in an employer-sponsored health plan. An employee's participation in the health plan would be optional."[10] Her proposal would also require employers to allow part-time and temporary workers who work 500 or more hours a year to participate in their firms' retirement plans. Her goal is to make part-time employment a viable option to workers by increasing their benefits and by forcing employers to treat part-time workers with the "same dignity and respect" accorded full-time workers.[11] Representative Schroeder told her listeners at the hearings that, when forced to provide mandated benefits, "employers will be rewarded with higher productivity, higher morale and higher retention," implying that the mandated benefits would be cost-effective and profitable.[12]

The Growing Importance of Part-Time Workers

Part-time workers—those Americans who work for pay one to 34 hours a week—have always been a significant component of the U.S. labor force, and since the 1950s their importance has generally grown, both in absolute and relative terms. Figure 7-1 shows the absolute growth in use of part-time workers. At the start of 1956, part-time workers accounted for close to 6 million of the 57 million employed nonagricultural workers in the country. The total count of part-time workers exceeded 11 million by 1970 (when the total employed labor force was 81 million) and exceeded 16 million in 1980 (when the total employed labor force exceeded 101 million). At the end of 1991 (when the total employed work force was 118 million), the count of part-workers was approaching 21 million, three and a half times the part-time count in 1956.

A substantial majority of these part-time workers actually wanted part-time work, as opposed to full-time work, a fact that is evident in figure 7-2. Four million of the 6 million part-time workers in 1956 had voluntarily sought part-time work, which means that only a third of the part-time workers had assumed their part-time work "involuntarily," that is, because of slack work at their full-time jobs or because they could not find full-time employment. At the end of 1991, over 14 million Americans—just under 70 percent of the part-time labor force—had assumed their part-time jobs voluntarily. Close to 6 million workers were on their part-time jobs involuntarily, and perhaps a million of these workers were involuntarily employed at part-time jobs because of the recession that started in 1990 and the 27 percent mandated increase in the minimum wage between 1990 and 1991.

Over the past three decades, the trend in part-time workers as

Figure 7-1 Total Number of Part-Time Workers in Nonagricultural Industries, Monthly, 1956–1991

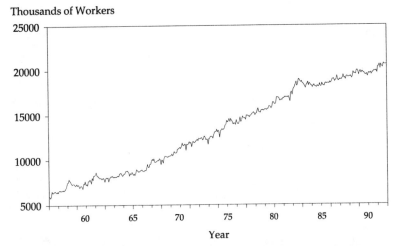

Thousands of Workers

Source: CITIBASE: Citibank economic data base (machine-readable magnetic tape file), 1946–present (New York: Citibank, N.A., 1991).

Figure 7-2 Voluntary and Involuntary Part-Time Workers, Monthly, 1956–1991

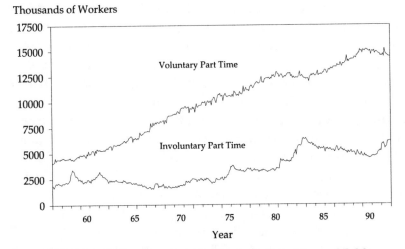

Thousands of Workers

Source: CITIBASE: Citibank economic data base (machine-readable magnetic data file), 1946–present (New York: Citibank, N.A., 1991).

Figure 7-3 Employed Nonagricultural Part-Time Workers as a Percentage of Total Employed Nonagricultural Workers, Monthly, 1956–1991

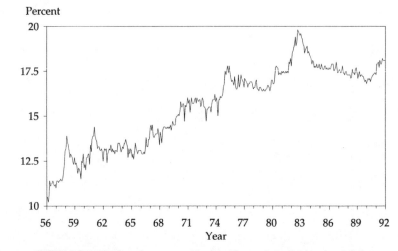

Source: CITIBASE: Citibank economic data base (machine-readable magnetic data file), 1946–present (New York: Citibank, N.A., 1991), pp. IX-1-2 and OX-1-5; and author's calculations.

a percentage of the employed (nonagriculture) labor force has been upwards, a fact that is evident in figure 7-3. At the start of 1956, part-time workers represented slightly more than 10 percent of the employed labor force. By the beginning of 1970, their share had grown by a factor of almost 50 percent, to over 15 percent of the labor force. By the depth of the recession in the early 1980s, their share was very close to 20 percent of all employed nonagricultural workers (partially because the employment of part-time workers during the 1981–1982 recession grew by a million while the employment of full-time workers fell by more than a million).

What is notable, perhaps surprising, about figure 7-3 is the decline in the share of workers who worked part time in the 1980s. Part-time workers represented 19.8 percent of the employed labor force in late 1982, only to fall to under 18 percent by early 1984. The part-time share continued to fall a few tenths of a percent, reaching 16.9 percent in mid-1990—a decline in share of 15 percent between

1982 and 1990. By late 1991, the share of the employed labor force represented by part-time workers was back up to 18.1 percent. Obviously, the ups and downs of the business cycle have a powerful influence on part-time employment. The run-up in part-time employment since 1990 should, in other words, not be surprising. I would also expect a decline in the part-time share with the expansion phase of the business cycle that began in early 1991.

Conventional wisdom appears to hold that people take part-time jobs only because they have no other choice and that involuntary part-time workers grew substantially as a share of the labor force during the 1980s because "good" full-time, full-paying jobs were being destroyed because the country turned, supposedly, toward free-market, anti-union policies when Ronald Reagan took office. In his 1988 critique of the Reagan administration's policies, Harvard economist Benjamin Friedman wrote:

> *Although it is easy enough to think of circumstances in which part-time work is preferable—mothers with small children, for example, or students continuing their education—surveys show that half of the Americans who have taken these part-time jobs in the 1980s would prefer full-time work. The prevalence of involuntary part-time work also suggests that to an unusually great extent the jobs created in recent years lack not just high pay but also prospects for significant advancement in the future.*[13]

M.I.T. economist Bennett Harrison and University of Massachusetts economist Barry Bluestone argue that practically all, if not all, the growth in the temporary and part-time work force has been imposed on workers, all of whom would presumably want full-time work, along with the pay, benefits, and responsibilities that go with full-time work. Or, in their words,

> *In recent years, business lobbyists have often argued that part-time jobs, usually in the service sector, are exactly what most people (especially women) desire. Yet official data on part-time work make it clear that practically 100 percent of the net additional part-time jobs created in the United States since the late 1970s are held by*

people who would have preferred full-time jobs but could not find them.[14]

Figures 7-4 and 7-5 chart the number of involuntary part-time workers as a percentage of all part-time workers and as a percentage of the employed labor force from 1956 to the end of 1991. Figure 7-4 shows that involuntary part-time employment fell from a high of 43 percent of employed part-time workers in 1958 to a low of 16 percent in 1968, after which it began to grow in the 1970s. However, the rise in involuntary part-time employment peaked at 34 percent of all employed part-time workers during the recession of the early 1980s, and then began to fall. This is contrary to what Friedman, and Harrison and Bluestone have claimed. In 1990, involuntary part-time employment dropped to less than 24 percent of all part-time workers, which was less than a third of the voluntary part-time work force.

According to Harrison and Bluestone, in the 1980s employers were seeking to "zap" the bargaining power of workers by shifting them, involuntarily, to part-time status.[15] Granted, the absolute number of involuntary part-time workers in 1990 did begin to rise as did their proportions relative to the total number of part-time workers and relative to the total number of workers, but that rise occurred because of the recession, not because employers planned, deviously, to "zap" their workers.

More notably, if employers were "zapping labor" by relegating them to part-time work, the unemployment rate of part-time workers, in general, should be rising relative to the unemployment rate of full-time workers. It is not. Figure 7-6 shows a strong downward trend in the unemployment rate of part-time workers relative to full-time workers for the 1963–1991 period (the inclusive dates for available data). In 1968, the unemployment rate of part-time workers peaked at more than 240 percent of the unemployment rate of full-time workers, after which the ratio moved downward with strong pro-cycle swings. By the end of 1991, the unemployment rate of part-time workers (8.6 percent) was only a third higher than the unemployment rate of full-time workers (6.5 percent).

Figure 7-4 Involuntary Part-Time Nonagricultural Workers as a Percentage of Total Part-Time Nonagricultural Workers, Monthly, 1956–1991

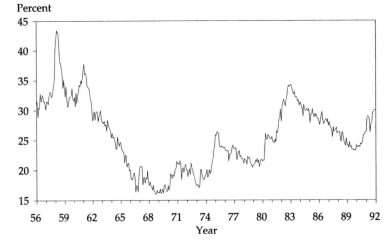

Percent

Figure 7-5 Involuntary Part-Time Workers as a Percentage of Employed Nonagricultural Workers, Monthly, 1956–1991

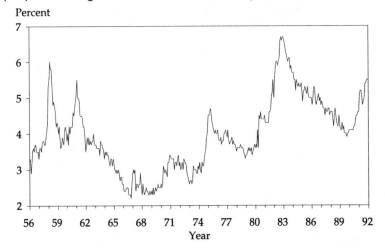

Percent

Source: CITIBASE: Citibank economic data base (machine-readable magnetic data file), 1946–present (New York: Citibank, N.A., 1991), pp. IX-1-2 and OX-1-5; and author's calculations.

Figure 7-6 Unemployment Rate of Part-Time Workers as a Percentage of the Unemployment Rate of Full-Time Workers, Monthly, 1963–1991

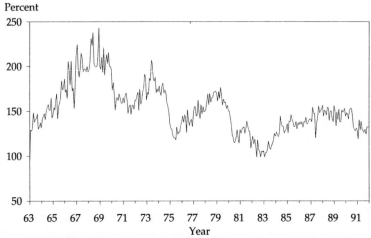

Percent

Source: CITIBASE: Citibank economic data base (machine-readable magnetic data file), 1946–present (New York, 1991), pp. IX-1-6; and author's calculations.

The Value of Part-Time Employment to Workers, Firms, and the Country

The part-time sector of the economy is often portrayed as second-rate, the lower tier in an expanding two-tiered economic order. Nevertheless, people continue to demand and hold part-time jobs, and this benefits both employers and employees.

Demand for Part-Time Jobs

In lamenting the growth in the part-time work force, Professor Friedman acknowledges how easy it is to imagine circumstances in which part-time work is beneficial, but then he cites only two examples—mothers who need to care for their children and students who need to pay for school. These cases are not inconsequential to total economic activity, given the growing number of women in the labor force, many of whom have entered the labor force in their prime child-bearing and child-rearing years, and given the increasing costs of higher education. Between 1956 and 1991, the number of women in the labor force increased from 20 million to 53 million, or two and a half times. Their labor force participation rate rose from 37 percent in 1956 to 57 percent in 1991, meaning that women jumped from representing 32 percent of the labor force in 1956 to 46 percent in 1991. The average cost of a college education rose four and a half times between 1965 and 1989, while the consumer price index rose significantly less.

However, there are far more than two reasons for the large number of part-time workers in the country. In two-income families, one parent often seeks a part-time job, thus fostering a sizable child-care industry that draws on the part-time labor force, many of whom are also parents. The substantial growth in the number of retirees who are living longer has also added to the part-time labor force. Many older workers do not want full-time work or the responsibilities and demands that often go with full-time jobs. Still, they have skills that are tremendously valuable to employers, and they want to continue creating and renewing the social contacts that go with jobs, even if their employment and benefits are limited. Other elderly people need special care, which means that family members may seek part-time employment not only to cover expenses but as a break from the demands of caregiving.

Many full-time jobs occupy the people who have them more than the conventional 40 hours per week. However, many full-time workers wish for additional work beyond the traditional 40 hours to earn additional income. "Moonlighting" satisfies this wish. Airline pilots are classic examples of "full-time" professionals with a great deal of time on their hands to work at other jobs on a part-time basis. So are fire fighters.

Many blue-collar workers also want more than the traditional 40 hours of work, which means they too seek part-time employment. The Current Population Survey found that in 1985 nearly 4 million workers had a part-time job as well as a full-time job; more than an additional million workers had two part-time jobs.[16] Of course, the employers of such full-time production workers may not be able to justify providing overtime work, mainly because they cannot afford the required time-and-a-half pay. Their workers must then look to the part-time sector of the economy for additional work hours.

Other workers—for example, freelance writers, actors, and artists (many of whom are low-paid)—desire very flexible work schedules so they can be available for unpredictable opportunities to make the "big time." Still other workers seek experience in a variety of jobs to help them achieve their long-term career goals.

Many seasonal workers in agriculture and tourism need at least part-time jobs in the "off season." These workers may put in far more than 40 hours a week on their seasonal jobs, during which periods they are counted as full-time workers. However, when they are working much less than 35 hours a week in the off season, they are counted as part-time workers though they may average more than 35 hours a week for the entire year.

Critics of the part-time economy seem to think that all workers regard all part-time work, especially when it is classified as "involuntary," as undesirable. However, many workers accept part-time employment to make ends meet while they search for a high-paying, full-time job; a job in a field with a very limited demand; or when starting a business of their own. Workers may want extra time to improve their chances of getting a really desirable job at a higher pay level, with even greater benefits. In such cases, we (and they) would regard their so-called involuntary part-time employment as voluntary, because without their "involuntary" part-time work, they might have had to truncate their search for higher paying full-time jobs and accept lower lifetime income paths. In this regard, part-time jobs contribute more to people's lifetime incomes than may be imagined simply by looking at the part-time wages and benefits.

Not all part-time workers need full-time work. Their part-time wage may be extraordinarily high, leaving them with a great deal of income potential that they can, so to speak, spend to buy more leisure or more time to do more work without pay for their families and communities. Certainly many actors, artists, and business owners do not want more than part-time work. Furthermore, some people seek

part-time jobs because they can move where their spouses are trans-
ferred without giving up the considerable personal investment that
must be made to develop and retain a full-time, career-oriented job.
If they already have fringe benefits through their spouses, the benefits that would accompany a full-time job may be of little concern to
such workers.

Naturally, a family's plans may require sacrifice, but not necessarily a full-time sacrifice. With one full-time and one part-time job,
many couples can cover the planned purchase of an automobile or
a college education with the same amount of work. Health crises may
shift wage-earning burden and force some family members back to
the labor force on a temporary, part-time basis to pay medical
expenses. Parents who consider it important that their children have
work experience from an early age may require their children to find
and hold part-time jobs; in their case, the money is relatively unimportant, but the experience and responsibility are of primary importance.

The cold facts are that many markets, especially in rural areas
and small towns, are not large enough to employ even one worker
full time, or a job market may be so divided among competitors that
no one person can be fully employed at the job. Such workers must
put together a "portfolio" of part-time jobs. In small towns, it is
altogether reasonable that one person may delivery newspapers, put
in lawns, and sell sweatshirts—all part time. Indeed, some part-time
entrepreneurs around the country are so good at finding part-time
niches in the work force that they make their own living by employing a number of part-time workers. This part-time work makes a net
contribution to total economic activity.

Temporary, and often part-time, clerical services have grown
into an industry because of the entrepreneurship of American firms,
and the growth in that industry has been a boon to part-time and
temporary workers. The growth meets the demand and adds to the
demand for part-time workers, hence, raising the wages of part-time
workers and making a net contribution to the nation's output and
families' disposable incomes.

Regrettably, because of mental or physical impairments, not all workers are capable of handling full-time work. Nevertheless, the income and experience of part-time work is important to them.[17] These individuals also benefit from part-time work.

In short, the demand for part-time jobs is real, important, and even vital to the people who fill those jobs. Indeed, the reasons for working part time and the benefits derived from part-time work may be as diverse as the people who hold and seek such employment. One argument for maintaining an unfettered part-time labor market is that no one can fully appreciate the diversity of interests of the 20 million part-time labor market participants. It is they who understand what combination of benefits and wages they want and are willing to accept. Clearly, the government should not adopt policies that undercut opportunities for part-time work, which are grounded in the costs of hiring part-time workers relative to their next-best alternatives.

Supply of Part-Time Jobs

The most all-inclusive explanation for why employers provide part-time employment opportunities is that part-time workers enable them to cope more successfully with the constant shifts in the markets for the goods and services they produce. A fact of economic life in most markets is transparently obvious: Product and service demands vary, often by the day, most often by the season, and almost always by the business cycle. Part-time workers enable many employers to handle the swings in their market demands. Accordingly, the Post Office and private, overnight delivery services add part-time delivery people during the Christmas season. Farmers add pickers at harvest time. Mail order firms add workers when there is a rush on advertised items, and restaurants add waiters and waitresses for special weekly brunches.

Part-time jobs are supplied because they enable the firm to deal with its peak load periods in a cost-effective manner. How do they do that? For one, part-time workers are often cheaper than their mechanical or full-time substitutes. Part-time workers also enable firms to carry less inventory and add flexibility that enables employers to hold down other costs, not the least of which is the sizable and costly commitment that must be made to keep full-time workers employed full time. In short, productive innovations in management, for example, "just-in-time" inventory control systems, have helped increase the demand for part-time workers. Part-time workers enable firms to meet their competition in both domestic and foreign markets, and it needs to be stressed that part-time workers are used extensively in other countries. One study found that part-time workers represented slightly more than 17 percent of American workers in 1987. They represented above 15 percent of the labor force in New Zealand and Canada, more than 20 percent in Australia, above 25 percent in Sweden and the United Kingdom, and nearly 26 percent in Norway.[18]

However, part-time jobs permit firms to do more than meet ever-changing external market forces. They allow businesses and community organizations to staff one-time events, and they permit firms to test and develop untried markets. For example, a newspaper or magazine interested in expanding its coverage into surrounding areas might hire a part-time freelance writer to cover the target area on a trial basis until circulation warrants more. A new company that installs sprinkler systems might have to start with part-time workers until there is a steady flow of business large enough to occupy full-time workers.[19]

Critics who see the part-time economy built on the oppression of workers by their employers do not seem to realize that many employers of part-time workers are actually responding to the demands of workers for part-time work. Discount stores, such as Wal-Mart, hire elderly greeters because of the number of elderly workers who *want* to work. Federal Express hires college students at Christmas because the students *want* the extra money that comes from being employed during school breaks. These workers, many of whom have valuable skills, could not be employed on a full-time basis. Surely, Wal-Mart and Federal Express do not exploit this part-time work force; rather, they give individuals much desired employment opportunities that they would not otherwise have. In addition, employers of part-time workers drive up the demand for part-time workers, thus raising their wages above what they would otherwise have been.

Somewhat ironically, full-time company employees have a demand for part-time help. Part-time workers reduce the pressures on full-time people. To the extent that part-time workers make production more cost-effective, they can drive up the demand for products and services, thus increasing the incomes of the firms' owners and of the full-time workers. On the other hand, when firms are under competitive pressures and are being forced to contract, the addition of part-time workers can ameliorate the pains of the contraction.

The Value of Part-Time Work to the Country

Part-time employment opportunities contribute to the ability of American firms to meet fluctuating market demands. The use of a part-time work force permits lower cost production, thus helping to meet the challenges of foreign competition. Part-time work also enables American workers and families to satisfy an array of objectives known only to them, not to people in Washington. Such work also affords workers an opportunity to make additional trades in their payment packages. While the wages of part-time workers may, on average, be lower than that of full-time workers, it could be that many part-time workers prefer receiving most (if not all) of their compensation in money wages. This affords them more opportunities than they would have if part-time work were not available, and they are also better off than they would be otherwise. Besides, as noted, the work opportunities available in the part-time sector of the economy ensure that many workers are able to reach a higher lifetime income growth path than they could otherwise achieve. Hence, the growth of the economy, national income, and even government tax revenues are greater than they would be if part-time jobs vanished because of cost-prohibitive mandates.

Economic Consequences of Mandated Benefits for Part-Time Workers

Representative Schroeder and other proponents of mandated benefits for part-time workers express heartfelt concern for workers who may have low wages and no fringe benefits. It is, indeed, an economic fact of life that part-time workers on average earn two-thirds as much as their full-time counterparts. It is also a fact that a much higher percentage of full-time workers have employer-provided fringe benefits. While the proponents advocate raising the economic status of part-time workers, they also want to ensure that part-time work remains a viable employment option. As is true of proponents of almost all mandated benefits, the proponents of mandated benefits for part-time workers want to see federal mandates as a means of making part-time work more attractive, more of an option. However, the proposed mandates will have exactly the opposite effect, even for those workers who retain their part-time jobs once mandates are in place. The mandates will be particularly oppressive for part-time workers, precisely because so often it is their lower wages and fewer benefits that have induced employers to turn to them to provide a competitive advantage. The proposed federal laws will take that advantage away. For a better understanding of this, we need to consider the many ways all workers, part-time and full-time, are paid.

The Ways Workers Are Paid

Almost all workers are paid in a variety of forms, and money wages is only the most obvious form. Workers also receive varying bundles of other benefits—some mandated, some voluntary. These may include tips, health and life insurance, pension plans, production and nonproduction bonuses (dependent upon company profitability), paid vacations, payment-in-kind, free room and board, sick-leave days, Social Security, workers' compensation, and unemployment compensation. But part of an employee's compensation package is made of less easily noticed employment-related benefits—rarely acknowledged fringes such as flexible hours, slack work demands, low-risk work, free uniforms, discounts on purchases from the company, on-the-job training, company parties and picnics, office amenities (pleasant surroundings, lighting, and air conditioning), personal use of company equipment (from computers to saws to copying machines), work breaks, and break and lunch facilities (special rooms, tables, and kitchen equipment).

One fringe benefit of working part time frequently goes unrecognized: the absence of any demand to make a long-term, or even an intermediate-term commitment to the firm or to pursue tasks with the degree of dedication expected of full-time workers. This is an implicit fringe that enables part-time workers to retain maximum flexibility to do other things and to take other jobs with little or no notice.

The point is, money is not everything to workers or to their employers. Nonmoney forms of compensation rose in importance rapidly during the 1960s and 1970s, partially because rising tax rates took a bigger bite from money income while fringes were not even taxed. In 1960, a list of identified "supplements to wages and salaries" (consisting primarily of employers' contributions to social insurance and private pension, health, and welfare funds) represented just under 9 percent of total worker compensation. In 1975, the supplements represented a little more than 16 percent. In the 1980s, supplements as a percentage of compensation leveled off, but in 1990 the supplements were still 20 percent of total worker compensation. Still, the listed "supplements" did not include many of the noncash employment-related benefits mentioned, such as the value of the subsidized lunches or flexibility in scheduling work.

The Losers from Mandated Benefits: The Targeted Workers

Why does it matter that workers are paid in a combination of ways that varies from workplace to workplace? The answer is threefold. First, the effect of mandates will be uneven across firms. Some firms may offer the identified mandated benefit in the amount specified but few of other benefits; these will not be affected adversely. However, firms offering total compensation packages of equal value with a small portion of the mandated benefit but lots of other benefits will be forced to incur the greater costs of meeting the mandates.

Firms employing mostly full-time workers typically will provide more of the mandated or standard fringes, such as health insurance and pensions, but less flexibility, at the same time requiring more dedication to the firm. On the other hand, firms employing part-time workers typically will be offering their workers a lot of two specific benefits, flexibility with no demands for dedication and few other benefits.

Second, by passing mandates Congress may believe that it is increasing total payments to workers. But, in fact, that will be very difficult, if not impossible, because workers receive a variety of benefits. To control their costs in the increasingly competitive global marketplace, employers can be expected to respond to mandates from Congress by altering the combination of benefits being paid—with more of the mandated benefit but less of other nonmandated benefits being offered—and without Congress ever knowing that the changes have been made.[20] Even if the alterations were known, Congress would probably not be able to prevent the alterations without greatly extending its intrusion into employer/employee relationships.

Third, the existing variety of benefits included in worker compensation indicates that employers are not unalterably opposed to providing their workers with a variety of benefits. The key is that the benefit must pay sufficiently in terms of making workers more productive or in terms of lowering wages to cover its cost. Indeed, the goal of greater profits should make firms attentive to worker needs and desires for various forms of compensation. If part-time workers truly wanted the proposed mandated benefits and were willing to pay the costs, firms should have no difficulty rearranging the payment bundles of their part-time work force.

Profit-making (and especially profit-maximizing) firms should be expected to seek to maximize the effectiveness of the "compensation bundle" in terms of promoting worker productivity and happiness. Even firms with market power (that is, those that do not operate in highly competitive labor markets) should want their compensation bundles to be as attractive to workers as possible and to carry the lowest possible costs to the firms and their employees. Attractive compensation bundles mean a greater supply of workers and subsequently lower total wage payments.

On the other hand, less attractive compensation bundles hurt the firms, not just the workers. Unattractive compensation bundles mean that the firms offering them will have to incur greater costs to get the quantity and quality of workers needed. It follows that firms have a built-in incentive to maximize the gain to their workers—even their part-time workers—for a given level of labor expenditures.

Of course, firms in highly competitive labor markets must make their compensation bundles as attractive as possible. If they do not, their workers will go elsewhere, to competitors with more attractive compensation bundles.

Newly imposed mandates necessarily increase the absolute and relative cost of hiring targeted workers (those covered by the law but without the identified benefit)—more specifically for this study, part-time workers.[21] The mandates will, therefore, reduce the relative cost of hiring workers who are not targeted, for example, full-time workers who already have the benefit and foreign workers who are not covered by the law.[22] In a competitive marketplace, the targeted workers may get more compensation in the form of a newly enacted mandated benefit, for example, health insurance. However, they will get less in some other form of compensation, for example, wages, on-the-job training, life insurance, subsidized meals and company purchases, and other difficult-to-measure employment-related benefits.[23]

The assessed value of the benefits forgone should, for several reasons, be greater than the value of the mandated benefit for the employee. First, a basic principle of economics will be at work: The lower the demand for any good or service, the lower the price paid. This principle applies to products as diverse as oranges and gasoline—and it is no less applicable to the part-time labor markets targeted by Congress. The lower demand for targeted workers caused by the mandated benefits implies a lower overall value for the compensation bundle that can be secured by workers. Therefore, if the acquired mandated benefits are worth $100 a month to the workers, the lost benefits must be worth more than $100.

If the benefits forgone are worth less to the employees than the mandated benefits and if there is no increase in cost of providing the mandate, then the mandate is actually unnecessary. Employers would happily provide the benefit without the mandate or would gladly switch benefits when told of an error. Employers would sow goodwill among their employees and would attract a larger labor supply, which, in turn, would enable them to reduce the cost of their total compensation package. When benefits must be mandated, we must assume they are worth less to the workers than the benefits that are taken away.

Proponents of mandated benefits have a fundamental inconsistency at the core of their argument. They contend that, for example, family leave is very important, even crucial, to workers' welfare, and workers know this. They also contend that the cost of the benefit is extraordinarily modest, especially since, to use Pat Schroeder's words, "employers will be rewarded with higher productivity, higher morale and higher retention." The juxtaposition of these propositions amounts to an acknowledgment that the federal mandate is unnecessary. The propositions suggest that employees should be willing to pay the modest cost by forgoing a few dollars a year in wages or other benefits. They are not willing, however, and this fact must make everyone wonder if the costs are as modest as indicated.[24] After all, the $7-figure quoted by some proponents as the annual cost per employee for a family-leave policy, for example, is basically the cost of lunch for one day. What employee wouldn't be willing to give up one day's lunch to have the opportunity to take three-months of family leave if needed? If fringe benefits do all the things that proponents say they will do for the employers, what profit-maximizing employer would not provide them voluntarily?

The questions answer themselves. The case for mandated benefits, especially just for part-time workers, is flawed in several regards. The cited average cost figure, which is calculated using the total labor force as the denominator, is a politically useful distortion of the true facts. The cost per employee for those who use the leave is far more than the price of a lunch, which explains why many employees and their employers have not negotiated a wages-for-leave trade.[25] And the cost for mandated health insurance and pension plans is probably far greater than the cost of a modest mandated-leave fringe benefit.

Whatever the likely impact of mandated benefits for the entire labor force, the effect is likely to be even more harsh for part-time workers. They are workers with the least commitment from their employers. Many have only low-level skills that frequently and easily can be duplicated by machines, robotics, and foreign workers—none of whom are covered by the mandates. For example, in the hotel and restaurant lab at the University of Wisconsin, researchers have developed a hamburger flipper that automatically flips hamburgers and puts them on buns. Suzumo Machinery Industries in Japan has developed a sushi maker that neatly molds balls of rice and passes the balls by conveyor belt to where the fish is added by machine, leaving only the garnish for a worker to add. Carnegie-Mellon's Center for Human Service Robots has also developed a "pizabot," which is a voice-activated robotic arm that makes pizzas to order. While the prototype has been pulled from service in need of further development, it remains a potential substitute for many part-time pizza parlor workers.

Part-time workers are frequently hired in lieu of placing greater work demands on full-time workers because part-time workers do not receive the same overtime benefits full-time workers must be paid. Federal mandates directed at part-time workers will obliterate a principal competitive advantage of part-time workers vis-à-vis full-time workers; they, therefore, place part-time workers at a competitive disadvantage.

No matter what the costs of the mandates are, the globalization of economic activity has increased competitiveness in all markets, including U.S. labor markets, especially the part-time market. In past decades, domestic firms did not have to worry about producers thousands of miles away. The U.S. economy was not yet dependent, to any large extent, on either foreign sales or foreign sources of supplies. It was far too expensive to engage in international trade. Now, however, transactions with firms in other parts of the world are not especially difficult. Indeed, competition forces firms to seek out the sources of supply at the lowest possible costs and to compete everywhere for market share. Firms no longer have the luxury of providing benefits that their competitors do not, a fact that is bound to mean that American workers will incur an even greater cost from the mandated benefits than they would have incurred in bygone eras.

Proponents contend that mandating benefits will ensure that workers cover the costs of social services they are already receiving. For example, one proponent maintains that "uninsured workers incur $15 billion in health care costs for which they do not pay."[26] The implication is that mandated health insurance would reduce government expenditures by $15 billion. That, of course, might be the result, but there are reasons for doubt. Congress has never been known to curb expenditures when additional taxes or mandates have been imposed in the past. Indeed, after Medicare was mandated in 1965, health care costs soared, pricing many people out of both health care and health insurance markets.[27] Furthermore, to the extent that worker welfare is undercut by the mandate, the case for an expansion of other government programs will be made stronger. Currently, proponents of expanded mandates and a variety of government services point to the reduction in real worker wages as a justification. However, a portion of faltering growth in workers' real wages over the past two decades can be attributed to an expansion of mandates. In short, this argument leads to the steepest of all slippery slopes in policy formulation.

The Winners from Mandated Benefits

Not everyone can be expected to lose from the mandates, which may help explain their political attraction. Some employers who already provide benefits will gain, primarily because their competition will have to suffer an additional cost of doing business. Accordingly, it is not surprising that the president and chief executive officer of Control Data, which provides a minimum of five months of leave at 65 percent of regular pay, has endorsed the family-leave legislation.[28] The parental leave bill, for example, is a means of saddling many of Control Data's competitors with some of the costs that Control Data has assumed. Some workers whose employers have already granted the mandated benefit will also probably experience an increase in the demand for their services and, therefore, in wages.

Firms that have not sought to gain competitive advantage by hiring part-time workers for less than 500 hours a year will also gain by the proposed mandates for part-time workers. Components of the proposed legislation will apply only to employers who hire part-time workers for more than 500 hours a year. The competition these worker groups face from lower cost targeted worker groups is reduced because the gap in relative costs between them and the targeted group will have been reduced.

Most congressional proposals to control labor markets typically end up applying only to "large" firms (as defined by the number of employees, say those with more than 50 or 100 employees). The reasons given for the exclusion of small firms is that they cannot endure the burden. In addition, there are too many small firms to control effectively. The sizable majority of employers of part-time workers who are "small" by the standards of the proposed part-time worker mandates will also see their competitive advantage improved.[29] Only "large" firms will suffer the mandated higher production costs. The proposed mandate will, of course, impose an additional cap on the ability and willingness of small firms to grow and become large, thus becoming subject to the mandate.

Foreign workers will also gain from the domestic mandates because mandates do not apply to overseas employment. To the extent that U.S. goods and services become relatively more expensive, the demand for imports should increase along with the incomes of foreign workers. Producers of robotics and automated machinery, as well as their work forces, are also likely to experience an increase in demand. And, of course, fringe benefits do not have to be paid to any robot even though it may work without a break night and day. These are not exactly the effects the backers of the mandated benefit bill have in mind.

The Empirical Connection between Benefits and Wages

Mandates have the same effect on the compensation package that a pinch has on a balloon: The air in the balloon may be reduced in one area, but that only intensifies the inside pressure for the balloon to expand elsewhere—in places that are not being pinched. In the case of mandates, however, the overall volume of the package will be reduced, much as the volume of the balloon will be reduced.

Showing the subsidiary, negative effects of mandated benefits is not an easy task. The impact of mandates can be felt in several easy-to-measure dimensions of the labor contract, for example, in wages. But they can also be realized in many not-so-easy-to-measure dimensions, for example, in greater work demands. Also, it is difficult to measure the potential effects, both positive and negative, of proposed mandates that have not been enacted. Nevertheless, a few empirical labor market studies have been undertaken that indicate the likely impact of any new mandates.[30]

Many states have mandated that if employers provide health insurance coverage the coverage must be relatively complete, including payment for services such as those provided by chiropractors and psychiatrists. Employers do not have the option of providing policies with limited coverage at a modest cost. In effect, employers must offer Cadillac health insurance policies or none at all. The effect of the growing array of mandates has pushed the cost of health insurance up, pricing perhaps as many as 9 million Americans out of the health insurance market.[31] In other words, perhaps a fourth of Americans without health insurance do not have coverage because of government mandates—a perverse, unintended effect of mandates.

While findings related to the impact of past mandates on the wages paid by private sector employers is mixed (with some studies showing negative effects and others positive effects), one study does show a one-for-one tradeoff of wages for mandates. That is to say, a 10 percent increase in the cost of a mandate leads to a comparable reduction in wages.[32] Another study found that an increase in the nonwage costs among targeted workers caused a shift in employment to areas not targeted,[33] which suggests that in the case of mandates for part-time workers, the demand for work will shift away from part-time workers. It also suggests that if "small" businesses are not covered by the mandates for part-time workers, then work will be shifted toward small firms who hire part-time workers (who will then hire more part-time workers), meaning that the coverage of the law will not be nearly as complete as proponents might think.

Mandating benefits can also encourage some employers to increase, albeit slightly, the number of hours of work by existing workers rather than hire additional workers.[34] Additional workers may increase a firm's costs for the benefits covered by the mandate, whereas additional hours may not. In other cases, the mandates for part-time workers will reduce the work demands of full-time workers simply because their firms will be forced to raise prices to accommodate higher production costs, thus diminishing their sales.

Other indirect effects have probably never been considered by the proponents of mandates. For instance, there will probably be a greater level of absenteeism among part-time workers because less of the worker's total income will be in wages. When more of their compensation is in the form of fringe benefits—the costs of which do not vary with the work performed—covered workers will have less incentive to report to work.[35] Employers of part-time workers will be in a better bargaining position, of course, due to work being more scarce. This implies that employers can force part-time workers to give up some of their flexibility with regard to the number and scheduling of hours worked.

There are two indirect empirical tests of the likely impact of mandated benefits for part-time workers. The first involves evidence on the effects of a historically important mandated benefit for low-wage/low skilled workers—minimum wage laws. The second is the recorded divergence over time of money wages from total compensation as fringe benefits have grown in importance.

Consider the second test, the impact of the increasing importance of fringe benefits in worker compensation packages. A number of economists, including Barry Bluestone and Bennett Harrison in one book and Robert Reich in another, have noted the widely recognized "U-turn" in average worker wages.[36] In arguing for increased income redistribution, these researchers stress that the real wages of nonsupervisory production workers in 1959 averaged $9.07 an hour in constant (1990) dollars. Real average wages rose by 26 percent over the next 13 years, reaching $11.60 in 1973. However, after 1973, real average wages began to fall precipitously, hitting $10.57 in 1980 and then $10.02 in 1990, resulting in a total percentage decline of 14 percent between 1973 and 1990.

Although not fully understood, the U-turn in average real wages was caused by many forces, not the least of which was the reduction in the economic clout of unions. The slowdown in productivity growth in the 1970s, the increased number of female and younger workers, the unexpected escalation in inflation rates, and the growth of service employment probably also played significant roles in reducing the average wage of workers (at the same time that many people were gaining in real wages).

However, a portion of the decline between 1973 and 1990 can be explained by the methodology used to compute the consumer price index (CPI) before 1983.[37] A portion of the decline in real worker wages in the 1970s is a statistical illusion. When a different index is applied to worker wages, the U-turn is not as pronounced. Real average wages did not peak until 1978, and then at $11.01, after which they began a less marked decline. The total decline between 1978 and 1990 was 9 percent.

A portion of this decline can also be explained by the growing importance of fringe benefits over the last two decades. As noted, between 1960 and 1990, total private supplements to pay (those fringes provided voluntarily by employers) and social supplements (those fringes required by law) increased from 9 percent to 20 percent of wages and salaries. After adjusting for inflation and the growth in wage and salary supplements, there is no apparent U-turn in real total compensation per hour.[38] Granted, the growth in wages and salaries slowed in the 1970s and 1980s. However, the slowdown can be partially attributed to workers' attempts to switch their compensation from taxed to nontaxed forms. Workers were earning more but taking a progressively larger portion of their pay in nontaxable forms, which implies that their spendable income was rising more rapidly than is suggested by the data.

It is not unreasonable to suggest that a portion of the slowed growth in wages was the result of federal legislation that increased employer payments for federal mandates, such as Social Security, Medicare, and unemployment insurance. Over the past three decades, mandated federal supplements doubled as a share of wages and salaries, rising from 3.2 percent of wages and salaries in 1960 to 7.6 percent of wages and salaries in 1990. During the 1970s and 1980s, government regulations intended to make work safer and to free the workplace from sexual and racial discrimination and harassment probably also took their toll on workers' wages.

The association of growth in mandated supplements with suppressed growth in money wages and salaries does not imply causation, but it does provide reasons for suspicion. If employers are forced to pay mandated contributions to the Social Security trust funds, fewer dollars are available for payment in cash or fringe benefits.

Moreover, several economists have shown empirically that the benefits of the minimum wage increase—a mandate in the form of cash—are offset by reductions in other benefits. One study found that, under the 1967 minimum wage hike, workers gained 32 cents per hour in money income but lost 41 cents per hour in training benefits—a net loss of 9 cents an hour in full-income compensation.[39] Another study came to a similar conclusion: Increases in the minimum wage reduce on-the-job training and, as a result, thwart growth in the real long-term income of covered workers.[40]

The flip side of this comes from another report that showed that the minimum wage caused retail establishments in New York to increase work demands on workers. Employees were given fewer hours to do the same work.[41] Three other researchers concluded that minimum wage increases lead to large reductions in fringe benefits and to worsening working conditions. Many New York stores reduced commission payments, eliminated year-end bonuses, and decreased paid vacations and sick leave. One of the researchers found that for every 1 percent increase in the minimum wage, restaurants reduced shift premiums by 3.6 percent, severance pay by 6.9 percent, and sick pay by 3.4 percent.[42]

If the minimum wage does not cause employers to make substantial reductions in nonmoney benefits, then increases in the minimum wage should make jobs more attractive. Hence, any increase in the minimum should result in an increase in the labor force participation rates of covered workers, a reduction in the rate at which covered workers quit their jobs, and a significant increase in prices of production processes that rely heavily on low-wage workers. However, Wessels found little empirical support for such conclusions. Indeed, in general, he found that minimum wage increases had the exact opposite effects: participation rates went down, quit rates went up, and prices did not rise appreciably—findings consistent only with the view that higher minimum wages make workers worse off. After reviewing a number of studies on the negative effects of the minimum wage, Wessels concluded that covered workers experienced a reduction in their total compensation of 2 percent for every 10 percent increase in the minimum wage.[43] Findings of such negative offsets to increases in the minimum wage help explain why economists have concluded that job losses are relatively minor. The offsetting reductions in fringe benefits and increased work demands minimize the increase in labor costs incurred by employers.[44]

The Growth in Contract Workers

Proponents of federally mandated benefits for part-time workers have extended their concern to so-called contract workers, those Americans who work for firms who in turn are under contract to provide a part or service to another firm. Representative Lantos acknowledged that contract work is a valuable source of income for many Americans. At the same time, he bemoaned the exploitation of such workers: "International competitiveness does not justify a major bank subcontracting its janitorial work to avoid unionization, nor is it a basis for a large office building management company to convert from a full-time janitorial work force to part-timers to cut wages and eliminate benefits."[45]

Whether international competitiveness justifies the actions cited is obviously more disputable than Mr. Lantos indicates, especially if the financial health, if not the company's basic survival, is at stake. Clearly, many firms out-source production of parts and services to firms under contract. Such interconnections among producers and suppliers are an integral component of American economic activity. Just as clearly, some of those firms who out-source do so to reduce labor costs (including the provision of fringe benefits) and materials costs.[46] However, this is hardly all bad. Indeed, there can be broad-based gains to the economy from such cost reduction, which is the principal justification for doing practically everything in business. Such competition from outside sources of supply may constrain the wage and fringe demands of many workers. However, such an argument from the proponents of mandated benefits bolstered the case against past mandates—and especially new mandates for part-time workers. Such mandates will force firms to seek alternative modes of production, which will generally mean that business will be driven to sectors of the economy not covered. It will also force the covered workers to make a trade of fringes for wages that they would not have freely chosen to make. (If they had been willing to make the trade voluntarily, because the fringes subject to mandate were worth their cost, then the mandate would not have been necessary.) Critics and researchers may view low-wage jobs with few fringe benefits as bad, but they may be considered very good jobs when the persons holding the jobs compare them to their next best alternative—jobs with more fringe benefits but even lower money wages.[47]

In addition, competition from all sources, inside and outside the country, is a powerful force that drives economic improvement, resulting in products that are produced at lower costs and sold in greater quantities at lower prices. Consumers gain, but so do the workers whose wage and fringe demands are constrained by the competition. They may receive lower wages and fewer benefits than otherwise because of the outside competition, but they gain indirectly from the lower priced goods and services that they can buy from the rest of the economy that is subject to the same competitive drive to lower costs and prices. Workers also gain indirectly because the overall competitive drive in the economy leads to greater American incomes and greater demand for goods and services.

Not all workers gain from the competitive market process. Having conceded that point, it does not follow that all workers lose just because of the potential competition from contract firms and their workers. Workers employed by contract firms obviously face a higher demand for their services than otherwise, and workers within firms that use out-sourcing also gain because their firms compete more successfully in both domestic and foreign markets.

Those who bemoan the rise of out-sourcing and contract work are tilting against the winds of technological and global change. Production is becoming more and more technical, sophisticated, and complicated. Managers cannot know enough to control all aspects of modern economic activity. They must delegate and decentralize many decision-making responsibilities. When they delegate, their problems multiply—specifically, problems of monitoring and maintaining cost-effective control over their workers and of preventing abuse of delegated authority by the employees granted the decision-making power. To deal with the growing complexity of producing products and managing a firm, many firms must concede some production to outside suppliers and then monitor and control their sources by competitive contract.

If the federal government impairs the trend toward out-sourcing and contracting-out in any way (for example, through mandated benefits for part-time workers), it will impair the ability of the affected firms to compete in the global economy. With every federal mandate that is passed, firms in other countries will acquire a competitive advantage over American firms.

Concluding Comments

Policymakers often harbor the delusion that the policies they adopt have the intended effect, more or less. This delusion is nowhere more apparent than in the contemporary political tussles over proposed legislation that would require employers to provide many of their employees (namely, part-time workers) with a variety of fringe benefits. Political fervor for labor policies that, if enacted, would play to this delusion reached new heights in the 1980s. However, few policy commentators, regardless of their stand on the issues, grasp the fact that politicians do not have as much control over worker welfare as is commonly thought, and the control they do have is fading in the intense light of the globalization of economic activity. As has been argued, government-required benefits would, indeed, make many of the targeted part-time American workers worse off, and the negative effects of the requirements are likely to grow with time. Before enacting such legislation, members of Congress should question whether they will be doing more harm than good. Theory and evidence, much of which was developed and refined in the 1980s, come together to suggest that mandated benefits for part-time workers will result in more harm than good.

Certainly, low-skilled and low-income workers deserve attention from policymakers and help from government. But the proposed legislation will, in fact, worsen the welfare of part-time workers, the exact opposite effect of the one intended. Surely the proponents of such legislation do not want to be held accountable for those consequences. These lawmakers can no longer simply wish their will on the progressively more competitive global economy of the 1990s.

Notes

1. As found in U.S Department of Commerce, *The Statistical Abstract of the United States: 1991* (Washington, DC: U.S. Government Printing Office, 1991), p. 418.

2. See Janet L. Norwood. Commissioner, Bureau of Labor Statistics, U.S. Department of Labor, a statement before the Employment and Housing Subcommittee, Government Operations Committee, House, U.S. Congress, May 19, 1988, pp. 4–7.

3. Opening remarks of Representative Tom Lantos, U.S. Congress, House, Employment and Housing Subcommittee of the Committee on Government Operations, *Hearings* (Washington, DC, May 19, 1988), pp. 1–2.

4. Ibid., remarks of Representative Joseph J. DioGuardi, p. 3.

5. Ibid., remarks of Representative Pat Schroeder, p. 4.

6. Ibid., p. 4.

7. Ibid.

8. Ibid., p. 5.

9. Ibid.

10. Ibid., p. 7.

11. Ibid., p. 8.

12. Ibid., p. 8.

13. Benjamin M. Friedman, *Day of Reckoning: The Consequences of American Economic Policy Under Reagan and After* (New York: Random House, 1988), p. 160. Friedman cites unspecified data from the Bureau of Labor Statistics, but apparently also relies on the work of Bennett Harrison and Barry Bluestone who, as will be seen, are also loose with their data sources.

14. Bennett Harrison and Barry Bluestone, *The Great U-Turn, Corporate Restructuring and the Polarizing of America* (New York: Basic Books, 1988), p. 47.

15. Harrison and Bluestone title one of their chapters "Zapping Labor" as a way of alerting readers to their theme that the supposed "great U-turn" in workers' wages could be attributed totally to the growing dominance of firms over labor, backed up by government policies (Ibid., chap. 2).

16. As reported in Norwood, a statement before the Employment and Housing Subcommittee, p. 5.

17. The benefits of part-time employment have been recognized in The Federal Employees Part-Time Career Employment Act of 1978,

enacted specifically "to provide increased part-time career employment opportunities throughout the federal government." *Part-Time Employment*, Federal Agencies' Part-Time Employment Programs, GGD-86-103BR, B-208025 (Washington, DC: Government Accounting Office, July 7, 1986), p. 3.

18. The part-time workers' share of the labor force in other industrial countries is hardly inconsequential, although a lower percentage than in the United States: Germany, under 13.6 percent; Japan and France, 12 percent; and Ireland, 10.2 percent. Overall, the part-time labor force in industrialized economies totalled 48 million in 1987, 35 million (or 73 percent) of whom were women. See Joseph E. Thurmond and Gabriele Trah, "Part-Time Work in International Perspective," *International Labor Review*, January/February 1990, p. 27.

19. For additional examples of how part-time and temporary workers increase productivity and reduce costs, see Audrey Freedman, a statement before the Employment and Housing Subcommittee, Government Committee on Operations, House, U.S. Congress, May 19, 1988, pp. 2–5.

20. The Labor Department keeps fairly accurate records of wages and fringe benefits. However, it does not even try to assess the extent of other employment-related benefits such as flexible scheduling, workplace amenities, and work demands.

21. As both proponents and opponents acknowledge, mandated benefits are costly (with the costs varying with the scope of the coverage and the details of the mandates). If they were not costly, benefits would be voluntarily provided by firms, meaning they would not have to be required. Even the greediest, most profit-concerned employers would provide workers with fringe or employment-related benefits if there were no attendant costs.

22. This line of analysis was initially and more fully developed in the context of the effects of minimum-wage increases on fringe benefits by Richard B. McKenzie, "The Labor Market Effects of the Minimum Wage," *Journal of Labor Research*, Fall 1980.

23. In effect, the mandates act like a head tax on labor that, as economists have long argued, drives a wedge between the labor cost to the employer and the payment received by the employee. This line of argument is developed by Marvin H. Kosters, "Mandated Benefits—On the Agenda," *Regulation*, no. 3, 1988, pp. 21–27; and Franke B. McArdle, "The Pressure for New Legislated Mandates," in *Government Mandating of Employee Benefits* (Washington, DC: Employee Benefit Research Institute, 1987).

24. Proponents of mandated benefits may respond by arguing that what

they really want is a simple redistribution of company funds from employers to targeted workers. But that cannot be if the proposals hike costs by more than the value of the benefits to workers and reduce the demand for workers. Logic suggests that the effect of the proposed mandates is far more negative: both employers and targeted employees lose from the mandates. The employers lose because they incur additional labor costs that are not offset fully by the reduction in other work-related benefits and wages. They also produce and sell less at the higher prices they must charge. The employees lose because they are forced to concede work-related benefits and wages that are worth more than those mandated by Congress. The real value of whatever wages they receive is also reduced by the higher prices charged for the goods and services they buy.

25. According to the Small Business Administration, the total cost of leave will be at least $1.2 billion a year, which means that the cost per employee who uses the leave can easily be several hundred dollars, a nontrivial amount for many workers and their firms [as reported by Paul Taylor, "Family-Leave Report Creates Commotion," *Washington Post*, April 15, 1991].

26. Lawrence H. Summers, "Some Simple Economics of Mandated Benefits," *American Economic Review* (May 1989), p. 178.

27. Milton Friedman, "Gammon's Law Points to Health-Care Solution," *Wall Street Journal*, November 12, 1991.

28. Lawrence Perlman, "Family Leave—It's Good Business," *Washington Post*, July 25, 1990.

29. There gain should be inversely proportional to how extensive the mandate is. The greater the cost and coverage of the mandate, the greater the improvement for the untargeted worker groups.

30. These studies are reviewed by Olivia S. Mitchell, *The Effects of Mandating Benefits Packages* (Cambridge, MA: National Bureau of Economic Research, working paper no. 3260, February 1990).

31. John C. Goodman and Gerald Musgrave, *Policy Report: Freedom of Choice in Health Care* (Dallas: National Center for Policy Analysis, November 1988).

32. R. G. Ehrenberg and R. S. Smith, "Who Pays for Pensions in the State and Local Sector: Workers or Employers?" *IRRA 32nd Annual Proceedings* (Madison, WI: IRRA, 1979).

33. See R. G. Ehrenberg, P. Rosenberg, and J. Li, "Part-Time Employment in the United States," in *Employment, Unemployment, and Labor Utilization*, edited by R.A. Hart (Boston: Unwin Hyman, 1988); and D. S. Hamermesh, "The Demand for Workers and Hours

and the Effects of Job Security Policies: Theories and Evidence," in *Employment, Unemployment, and Labor Utilization*, edited by R.A. Hart (Boston: Unwin Hyman, 1988).

34. Hamermesh, "The Demand for Workers and Hours and the Effects of Job Security Policies."

35. S. F. Allen, "Compensation, Safety and Absenteeism: Evidence from the Paper Industry," *Industrial and Labor Relations Review*, January 1981, pp. 207–218.

36. Harrison and Bluestone, *The Great U-Turn*; and Robert B. Reich, *The Work of Nations*, (New York: Alfred A. Knopf, 1991).

37. Because of the way housing costs were included in the CPI, inflation was exaggerated; and the greater the rate of inflation, the greater the exaggeration. Inflation began to take off in the 1970s, which meant that wages began to be deflated excessively [Richard B. McKenzie, *The Mythical "Great U-Turn" in Worker Wages* (St. Louis: Center for the Study of American Business, Washington University, 1989)]. See also Marvin H. Kosters, "The Measure of Measures," *The American Enterprise*, January/February 1991, pp. 58–65.

38. See McKenzie, *The Mythical "Great U-Turn" in Worker Wages.*

39. Masanori Hashimoto, "Minimum Wage Effect on Training to the Job," *American Economic Review*, December 1982, pp. 1070–1087.

40. Linda Leighton and Jacob Mincer, "Effects of Minimum Wages on Human Capital Formation," in *The Economics of Legal Minimum Wages*, edited by Simon Rothenberg (Washington, DC: American Enterprise Institute, 1981).

41. Walter J. Wessels, "Minimum Wages: Are Workers Really Better Off?" paper prepared for presentation at a conference on the minimum wage, Washington, DC, National Chamber Foundation, July 29, 1987).

42. Belton M. Fleisher, *Minimum Wage Regulation in Retail Trade* (Washington, DC: American Enterprise Institute, 1981); William T. Alpert, "The Effects of the Minimum Wage on the Fringe Benefits of Restaurant Workers" (Bethlehem, PA: Lehigh University, 1983); and L. F. Dunn, "Nonpecuniary Job Preferences and Welfare Losses among Migrant Agriculture Workers," *American Journal of Agriculture Economics*, May 1985, pp. 257–265.

43. Wessels, "Minimum Wages: Are Workers Really Better Off?"

44. The supporting graphical analysis of this new view of minimum wages is developed in greater detail in Richard B. McKenzie, *The Fairness of Markets* (Lexington, MA: Lexington Books, 1987), chap. 7.

45. Lantos, "Rising Use of Part-Time and Temporary Workers," p. 2.

46. See Chris Tilly, "Reasons for the Continuing Growth of Part-Time Employment," *Monthly Labor Review*, March 1991, pp. 10–17.

47. One labor department researcher does declare that the overwhelming majority of part-time jobs are indeed "bad" (her choice of words). One must wonder how she can make such a designation when she knows little of the workers' individual circumstances and knows nothing of their willingness to take fringe benefits for wages (see Tilly, "Reasons for the Continuing Growth of Part-Time Employment," p. 11).

8

THE REAGAN RECORD

Critics of the 1980s never get more exasperated than when discussing the policies of the Reagan administration. Ronald Reagan is credited with orchestrating the economic, political, and moral decline of the country. More specifically, critics charge that his free-market, militaristic policies—the center pieces of which, presumably, were tax cuts for the rich, broad expenditure cuts (except in defense), and deregulatory efforts—not only throttled economic growth, but also intentionally redirected the country's income away from the poor and the middle classes and toward the rich.

Philadelphia Inquirer reporters Donald Barlett and James Steele maintain that government fiscal policy during the 1980s had the intended effect of "dismantling the middle class" as well as causing practically everything else to go wrong in America.[1] Political analyst Kevin Phillips catalogued the various dimensions of the country's supposed economic malaise during the 1980s—which, as I have shown, was more a function of political rhetoric than of economic reality. Nevertheless, he insists that the "accelerating inequality under the Republicans was more often a policy objective than a coincidence."[2] Although Phillips at one point wrote that "free-market philosophy," not greed, guided the administration's policy actions,[3] he later sketched the tendency of Republicans to elevate "avarice" to a new form of "achievement."[4] He then concluded his reflections on political history, arguing

> What conservatives found difficult to admit, even by 1989, was that the capitalist exuberance of the 1980s—bolstered by a supportive culture and well-placed allies in Washington—had begun, inevitably, to create its own economic and social imbalances.... During the 1980s the bucket of liberty and economic freedom rose, while the bucket of income equality fell. Upper-tier Americans significantly expanded their share of national wealth while low-income citizens lost ground, and Reagan policies were critical to this shift.[5]

Harvard professor Benjamin Friedman can imagine only two alternatives for the origin of what were, in effect, Reagan's bankrupt fiscal policies, including mounting deficits despite presumed cuts in social welfare programs: "On the one construction, it was an intellectual error of the first magnitude. On the other, it was deliberate moral irresponsibility on a truly astonishing scale."[6]

What did Reagan do? Phillips and a host of other critics have told us that he slashed federal spending, especially on domestic programs (particularly those aiding the poor); he cut the taxes of the rich, shifting the federal tax burden off the shoulders of the rich and onto the backs of the poor and middle classes. At the same time, he managed to pile up federal debt, mainly because of the defense build-up and tax cuts for the rich, further crimping the ability of government to tend to the needs of the poor and to rebuild the nation's infrastructure. A major part of the problem was that Reagan had "doubled America's military budget in the first half of the 1980s."[7] The critics eagerly jumped on probably the most inane policy move of Reagan administrators as fully descriptive of the administration's fiscal approach to solving social problems—classifying ketchup as a vegetable to save a few dollars on federal support of school lunch programs.

From the tone of such commentaries, the Democratically controlled Congress had nothing to do with anything that went wrong in the 1980s. Reagan was an unmitigated curse on the country; his overwhelming victory in 1984 was something of an electoral fluke. The facts of the budget spoke for themselves. The country was being taken through fiscal hell in a free-market, no-government hand-basket—solely because of the uncanny power of one person to communicate effectively with an unwary public.

As has been the case with so many other claims about the 1980s, the Reagan fiscal record does not live down to its billing. A part of the problem is that the critics have played shrewd statistical games. For example, the claim that Reagan "doubled" the military budget is approximately true only if you assume that Reagan was responsible for the 1981 military budget, which had been passed by Congress before he took office, and then only if no adjustment is made for inflation. I will show that the increase was far more modest than claimed, although consequential.

Ronald Reagan simply did not have the impact on federal budget policies that his critics have claimed. Federal expenditures and taxes continued to rise in real dollar terms during the 1980s. The total federal tax burden covered by the "rich" rose during the decade. If he accomplished anything in getting "government off the backs of Americans," it was mainly in checking the growth of federal expenditures and taxes relative to national production. Federal income tax rates faced by the poor fell by more than the tax rates paid by the poor. Even then, as will be argued, the credit (if that is the appropriate term) should not be all Reagan's. Congress (both houses of which were controlled by Democrats for all of the 1980s, aside for two years) did have a hand in tax policy and the budget process.

Moreover, it may be more accurate to say that the Reagan presidency was more a product of the times than vice versa. The United States no longer exists in a governmental vacuum; its policies in the 1980s, if not before, had to be determined with an eye toward the policies adopted by other world governments with whom the United States had to compete more fiercely for the world's capital stock. That capital (in both physical and human forms) became progressively more fluid during the decade—far more able to jump governmental jurisdictions when cost and tax conditions required it to do so. Many of the fiscal and regulatory policies followed by the Reagan administration had to be enacted—because other countries were enacting similar policies. In fact, many of them would probably have been enacted had Jimmy Carter or any other Democrat been in office.

As is widely recognized, emergence of the global economy forced American firms to become competitive on a global scale. As is not so widely recognized, the global economy also forced governments, including the United States, to become more competitive vis-à-vis other world governments.[8] That meant that the country had to adjust its policies to account for policy adjustments in other countries. The tax reform, deregulation, and privatization policies that were the hallmark of the Reagan presidency were also hallmarks of government policies in most other industrial countries around the world across the ideological spectrum. Forces other than Reagan were at work on the governmental policy process in the 1980s; those forces remain active in the 1990s.

The Federal Budget

The data on federal outlays and taxes during the 1980s reveal growth in real dollar terms; the federal government was larger in absolute terms in 1990 than in 1980. For that matter, it was larger in absolute terms (by several hundred billions of real dollars) when Reagan left office in 1989 than when he assumed the presidency in 1981. Total federal spending averaged a higher percentage of GDP under Reagan than under Carter. Nevertheless, there was some slight downward trend in federal spending relative to the size of the national economy (measured in tenths of a percent per year) during the Reagan years. That is the important, but limited, extent to which Reagan actually "cut" (if the meaning of that term can be stretched) the size of government.

Outlays and Taxes in Constant Dollars[9]

Figures 8-1 and 8-2 show what actually happened to total federal outlays and receipts (which will be interchanged with "taxes," since taxes make up the overwhelming share of receipts). As is shown in figure 8-1, federal outlays in constant (1990) dollars rose by a third ($313 billion), from $939 billion in 1980 to $1,252 billion in 1990. The Reagan administration was responsible for the budget from 1982 to 1989.[10] Total outlays rose by 22 percent ($215 billion) in real dollar terms (or by two-thirds of the increase for the decade) during those years, from $979 billion in 1981 (the last Carter budget) to $1,194 in 1989 (the last Reagan budget). Given the criticisms about supposed budget cuts during the Reagan years, what may be surprising is that total federal outlays were slightly above the values predicted from the trend established in the 1970s. The Reagan budgets (1982–1989, averaging $1,107 billion in 1990 dollars) exceeded the Carter budgets (1977–1981, averaging $901 billion) by 23 percent.

As can be seen in figure 8-2, total federal receipts dipped in the early 1980s with the recession and, probably to a lesser extent, due to the effects of the 1981 tax cuts, but then increased markedly after 1983, reaching record levels by the mid-1980s. Indeed, total federal receipts expanded by 26 percent in real dollars between 1980 and 1990. Receipts totaled $822 billion in 1980 and $1,031 in 1990, an increase of $209 billion. During the 1980s, receipts oscillated around the upward trend charted in the 1970s, but were above the trend by the late 1980s. Receipts under the eight Reagan budgets rose in real dollars by $189 billion, or by 19 percent (equaling 73 percent of the percentage increase in receipts for the decade). The Reagan receipts, averaging $898 billion, were 13 percent above the receipts under the four Carter budgets, averaging $797 billion.

The most important finding is that the size of the federal government, whether measured by outlays or receipts, did not contract during the 1980s. Indeed, it increased significantly in actual command over resources.

Figure 8-1 Total Federal Outlays, Actual and Predicted from 1970–80 Trend

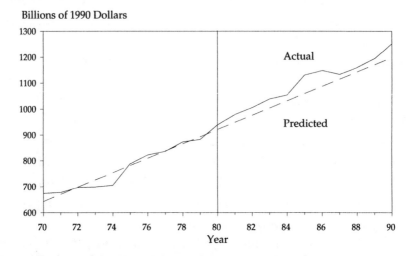

Source: Budget of the United States Government: Supplement, February 1992 (Historical Tables); and author's calculations.

Figure 8-2 Total Federal Receipts, Actual and Predicted from 1970–1980 Trend

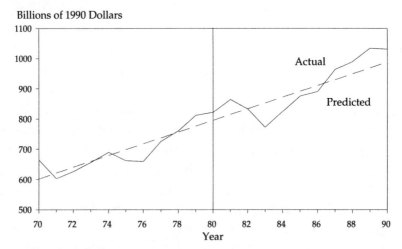

Source: Budget of the United States Government: Supplement, February 1992 (Historical Tables); and author's calculations.

Relative Outlays and Receipts

If there was any significant change in budget policy during the 1980s, it was in the trend of federal outlays and receipts relative to national production. Outlays and receipts as a percentage of gross domestic product (GDP) had been rising more or less steadily since at least World War II. Figure 8-3 shows that the upward trend was probably broken and possibly capped in the 1980s. In 1970, total federal outlays represented just under 20 percentage of GDP. By 1983, total outlays reached 24.4 percent, the peak for the decade. Then, outlays fell as a percentage of GDP and stayed under 23 percent through 1990.

On the other hand, it must be stressed that federal outlays represented a greater share of GDP in 1990 (22.9 percent) than in 1980 (22.3 percent). Outlays as a share of GDP in 1989, 22.1 percent under the last Reagan budget, were just .8 of a percentage point below the share in 1981, 22.9 percent under the last Carter/Reagan budget.

Figure 8-3 Federal Outlays and Receipts as a Percentage of Gross Domestic Product, 1970–1990

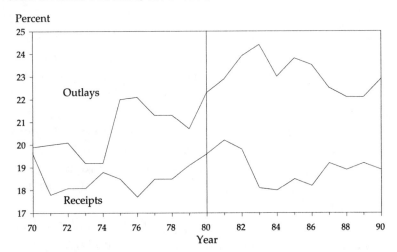

Source: Budget of the United States Government: Supplement, February 1992 (Historical Tables); and author's calculations.

Total receipts as a percentage of GDP peaked in 1981 at 20.2 percent, only to fall to 18 percent in 1984 and then rise to 19.2 percent three years later. In 1990, receipts represented 18.9 percent of GDP.

How much were federal taxes cut? On balance, the reduction was not nearly as great as may have been thought, given the ferocity of the criticisms. Relative to the national economy, the reduction was only .7 of a percentage point over the decade, from 19.6 percent in 1980 to 18.9 percent in 1990, and then there were a couple of years during the late 1980s when the share reached 19.2 percent. Moreover, although critics may disdain the thought, the slight reduction in share may be attributable, at least in part, to the fact that tax rate reductions in the 1981 and 1986 tax bills may have stimulated the economy, increasing revenues in real dollars but reducing revenues as a share of income. The debate over the efficacy of tax policy in the 1980s has hardly been settled at this juncture. The critics are not necessarily correct when they claim that tax policies reduced tax collections—just because the overall average income tax rate was cut and because tax revenues may have fallen slightly as a percentage of income.

Defense Spending

The critics are right on one score. Defense spending rose substantially during the 1980s, a point that is self-evident in figure 8-4. In the 1980s, defense spending rose in real dollars by 41 percent, or by $86 billion, from $213 billion in 1980 to $299 billion in 1990 (after peaking at $318 billion in 1987). But the defense buildup did not begin with Reagan, a point that is also clear in the figure; rather, it began with Carter after 1978. Carter raised defense spending by 14 percent between 1977 and 1981. The increase in the defense budget under Reagan was almost 40 percent, from $227 billion in 1981 to $317 billion in 1989.

Critics of the 1980s often suggest that the defense buildup continued throughout the decade and, accordingly, progressively crippled the economy and curbed the growth of nondefense spending. That is obviously not the case. Figure 8-4 shows that defense

Figure 8-4   Federal Defense Outlays, 1970–1990

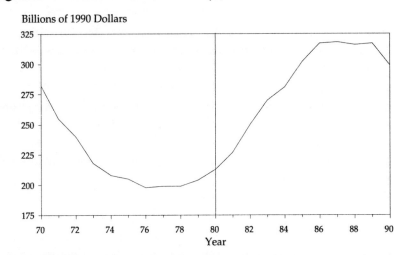

Billions of 1990 Dollars

Source: Budget of the United States Government: Supplement, February 1992 (Historical Tables); and author's calculations.

spending leveled off after 1985 and actually decreased in 1990 by close to 6 percent. Relatively speaking, defense spending rose from 5.1 percent of GDP in 1980 to 5.9 percent in 1982, peaked at 6.5 percent in 1986, and then fell, returning to 5.5 percent in 1990. Since total real spending rose throughout the decade and declined little relative to national production, it follows that there must have been some growth in some nondefense area of government.

Was the defense buildup truly the horrific burden on the American economy the critics claim? Perhaps in one sense it was: More resources were diverted from investment and from pursuit of other social programs. Given the rapidity of the buildup, a great deal of waste probably resulted in the actual preparedness of the defense establishment rising. As a consequence, the country was probably poorer than it could otherwise have been.

That is, however, a short-run perspective. It is not unreasonable to argue that the buildup contributed to the downfall of the Soviet Union. The U.S. defense buildup confronted Soviet leaders with a challenge—the prospects of an arms race at an unprecedented peacetime level that would impose such high costs on their economy that they could not effectively compete. Seen from this perspective, the defense buildup of the 1980s has yielded peace dividends for the 1990s, which converts to a chance to divert resources away from defense and toward investment and the pursuit of other social programs. Critics of the 1980s may not find these thoughts congenial. Nonetheless, they are thoughts that were central to the "new thinking" of Mikhail Gorbachev and other Soviet leaders.[11] In short, total defense spending for the entire 1980s and 1990s (and beyond) could be lower than it would have been had defense spending not been increased significantly in the 1980s.

Nondefense Outlays

The critics are probably correct that the increases in defense spending and the greater interest payments that the growing federal debt required during the 1980s reduced federal expenditures on nondefense spending. However, they are wrong to deduce that the total of outlays minus defense and net interest actually declined. As shown in figure 8-5, the total of "other" outlays (all federal outlays other than defense and net interest) actually rose, albeit at a reduced pace, between 1980 and 1990. Indeed, other outlays rose from $642 billion in 1980 to $768 billion in 1990, or by almost 20 percent after adjusting for inflation. During the Reagan budgets, the other outlays rose by 9 percent (in 1990 dollars). That small increase is only notable because it stands in sharp contrast to claims of actual real dollar decline.

Social Security could have accounted for the increase, and actually did during the Reagan years. Figure 8-6 reports others outlays (as in figure 8-5) minus Social Security payments. Still, this measure of other outlays in 1990, $520 billion, was 14.5 percent above the level of 1980, $454 billion. However, as is evident in the figure, this measure of other outlays was below the 1980 level in every year between 1980 and 1989. On average, the 1981–1988 budgets were $19 billion, or 4.2 percent below, the 1980 level. Does this imply cuts in welfare spending? I will show that the answer is clear, No!—mainly because cuts occurred elsewhere in the budget.

Figure 8-5 Federal Outlays Minus Defense and Net Interest, 1970–1990

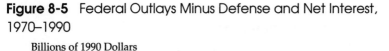

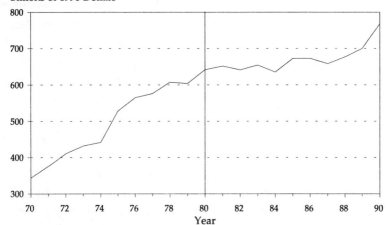

Source: Budget of the United States Government: Supplement, February 1992 (Historical Tables); and author's calculations.

Figure 8-6 Federal Outlays Minus Defense, Net Interest, and Social Security, 1970–1990

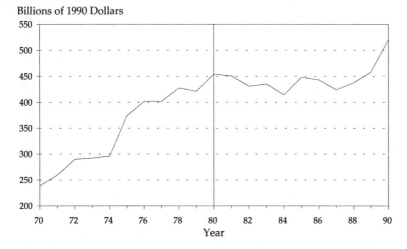

Source: Budget of the United States Government: Supplement, February 1992 (Historical Tables); and author's calculations.

Nondefense Public Investment
and Research and Development

As is evident in figures 8-7, 8-8, and 8-9, the outlay cuts were centered on three areas: major nondefense public physical investment (roads, bridges, and airports), research and development, and grants to state and local governments. Nondefense public physical investment (via direct outlays or grants) fell by almost 20 percent, from $48.5 billion in 1980 to $40.9 billion in 1990. Federal nondefense spending on research and development was close to $22.5 billion in both 1980 and 1990, but figure 8-8 reveals a sharp decline in these outlays during most years in the 1980s. Similarly, outlays for grants to state and local governments in 1990, $135 billion, were only 7 percent below their 1980 level, $145 billion. But that small decline hides the initial significant drop in such outlays in the first few Reagan budget years.

Figure 8-7   Federal Outlays in Major Nondefense Public Physical Investment, 1970–1990

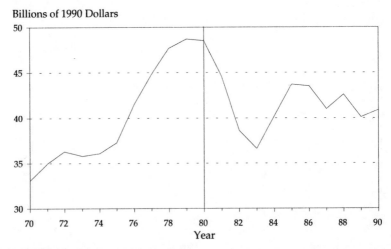

Note: Outlays include direct and grants.
Source: Budget of the United States Government: Supplement, February 1992 (Historical Tables), p. 108; and author's calculations.

Figure 8-8 Federal Outlays for Nondefense Research and Development, 1970–1990

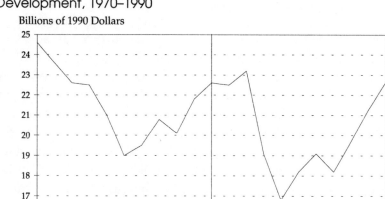

Billions of 1990 Dollars

Source: Budget of the United States Government: Supplement, February 1992 (Historical Tables), p. 127; and author's calculations.

Figure 8-9 Federal Outlays for Grants to State and Local Governments, 1970–1990

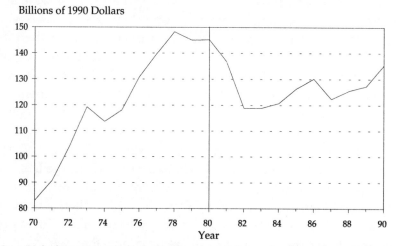

Billions of 1990 Dollars

Note: Includes payments for individuals, capital investment, and remainder.
Source: Budget of the United States Government: Supplement, February 1992 (Historical Tables), pp. 164–165; and author's calculations.

If there are grounds for criticism of the Reagan programs, it is in these areas, but criticism must be tempered somewhat by the prospects that some of the drop in nondefense expenditures could have been offset by increases in military expenditures. In addition, about half of the decline in physical investment expenditures was in lower expenditures on water (reduced by 17 percent between 1980 and 1990) and on community and regional development projects (cut by 52 percent). Both of these budget areas came under serious criticism during the 1980s. There were concerns that the country did not need to dam any more of its free-flowing rivers, and many of the community and regional development projects were viewed as being filled with nothing more than Washington "pork." Federal grants for transportation stagnated during the decade, but the debate over whether paving more of the country's acreage would contribute to growth has continued into the 1990s.[12]

Payments to Individuals

During the 1980s, real federal outlays were not just shifted from nondefense to defense, interest, and Social Security; they were also shifted from buying things to paying people. Figure 8-10 shows what happened to payments to individuals for purposes other than defense and Social Security. These payments rose significantly, from $254 billion in 1980 to $336 billion in 1990, or by close to a third in real terms. On balance, non-Social Security federal payments to individuals averaged 22 percent higher in the Reagan years than in the Carter years.

Did social welfare programs suffer during the Reagan era? The figures on total payments to individuals cast doubt on the fear that the welfare net was pulled from under the most needy. In fact, contrary to what may be surmised from the critics' claims, between 1981 and 1989 several key social programs prospered. Other programs did not grow, and a few welfare programs that help children and families contracted. On balance, growth was evident in welfare benefits. Consider table 8-1, which itemizes the federal expenditures on thirty-eight federal programs that target children and families and then gives the changes in constant 1989 dollars and in percentages between 1981 and 1989, the end years for the Reagan budgets. The most notable is that expenditures on twenty-three of the programs expanded, and only ten declined by more than 5 percent. Of these ten, three of the large percentage declines were in block grants to state and local governments, which were often offset by increases in other programs. Overall, total real dollars on all children/family programs combined expanded by $19 billion and by 18 percent. This was during the same period that the country's population expanded by 10 percent and the number of poor people declined by 300,000 (or 1 percent), falling from 31.8 million in 1981 to 31.5 million in 1989 (after peaking at 35.3 million in 1985).[13]

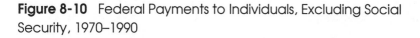

Figure 8-10 Federal Payments to Individuals, Excluding Social Security, 1970–1990

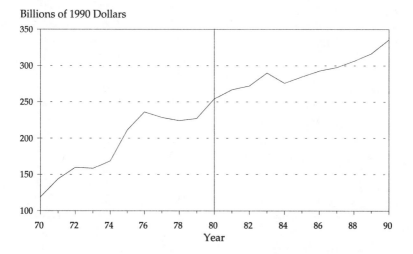

Note: Federal payments includes direct federal and grants to states and local governments for payments to individuals.
Source: Budget of the United States Government: Supplement, February 1992 (Historical Tables), pp. 135–136; and author's calculations.

Table 8-1 Real Spending on Programs that Include Children and Families, 1981 and 1989

	Year		Change	
Spending Program	1981	1989	In $	In %
AFDC	9,112	9,000	-112	-1
EITC	2,661	5,368	2,707	102
Child Support Enforcement	588	941	353	60
Supplemental Security Income	8,676	11,300	2,724	32
Social Security Dependents	15,410	11,000	-4,410	-29
Military Survivors	441	804	363	82
Workers' Compensation—Federal	840	988	148	18
Black Lung	2,144	1,400	-744	-35
Income Support Subtotal	39,772	40,801	1,029	3
Food Stamps	10,988	10,300	-688	-6
School Lunch	3,216	3,100	-116	-4
School Breakfast	430	510	80	19
Child Care Food	390	669	279	72
Commodity Assistance	847	530	-317	-37
Women, Infants, and Children	1,206	1,900	694	58
Nutrition Subtotal	17,077	17,009	-68	0
Social Services Block	4,020	2,700	1,320	-33
Dependent Care Credit	1,260	3,500	2,240	178
Head Start	1,072	1,200	128	12
Foster Care	407	1,023	616	151
Community Services Block	705	381	-324	-46
Social Services Subtotal	**7,464**	**8,804**	**1,340**	**18**
Education of Disadvantaged	3,484	4,000	516	15
Education Block Grant	686	463	-223	-33
Handicapped Education	1,182	1,475	303	26
Vocational Education	820	826	6	1
Impact Aid	914	733	-181	-20
Defense Schools	512	821	309	60
Training Disadvantaged	2,814	1,800	-1,014	-36
Job Corps	752	742	-10	-1
Summer Youth Training	1,124	709	-415	-37
Education/Training Subtotal	12,278	11,569	-709	-6
Medicaid	5,494	7,700	2,206	40
Maternal and Child Block	519	554	35	7
Community Health Centers	434	415	-19	-4

Table 8-1 Real Spending on Programs that Include Children and Families, 1981 and 1989 *(continued)*

| | Year | | Change | |
Spending Program	1981	1989	In $	In %
Alcohol, Drug Abuse Block	695	806	111	16
Indian Health	925	1,081	156	2
Federal Employees	3,350	7,800	4,450	133
Military Health	7,638	12,700	5,062	66
Health Subtotal	19,055	31,056	12,001	63
Public Housing	3,216	3,200	-16	-1
Leased	4,154	9,800	5,646	136
Rental	891	626	-265	-30
Housing Subtotal	**8,261**	**13,626**	**5,365**	**65**
Grand Total	**103,907**	**122,865**	**18,958**	**18**

Note: Figures are in millions of constant 1989 dollars. Does not include unemployment compensation or Cuban/Haitian refugee assistance or programs with funding less than $500 million.

Source: S. L. House, *Federal Program for Children and Their Families* (90-101-EPW), Washington, DC: Congressional Research Service, 1990), pp. 25–29; as cited in House Wednesday Group, U.S. Congress, *Moving Ahead: Initiatives for Expanding Opportunities in America*, October 22, 1991, p. 6.

Between 1981 and 1989, Aid to Families with Dependent Children declined by 1 percent, and food stamps and school lunch programs declined by 6 percent and 4 percent, respectively. At the same time, total income and nutrition support stayed more or less constant. Furthermore, dependent-care credit expanded by 178 percent; head start increased by 12 percent; and foster care expanded by 151 percent. And, it must be stressed that a goal of the administration was to relate federal benefits to work and earnings, which was partially achieved by expanding the earned-income tax credit (listed as EITC in table 8-1), which rose 102 percent. Moreover, there were more poor Americans in the mid-1980s, which caused some temporary dilution of federal aid, but one fact stands out: There was no wholesale destruction of the federal safety net during the 1980s.

Finally, in evaluating the shifting federal expenditures on welfare, it must be remembered that when Reagan came into office (even long before) many welfare programs were under severe criticism for being misguided and ineffective. Even so-called liberal commentators recognized welfare failures. For example *New Republic* senior editor Mickey Kaus acknowledged, after a stint in the Carter administration:

> *From there I had watched as the best minds of the Democratic party ran the liberal enterprise into the ground. They had put liberalism on the side of welfare rather than work. They funded housing projects that were among the most hellish places on earth. They defended absurd extensions of criminals' rights. They funneled billions to big-city mayors who gave the money to developers who build hideous, bankrupt downtown malls. They let the teacher's union run the education department and the construction unions run the labor department. I hadn't wanted Reagan to win; I'd voted for Carter without hesitation. But as I waited for Carter to show up [in a Washington hotel ballroom to announce his defeat], and looked up at the outgoing Democratic officials gathered at the stage, I realized there was not one of those people I wasn't happy to see go.*[14]

Nevertheless, critics do not seem able to consider that the reorganization of welfare spending may have been for the benefit of most poor people, or that various programs have differing effects on reducing poverty and that some reorganization of benefits could actually lower the poverty rate. Instead, critics continue to focus on the cuts, as if they were not part and parcel of real-life political bargains that involved increases elsewhere.

Nonetheless, recent research has revealed a commonsense policy position: Not all social welfare policies are created equally, and not all have the same effect.[15] According to the Joint Economic Committee in Congress, the earned-income tax credit—which does reward low-income workers and which was substantially expanded under Reagan—had a far more positive impact on poverty relief during the 1980s than did other programs. Specifically, the committee concluded that an additional billion dollars of earned-income tax credit reduced the poverty count by 258,000—at a cost of $3,870 per person removed from poverty. An additional billion dollars spent on Medicare and Medicaid removed, respectively, only 5,400 and 10,800 people from the poverty rolls, at a cost, respectively, of $185,000 and $93,000 per person. Changes in federal expenditures on other welfare programs did not have a statistically significant impact on the poverty rate, a fact that suggests that the redirection of welfare aid away from many means-tested programs toward the earned-income tax credit was socially productive.[16] Perhaps the most important criticism that can be leveled against Reagan's policies is that Reagan (and Congress) did not do enough to shift welfare expenditures from conventional means-tested welfare programs to work-related programs like the earned-income tax credit.

Total Government Spending

Total expenditures of all levels of government—federal, state, and local—continued to rise during the 1980s. Per capita total government expenditures in constant (1990) dollars rose by 28 percent, from $6,741 in 1980 to $8,641 in 1990.

Indeed, total government expenditures in constant dollars rose faster than the economy between 1980 and 1990. This means that total government spending represented a higher percentage of GDP in 1990, 33.1 percent, than it did in 1980, 31.5 percent (see figure 8-11). At the same time, total government spending was only slightly higher in 1989, 32 percent, than in 1981, 31.9 percent (the last Carter budget). Total government spending rose to a peak of 33.8 in 1983, but the rise in 1982 and 1983 was, to a significant extent, a reflection of the 1981–1982 recession. On balance, total government spending during the Reagan presidency averaged 32.7 percent of GDP, a 6 percent higher share than during the Carter presidency, 30.9 percent.

Federal Tax Policies

Escalating rates of inflation during the 1960s and 1970s gave rise to progressive "bracket creep," a rise in the marginal tax rates without

Figure 8-11 Total Government Expenditures as a Percentage of Gross Domestic Product, 1970–1990

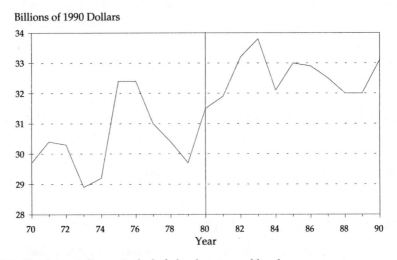

Billions of 1990 Dollars

Note: Total expenditures include federal, state, and local governments.
Source: Budget of the United States Government: Supplement, February 1992 (Historical Tables), p. 217.

any special tax legislation being enacted. Indeed, the average American's marginal tax rate rose from the low 20 percent range in the 1960s to the low 40 percent range by the start of the 1980s. One of Reagan's first fiscal initiatives was to propose a reduction in the marginal tax rates—a move grounded in the supply-side theory that lower marginal rates would encourage growth. Congress passed a series of three annual reductions in tax rates in 1981, supposedly totalling a 25 percent reduction in marginal rates, which included dropping the top marginal rate from 70 to 50 percent by 1984. However, because the new tax law did not index tax rates to inflation, commentators of the period figured that the reduction would merely offset "98 percent of the [expected] bracket creep" that had come with the escalating inflation rates in the 1970s and early 1980s.[17] Nevertheless, fearful of increasing the deficit, the Congress and the Reagan administration returned in 1982 with a tax increase (in the form of the Tax Equity and Fiscal Responsibility Act) of more than $100 billion and again in 1984 with another tax increase (in the form of the Deficit Reduction Act) that proposed to reduce the deficit with yet another tax increase—legislation that had to mute the effects of the 1981 tax act.

Nevertheless, in 1986, a fourth major tax bill was passed (the Tax Reform Act), the effect of which was to lower the marginal rates further (including dropping the top marginal rate from 50 percent to 28 percent). At the same time, this new law broadened the tax base through elimination of so-called loopholes (which critics rarely mention but that had the effect of increasing the tax burden of high-income earners by an estimated $227 billion[18]) while it shifted the tax burden from individuals to corporations through repeal of the accelerated depreciation and investment tax credits, central features of the 1981 law.[19]

Because of media attention to the decline in the top marginal rates, which fell by 60 percent from a high in 1980 to a low in 1986, critics have concluded that the tax burden was greatly reduced for the rich. This is the case, however, only when comparing tax payments under the new laws with what various income groups would have paid under the old tax laws if they had remained in force throughout the 1980s—and if incomes had continued upward, as they did with the tax rate changes.

For example, *Philadelphia Inquirer* reporters Barlett and Steele make a great deal of the fact that the 1986 Tax Reform Act had lowered the taxes of those with less than $10,000 of income by an average of only 11 percent (or $37), whereas it had lowered the taxes of those with incomes between $500,000 and $1 million by an average of 34 percent (or $86,084). It had also lowered the taxes of taxpayers with more than $1 million in income by an average of 31 percent (or $281,033).[20] From such statistics has grown the myth that the rich paid fewer taxes at the end of the 1990s than at the start and that the burden of federal taxes had been effectively shifted to the shoulders of the middle class and the poor.

While there is no doubt that the federal tax burden of some low-income taxpayers was raised significantly during the 1980s and

the burden of some high-income taxpayers was lowered significantly, data on the net effect of *all* tax policy changes adopted during
the 1980s (even the data organized by congressional Democrats
concerned about the welfare of the lower income groups) does not
support the sweeping class-based conclusions that have been drawn.

Consider table 8-2, which contains the effective average tax
rates (including all forms of federal taxes) for families divided into
income classes. It shows an increase in the average tax rate for people
in the lowest income group from 8.1 percent in 1980 to 9.3 percent in
1989 (the last year of available data). The tax changes in the 1980s
had the effect of returning the lowest quintile's average tax rate to
the level of 1977 (after hitting a high of 10.3 percent in 1985).

The critics are correct when they conclude that the tax burden
on the poor was increased, although they probably exaggerate the
extent of the increase. However, it must be noted that the greater
percentage rate is not attributable to changes in the federal personal
and corporate income tax rates. On the contrary, the lowest quintile's
average federal income tax rate fell from -.5 percent in 1980 (because
of the earned-income tax credit) to -1.8 percent in 1989. Federal
corporate income taxes had the effect of taking (through higher
prices and lower wages) an estimated 1.3 percent of the lowest
quintile's income in 1980 and 1.1 percent of the group's average
income in 1990.[21]

Table 8-2 Total Federal Tax Rates for Families for Selected Years

Quintile	1977	1980	1985	1988	1989
Lowest	9.3	8.1	10.3	9.3	9.3
Second	15.4	15.6	15.8	15.9	15.7
Middle	19.5	19.8	19.1	19.8	19.4
Fourth	21.8	22.9	21.7	22.4	22.0
Highest	27.2	27.5	24.1	26.0	25.6
Overall	22.8	23.3	21.7	22.9	22.6

Source: U.S. Congress, Committee on Ways and Means, *1992 Green Book*
(Washington, DC: U.S. Government Printing Office, May 15, 1992),
p. 1526.

The real hardship for the lower income groups, if there was one, was the increase in Social Security taxes, which raised the tax rate of the lowest quintile from an average of 5.6 percent in 1980 to an average of 7.6 percent in 1989.[22] But lower income taxpayers get a disproportionate amount of Social Security benefits, which explains why they are required to pay the taxes.[23] Any increase in Social Security taxes should not be blamed on Reagan. If he had had his way, Reagan probably would have reduced benefits and taxes for everyone, which he initially tried to do, albeit timidly (given the force of elderly interest groups).[24]

Furthermore, it must be remembered that not everyone in the lowest quintile is poor. People are often in the lowest quintile for a short period of time, and others have sources of support that are not reported as income. The estimated average tax burden of Americans at the poverty-income threshold (covering only federal income and payroll taxes) actually fell significantly during the 1980s—at least as estimated by the staff of Democrats on the House Ways and Means Committee.[25]

The tax burden in constant (1990) dollars of one-person families at the poverty threshold changed little in the 1980s; the burden was $714 in 1982 and $712 in 1990 (the first and last years of available data for the 1980s). However, the real tax burden of larger families at the poverty income threshold fell substantially. The average burden of two-person families fell from $710 in 1982 to $651 dollars in 1990, or by 8 percent. The real tax burden of three-person families fell by almost 75 percent, from $1,275 in 1982 to $331 in 1990. The real tax burden of six-person families at the poverty threshold declined by 39 percent, from $1,858 in 1982 to $1,136 in 1990. The average tax rates faced by all family sizes at the poverty threshold declined markedly.[26]

Table 8-2 also shows that between 1980 and 1989 the actual shifts in the average tax rates of the other income classes, aside from the top quintile, were relatively minor. The average tax rate of the top group declined from 27.5 percent in 1980 to 25.6 percent in 1989, a decline in rate of 7 percent.

Does this mean that the rich paid fewer federal taxes at the end of the 1980s than at the start? Not really. Average rates can fall from increases in earned and reported incomes just as they can fall from changes in the statutory rates. Also, at the same time rates were lowered in 1986, the taxable income base was expanded, mainly by elimination of loopholes that when they were available, tended to benefit the higher income groups. We have already noted that total federal tax collections in real dollars continued to rise during the decade. The question critics often overlook is, Who actually paid the taxes?

Table 8-3 answers that question with some surprising results. The actual share of all federal taxes paid by the higher income groups went up, while the share of the lower income groups went down. The share of taxes paid by the lowest quintile fell slightly from 1.6 percent in 1980 to 1.5 percent in 1989 (after peaking at 1.8 percent in 1985). The share of the second quintile went from 6.9 percent in 1980 to 6.4 percent in 1989. The share of all federal taxes paid by the highest quintile rose from 56.1 percent in 1980 to 58.6 percent in 1989. Similarly, the share of taxes paid by the top 10 percent rose from 39 percent in 1980 to 42 percent in 1989; the top 5 percent, from 27.3 to 30.4 percent; and the top 1 percent, from 12.9 to 15.4 percent.

Table 8-3 Shares of Total Federal Taxes Paid by All Families for Selected Years

Quintiles	1977	1980	1985	1988	1989
Lowest	2.0	1.6	1.8	1.5	1.5
Second	7.2	6.9	6.8	6.2	6.4
Middle	13.4	13.2	13.0	12.5	12.5
Fourth	21.6	22.2	22.0	20.8	20.8
Highest	55.7	56.1	56.1	58.9	58.6
Top 10 percent	39.0	39.0	39.2	42.5	42.0
Top 5 percent	27.7	27.3	27.3	30.9	30.4
Top 1 percent	13.6	12.9	13.3	15.9	15.4

Source: U.S. Congress, Committee on Ways and Means, *1992 Green Book* (Washington, DC: U.S. Government Printing Office, May 15, 1992), p. 1528.

55 ↑ a lot.

Table 8-4 Percentage of Federal Income Taxes Paid by Various
Income Groups, 1981–1988

			Income Group		
Year	Top 1%	Top 5%	51st-95th Percentile	Bottom 50%	Burden Ratio*
1981	18	35	57	8	118
1982	19	36	56	7	129
1983	20	37	56	7	142
1984	21	38	55	7	143
1985	22	39	54	7	152
1986	25	42	52	7	191
1987	25	43	51	6	202
1988	28	46	49	6	240

Note: Based on IRS tax return data; income data is for families.
*Computed by dividing the average tax paid by families in the upper 1 percent
by the average tax paid by families in the bottom 50 percent.

Source: C. Frense, _The Federal Income Tax Burden, 1981–1987: A Senate Staff
Report,_ Washington, DC: Joint Economic Committee, Republican Staff,
1990.

Taken by itself, the actual share of federal income taxes paid by
the top income groups rose even more dramatically during the 1980s.
As is evident in table 8-4, the share of the top 1 percent rose by a
remarkable 56 percent between 1981 and 1988, from 18 percent in
1981 to 28 percent in 1988. The share of the top 5 percent rose by 31
percent, from 35 percent in 1981 to 46 percent in 1988. The share paid
by the bottom 50 percent of the population fell by 25 percent, from
the already low level of 8 percent in 1981 to 6 percent in 1988. In 1981,
the average tax burden of the top 1 percent of families was 118 times
the average tax burden of the lowest quintile. By 1988, the multiple
had more than doubled to 240.

Some of the increase in tax share paid by the higher income
groups is, no doubt, attributable to the relatively more rapid increase
in the incomes of higher income families. However, some of the rise

in income of the higher groups is attributable to the upward mobility of families. Of course, it's not possible to know how much of the increased income of the higher income groups was caused by the incentives incorporated in the tax code changes made during the 1980s that stimulated taxpayers to earn more income and to report more of what they earned. What is clear from the data is that the poor and the middle class did not suffer under a heavier share of the federal tax burden. In 1980, the top quintile's share of all federal taxes was 35 times the lowest quintile's share. By 1989, the top quintile's share had risen to 39 times the lowest quintile's share.

Part of the explanation for these changes is that the actual rates of the lower income groups were lowered more than were the rates of higher income groups. Consider table 8-5, which compares the federal income tax rates families in the different quintiles will pay on their 1992 incomes, given current tax laws, with what they would have paid if the 1980 tax laws had not been changed. Again, the results are surprising. The tax rates were lowered for every quintile.

Table 8-5 Effective Federal Income Tax Rates in 1992 Under 1980 and 1992 Tax Laws

Income Group	Effective Tax Rate Under 1980 Tax Law	Under 1992 Tax Law	% Difference 1980 &1992
Lowest Quintile	1.7	-2.8	-263.6
Second Quintile	7.3	2.6	-64.1
Middle Quintile	11.7	6.3	-46.3
Fourth Quintile	15.6	8.7	-44.2
Highest Quintile	25.2	16.3	-35.2
Top 1 Percent	33.9	23.7	-30.2
Average	18.9	11.5	-39.5

Note: Incomes are projected for 1992 by the Congressional Budget Office tax model; families with zero or negative incomes are excluded from this bottom quintile.

Source: Congressional Budget Office.

Moreover, the rates were lowered less for the higher income groups than for the lower income groups. The tax rates for the lowest quintile fell by 264 percent, while the average tax rate for the highest group fell by 35 percent. The average tax rates of the top 1 percent fell by 30 percent. Of course, the analysis does not account for the increase in Social Security taxes, but it does undercut the myth that federal income tax rates for the rich were cut more than the rates for the poor. In short, the income tax code changes were progressive.

The Reagan Effect

Did the Reagan administration cut the federal budget? The answer is—remarkably—both yes and no (which may explain why liberals and conservatives both have complained about what Ronald Reagan did and did not accomplish). The answer is yes in the sense that total federal expenditures during the 1980s were probably less than they would have been had Carter continued in office. How much the budget was curbed from the levels that would have been achieved under Carter is anybody's guess. Carter probably would not have continued to increase the budget by as much as he did during his first four years and certainly not as much as he had planned in his last budget proposal. He also probably would have continued to shift resources from nondefense to defense purposes, given the remaining Soviet threat and the growing concern in the country that defense spending had declined too rapidly. As noted, Carter had begun to raise defense spending before his defeat.

The answer is also no in the sense that total real federal outlays and real federal per capita outlays continued to mount during the 1980s. Total federal outlays averaged 23 percent of GDP in the 1980s, 11 percent higher than the average share of GDP in the 1970s (20.7 percent). They averaged a 7 percent greater share of GDP during the Reagan presidency (23.2 percent) than during the Carter presidency (21.7 percent). I have noted that all levels of government were spending more in real terms and relative to GDP in the 1980s under Reagan than in the 1970s under Carter.

What Reagan did, with the approval of Congress, was reallocate spending from nondefense programs to defense programs and to interest payments. In this sense, defense and interest payments crowded out some nondefense spending. But, it is also apparent that increases in Social Security payments, which were being driven by the continuing growth in the elderly population not by increases in benefits per elderly person, also crowded out outlays on nondefense programs. Health care costs under Medicare and Medicaid were also on automatic pilot, being driven extensively by medical technology and the threat of lawsuits. These rapidly expanding federal programs also crowded out outlays that could have gone for infrastructure or research.

On balance, Reagan did not stop the growth of government, nor did he stop the growth of entitlements to the poor. At best (or worst, depending on one's perspective), his administration managed to slow the pace of increase in the size of government at all levels and, possibly, to cap the growth in government as a percentage of GDP. During the 1980s, total government expenditures as a percentage of GDP fluctuated around a more or less flat trend, a significant break from the upward trend of the 1960s and 1970s.

Was it all Reagan? Hardly. Some budget cuts in some programs were simply the result of the realigning political power of interest groups, for example, the elderly, the homeless, and AIDS victims. Without question, Reagan had an effect, but his personal influence per se was nowhere near as large as has been imagined by his critics. Moreover, the fiscal policies followed during the 1980s were the product of a myriad of economic forces, the power of which extended to all points on the globe. In short, the so-called Reagan Revolution was part and parcel of a world technological revolution that was slowing the growth of governments around the world and was forcing governments to radically alter the way they do business.

The Economic Report Card for Presidents

Given the vocal criticisms about the 1980s, one might think that Ronald Reagan supervised the poorest performance of the economy since World War II. Harvard University economist Robert Barro evaluates the economic performance under Reagan with its performance under other presidents in the post-World War II period through changes in the so-called misery index originally developed by the late Arthur Okun, an adviser to Democratic presidents, and in a variation of the misery index that Barro devised.[27]

Barro's economic report card for the presidents is provided in table 8-6. The misery index adds the change in the inflation and unemployment rates (equal to the average rate during the term) minus the rate at the end of the previous term. The change in the misery index is reported in column V with the ranking of the presidents in column VI. Notice that the two Reagan terms rank 1 and 2, while the combined terms of Richard Nixon and Gerald Ford and the term of Jimmy Carter ranked last and second-to-last, respectively.

When the index is revised to include changes in long-term interest rates (column III), which Barro believes to be a better indication of the change in long-term inflation expectations, and the shortfall in economic growth from the long-run average of 3 percent, the ordering changes very little. Reagan's two terms still rank 1 and 2, respectively. Nixon/Ford and Carter switch places at the bottom of the ranking.

The downward shift in the ranking of Dwight Eisenhower's second term, from fifth to eighth, is the single largest change. George Bush's term in office, which covered the last years of the decade, ranked fifth in the new ordering despite the fact that a recession began in 1990 and growth was sluggish through 1992.[28]

Table 8-6 Economic Report Card on the Presidents

Administration	Inflation Change (I)	Unemploy- ment Change (II)	Interest Rate Change (III)	Shortfall in GNP Growth (IV)	Misery Index Change (V)	Rank (VI)	Expanded Misery Change (VII)	Rank (VIII)
Truman II 1949–52	-0.4	0.4	0.3	-2.6	0.0	4	-2.3	4
Eisenhower I 1953–56	0.3	1.6	0.6	0.7	1.9	9	3.2	9
Eisenhower II 1957–60	-0.8	1.3	0.5	1.1	0.5	5	2.1	8
Kennedy/Johnson 1961–64	-0.5	-0.8	0.3	-1.7	-1.3	3	-2.7	3
Johnson II 1965–68	2.2	-1.1	1.5	-1.4	1.1	7	1.2	6
Nixon I 1969–72	0.0	1.6	0.0	0.0	1.6	8	1.6	7
Nixon/Ford 1973–76	4.8	1.5	0.8	1.1	6.3	11	8.2	10
Carter 1977–80	3.9	-1.3	5.5	0.3	2.6	10	8.4	11
Reagan I 1981–84	-5.7	1.4	-0.7	0.7	-4.3	1	-4.3	1
Reagan II 1985–88	-0.6	-0.8	-2.1	-0.2	-1.4	2	-3.7	2
Bush 1989–92 (est.)	-0.2	1.0	-2.1	2.1	0.8	6	0.8	5

(I) Average CPI inflation rate (exclusive of shelter) during term, less rate in final year of previous term.

(II) Average unemployment rate during term, less rate at end of previous term.

(III) Change in long-term government bond rate from beginning to end of term.

(IV) Long-term average value of 3.0 less average real GNP growth rate during term.

(V) (I) + (II).

(VI) Misery index rank (1 is best).

(VII) (V) + (III) + (IV).

(VIII) Expanded Misery index rank (1 is best).

Source: Robert J. Barro, "A Gentleman's 'B-' for Bush on Economics," *Wall Street Journal,* September 30, 1992, p. A16.

Concluding Comments

A careful examination of the government record of the 1980s reveals important conclusions. The Reagan administration did not gut government by nearly as much as supposed by the critics of the decade, and its policies did not engineer a massive redistribution of government benefits from the poor to the rich. There was, however, some redistribution from nondefense to defense programs and from the purchase of goods and services to payments to individuals. Overall, the Reagan administration probably slowed the growth of government, helping to hold government expenditures, more or less, to a constant percentage of national production. The Reagan administration affected the private sector more through hiring policies and regulations than through expenditure policies.

Reagan did well misery index.
Also, Clinton

Notes

1. Donald L. Barlett and James B. Steele, *America: What Went Wrong?* (Kansas City, MO: Universal Press Syndicate, 1992), especially chap. 1.

2. Kevin Phillips, *The Politics of the Rich and Poor: Wealth and the American Electorate in the Reagan Aftermath* (New York: Harper Perennial, 1991), p. 52.

3. Ibid.

4. Ibid., p. 59.

5. Ibid., p. 73.

6. Benjamin Friedman, *Day of Reckoning: The Consequences of American Economic Policy Under Reagan and After* (New York: Random House, 1988), p. 24.

7. Lester Thurow, *Head to Head: The Coming Economic Battle among Japan, Europe and America* (New York: William Morrow, 1992), p. 12.

8. This theme is covered in detail in Richard B. McKenzie and Dwight R. Lee, *Quicksilver Capital: How the Rapid Movement of Wealth Has Changed the World* (New York: Free Press, 1991).

9. All current dollar figures have been converted to 1990 dollars by the gross domestic product deflator.

10. The federal government's fiscal year ends on September 30, and the budget year is defined by the ending year. Hence, the federal budget for 1982 covered outlays and receipts for the period from October 1, 1981, to September 30, 1982.

   Reagan came into office in January 1981, which means that planning for the 1982 budget had been started by the Carter administration. The Reagan administration was only able to influence the 1982 budget by submitting revisions to the budget proposal that had already been sent to Congress.

11. See Mikhail Gorbachev, *Perestroika: New Thinking for Our Country and the World* (New York: Harper & Row, 1987).

12. See Peter Passell, "Economic Scene: More Concrete, More Growth?" *New York Times,* July 30, 1992.

13. In addition, while the poverty rate rose with the recession in the early 1980s, peaking at 15.2 percent in 1983, it must be acknowledged that the poverty rate in 1989, 12.8 percent was slightly less than what it was in 1980, 13 percent. For the decade, however, the number of poor people expanded by close to 15 percent, from 29.3 million (or 13 percent of the population) in 1980 to 33.6 million (or 13.5 percent of the population) in 1990 [Executive Office of the

President, Council of Economic Advisers, *Economic Report of the President: 1992* (Washington, DC: U.S. Government Printing Office, 1992), p. 330 (statistical appendix)].

14. Mickey Kaus, *The End of Equality*, as quoted in "Notable and Quotable," *Wall Street Journal*, August 8, 1992.

15. Lowell Galloway, "The Effectiveness of Income Transfers in Reducing Poverty" (Washington, DC: Joint Economic Committee, U.S. Congress, December 29, 1992).

16. Ibid, pp. 6–13.

17. Robert L. Bartley, *The Seven Fat Years and How to Do It Again* (New York: Free Press, 1992), p. 101.

18. Norman Ture, "To Cut and to Please," *National Review*, August 31, 1992, p. 39.

19. The intention of the law was to reduce the tax payments of individuals by $11 billion over a five-year period at the same time it proposed to increase the tax payments of corporations by $120 billion (Ture, "To Cut and to Please," p. 39).

20. Barlett and Steele, *America: What Went Wrong?*, p. 6.

21. U.S. Congress, Committee on Ways and Means, *1992 Green Book*, (Washington, DC: U.S. Government Printing Office, May 15, 1992), pp. 1529–1530.

22. Ibid.

23. In 1989, families in the lowest quintile received benefits that equaled on average to 23.4 percent of their incomes and paid taxes equal to 5.8 percent of their incomes, whereas the highest quintile paid taxes equal to 5.5 percent of their incomes and received benefits equal to 1.9 percent of their incomes (Ibid., p. 1547).

24. Murray Weidenbaum, *Rendezvous with Reality: The American Economy after Reagan* (New York: Basic Books, 1988), pp. 33–37.

25. U.S. Congress, House, Committee on Ways and Means, *1992 Green Book* (Washington, DC: U.S. Government Printing Office, May 15, 1992), pp. 1481–1482.

26. Ibid., p. 1482.

27. Robert J. Barro, "A Gentleman's 'B-' for Bush on Economics," *Wall Street Journal*, September 30, 1992.

28. Conservatives continue to echo 1970s concerns of rapid and unchecked growth of government. However, as we approach the twenty-first century, a remarkable change is taking place around the world. Government is in retreat, and not just in the United States. The rate at which governments around the world have been growing

has slowed dramatically, and in some cases the size of government is actually shrinking.

Except in communist countries, this change is not occurring because there is widespread demand for smaller government. Instead, governments around the world are privatizing, deregulating, lowering tax rates and moderating spending increases to make their countries more attractive to investors and workers. The experience of the United States under Ronald Reagan was, to one extent or another, duplicated in many other countries, a fact that suggests that the "Reagan Record" was not the consequence of Ronald Reagan's efforts alone. A comprehensive discussion of this worldwide phenomenon can be found in McKenzie and Lee, *Quicksilver Capital*.

9

THE BRIGHT SIDE OF GOVERNMENT DEFICITS[1]

Ronald Reagan has been brutalized in media and policy circles for what is perceived to be rank political hypocrisy. Before and after his 1980 election, Reagan spoke eloquently against deficit spending by the federal government. This rhetoric was followed by a series of massive deficits during his eight years in office. The critics say history will not be as kind to Ronald Reagan as were the voters in 1980 and 1984.

Without much question, the Office of Management and Budget under Ronald Reagan must have maintained a storehouse of red ink. As is evident in figure 9-1, during the Reagan years the smallest increase in the federal debt was $113 billion (in 1990 dollars), and that increase occurred in 1981 and was certainly more attributable to Jimmy Carter's fiscal "prudence" than Reagan's. In the remaining seven Reagan years, the annual budget deficit never again went below $160 billion.[2] In the end, the federal budgets of the 1980s added nearly $1.7 trillion (in 1990 dollars) to the total federal debt, an amount equal to nearly one and a fifth times the real total federal debt accumulated in all years prior to 1982.

Figure 9-1   Federal Deficits (in Constant 1990 Dollars), 1970–1990

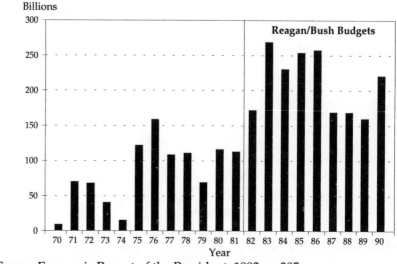

Source: Economic Report of the President: 1992, p. 385.

My purpose here is not to bury the federal deficit spending of the 1980s but to put it into perspective by recognizing favorable attributes of deficits not normally considered and by acknowledging the unfavorable attributes of viable fiscal policy options during the 1980s. For a government sector of a given size, budget deficits have three main advantages over alternative methods of raising revenue:

1. As deficits accumulate, an increasing proportion of the federal budget must be allocated to the payment of interest on the national debt. These increased interest payments bind the fiscal hands of Congress, constraining the growth of spending on other budgetary line items that arguably may have a greater distortive impact on the private economy than the deficit. From this point of view, deficit spending is of greatest value in lightening the burden of government when borrowing is required to meet existing principal and interest obligations.

2. Not all deficits are equal, even when they total the same dollar amount. The effect of particular deficits on the economy depends upon why they were incurred, whether as an out-

growth of greater spending or as a necessary part of a broader political package that includes policies designed to spur economic growth. When budget deficits are accompanied by reductions in the progressivity of the income tax, as they were in the early 1980s, the deficits themselves may help to flatten tax rates. This follows because interest income tends to be highly correlated with other types of income. If budget deficits do in fact raise real interest rates in the economy, higher income individuals would benefit disproportionately, meaning that their effective tax rate is reduced.

3. When government spending is financed by borrowing, revenue is raised from willing lenders both at home and abroad rather than from unwilling taxpayers.

The Reagan budget deficits have been unduly maligned. Deficits may be "bad" in themselves, but that does not mean that they were the worst thing to do under the political and economic circumstances of the 1980s. Far from representing the greatest fiscal disaster of the Reagan years, the massive debt accumulated during the 1980s may in fact be an achievement of sorts, given the goals of the Reagan administration. Of course, those who disagree with Reagan's objective of restraining government still have much to fret about.

The Opinions, Lots of Them

David Stockman, Reagan's first budget chief, maintained (with the political chivalry assumed by government officials only after they leave office) that the Reagan deficits reflected the administration's pervasive lack of political guts or the will to fight for the desired cuts in many domestic entitlement programs, among the most important of which was Social Security. The deficits were nothing less than a conscious strategy, Stockman tells us, to force the budget cuts out of Congress under the threat of charges of fiscal irresponsibility when the expected large deficits emerged.[3] In his reflections on the Reagan years, Murray Weidenbaum, the administration's first chief economic adviser, criticized the Reagan administration for its fiscal improvidence and advised that "the party will soon be over":

[The] chips are being called in; the bills are coming due. Citizens concerned with the future of America must take on a role akin to that of the cleanup crew the morning after the big blast. There is no substitute for tackling those lingering problems that have been swept under the national rug—the unparalleled string of huge budget deficits that would have threatened any less popular President, the large pockets of distress in many urban areas, and the tremendous weakening of this nation's position in world trade as symbolized by its becoming the world's largest debtor nation.[4]

Weidenbaum appears to agree with Stockman on one essential point—the Reagan deficits reflected an unwillingness to go for broke and take on powerful, entrenched lobbies for federal entitlement programs and subsidies for the nonpoor.

Harvard University Professor Benjamin Friedman has been far less kind in his assessment of the Reagan years, arguing that "since 1980 we have broken with that tradition [founded on the belief that our children would inherit a better world] by pursuing a policy that amounts to living not just in, but for, the present. We are living well by running up our debt and selling off our assets. America has thrown itself a party and billed the tab to the future."[5] Like many others, Friedman claims the locus of the blame is self-evident: "The tax and spending policies that the U.S. government has pursued throughout Ronald Reagan's presidency have rendered every citizen a borrower and every industry a liquidator of assets."[6] The fact that the Reagan fiscal policies were "clothed in the rhetoric appealing to traditional values that most Americans hold important"[7] is no excuse for blatant irresponsibility and no counterweight for the Americans' lost hopes and dreams for their children and grandchildren.

Like Friedman, a host of other policy commentators, mainly from the political left, have attributed many of our current economic problems to federal budget deficits of "unprecedented proportions."[8] They tell us that "American policy in recent years has been more and more addicted to wishful thinking. Economically... the era of comfortable self-indulgence appears near its close. Today the United States is on a collision course with history. The American fiscal dilemma must be resolved, and the perpetual instability of the dollar that is the consequence must cease."[9] We have been told repeatedly that the budget deficits, in themselves a barometer of national political bankruptcy, have "mortgaged" the country's future. They have soaked up the country's dwindling savings and forced Americans to maintain their standard of living by selling off their "seed corn"—that is, their industrial plants and equipment, farms, office towers, and hotel—to foreigners.

The critics warn that the deficits are both the symptom and the cause of America's continuing economic decline in the global economy. Our military spending has reflected the nation's "imperial overstretch," meaning the assumption of too many geopolitical obligations around the world that have, in turn, imposed a drag on the ability of the American economy to expand apace with many other countries, most notably countries on the Pacific Rim. Also, since the deficits were, or so it is argued, the product of tax cuts passed at the behest of the Reagan administration in 1981, they have forced, albeit indirectly, a substitution of consumption goods for capital goods.

According to others, the Reagan deficits have increased the total demand for borrowed funds and, therefore, have hiked real (inflation adjusted) domestic interest rates. The higher real interest rates have supposedly crowded out business borrowers from financial markets and impaired the growth in America's capital stock and future income stream.

Higher interest rates have also attracted foreign investors whose demand for dollars has put upward pressures on the international value of the dollar; and the boost in the dollar's international value has discouraged exports, especially of manufactured goods, and increased imports, causing many American exporting and importing companies to fold. The critics have told us so often and with such great eloquence that America can't compete[10] and that America is in long-term decline in the world economy[11] that many have begun to believe the lyrics of the new national swan song—despite all the cheery economic news to the contrary.

The Facts—Only the Facts

This dismal economic picture of contemporary America is not founded on sound logic and does not square with the facts, the most important of which are that the country's domestic production continued to rise, unemployment continued to fall, and measures of industrial production, manufacturing sales, and exports continued to grow during the 1980s precisely when the federal deficits were mounting. Moreover, U.S. national production held its own as a major share of the expanding world economy.

Admittedly, the dollar appreciated dramatically (by more than 60 percent) during the first half of the 1980s when annual federal deficits exceeded $200 billion. However, the dollar's value fell almost as precipitously after 1985—when annual federal deficits were still above $200 billion and were rising, albeit temporarily.[12]

The national saving rate (saving as a percentage of national income) fell during the Reagan years, despite the 1981 tax cut bill that was supposed to have the opposite effect. However, the investment rate (total investment as a percentage of total production) has not fallen.[13] In fact, while investment was erratic during the 1980s, the average investment rate during the 1980s was higher than the average investment rates during the 1960s and 1970s, and the 1960s has been widely acclaimed as a period of enviable growth.[14]

Real (inflation adjusted) interest rates rose dramatically from the late 1970s to 1981 along with the escalating budget deficits, but they fell just as dramatically after 1981, which is not what would be expected from arguments proffering a positive relationship between the rising deficits of the mid-1980s and real interest rates. Similarly, real interest rates and exchange rates have not moved consistently in the directions predicted. The dollar appreciated during the first couple of years in the 1980s when real interest rates were rising. However, confounding conventional wisdom are the facts that the dollar also continued to appreciate through 1985 when real interest rates were falling, and it began to depreciate after 1985 as real interest rates continued to fall.

Granted, real world events are the residue of a multitude of economic forces, with budget deficits only one factor. The predicted effects of the budget deficits could be obscured by other more important domestic and international forces moving in offsetting directions. For example, slack domestic investment demand could have more than offset the federal government's increased demand for loanable funds, causing real interest rates to fall during most years of the 1980s. Reductions in political instability abroad could have hiked foreign investment in the United States, inducing a reduction in the value of the dollar on international money markets, despite continued high and mounting deficits after 1985.

Obviously, the economic linkages between budget and trade deficits can be obscured by "noise" in the data. Indeed, I suspect that economic linkages probably do exist, although I have some doubt as to the strength of those linkages. The simple fact remains: The U.S. economy did not crumble under the weight of the additional debt piled up under the Reagan administration. Life in the United States in the 1980s got better, not worse, for most Americans. And the federal deficit as a percentage of total production tumbled from over 6 percent in the early 1980s to under 3 percent by the late 1980s.

At the very least, by now the harbingers of the budget deficit problem should have moderated their forecasts of a calamitous future for the U.S. economy. They have not done so. Instead, their rhetoric has escalated in a series of recent "doom-and-gloom" books. The most recent policy fad is to predict that the consequences of 1980s deficit spending will throttle growth in the 1990s. All the rhetoric about budget deficits is grounded in the very same political process that the deficits are. And political rhetoric about deficits have many of the same flaws that the critics say deficits have. In addition, the rhetoric is misguided because the full impact of deficits—measured in the light of both the pluses and minuses relative to alternative policy options—is misunderstood and infrequently appreciated.

A Reconsideration of Federal Deficits

No one need question claims that federal deficit spending is "bad." Just like very hot weather, most Americans would prefer to do without it, everything else being equal. By suggesting that budget deficits may be an unnoticed economic legacy of the Reagan administration, I do not wish to dispute claims that politicians are fiscally irresponsible or are forever seeking new and creative means of hiding the costs of government programs Congress votes their constituencies. I probably harbor a lower assessment than most of congressional fiscal integrity and the willingness of members of Congress to defraud voters. To say that deficits are bad, or just undesired is not to say that they should not be incurred, given a particular set of circumstances. The only relevant fiscal question is, "Compared to what?" Just as very hot weather might be chosen (eagerly) when set in contrast to very cold weather, deficits may be chosen when the full consequences of alternative policies are appreciated. Deficits might do damage to the national economy, but they may do less damage than the only other viable policy options. To damn deficits because they do not match policies chosen by angels is one of the more delusionary efforts of our time.

A key to the proper assessment of the true impact of deficits lies in understanding that federal expenditures on real goods and services constitute the ultimate tax on the American public. Those expenditures draw resources away from the private sector and cause a reduction in the ability of Americans, in the aggregate, to have the things they want. The net burden of the federal government will, ultimately, rise and fall with the effectiveness of federal expenditures. If the federal government buys more tanks, roads, or dams, then private citizens will have fewer TVs, VCRs, and automobiles to buy. And Americans will be better or worse off depending on whether the goods and services purchased by government are worth more or less than the private goods and services forgone.

The method of financing federal expenditures is not totally unimportant. The method of taxation can be more or less efficient; it can raise or lower incentives to work, save, and invest. As economists have long argued, so-called "lump-sum" taxes (which do not change with circumstances) can lead to greater national production than an equivalent income tax that rises with income. The income tax reduces people's after-tax return on additional work and, therefore, reduces their incentive to work longer and harder. Similarly, an income tax rate system that has a constant marginal rate schedule can lead to more national production than a rate schedule that is highly progressive but results in the same tax collections. Because the after-tax return to additional income goes down as the marginal rate rises under a progressive tax rate structure, the incentive to invest (to earn more future income) can be lower under the progressive income tax rate structure than under the constant rate structure.

Having said that, however, I have not said that taxation should be preferred to deficit spending, at least within bounds. Deficit spending has detrimental effects, of course. It reduces the funds available to the private sector, even the investment sector. But so do taxes. By lowering after-tax earnings, higher taxes to cover the deficit gap can also lower savings, reducing the funds available to private investors. The reduced supply of available funds could also cause the sequence of detrimental effects widely advertised for budget deficits: higher real interest rates, lower investment, increased inflow of foreign funds, a higher value for the dollar on international money markets, and an expanded trade deficit.

In short, the important issue is not that both deficits and taxes have detrimental effects but which has the greatest detrimental effect, given governmental expenditures. Cannot taxes be lowered and deficits increased within bounds with a net improvement in economic efficiency and growth of the economy?

The Reagan administration put forth a reasonably sound justification for its deficits. Given the political circumstances of the early 1980s, an increase in taxes (or no reduction in taxes) might have had greater detrimental effects than the deficits did because the greater tax revenue might have gone up in the fiscal smoke of higher government spending. Reagan might very well have been orchestrating a policy of "least destruction" by leaving the country with such a large increase in its national debt. This may be true because the annual deficits, as planned, tied the hands of Congress, impaired their ability to expand expenditures, and thereby increased the pool of national resources for the private sector. As opposed to having crimped economic growth, the massive deficits may have spurred it—*relative to what it would have been,* which is the only meaningful political and economic standard by which to judge the deficit. Some empirical evidence does support the administration's concern that more government revenue would simply have led to more spending, and vice versa, and that the increase in spending might exceed the increase in tax revenue.[15]

The Reagan administration's estimate of the relative advantage of deficits may not be the correct one. Politicians have been known to make incorrect political judgments (at least 50 percent of them lose every election). It might be, as distinguished economists have argued, that the deficits had the opposite effect of that intended. The breakdown of fiscal norms against deficit spending in virtually unlimited amounts may have granted members of Congress an opportunity to expand expenditures and draw resources away from the private sector. Furthermore, the deficits may have seduced voters into thinking (incorrectly) that they were getting something for nothing (or at a lower perceived cost than if the expenditures were covered by explicit taxes on incomes or purchases), a result that may have increased demand for federally provided programs.[16] However, recent research indicates that deficits enacted because of tax reductions can have the effect Reagan and his advisers wanted—a reduction in government spending.[17]

At best, this debate over the relative efficacy of deficits and taxes has not been settled, and very likely will not be settled for years to come. Under the circumstances, it might be best to look at the historical record. That record tells us that, gloom-and-doom forecasts to the contrary, as the deficits mounted, economic conditions got better for most Americans.

Furthermore, amidst all the rhetoric about the detrimental effects of federal budget deficits, federal expenditures as a percentage of national production stopped rising and remained more or less level during the 1980s (staying within a range of 22.3 to 24.3 percent of national production). I suggest that the deficits may have had the promised impact—they throttled Congress's ability to raise expenditures, and they spurred economic growth because they reduced federal expenditures on real goods and services and because they covertly but effectively led to lower marginal tax rates. Such real-world observations should shift the burden of argument onto the shoulders of those who, with deep convictions, maintain that deficits were a bad choice made by an intellectually bankrupt administration during a disastrous decade.

There are other good reasons for believing that deficit spending was not all that bad a choice for a president who aligned himself early on with supply-side economics, which holds that incentives matter and that marginal incentives matter more than just any incentives. As noted, Reagan and his advisers were concerned that the highly progressive U.S. tax rate schedule imposed an unwarranted drag on the American economy. After taxes were withdrawn from paychecks, Americans did not have enough incentive to work longer and harder and to do those things that would increase their human and physical capital stock and raise their future incomes. Government took too much from people and would extract a growing proportion of people's growing incomes. Accordingly, Ronald Reagan set out to "flatten" the tax rate structure in 1981, and did it with a bill that lowered the top marginal rate from 70 to 50 percent. Eventually, the administration was able to get the top marginal rate all the way down to 28 percent (before it was raised again in 1990).

However, the administration probably flattened the overall tax rate schedule by more than was advertised. This is because the deficit is also, indirectly, a form of taxation—a "deficit tax" that just as surely as the Internal Revenue System draws resources away from the private sector. No one knows the incidence of the deficit tax, but almost everyone is certain that it is imposed in an uncertain manner through the pricing system: possibly by higher interest rates, which can cause a reduction in investment and in people's incomes (due to the fact that the capital stock is reduced), and possibly through higher prices for goods and services attributable to the increased federal expenditures. Frankly, we also do not know who bears the deficit tax; but it would not be unreasonable to imagine that the burden of the deficit tax is spread so thinly and widely (without regard to incomes) through the pricing system that it is, for all practical purposes, a "proportional (or flat) tax" if it is not a "regressive tax."

I make this claim for several reasons. First, I suspect that higher income earners are generally more adept at avoiding all taxes (including deficit taxes) than lower income earners, and higher income earners (because of their demonstrated ability to work with markets) should have a comparative advantage in coping with changing prices. In addition, interest income tends to rise with other forms of income. If deficits do raise real interest rates across markets, higher income people would benefit disproportionately, which means that the net burden of government borne by higher income people might fall with deficits, lowering the effective tax rates faced by higher income groups. The net burden on lower income people might rise, increasing their effective tax rates.

Second, I suspect that Congress is capable of intentionally structuring a more progressive tax schedule for the IRS than would be found in the pricing system distorted by the deficit tax.

Third, I suspect that Congress accepted the deficits because it did not want to pass an increase in taxes that would confound its intentions to flatten taxes.

In summary, it is quite possible and plausible that a shift from explicit taxation through the IRS to implicit taxation through federal deficits helped to flatten the overall tax rate schedule and, according to supply-side principles, spurred economic growth, albeit marginally. Without the option of incurring deficits, the 1981 and 1986 tax bills might never have been passed.

The Crowding Out Effects of Interest Payments

I have noted the considerable attention economists and policy commentators give to the way deficits "crowd out" private investment.

By raising interest rates, the federal government borrows funds that would have, in the absence of the deficits, financed private capital projects. The fewer private investment projects undertaken spells a lower rate of economic growth and possibly greater inefficiency in the allocation of resources, assuming the federal expenditures the deficits finance are largely wasteful. Nonetheless, I must insist that the effects of deficits do not stop with their direct or indirect effects on private investment.

Few deficits critics have recognized a potential boon of deficits: They do indeed expand federal interest payments for the new and old debt. During the Reagan years, federal interest payments increased more than threefold, from $114 billion (in 1990 dollars) and 11 percent of total federal outlays in 1982 to $184 billion and 15 percent of total federal outlays in 1990. Without compensating increases in taxes, the dramatically greater interest payments must have "crowded out" of the federal budget other expenditures. Other budget lines either fell in real dollar and percentage terms, or they increased by less than they would have otherwise. From the analysis of the federal budget in chapter 8, it is clear that some federal expenditures were crowded out. In addition, I noted that total federal expenditures as a percentage of national production remained more or less constant in the 1980s. That means that non-interest expenditures of the federal government must have fallen under Reagan, and they did, at least slightly relative to national production. All government expenditures, excluding net interest payments, fell from 20.9 percent of national production in 1982 to 19.5 percent in 1990, a drop of nearly 7 percent in share of national production in eight years but a nontrivial capping of the upward trend in government expenditures as a percentage of national production in the three decades prior to 1980.[18]

Since the Reagan administration favored defense, which increased by more than a third in real dollar terms between 1980 and 1990, the nondefense expenditures of the federal government must have taken the brunt of the relative decline (see chapter 8). More important, between 1980 and 1990 nondefense discretionary spending actually fell in real (1990) dollar terms by 10 percent, from $224 billion in 1980 to $202 billion in 1990. These discretionary expenditures fell even more relative to GNP, from 8.2 percent in 1980 to 3.7 percent in 1990, a decline of 55 percent in share. In other words, Congress had fewer real dollars of discretionary funds to allocate over an expanding population and economy, a result that caused advocates of expanded government great consternation.

The progressive tightening of congressional discretion—due to the double-barreled effects of the growth in deficits and in defense spending—may help explain why many liberal politicians and political analysts have apparently switched from intense affection toward deficits in the 1960s to equally intense distaste for deficits in the 1980s. The earlier deficits accompanied an upward trend in taxes. The Reagan deficits were partly a consequence of reductions of marginal tax rates that helped to check upward growth in expenditures.

Obviously, I do not wish to praise federal interest payments, per se, any more than I wish to praise federal deficits per se. At the same time, relatively speaking, federal interest payments may be among the least distorting and destructive forms of federal expenditures. Many other expenditure categories can create massive disincentives to work, save, and invest, and massive incentives to retire, to live on the dole (either as a welfare claimant or farmer or university researcher), and to waste resources trying to get even more money from the federal government. On the other hand, through bonds held by banks, insurance companies, mutual funds, and individuals, interest payments are very likely spread thinly across the citizenry and, if they are not spread totally evenly, they at least provide government-inspired differential rewards for frugality (a virtue that even the decade's critics appear to hold with some reverence).

To my way of thinking, any given level of federal outlays would have a less destructive effect the more it is dominated by interest payments, at least to a point.[19] To the extent that interest payments actually lower non-interest outlays, they can reduce the disincentives of federal programs and expand positive incentives to work, save, and invest. Therefore, the interest payments can reduce the net drag of the federal budget on the economy, thus spurring greater economic growth than would otherwise exist. To that extent, while wasteful government expenditures may burden future generations, the deficits per se have not added to that burden and may have lowered it.

Finally, in defense of the relative (but only relative) merits of deficits, it needs to be noted that the purchase of debt is voluntary, whereas the collection of taxes by the IRS is a matter of official coercion. I do not wish to make too much of the economic value of voluntary actions, at the same time, I do not think its economic value should be ignored either just because it may be limited. If nothing else, no enforcement resources are required to sell a bond; the cost of raising $1 in the capital market is lower than the cost of raising $1 in taxes. To that extent, the government or the private sector has more resources for doing other more productive things.

Efficient Deficits

By finding something to praise about deficits, I do not mean to suggest that all government expenditures, no matter what the type or the circumstances, should be financed by debt. That would be silly, if for no other reason than that most real world governments must have and use their powers of taxation just to maintain their creditworthiness, which permits the deficits in the first place. The only governments that could finance all government expenditure by borrowing would be those that make outlays exclusively on profitable capital projects. The expected return on the investment, generated by sales, would be all the security lenders would need to be enticed into buying government bonds at going market interest rates. In principle, the interest on the debt and the principal could be covered by the future income stream.

However, governments that made only those types of outlays would be acting like private businesses, investing in projects that other private businesses would. Their capacity to make transfers and provide public goods and services (the types of goods and services that cannot be readily sold at market prices) would be limited, possibly no greater than the capacity of private businesses to make, for example, charitable contributions.

Real world governments orchestrate extensive transfers among various income classes and special interest groups, for example, transfers to nonpoor senior citizens. Most governments also produce a variety of public (and private) goods and services, including systems of national defense, education, and justice. And most governments are downright wasteful. Before such governments can borrow extensively, they must demonstrate a capacity to obtain an income stream that can be used, at least in principle, to cover the obligatory interest payments and the debt principal. Many of governments' outlays simply do not have an expected income stream from private market sales. Thus, taxation is mandatory—but only up to a point.

While moderation in the use of debt is a reasonable rule for all governments, the capacity of any particular government to issue debt depends upon its circumstances. One of the most important considerations is the extent to which the government makes transfers and obstructs or supports the national economy's capacity to prosper and grow. Any policy agenda designed to make government or the economy more efficient should translate into an increase in the ability of the government to incur debt (without adding an additional risk premium to the interest rate on the government bonds). This is true simply because the efficiency-enhancing policies increase the expected income stream from any given set of tax rules and rates.

You do not have to agree with the full spectrum of Reaganomics to concede that greater debt may have been consistent with the *intent* of the Reagan policy agenda, at least as articulated. The Reagan administration had five principal economic planks in its platform:

1. Under the banner of "flat(ter) taxes," to lower marginal tax rates and, in other ways, make the tax code more efficient.

2. In an effort to get the "government off the backs of Americans," reduce government expenditures, especially as a

percentage of GNP and especially those that have built-in dis-incentives to work, save, and invest.

3. Under the banner of "federalism," to devolve federal programs to state and local governments where they would be controlled, to a greater degree, by intergovernmental competition.

4. To promote free international trade.

5. Where possible, to deregulate additional industries and privatize as many governmental services as possible.

The Reagan administration was not always successful in its efforts to accomplish these objectives, as the administration's own economists have recognized.[20] The administration did allow some trade barriers to rise and accomplished little in the way of deregulating additional industries. Nevertheless, several nontrivial accomplishments can be acknowledged. Tax rates were lowered. The flow of federal funds to states was reduced. Government expenditures as a percentage of GNP stagnated, and the discretionary spending authority of Congress was reduced. The trend in the promulgation of additional federal regulations was throttled, and a major new drive to privatize government services was initiated.[21]

To the extent that the Reagan administration was successful in adopting policies that improved the economy's efficiency, more debt could be justified on economic and political grounds. The debt has been, and will continue to be, less of a burden than has been imagined. To the extent that the debt was actually necessary (given political constraints in the 1980s) to improve economic efficiency via the passage of key tax and regulatory bills, the debt was no net burden at all. Indeed, it might be construed as enhancing the overall efficiency of the current and future U.S. economy since it was part and parcel of the whole political package, which might not have been adopted if the debt had not been incorporated.

Finally, we must recognize a frequently heard concern about deficits—they give members of Congress the power to extend spending without having voters pay a direct cost. From this perspective, federal deficit spending needs to be controlled to contain federal expenditures.[22] However, it needs to be noted that external, international controls on the fiscal proclivities of governments have been tightened during the past decade or two. Capital and people have become more mobile, and the greater mobility has imposed a check on the power of governments to tax and regulate in flagrant disregard for the economic efficiency of the adopted policies.[23] As never before, people can "vote with their feet"—or with their computers, since they can now transfer their financial capital (or other income-earning assets) to other more hospitable governmental jurisdictions via modems and telephone lines. To the extent that international capital mobility constrains government, the capacity of governments to engage in inefficient levels of deficit spending is contained (perhaps more effectively than by any formal, constitutional check on government's fiscal powers).

In summary, deficit spending might be less dangerous and burdensome than in earlier periods when capital and people were not so mobile and deficits were a smaller percentage of the budget or of GDP. For decades, economists and policymakers have decried (or, in the case of Keynesians, praised) deficits as if deficits of equal amounts are, in fact, equal. A $200 billion deficit incurred at one time is equal to a $200 billion deficit incurred at another time (so long as the major macroeconomic variables—for example, the unemployment and growth rates—are the same). A greater deficit is necessarily "worse" than a smaller deficit. If nothing else, my approach to deficits unsettles such presumptions. A deficit incurred when expenditures go up may be part and parcel of a totally different policy agenda with drastically different social and economic objectives than a deficit of an equal amount incurred when tax rates are falling. The former policy agenda might inhibit growth, while the latter policy agenda might spur growth. As a consequence, the Reagan deficits, as large as they were, might have been superior to much smaller deficits incurred under other administrations with different policy agendas.

Concluding Comments

Keynesian economics became immensely popular among policy-makers because of a basic tenet: Deficits stimulate the national economy. I agree, but not for the reasons postulated by Keynes. Keynesians maintained that budget deficits expand aggregate demand by injecting more expenditures into the national income stream than are withdrawn in the form of taxes. From my perspective, budget deficits marginally expand aggregate supply from what it would otherwise be, given government expenditures, which may be construed as the ultimate source of federal drag on the economy. Under certain conditions, deficits may stimulate aggregate supply *marginally* in three principle ways. First, they can marginally constrain the growth in government expenditures (and therefore the expenditure drag on the economy). Second, when deficits are created by reductions in the progressivity of the IRS tax rate structure, deficits themselves can contribute to a flattening of the aggregate tax rate structure (the combined effect of the IRS tax rate structure and the deficit tax rate structure). Third, the increased federal interest payments bind the fiscal hands of future Congresses, constraining the planned growth in non-interest federal expenditures that may have had inherent disincentives to work, save, and invest and may have impaired economic growth.

Ronald Reagan campaigned for the presidency on a platform that promised to get the federal government off the backs of American taxpayers. Faced with entrenched bureaucracies and powerful interest groups implacably opposed to reductions in entitlements and other subsidies, direct spending cuts and the wholesale elimination of programs were politically unrealistic. (Remember his plans to do away with the Department of Education and the Legal Services Corporation and his proposal to lower Social Security payments?) Rather than attack directly on a legislative battleground where defeat was likely, Reagan undertook a strategy, purposefully in my view, to accomplish these same goals, albeit partially and indirectly. This strategy consisted of engineering a marginal but significant shift in the method of financing the federal government. By shifting toward greater reliance on borrowing, Reagan imposed a more effective and lasting constraint on discretionary congressional spending and the growth of government than any statutory or constitutional limitation could hope to be.

Interest payments on the debt represent the ultimate entitlement program—to maintain the federal government's creditworthiness, interest payments must be met before any other outlays, including Social Security and defense, can be contemplated. Growing interest payments, more than any other cause, has forced Congress and the public to think seriously about federal spending priorities, of picking somewhat more carefully among competing programs. For this reason alone, the debt can be construed as a necessary component of redirecting the course of government for the 1980s and decades beyond. Many critics of the Reagan deficits seem to agree—but with grave regrets.

Notes

1. The author is indebted to William Shughart of the University of Mississippi for the considerable contribution he made to the policy paper from which this chapter is developed with revisions.

2. In August 1989, the Congressional Budget Office (CBO) predicted that the federal budget deficit would remain above $140 billion through 1993, despite much lower deficit limits legislated under the Balanced Budget Act [Nathaniel C. Nash, "Congressional Budget Panel Fears Long-Term $140 Billion Deficits," *New York Times* (August 18, 1989). In March 1992, the CBO estimated that the deficit would be $332 billion if administration policies were continued [U.S. Congress, Congressional Budget Office, *An Analysis of the President's Budgetary Proposals for Fiscal Year 1993* (Washington, DC: U.S. Government Printing Office, March 1992), p. 2].

3. See David Stockman, *The Triumph of Politics: Why the Reagan Revolution Failed* (New York: Harper and Row, 1986), chap 12.

4. Murray Weidenbaum, *Rendezvous with Reality: The American Economy after Reagan* (New York: Basic Books, 1988), pp. 3–4.

5. Benjamin Friedman, *Day of Reckoning: The Consequences of American Economic Policy Under Reagan and After* (New York: Random House, 1988), p. 5.

6. Ibid., p. 6.

7. Ibid., p. 9.

8. W. Michael Blumenthal, "The World Economy and Technological Change," *Foreign Affairs*, vol. 66, no. 3 (1987/1988), p. 529.

9. David P. Calleo, Harold van B. Cleveland, and Leonard Silk, "The Dollar and the Defense of the West," *Foreign Affairs*, vol. 66, no. 4 (Spring 1988), p. 845.

10. Daniel A. Sharp, "America is Running Out of Time," *New York Times* (February 7, 1988), as reprinted in *The World Trade Imbalance: When Profit Motives Collide* (Washington, DC: Executive Council on Foreign Diplomats, U.S. Department of State, 1988), p. 25.

11. Paul Kennedy, *The Rise and Decline of Great Nations: Economic change and Military conflict from 1500 to 2000* (New York: Random House, 1987).

12. For charts of the relevant data series, see Richard B. McKenzie, *The American Job Machine* (New York: Universe Books, 1988), chap. 6.

13. John A. Tatom, "U.S. Investment in the 1980s: The Real Story," *Review* (Federal Reserve Bank of St. Louis; March/April 1989), pp. 3–15.

14. Admittedly, as Tatom shows, *net* investment (gross investment minus depreciation) as a percentage of gross national product was on a downward trend in the 1980s. However, Tatom argues, I think appropriately, that net investment does not account for the improvements in technology that are incorporated in replacement investment (Ibid., p. 12).

15. See Neela Manage and Michael L. Marlow, "The Causal Relation between Federal Expenditures and Receipts," *Southern Economic Journal,* January 1986, pp. 617–629; William A. Niskanen, "Deficits, Government Spending, and Inflation," *Journal of Monetary Economics,* August 1978, pp. 594–602; and Richard Veddar, Lowell Galloway, and Christopher Frenze, "Federal Tax Increases and the Budget Deficit, 1947–1986," *Congressional Record,* April 30, 1987, pp. S5754–S5755.

16. This view is developed in James M. Buchanan and Richard E. Wagner, *Democracy in Deficits: The Political Legacy of Lord Keynes* (New York: Academic Press, 1977).

17. See Dwight R. Lee and Richard K. Veddar, "Friedman Tax Cuts vs. Buchanan Deficit Reduction as the Best Way of Constraining Government,: *Economic Inquiry,* October 1992, pp. 722–732.

18. Figures on government expenditures as a percentage of GNP are taken from Congressional Budget Office, U.S. Congress, *The Economic and Budget Outlook: An Update* (August 1989).

19. Milton Friedman has made this same point, arguing that "the deficit has been the only effective restraint on congressional spending" [Milton Friedman, "Why Deficits Are a Blessing," *Wall Street Journal* (December 15, 1988)].

20. See Weidenbaum, *Rendezvous with Reality;* and William Niskanen, *Reaganomics: An Insider's Account of the Policies and the People* (New York: Oxford University Press, 1988).

21. For a review of the government policy record during the last three decades, see Richard B. McKenzie and Dwight Lee, *Quicksilver Capital: How the Rapid Movement of Wealth Has Changed the World* (New York: Free Press, 1991).

22. This view has been most effectively and completely developed by Buchanan and Wagner, *Democracy in Deficit.*

23. See McKenzie and Lee, *Quicksilver Capital.*

10

THE ASSAULT ON DEREGULATION

AIRLINES AS A CASE STUDY[1]

Critics of the 1980s were concerned about the changing distribution of income and wealth. However, as I have shown, the reality of the 1980s did not square with the critics' rhetorical claims, often made for political purposes. Nevertheless, the critics' attention to income and wealth statistics appears to have been directed by a more deep-seated and abiding resentment—the shift away from government solutions to social and economic problems and toward greater reliance on markets. For this reason, those who criticized the changing distribution of income and wealth often found fault with practically every form of government deregulation as well, whether in the banking, securities, or transportation industries or in labor and import-protection policies.

Indeed, critics have resolutely charged that worker income suffered precisely because of the deregulation movement and curbs in the growth of many forms of government regulation, all of which was attributed to the advent of Ronald Reagan—despite the fact that

Reagan had little to do with many of the more prominent forms of deregulation and may, in fact, have slowed the pace of deregulation.[2] Critics have recommended with equal vigor and conviction that the nation's income problems could be solved with relative ease, in part by reregulation of deregulated industries and in part by extending government's regulatory arm further—that is, by reversing the so-called Reagan Revolution.[3]

The regulatory legacy of the 1970s and 1980s has been reviewed at length in *Quicksilver Capital,*[4] which deals with the charges critics have made regarding deregulation of a variety of industries. The full breadth of the charges against the free play of markets can be appraised here, however, with a study of the very serious and emotionally charged complaints made against the performance of the deregulated American airline industry in the 1980s. In the view of many critics, airline deregulation was a disaster, the results of which are supposedly revealed in congested planes and airports, money-losing and bankrupt airlines, and reduced safety. According to the critics, the performance of the airline industry during the 1980s was a pluperfect example of how Americans can be literally and figuratively hurt by greater reliance on the free flow of market forces. *Washington Post* columnist Hobart Rowen chafed in 1987, "As the grim record of near collisions on the nation's airways proliferates, you and I are taking a bigger chance flying than ever before."[5] Nevertheless, upon hearing similar claims in the mid-1980s, Alfred Kahn, the Carter administration's executor of U.S. airline deregulation, and Daniel Kasper, a management consultant, bristled that any "argument that deregulation has made airline travel more hazardous—despite the fact that there has been no dilution in the Federal government's responsibility for safety—represents a triumph of preconceptions over fact."[6]

Without much question, preconceptions have fueled the public debate over the safety effects and other consequences of deregulation and proposals for reregulation. Drawing a distinction between the impression of reduced safety—spawned, say, by the horrendous television pictures of a DC-10 tumbling down an Iowa runway—and the airline industry's actual safety record, spanning a growing number of flights over more than a decade of deregulated airways, is crucial to the future of transportation policy in the United States. The reregulation of airlines—along with effects on ticket prices, flight schedules, and even safety—hangs in the balance of the continuing debate. The Clinton administration has expressed some interest in reregulating the airline industry, and CEOs of some airlines, no doubt tiring of huge losses and cut-throat competition, have made positive remarks about the possibility of reregulation.

The airline industry is a paradigm of a modern complex marketplace and makes an excellent case study of how deregulation has actually worked, in part because airline deregulation is one of the things that, on balance, went *right* in the 1980s, and in part because of the way partial deregulation (which is what really happened with the airline industry) misleads opinion leaders in making judgments about this and other regulatory issues.

The Record of Accomplishment

According to a growing body of scholarly and policy studies, airline deregulation (which actually began with the passage of the Airline Deregulation Act of 1978) achieved many of its goals in the 1980s.[7] These goals were:

> more intense airline competition,

> lower air fares,

> greater air travel, and

> enhanced consumer welfare and airline profits.

According to an early study of the effects of airline deregulation by President Ronald Reagan's Council of Economic Advisers, airline deregulation from 1978 through 1986:

> increased the number of city-pairs served by more than one airline by 55 percent, and expanded the flights to smaller cities by 20 to 30 percent;

➤ extended service to 140 additional airports, slowed the rate at which smaller communities lost service, and (because of the development of the commuter airline system) reduced the need for federal airport subsidies in smaller communities after 1981;

➤ expanded the service in markets with the lowest passenger volume more than larger markets;

➤ lowered fares across the board by 15 percent (with fares on short flights reduced by 10 percent and fares on longer flights reduced by 35 percent);

➤ extended the use of discount fares from 15 percent of travelers in 1976 to 90 percent in 1987;

➤ reduced the percentage of passengers having to change planes from 68 percent in 1977 to 12 percent in 1986; and

➤ increased airline productivity by 7 percent.

On balance, Reagan's economic advisers accepted others' estimates that for the 1978 to 1986 period airline deregulation increased annual consumer benefits by $11 billion.[8] The Federal Trade Commission (FTC) has since estimated the annual welfare gains from deregulation to be equal to half of airlines revenues in 1977.[9]

Increased Airline Travel

Reagan's Council and the FTC may actually have underplayed the net consumer benefits from deregulation. Many of the benefits of deregulation are evident in a simple plotting of revenue passenger miles flown in domestic markets by major airlines in scheduled service.[10] In figure 10-1, the solid line depicts the actual revenue passenger miles flown, while the dashed line shows predicted values for revenue passenger miles. The projected values for 1978 through 1988 indicate how many revenue passenger miles would have been flown in the domestic market had deregulation not occurred and had airlines continued to follow flight patterns established prior to 1978.

Figure 10-1 Actual versus Projected Revenue Passenger Miles,
1960–1988

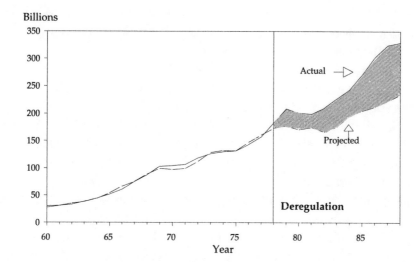

Note: The predicted values were generated by making revenue passenger miles for 1960 through 1988 a function of constant dollar GDP per capita, population, a time trend, a deregulation dummy variable, an interaction term (equal to the time trend times the deregulation dummy variable), and a correction term for serial autocorrelation. After computing the estimating equation, the projected values were obtained by setting the deregulation dummy and the interaction variable equal to zero. The interaction term indicates that deregulation expanded air travel at a rate of nearly 9 billion miles a year. All variables are statistically significant at less than the 5 percent confidence level. The adjusted R-square for the equation is .994.
Source: Federal Aviation Administration and author's calculations.

Passenger miles actually flown in the post-deregulation period rose dramatically above the projected trend. By 1988, the actual passenger miles flown were 329 billion, or 41 percent above the 234 billion projected for 1988.[11] During the 1978 to 1988 period, actual passenger miles flown on major carriers exceeded the predicted miles flown by an annual average of 61 billion (or 31 percent). This means that deregulation added 671 billion miles of air travel, an amount equal to slightly more than twice the total travel for 1988.

These figures do not include the growth in revenue passenger miles flown by major carriers in nonscheduled service or the passenger miles flown by the many commuter airlines and air taxis in scheduled and nonscheduled service,[12] which cannot be similarly analyzed because of data unavailability.

While some of the growth of air travel may reflect economies of scale and greater utilization of existing airport capacity, the failure to expand the air transport system has shown up in increased congestion on the runways and in the terminals and in longer take-off delays, facts that have often given deregulation a bad reputation in policy and media circles.[13] The growing congestion no doubt lowered the net reduction in the total cost of air travel (the sum of fares and value of time in transit) and curbed the benefits of deregulation.

Some of the gains in miles flown can be attributed to a number of economic factors not directly related to deregulation, for example, the increase in the rate of economic growth.[14] However, the spurt in the growth of air travel in the post-deregulation period was also the product of three forces set in motion by deregulation.

First, airlines were given the authority to use their limited number of planes more extensively by flying them more fully loaded and by reallocating them to serve the more heavily traveled routes. In 1976, airlines filled an average of 55 percent of their seats. With more seats added to planes, the so-called load factor reached 61.4 percent in 1988.[15]

Second, airlines developed hub-and-spoke systems that made trips less direct for many travelers, a factor that may have increased travel distances by an estimated 5.4 percent.[16]

Third, airline deregulation appears to have reduced air fares, although that issue has been and remains hotly disputed.[17] Brookings Institution economists Steven Morrison and Clifford Winston, supporters of deregulation, initially estimated that had airlines been deregulated in 1977, air fares would have been 30 percent below what they actually were.[18] On the other hand, University of Denver law professor Paul Stephen Dempsey maintains emphatically that an array of adverse service and safety effects of deregulation *"have not been accompanied by lower ticket fares"* (emphasis in the original).[19] After adjusting for the downward trend in revenue per passenger mile under way before deregulation and also for changes in inflation and fuel prices, Dempsey estimates that "ticket prices today [1990] are at least 2.6 percent *above* the level for which they were headed before deregulation took place."[20] He stresses that the substantial declines in air fares claimed by deregulation proponents are actually the product of the "totally fortuitous 2.8 percent annual *decline* in real fuel prices during the 78–88 period,"[21] which permitted airlines with lower costs to drop their prices.

However, Dempsey concedes that "deregulation was responsible for a one-time reduction in fares on the order of 13 percent,"[22] which he attempts to attribute to fuel prices or dismiss as being very temporary and having little or no consequence. Dempsey stresses that "by 1988—due to the slower rate of decline of real fares—all the gains of this one-time shift had been dissipated. By 1988, that is, consumers were paying 'net' prices (net of the effects of fuel) exactly equal to what they would have paid had pre-deregulation trends continued."[23]

Dempsey's conclusions are founded on statistical techniques that, upon close examination, cannot escape serious criticism. The just-cited conclusion regarding 1988 air fares is grounded in a simple extension of the downward 1967 to 1977 linear trend in real air fares to 1988 (measured by an index for real revenue per passenger mile). What Dempsey does not emphasize is that his "one-time reduction" lasted from 1978 through 1987, the next to the last year covered by his statistical analysis.[24]

By using Dempsey's data and improving on his econometric techniques, a decidedly different picture of the impact of deregulation on air fares is developed.[25] The lower line in figure 10-2 is Dempsey's actual index for real revenue per passenger mile (1978 = 100). The top line plots the projected values for his index estimated from a regression equation that includes variables to assess the separate effects of the downward trend, the radical swings in fuel prices during the 1967 to 1988 period, and the somewhat gradual deregulation of fares and routes beginning in 1978.[26] The striped area

Figure 10-2 Index of Real Revenue per Passenger Mile and Projected Index of Real Revenue per Passenger Mile (assuming deregulation did not occur)

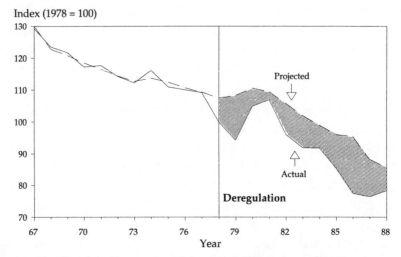

Source: Paul Stephen Dempsey, *Flying Blind: The Failure of Airline Deregulation* (Washington, DC: Economic Policy Institute, 1990); and author's calculations.

represents the difference between the higher projected values for real revenue per passenger mile, assuming deregulation had not occurred, and the lower actual values.

In the 1978 to 1988 period, the projected values (which were computed assuming deregulation did not take place) range from 2.4 to 23 percent above the actual fare index values (bottom line). Without deregulation, the air fare yields would have averaged 10.8 percent above the actual index values. Contrary to what Dempsey found, the econometric approach represented in figure 10-2 suggests that airline deregulation had the effect of progressively lowering air fare yields by slightly more than one-half percent a year. This finding also weakens Dempsey's other major claim—that the industry was becoming more concentrated in its structure and more monopolistic in its pricing behavior.[27] Also contrary to Dempsey's finding that actual and predicted prices were the same in 1988, figure 10-2 shows that if deregulation had not happened, air fare yields in 1988 would have been 9.3 percent higher than what they actually were.[28]

In addition, Dempsey stresses that airline deregulation initially unleashed "intense price competition" that imposed "economic strains" on carriers, causing them to willfully sacrifice safety.[29] However, he claims, the competition was eventually destructive, leading to monopolization of the industry by a few megacarriers. By 1988, these megacarriers were capable of forcing consumers to pay "tribute to a private monopoly to obtain a level of safety taken for granted prior to 1978."[30] This description of the competitive process at work in the airline industry does not conform to Dempsey's picture of the abrupt change in air fares after 1978. "Intense price competition" cannot be expected to lead to an immediate jump in relative air fares (after adjusting for fuel cost changes). As opposed to air fares falling with the advent of the acknowledged intense competition and then increasing at a progressively faster pace with the supposed monopolization of the industry in the mid- to late-1980s, Dempsey shows air fares rising very rapidly between 1979 and 1981 (when there was, supposedly, intense price competition), rising less rapidly between 1981 and 1986, and then falling between 1986 and 1988. Obviously, Dempsey's theory and evidence do not meld.[31]

Morrison and Winston used another technique to assess the impact of deregulation on air fares.[32] They compare actual air fares (measured, as Dempsey does, by "yields" or cents per mile) between 1978 and 1988 with what they would have been had the CAB continued in operation and continued to use its Standard Industry Fare Level method for setting fares, as computed by Morrison and Winston. Morrison and Winston found that their measure of air fares fluctuated over the 1978 to 1988 period, rising substantially between mid-1986 and 1988. However, the Brookings researchers determined that over the 1978 to 1989 period air fares were on average 18 percent lower than they would have been under CAB control.[33] The run-up in air fares in the late 1980s would have occurred under a continuation of the pre-1978 regulatory regime.[34] Morrison and Winston found, however, that the average decline in fares hides fare reductions for long-haul flights (more than 900 miles), which were artificially inflated by regulation, and increases in fares for short-haul flights (less than 900 miles), which were artificially suppressed by regulation.[35]

The decline in air fares attributable to deregulation undermines claims of counterproductive monopolization within the airline industry. Few monopolies have been known to exert their destructive will over consumers by lowering prices and increasing sales. Almost all counterproductive monopolies do the exact opposite, which is why so much attention has been given to air fares.[36]

Nonetheless, the calculated lower prices suggest that the industry may still be more competitive—not so much in terms of observed structure but in terms of result—than it would have been if fare and route regulation had continued. Although new airlines may not be forming as frequently as they once were and established airlines may have slowed their pace of entry into new markets, the pace of change in the industry in the 1980s must be compared not with some competitive market ideal, but with the pace of change prior to 1978. As already noted, fewer than 10 percent of route applications in the decades prior to deregulation were approved by government. After 1981, all proposed route changes were effectively approved by government carte blanche.

Indeed, competition among airlines appears to have increased, although competition and consumer benefits might have been greater had not six major mergers occurred,[37] the principal ones were Northwest/Republic, Delta/Western, and USAir/Piedmont). Admittedly, competition among major scheduled airlines declined between 1978 and 1988, at least in terms of one widely accepted measure. One researcher found that the number of "effective competitors" rose from 8.7 in 1978 to 11.2 in 1985 and then fell back precipitously to 7.7 in 1988, a decline of 31 percent from 1985.[38] Furthermore, the General Accounting Office (GAO) found that deregulation led to more concentration, especially at major airports, between 1985 and 1988,[39] although some of the increased concentration can apparently be attributed to the Department of Transportation "buy/sell" rule that has not permitted new entry at the four airports in the country at which the landing slots are controlled and to airport noise restrictions that affect the expansion of the number of airport gates and the entry of new competitors.[40]

Such concentration statistics caused Senator John Danforth (R-MO) to complain in 1989, "The issue is not deregulation or regulation. The issue is lack of competition."[41] At least in the early years of deregulation, however, competition in the airline industry as a whole clearly escalated with the entry of new firms.[42] Prior to deregulation there were 36 noncommuter airlines that provided certified service. In 1984, the number was up to 100. Including commuter airlines, the number of airlines jumped from 219 in 1978 to 419 at the end of 1984.[43] By 1988, more than 200 new airlines may have folded or been merged out of existence.[44]

Statistics on growing concentration do not, contrary to what is claimed, necessarily mean that deregulation has made the airline industry less competitive or that the airline industry has been extensively monopolized. While the vast majority of the new entrants to the airline industry were small (necessarily so since they were new) and many of them have since gone out of business or been absorbed by larger airlines, the very fact that they did emerge suggests that some new airlines can emerge and can be successful enough for the larger established airlines to consider them worthy of being absorbed. The new entrants in the 1980s may also suggest to the established airlines that the threat of competition from new, potentially successful airlines is worthy of serious consideration in establishing fares and service levels.

The most important determinant of competition is not how many independent airlines exist at any point in time for the country as a whole, but how many airlines do compete, or can compete, on individual routes between "city-pairs." Several studies have found that competition at the route level has increased, although they disagree on the extent of the increased competition. The Congressional Budget Office (CBO) concluded that the number of competitors on city-pair routes of more than 200 miles with 25 or more passengers a day increased, albeit slightly, from 2.4 carriers in 1983 to 2.5 carriers in 1987.[45] The CBO's finding is also supported by a study from the Department of Transportation that found that city-pair markets served by one airline fell by 15 percent between 1978 (4,093) and 1988 (3,481), while the number of city-pair markets served by two or more airlines expanded by 45 percent between 1978 (1,266) and 1988 (1,833).[46]

Morrison and Winston found that "the number of effective competitors at the route level, where competition actually takes place, rose from 1.52 to 1.90 during this period (with a peak of 1.96 in 1986),"[47] an increase in effective competitors on individual routes of 25 percent from 1978 to 1988. The Brookings researchers also stress that "the percentage of travelers flying on carriers with a 90 percent or greater market share has fallen from 28 percent in 1978 to 17 percent in 1988; the percentage of travelers flying on carriers with 20 percent or less market share has risen from 7 to 17 percent during the same period."[48] They figure that travelers saved an average of $6 billion a year from the extended competition and the lower fares.[49]

The Persistent Complaints

Despite all the cheery news, airline deregulation has hardly been cheered by a substantial share of air travelers in the United States. One columnist, in a fit of hyperbole, wrote in 1987, "The horrors of airline travel are overtaking crime and real estate on the small-talk agenda. Everyone has a war story."[50] And even Brookings economist Robert Crandall, who does not support reregulation, acknowledges, "Anyone who flies these days—and anyone who turns on a TV or reads a newspaper—is well aware that things have gotten out of hand. The skies and airports are crowded and the entire system is creaking as airlines seek to accommodate the waves of customers brought to their ticket counters by deregulation and cheap fares."[51]

Partial Deregulation

Why the highly negative perception of the effects of airline deregulation? A part of the explanation may be found in the observation that air travel in the United States was never totally deregulated.

Hence, many complaints are misdirected. Airport landings and takeoffs have not been subjected to the forces of free-market pricing. As a consequence, below-market prices for access to runways remain common, and peak-load pricing, which could alleviate much congestion, is rarely employed. In 1987, peak-load pricing was used only at airports controlled by the New York, New Jersey, and Massachusetts Port Authorities, facts that caused Alfred Kahn to note, "The uniform charge for landing at Washington National Airport is 57 cents a thousand weight. My local charter operator tells me that this comes to between $2.75 and $6 for the kinds of planes he uses. When I asked him how he would find a place for me if I wanted to charter a flight to Washington, he said all he had to do was call 24 hours in advance and reserve a spot. No wonder the demand exceeds the supply!"[52]

It is not surprising that a number of carriers that existed at the time of deregulation, such as Continental, Eastern Airlines, TWA, and Pam Am, have since faltered financially or have gone bankrupt. The Civil Aeronautics Board (CAB) was in the business of maintaining a stable airline system, which was often interpreted to mean helping distressed carriers with the allocation of profitable routes and protecting all airlines from price and route competition. Carriers and their employees, many of whom may have grown accustomed to surviving without close attention to costs, may not have been able to compete effectively without regulation. In addition, these airlines may have been encumbered with a fleet of planes and the attendant fixed costs that are suitable in a regulated airline industry but not in a deregulated arena.   *De-regulation caused mergers but prices now ↓.*

Perceptions of Costs and Benefits

The crowded scenes of people and planes at airports may actually be evidence of how well deregulation has worked. Nevertheless, those scenes, along with the deterioration of airline services, fortify the impression that the nation's air transport system is not working very well and may cause travelers to doubt the magnitude of claimed benefits from deregulation. Of course, the benefits of deregulation cannot be measured solely by adding up the savings on an expanding number of tickets sold on more flights. Rather, the benefits must be the net of such a sum minus the lost pre-deregulation benefits for some passengers who were able to ride in half-empty planes, receive high-quality meals, take trips on large planes, and not fight the crowds for positions in the ticket counter queues.

Any process of deregulation will have winners and losers. In the case of airline deregulation, the winners were the long-distance flyers and the losers were short-distance flyers. The losers are well aware of the relatively higher prices for their short-haul flights. They understand that they lost significant benefits from deregulation, although they may not know that what they lost were subsidies paid by long-distance flyers. To many such travelers, a loss is a loss, subsidy or not.

In addition, many travelers—especially business travelers—see themselves as net losers because they never paid directly for their tickets. Their air fares were always picked up by someone else, for example, their employers or clients. These travelers may not see the benefits of the breaks in prices, to the extent that the breaks are detectable, while they must endure the greater cost and inconvenience associated with reduced services and greater crowds and congestion.

The Safety Record: The Positive Perspective

The safety record for air travel by major carriers has, in general, improved substantially since airline deregulation. However, the late 1980s saw a spurt in airline accidents that gave rise to a jump in passenger fatalities (see table 10-1), a portion of which can be chalked up to the increasing carrier departures, landings, and miles flown and decreasing quality of transport facilities such as airports and radar systems. Table 10-1 and figure 10-3 include the basic data on total accidents, fatal accidents, and fatalities for major airlines flying in the domestic skies.

Table 10-1 Total and Fatal Accidents and Fatalities of Major
Domestic Airlines (FAA Part 121), Before and After Deregulation

	Regulation 1965–1977	Deregulation 1978–1990	Deregulation 1985–1990
Total Accidents	41.1	21.6	24.5
Fatal Accidents	5.7	3.8	4.5
Fatalities	163.8	121.9	140.8
Departures (millions)	4.9	6.1	7.0

Source: National Transportation Safety Board and Air Transport
Association.

Figure 10-3 Total Accidents and Fatal Accidents of Major
Domestic Airlines, 1955–1990

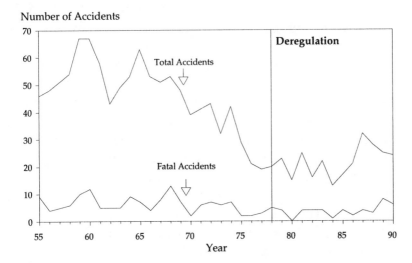

Source: National Transportation Safety Board and Air Transport
Association.

The total number of accidents (including fatal and nonfatal accidents) for major domestic airlines declined irregularly during the 1955–1990 period. The annual average number of all accidents during the first thirteen years of deregulation (1978–1990) was 21.6, close to half the annual average of 41.1 for the thirteen years prior to deregulation.[53] The average annual number of fatal accidents in the deregulated period (3.8) was one-third below the annual average for the regulated period (5.7). The average annual number of passenger fatalities in air accidents in the deregulation period (121.9) was also 26 percent below the annual average for the regulated period (163.8).[54]

However, as can be seen in the table, the average number of airline accidents and fatalities were higher in the latest six years of deregulation, 1985 to 1990, than in the whole period since deregulation. The increase in these counts can be attributed in part to the continuing growth in airline departures, which were 15 percent higher in the 1985 to 1990 period than in the 1978 to 1990 period. The jump in the number of air deaths can also be partially explained by the increase in the number of passengers carried on each departure.

One explanation for the generally improving safety record during the entire deregulation period is that airlines have continued to buy and use safer aircraft, to improve their maintenance, and to learn how to be safer through experience with a greater volume of air travel. Another reason may be that safety was never deregulated in the United States. The FAA continued to exist. Nevertheless, there have always been solid conceptual arguments underpinning the fear that deregulation could lead to less safe air travel. If airlines maintained better safety standards under CAB regulation than those required by the FAA, then it is possible that post-deregulation fare competition could have forced airlines to concede some of their safety margin. The greater volume of air traffic in the post-deregulation period could have raised the likelihood of air accidents above what would have happened otherwise.

James Miller, former director of President Reagan's Office of Management and Budget, is reported to have once said, "Sometimes you have to accept the facts no matter how cheery the news." That witticism may be worthy of some reflection by proponents of deregulation who appear nervous about accepting the tenor of the econometric findings to date.

Sophisticated statistical analysis is not necessary to appreciate the "cheery news." Consider figure 10-4, which shows the wide swings in air fatalities. Figure 10-5 is more revealing. It contains a plot of the air fatalities per billion passenger miles for large carriers.[55] Obviously, the fatality rate was lower after deregulation than before deregulation.

During the 1960 to 1977 period, total fatalities per billion passenger miles averaged 3.13. During the 1978 to 1990 period, they averaged .48 per billion passenger miles, 85 percent below the average for the earlier period. More important, there is no obvious break or even an upward tilt in the fatality rate curve after 1977 that might suggest that deregulation slowed the decline in the fatality rate.[56]

Figure 10-4 Total Fatalities of Major Domestic Airlines, 1955–1990

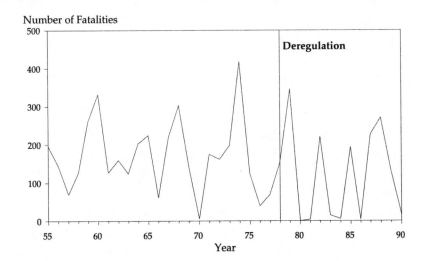

Source: National Transportation Safety Board and Air Transport Association.

That observation is firmly supported by econometric analysis reported elsewhere.[57]

Admittedly, econometric research on airline safety using deaths or accidents per billion passenger miles may be biased.[58] Most accidents, upwards of 90 percent, occur on takeoffs and landings, making the number of fatalities largely independent of the distance flown. Also, the number of fatalities is dependent upon many factors, such as the size of aircraft and the number of filled seats, which may be largely unrelated to the safety measures taken by airlines or the FAA.

Nevertheless, the conclusion of "no effect" has been supported by a growing body of statistical analyses that have used different data series and statistical techniques. M.I.T. economist Nancy Rose evaluated the impact of deregulation on accidents—fatal, nonfatal, and total—of major scheduled air carriers using the number of accidents per thousand departures as her measure of air-travel safety.[59]

Professor Rose uses complicated econometrics to argue that deregulation had no direct, statistically significant impact on airline safety through 1986.[60] However, her basic point is also easily seen in figure 10-5, which includes revised data extended to 1990. That figure contains the total number of fatal and nonfatal accidents per billion passenger miles from 1955 to 1990. The irregular line shows an obvious decline (at a decreasing rate of decline) over time. There is no apparent break (or upward kink) in the downward movement in data points in the 1980s.

While Rose was able to extend the trend only through 1986, I am now able to extend it through 1990. Given the observed relationship evident in figure 10-5 between actual and predicted values through 1986, it is understandable that for the 1978 to 1986 period Rose deduces that "accident rates after deregulation are all quite close to, or slightly below, the predicted trend line."[61] She draws much the same conclusion for the number of fatal accidents per thousand departures during the 1978 to 1986 period, a point that is evident in figure 10-6.

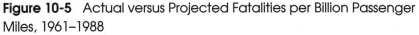

Figure 10-5 Actual versus Projected Fatalities per Billion Passenger Miles, 1961–1988

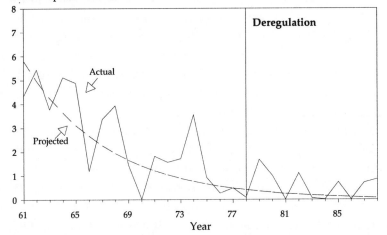

Source: Federal Aviation Administration, National Transportation Safety Board, and author's calculations.

Figure 10-6 Actual versus Projected Total Accidents per Million Departures, 1955–1990

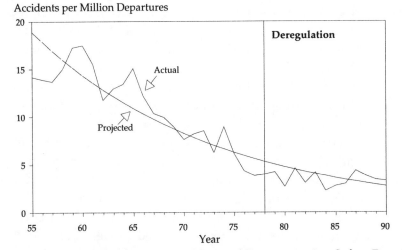

Source: Air Transport Association, National Transportation Safety Board, and author's calculations.

Rose's regression analysis suggests that the accident rate fell faster in the post-deregulation years than in the pre-deregulation years.[62] When her study is updated to include revised data for all years through 1990, there may be one cause for concern: total accidents and fatal accidents per million departures, especially, were above the downward trend after 1986. However, revised regression analysis leads to the same overall conclusion that Rose reached:[63] Deregulation has had no statistically significant effect on air safety as measured by total and fatal accident rates.

M.I.T. management professor Arnold Barnett and Pentagon analyst Mary Higgins evaluated safety records of the eighteen major national airlines that existed at the time of deregulation for the years between 1957 and 1986.[64] These researchers measured the risk of dying in an airline accident by the proportion of passengers who perish in given accidents divided by the number of flights. This means that if 25 out of 50 passengers on board a given flight died in an airline's only accident in a year in which the airline had 100 flights, the measure of aviation "death risk" would be .005 [(25/50)/100], or five in a thousand flights.[65] While Barnett and Higgins report safety failings on the part of several commuter airlines that began service after deregulation, they found statistically significant evidence of improved safety records since deregulation in 1978 for the eighteen domestic trunk-lines that "provided nearly all of the nation's interstate jet service in the mid-1970s."[66] Prior to deregulation, the death risk was 1 in 2.6 million flights or worse.[67] After deregulation, the death risk was 1 in 10.2 million or better. Their econometric analysis indicates no worsening of the safety records of the all-jet airlines in existence at the time of deregulation.

University of California, Berkeley, professors Adib Kanafani and Theodore Keeler also investigated the impact of deregulation on accidents and near misses per million departures, seeking to distinguish between the safety records of established carriers and new entrants.[68] They found that while the accident rate for new entrants was on average higher than for established carriers in the 1982 to 1985 period, the differences were not statistically significant. Hence, they conclude,

Our evidence consistently suggests that there is no difference in safety performance between the established carriers and new entrants who joined the market after airline deregulation. Neither aircraft safety nor traffic safety appears to be any different for these two groups of carriers. New entrants, if anything, appear to be spending more of their resources on maintenance than the large established carriers.[69]

Policymakers and commentators have noted that airline deregulation has been accompanied by the development of the hub-and-spoke system that relies heavily on commuter airlines whose safety records are, in general, inferior to the safety records of major trunk lines. Indiana University professors Clinton Oster and Kurt Zorn recognized a potential loss of safety from the substitution of commuter for trunk-line service, and of small propeller-driven planes for jets. However, they give three reasons why "there has not been a substantial reduction in safety for travelers to and from small communities as a result of the transition to commuter service."[70] First, the safety records of the larger commuter airlines, which have extensively replaced the major carriers, are comparable to the records of the majors. Second, commuter service to hubs is typically provided with fewer intermediate stops than was the case with major carriers before deregulation (whose subsidies for serving small communities were often dependent upon the number of stops), and most accidents occur during takeoffs and landings. Third, many commuter passengers, before deregulation, would have driven to a distant airport, making development of many commuter services a safer transportation alternative.[71]

Finally, private insurers of domestic airlines have economic incentives to monitor the safety records of airlines very carefully. Insurance companies can lose their financial shirts if their rates do not cover the risks involved in air travel. If airline deregulation had made the skies less safe, then we would expect insurance rates for passenger liability and for the airplanes themselves to increase. However, insurance rates have actually been reduced by 22 percent below what they would have been in the absence of airline deregulation, a finding that has caused Morrison and Winston to conclude emphatically in a separate study, "[A]irline insurers perceive that deregulation has actually enhanced safety."[72]

The Market as Regulator

Most critics of deregulation assumed that in the absence of direct government controls on airline fares, routes, and safety measures, airlines would be left unconstrained in the level of safety adopted; they could do more or less as they pleased in matters of safety. First, the FAA's control over air safety was never deregulated in the United States. In addition, airline safety is regulated by basic market forces, namely the drive of airlines to make profits and increase the wealth of stockholders. Safe, uneventful flights are in demand by both travelers and airlines. Most travelers are risk averse, meaning they would prefer to avoid accidents and are willing to reduce their chances of accidents. Airline managers and stockholders understand that accidents, and the injuries and fatalities that result, can translate into liability suits, reduced ticket sales, increased insurance premiums, lower profits, and depreciation of stock values.

Andrew Chalk found that following the 1979 Chicago DC-10 crash, the stockholders of the plane's manufacturer, McDonnell Douglas, lost about $200 million, or 22 percent, in the value of their stock.[73] In a more refined follow-up study, he estimated that accidents that implicated the manufacturer of an aircraft still in production reduced the market value of the company's stock by 3.8 percent, or the equivalent of slightly more than $21 million.[74]

The assessed economic effects of accidents and fatalities on the wealth of airline stockholders (as distinct from the stockholders of the aircraft manufacturer) is mixed (which is not unexpected, given the differences in the data sets and the statistical techniques employed). Arrow Air, whose aircraft went down in Canada in 1985, ultimately had to file for bankruptcy.[75] Other airlines had difference experiences. Air Florida had a highly publicized crash of a Boeing 737 on the Fourteenth Street Bridge in Washington, DC, in a winter snowstorm. The crash killed 74 of the 79 people on board. Blame was linked to pilot error and lack of pilot training provided by Air Florida. Nonetheless, "despite a slumping economy and virtually the same prices a year earlier, Air Florida carried 30 percent more passengers in the first quarter of 1982 than in the first quarter of 1981."[76] Still, Air Florida eventually went broke. On average, accidents reduced the involved airlines' passenger demand by 10.7 percent of one month's traffic, and on average, crashes reduce the firms' equity value by just under 1 percent, or $4.5 million, an amount Borenstein and Zimmerman assess as being "quite small relative to the total social cost of the accident" since there were an average of 40 fatalities in the crashes studied.[77] Don Chance and Stephen Ferris found that airline crashes had no statistically significant impact on the equity values of airlines not involved in the crashes.[78]

On the other hand, Clemson University economists Mark Mitchell and Michael Maloney found the effect of pilot-error crashes on the airlines' equity value to be, on average, substantially higher—approximately $27.3 million (1987 dollars), or about 2.2 percent of total equity two trading days after the crash—and most of the lost equity value was attributed to increases in insurance premiums.[79] These authors also found that the crashes had a statistically insignificant negative effect (-1.2 percent) on the equity of airlines not involved in the crashes and that the advent of deregulation had no detectible effect on the estimated equity losses, indicating that deregulation had not impaired safety, at least as measured by immediate stock market responses.[80]

Markets account for lack of attention to safety, to a degree, and the airlines' actual total cost incurred from crashes can be substantially more than the few million dollars of losses identified in these studies. A history of air accidents can hold the value of airline stocks down over time, while individual crashes (which have already been partially considered in people's decisions to buy or sell the stocks) only suppress the stock values marginally from the already low levels. In short, airline crashes could cost—and very likely do cost—stockholders more than these estimates suggest.

However, this is not the same as saying that markets take adequate or optimal account of accidents. Most airlines support safety regulation as a means of bolstering public confidence in air travel and to guard against the negative spillover effects they all may suffer as an industry when industry members take unnecessary risks. At the very least, the evidence indicates that the continuance of safety regulations might be socially desirable not only to reduce deaths but also to gain the necessary political acceptance of fare and route deregulation. But while the point is debatable—and liberals and libertarians continue to debate the philosophical grounds for and efficacy of safety regulation—it is important to remember that in the United States airline safety has not been deregulated.

The Take-Off and Crash in Near Misses

"Looking out the window when you're 30,000 feet up, statistics are of little comfort,"[81] worried Hobart Rowen. Paul Stephen Dempsey reckoned that by the end of the 1980s American airlines were literally "flying blind" as partially evident in the soaring count of near misses.[82] As is evident in figure 10-7 and as Dempsey stresses, "There were 311 near misses during 1982, 475 in 1983, 589 in 1984, 758 in 1985, 840 in 1986, and 1,058 during 1987"—an increase of no less than 240 percent between 1982 and 1987."[83] Even conservative Reason Foundation President Robert Poole, an avid deregulation proponent, confesses that the run-up in near misses during the 1980s was "alarming."[84] Both Rowen and Dempsey have a favored solution for making air travel safer: Bring back airline regulation. Poole recommends privatizing the nation's airports and air traffic control system, freeing the nation's air transportation system from congressional and bureaucratic budget restrictions so more resources can be devoted to making air travel safer.[85]

Figure 10-7 Near-Midair Collisions: Actual Count and 1972–1978 Trend

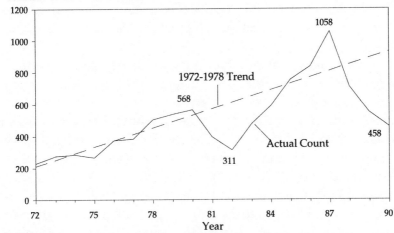

Number of Near-Midair Collisions

Source: Federal Aviation Administration and author's calculations.

A return to the type of regulation existing prior to 1978 is not likely to make American skies more friendly, however, because deregulation does not appear to be a significant source of the near-miss problem. In fact, the near-miss problem for commercial airline flyers has been greatly distorted by the frequently cited raw count of near misses. The count of near misses is heavily influenced by bureaucratic forces that have nothing to do with deregulation.

The Nature of a Near Miss

A near miss is more a judgment call than a source of hard fact. Indeed, officially, a near miss is an "incident associated with the operation of an aircraft in which the possibility of a collision occurs as a result of proximity of less than 500 feet to another aircraft," plus any other report of closeness of aircrafts that a flight crew member deems sufficiently hazardous to warrant reporting.[86]

Of course, not all near misses carry the same risk to passengers, not all near misses are reported, and not all near misses that are reported necessarily fit the required proximity of 500 feet. One explanation for the looseness of the data is obvious; it is difficult for crew members to judge distances between aircraft tens of thousands of feet in the air and at speeds attained by modern aircraft. And not all aircraft operations can be checked for failure to report near misses.

Furthermore, not all pilots judge the same set of conditions as being sufficiently hazardous to warrant reporting. No doubt, many pilots change their personal criteria for reporting near misses from time to time. The real threat of being within 500 feet of another aircraft depends critically on the angle of approach. A head-to-head proximity of less than 500 feet is radically more serious than a tail-to-tail proximity of the same distance. Hence, critics should acknowledge, at the very least, that between 1986 and 1990, near misses that were judged to be critical represented only 17 percent of the total count for the period, whereas near misses that were judged to present no hazard (but were still included in the reported count) represented 24 percent of the total.[87]

Misinterpreting Near Misses

The caveat that is rarely, if ever, mentioned in reports on the growth in near misses in the 1980s is that the rising count can reflect more danger in the skies, but it can also reflect a greater willingness and capacity to report actual near misses. People at the Federal Aviation Administration (FAA) who work with the near-miss data freely concede that the count appears to be heavily influenced by the general awareness of the near-miss problem and by the threat of penalty imposed on pilots for being cited in near misses.[88]

FAA analysts have noticed that if media attention to the count of near misses increases or if there is an actual midair collision there will be a sudden flurry of near-miss reports. In this regard, the collision between a private plane and an Aeromexico jet over San Diego in 1986 (in which 186 people were killed) probably contributed to the growth in near-miss reports in 1986 and 1987. Also, FAA officials report that the growth in the count was probably spurred by pilots' greater awareness of the near-miss problem that emerged from increased pilot training on midair-collision avoidance beginning in 1982.[89]

Clearly, the count of near misses is heavily influenced by the threat of penalties imposed on pilots for being cited in near-miss reports and by FAA monitoring of near-miss reports. Between 1968 and 1971, parties cited in near misses were granted immunity from penalties. As a result, the near-miss count quadrupled to 2,230 in 1968 from 559 in 1965 (the counts for 1966 and 1967 are not available). When the grant of immunity was withdrawn, the number of near-miss reports plunged in one year by 83 percent, from 1,350 in 1971 to 231 in 1972.

In 1985, the FAA expanded its monitoring of near misses, double-checking reports received in their regional offices with those received in Washington. The effect of the new monitoring system, FAA officials attest, was probably an increase in the near-miss count, mainly because of greater official emphasis on the near-miss problem and because of the implied greater threat of penalties for failure to report near misses.

In December 1985, the FAA issued its "transponder-on rule" that required airplanes equipped with transponders, which automatically report the aircraft's location to air traffic controllers, have them turned on when operating within controlled air spaces. The new rule probably increased the count of near misses because, as the FAA found, it "enhanced aviation safety by increasing controller awareness and facilitating controller recognition and resolution of potential traffic conflict situations between controlled and noncontrolled aircraft."[90]

Somewhat surprisingly, the count of near misses appears to be positively related to FAA resources, including the number of air traffic controllers. That is to say, the greater the number of air traffic controllers, the greater the number of reported near misses, and vice versa. This means that an increase in the number of controllers, which may improve the safety of the air transport system, can have the effect of increasing near misses—and inspire political demands for reregulation under the banner of greater safety.

When 10,000 air controllers were fired after they went on strike in mid-1981, the near-miss count took a nosedive, falling by 45 percent, or from 568 in 1980 to 311 in 1982 (see figure 10-7). The drop in the count should not be surprising since the FAA immediately began compensating for its lost manpower by restricting the number of flights and by spacing planes further apart. Similarly, as the FAA rebuilt its controller work force in ensuing years from 5,500 in 1982 to 10,200 in 1987, the number of near misses mounted because the reins on flights were loosened and because the distances between planes were once again narrowed. Ironically, calls for reregulation were being fortified by administrative efforts to make American skies safer.

The Impact of Deregulation

Did airline deregulation contribute to the near-miss problem, which, in turn, made America's skies less safe? It is altogether reasonable to expect airline deregulation to lead to greater air travel and thus to increased risk. However, if airline deregulation has worsened the near-miss problem, the effect has been too small to be detected by standard econometric analysis.

There has been a general upward trend in near misses over the past two decades, but that upward trend was under way prior to deregulation. Indeed, figure 10-7 plots the upward trend in near misses for the entire 1972 to 1990 period, computed from the near-miss data for 1972 through 1978. A comparison of the actual counts with the predicted trend values indicates that while the 1987 near-miss count was more than three times the unusually low count for 1982, it was only about 20 percent above the predicted count for 1987. And the actual number of near misses reported for the entire 1982 to 1987 period was less than would have been predicted for the period from pre-deregulation data. In addition, it should be noted that the 1990 near-miss count was less than half the predicted count for that year, given the 1972 to 1978 trend.

More important, econometric analysis reveals that the upward trend in near misses appears not to have been tilted further upwards to any statistically significant degree by the advent of deregulation in 1978 despite the dramatic growth in air travel reflected in the surge in the number of commercial airline operations (from 14 million in 1978 to 22 million in 1990). The number of near misses in 1990 per million airline operations (21 per million operations) was 42 percent below the rate of 1978 (36 per million operations). This suggests that factors not normally mentioned in the context of near-miss reports have weighed heavily in determining the counts.

The Role of Private Planes

Deregulation critics must recognize that the near-miss count they cite is for all types of aircrafts, including private and military planes, as well as the planes of commercial air carriers. Admittedly, air carriers were involved in 40 percent of the reported near misses in 1990, but over 80 percent of all reported near misses involve a private plane, which means that the growth in near misses can be far more easily contained by controlling travel by private plane, which is what the FAA began to do in earnest after 1987.[91]

The Airport and Airway Safety and Capacity Expansion Act of 1987 mandated that the FAA develop a rule requiring all planes operating close to major airports or in controlled air spaces to have Mode C transponders. These transponders automatically provide controllers with aircraft location and altitude information, continually predicting and updating the flight path of the aircraft. This alerts controllers to potentially hazardous situations.

Reasoning that its earlier "transponder-on rule" had made aircraft without transponders less easily identified and tracked by controllers,[92] the FAA ruled that aircraft operating within 30 miles of a "terminal control area" and 10,000 feet above sea level must have Mode C transponders. The rule did not become effective until 1989, but its formulation was widely known by mid-1988. The FAA expected its new rule would affect few commercial aircraft. However, the rule was expected to affect as many 85,000 single-engine planes and some helicopters (at an estimated total discounted cost of compliance of $140 million).[93]

Figure 10-8 Midair Collisions: Actual Count and Pre- and Post-Deregulation Trends

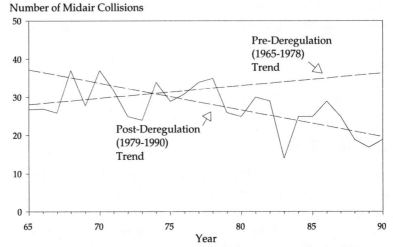

Number of Midair Collisions

Source: Federal Aviation Administration and author's calculations.

As a consequence of these new transponder rules, the near-miss count crashed, dropping 57 percent between 1987 and 1990 (from 1,058 to 458), at which time the count was 9 percent below its pre-deregulation 1978 level. The area covered by the Mode C transponder requirement was further tightened at the end of 1990; and during the first four months of 1991, near misses were reported at a rate more than 50 percent below the low rate of 1990.[94]

Actual Midair Collisions, The Litmus Test

Do the changes in the count of near misses mean that the American traveling public has been, in Rowen's words, "taking a bigger chance than ever before" on their commercial flights? A series of statistical studies reveal that the risk of air accidents generally fell during the 1980s, and the decline in the accident rates appears to have been unimpaired by airline deregulation.[95] However, the litmus test of the implied risk from the run-up and then crash in near misses in the 1980s lies in the count of actual midair collisions, plotted in figure

10-8. The number of midair collisions trended downward during the 1980s—a reversal of the evident upward trend in midair collisions under way from the mid-1960s through the 1970s, the period just prior to airline deregulation.

During the seven years prior to deregulation, 1972 to 1978, the number of midair collisions averaged slightly more than 30. During the last seven years of the 1990s, the average number of midair collisions was down to under 23 a year, 23 percent below the average for 1972 to 1978—in spite of much more air travel. The rate of midair collisions per million operations dropped 66 percent, from 2.5 midair collisions per million operations in 1978 to 0.9 midair collisions per million operations in 1990. America's skies have become safer for air travellers.

The Failure of Incomplete Deregulation

Despite the positive findings on the safety of airline deregulation, the airline industry remains beset with problems: a jump in accidents and fatalities after 1987, a growing concentration of air service at some major airports, and continually expanding congestion at other airports (the total cost of which has been estimated by the Department of Transportation to be $5 billion annually).[96] From one perspective, a major share of the blame for these problems can be attributed to the growth in travel, itself extensively due to deregulation.

However, from another perspective, a share of the recognized air-travel problems can be attributed to the structure, contractual arrangements, and budget procedures that shape the activities of the FAA and many airports. In short, constraints on the air-travel system, within which deregulated airlines have had to expand, appear to be restricting airline competition, reductions in air fares, growth in air travel, and possibly additional improvements in safety.

Airport expansions in the form of additional gates and runways are often dictated by contractual arrangements, called use agreements, between airports and their tenant airlines. To secure commitments from airlines to pay fees sufficient to cover operating costs (such as parking fees and shop rentals not covered by other revenue sources) and to repay bonds for airport expansion projects (the net effect of which could be a reduction in the interest rates on airport bonds), major airports have frequently, and understandably, agreed to give tenant airlines the right to approve or disapprove operating and capital budget decisions that affect the fees the tenant airlines may be called upon to pay. Many of these use agreements, which may cover periods as long as forty years, were negotiated prior to deregulation, at a time when they may not have restrained competition because the Civil Aeronautics Board was already restraining competition.

Indeed, the General Accounting Office found in a 1990 survey that 37 percent of the gates at large and medium-sized airports were leased under use agreements negotiated in 1978 or earlier. Furthermore, 60 percent of the gates in 1990 were leased under contracts that had ten or more years before expiration.[97] The existence of such agreements and the budgetary problems airports face can certainly inhibit the competitiveness of the airline industry for years to come. Such agreements also aggravate the congestion problem, impairing further improvements in air-travel safety records.

The problem of expanding the air transport system—and enhancing competition and safety—is compounded by the fact that the FAA has a potential conflict of interest. Since passage of the Federal Aviation Act of 1958, the FAA has been responsible for air-travel safety and for promoting civil aviation, which, according to one study, makes the FAA "the only federal safety regulatory agency also charged with promoting the economic interests of the industries it regulates."[98]

Furthermore, airports and the air-control system have never been deregulated. Airports remain the product of bureaucratic systems, sponsored by federal, state, and local governments. As such, their operations remain constrained by bureaucratic procedures that inhibit airport expansion and modernization. Reason Foundation president Robert Poole explains that "the tragic Feb. 1st collision between a USAir 737 and a commuter plane at Los Angeles International Airport was caused directly by the antiquated air traffic control system."[99]

Such problems are not unique to Los Angeles. They are endemic to most major airports, mainly because "the FAA is required to buy things according to cumbersome procurement rules."[100] According to Poole, the purchase of a new radar system requires four to seven years. The FAA's 1982 plan to modernize the nation's air traffic control system began as a ten-year project expected to cost $10 billion. But the project now will not be completed until 1998 and will cost $27 billion. The inability of airports to expand, the failure to adopt state-of-the-art technology in a timely manner, and continuing manpower shortages all help explain why "runway incursions" have risen by 49 percent during the three years (1987 to 1989) they have been counted.[101]

Because of the political problems airport expenditures encounter in Washington budget battles, the FAA has not been able to spend all the funds it collects from the 10 percent tax on ticket sales on improvements in the air transport system. The FAA trust fund grew at a rate of about $1 billion a year in the late 1980s. While departures grew dramatically after deregulation, the twin forces of budget and procurement constraints and air travel expansion resulted in a significant drop in real expenditures per departure, as can be seen in figure 10-9.

Total real federal outlays on the nation's air transportation system rose by 8.5 percent between 1978 and 1988, from $4.7 billion in 1978 to $5.1 billion in 1988. However, all scheduled airline departures expanded nearly 45 percent, from 7 million in 1978 to 10.2 million in 1988. The net effect of these budget and air-travel changes was that real outlays per departure fell by 33 percent between 1978 and 1982, only to stay close to the 1982 low through 1988. Admittedly, some of the reductions in FAA expenditures per departure may reflect cost savings associated with greater utilization of airport facilities. However, the growing number and length of air-travel delays and the expressed irritations of the public suggest that a failure to expand the air transport system is imposing real burdens on the air-traveling public in terms of lost purchasing power and wasted time.

Figure 10-9 Real Federal Outlays in Air Transportation per
Scheduled Airline Departure (FAA part 121 and 135), 1975–1988

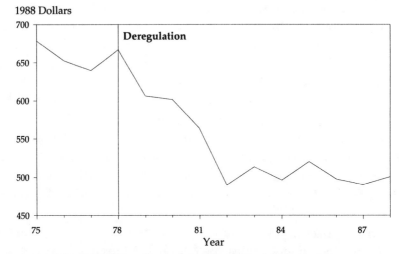

Source: FAA Statistical Handbook of Aviation (Washington, DC:
Government Printing Office, 1990); National Transportation Safety
Board; and author's calculations.

The source of current and future air safety problems, to the
extent that they exist, may be the inability of the airport system to
expand and to modernize, like other rapidly expanding industries.
More dollars alone may not solve these air transport problems.
Airports must have the flexibility and responsibility to collect and
use their own funds. Greater budget autonomy at the airport level
could mean that air-fare taxes are used more wisely, that airport
landing and departure slots are allocated more efficiently, and that
air-travel safety is further enhanced—or, at the very least, is not
sacrificed due to budgetary restrictions imposed by Congress, the
Civil Service Administration, or the FAA.

By way of the Aviation Safety and Capacity Expansion Act of
1990, Congress has sought to break the stranglehold over airport
expansion projects that some dominant airlines have through use
agreements negotiated prior to deregulation. The Capacity Expansion Act would give airports the right to impose "passenger facility

charges" without the consent of the dominant airlines. However, airports' rights to impose passenger facility charges will continue to be regulated extensively from Washington.[102]

The Air Transport Association and the National Academy of Public Administration suggest a different proposal, one that is already successful in Great Britain, New Zealand, and Switzerland. In the version proposed by Robert Poole of the Reason Foundation, the air traffic control system would be separated from other functions of the FAA and privatized under a federally chartered Airways Corporation, a "nonprofit, user-owned, and user-funded corporation federally regulated as to safety by the redefined FAA."[103] The proposal would place the nation's air traffic control system beyond the federal budget and procurement processes and the civil service system. Safety performance standards that must be met by privately run airports and air control systems would continue to be set and monitored by the FAA.

Such a privatized system has several advantages, not the least of which is that air travelers themselves pay for reductions in air-travel congestion and further improvements in air-travel safety. The proposed Airways Corporation would have greater flexibility over the amount of funds collected and over how the funds collected are spent. Political efforts to reduce the federal deficit or to increase expenditures on non-air-travel federal projects would not limit the ability of the flying public to reduce the total cost of air travel or air safety.

Concluding Comments

The scholarly and policy studies published to date strongly suggest that deregulation has significantly lowered air fares and has substantially increased air travel and consumer benefits from air travel. Of course, all of this good news also has given rise to airport congestion. While there was a jump in airline accidents and passenger fatalities in the late 1980s, deregulation has not made American skies less friendly. Nevertheless, critics of deregulation do have a point that cannot be dismissed easily, namely that the full safety effects of deregulation may not have had time to be felt. More time and additional research on the accumulating data is needed to settle the safety debate.

Clearly, problems abound in the U.S. airline industry. Planes have become so crowded that they, at times, compare unfavorably with crosscountry buses. Many terminals are unattractive and congested. In-flight services on many airlines have been drastically curbed. Air travel probably could be safer—at higher prices.

The American experience suggests that many of the problems brought on by deregulation can be averted by a concomitant expansion of the air transport system to accommodate the expanding volume of traffic and the appropriate use of peak-load pricing of available runways and other airport facilities. Policymakers interested in enhancing the convenience and safety of air travel should seriously consider finishing the deregulation project officially initiated in 1978 by privatizing airports and air control systems.

Furthermore, even if the rosy assessment of the safety record of deregulation changes in the future, it does not follow that widely touted "obvious" solutions like airline reregulation would improve travel safety. Available econometric research should remind members of Congress of an important lesson that is easy to forget: changes in economic (including regulatory) policies can have hidden, secondary effects. Regulatory policy undertaken in the name of safety may have the exact opposite effect of the one intended.

Notes

1. Much of this chapter was first published in Richard B. McKenzie, *Airline Deregulation Air-Travel Safety: The American Experience* (St. Louis: Center for the Study of American Business, Washington University, July 1991).

2. See William A. Niskanen, *Reaganomics: An Insider's Account of the Policies and People* (New York: Oxford University Press, 1988), chap. 4.

3. See Bennett Harrison and Barry Bluestone, *The Great U-Turn: Corporate Restructuring and the Polarization of America* (New York: Basic Books, 1988), chap. 4.

4. See Richard B. McKenzie and Dwight R. Lee, *Quicksilver Capital: How the Rapid Movement of Wealth Has Changed the World* (New York: Free Press, 1991).

5. Hobart Rowen, "Bring Back Regulation," *Washington Post National Weekly*, August 31, 1987, p. 5.

6. Alfred E. Kahn and Daniel M. Kasper, "Airline Safety without Re-Regulation," *New York Times*, April 14, 1986.

7. The Airline Deregulation Act of 1978 was a watershed in American regulatory policy, partly because the legislation, along with similar bills affecting trucking and busing that were being considered at more or less the same time, represented a dramatic break with the regulatory fervor of the 1960s and 1970s, and partly because the legislation was broadly supported by political and academic leaders from across the ideological spectrum, from Edward Kennedy to Milton Friedman [49 U.S.C. & 1301–1542 (1982)]. The act was passed in the Senate with a margin of 83 to 9 and in the House with a margin of 363 to 8, and it was signed into law on October 24, 1978.

   Contrary to widely held belief, however, airline deregulation did not commence with the passage of the 1978 bill. More important, it must be stressed that airline safety was never the object of deregulation and the 1978 legislation. The process of airline deregulation involved only decontrol of air fares and routes—pricing structures and entry into and exit from markets—not relinquishing federal responsibility for safety standards, inspections, and penalties for infractions. The deregulatory process actually began by administrative fiat two or three years before the passage of the 1978 deregulation law. The first important break with past regulatory procedures occurred in 1976. That year the Civil Aeronautics Board approved the sale of flights on charters with a required thirty-day booking but without restrictions on fares. Early in 1977, the CAB allowed Texas International to offer "peanut fares" in five selected markets for flights that had low-load factors. It also permitted American Airlines to offer "supersaver fares" at 45 percent below coach class to fend off competition from charters, a practice that was extended to other airline markets. By the fall of 1977, the CAB had effectively reversed its long-established pricing policy, making it "known to the carriers that the board would follow a liberal policy toward discount fares, approving any brought before it in a pro forma fashion," even though the low fares might be destabilizing to the market position of competitors [Elizabeth E. Bailey, David R. Graham, and Daniel P. Kaplan, *Deregulating the Airlines* (Cambridge, MA: M.I.T. Press, 1985), pp. 41–43].

8. Council of Economic Advisers, Executive Office of the President, *Economic Report of the President* (Washington, DC: U.S. Government Printing Office, 1988), pp. 199–229. For a summary of these findings by one of the then members of the Council of Economic Advisers, see William A. Niskanen, "Economic Deregulation in the United States: Lessons for America, Lessons for China," *Cato Journal*, Winter 1989, p. 659.

9. Federal Trade Commission, *The Deregulated Airline Industry: A Review of the Evidence* (Washington, DC: U.S. Government Printing Office, 1988), p. 30.

10. The data cover airlines classified by the FAA as Part 121, which excludes commuter airlines and air taxis. One "revenue passenger mile" equals one passenger flying one mile. A plane on a 100-mile trip with 60 paying passengers (with, say, a crew of four and five passengers flying free) would generate 6,000 revenue passenger miles (60 x 100). The analysis excludes revenue passenger miles of domestic airlines. In 1988, international revenue passenger miles represented 29 percent of domestic revenue passenger miles.

11. The actual passenger miles reached a peak of 102 billion, or 46 percent, above the predicted value in 1987. Also, it is worth noting that the annual growth in miles flown nearly doubled from the 1960–1977 period, which had an average annual growth rate of 7.4 billion passenger miles, to the 1977–1988 period, which had an average annual growth rate of 15.6 billion passenger miles.

12. The consumer and producer gains from deregulation would have no doubt been greater had it not been for the air traffic controllers' strike and their subsequent firing, as well as the twin recessions of the early 1980s, both of which put an obvious crimp in the growth of air travel. The benefits from deregulation also were likely reduced by the failure of airports to employ peak-load pricing (which requires that prices rise and fall with the volume of traffic) and by the failure of the federal government to expand airport outlays and facilities to

meet the growing demand. In spite of the growth in air travel, there has not been a single major airport built since deregulation. A complete analysis of the impact of airline deregulation on commuter and air taxi services is not possible because the FAA and the National Transportation Safety Board do not have the required data series extended back past 1975.

13. As a sample of the media attention to the emerging problem of airport congestion, see Kenneth Labich, "How to Cure Those #@*&1 Airline Delays," *Fortune*, October 1, 1984, pp. 34–38; Tom Morganthau, *et al.*, "Year of the Near Mid-Air Miss," *Newsweek*, July 27, 1987, pp. 20–27; Kenneth Labich, "Why Air Traffic Is a Mess," *Fortune*, August 17, 1987, pp. 54–58; and Jonathan Dahl and Judith Valente, "Airline Delays Rise Sharply after Earlier Improvement," *Wall Street Journal*, November 23, 1988.

14. My own research suggests that after adjusting for the upward trend in air travel and the growth in national economic activity, deregulation may have boosted passenger miles flown through 1986, after adjusting for other forces, by an annual average of 11.4 percent. See Richard B. McKenzie and William F. Shughart, *Deregulation's Impact on Air Safety: Separating Fact from Fiction* (St. Louis: Center for the Study of American Business, Washington University, September 1987).

15. U.S. Department of Commerce, *Statistical Abstract of the United States: 1990* (Washington, DC: U.S. Government Printing Office, 1990), p. 621.

16. As reported in Steven Morrison and Clifford Winston, *The Economics of Airline Deregulation* (Washington, DC: Brookings Institution, 1986).

17. For a thorough discussion of this dispute see McKenzie, *Airline Deregulation Air-Travel Safety.*

18. Steven Morrison and Clifford Winston, "Airline Deregulation and Public Policy," *Science* (August 18, 1989), p. 708.

19. Paul Stephen Dempsey, *Flying Blind: The Failure of Airline Deregulation* (Washington, DC: Economic Policy Institute, 1990), p. 1.

20. Ibid.

21. Ibid., p. 29.

22. Ibid., p. 30.

23. Ibid., p. 30.

24. See Dempsey's Figure 1 (Ibid., p. 30).

25. See Dempsey's data on real yields, unadjusted and adjusted for fuel price changes. Ibid., 28, Table 1.

26. The projected values in figure 10-2 were developed by making

Dempsey's index of real revenue per passenger mile (YIELD; 1978 =
100) a function of time (TREND), and Dempsey's index for real fuel
prices (FUEL; 1978 = 100), an interactive term (INTER; 0 for
1967–1977 and the value of TREND for 1978–1988), and a term to
correct for first-order serial correlation (AR) and then by setting
INTER equal to zero for 1978–1988 once the following equation was
computed:

YIELD = 122.20 - 1.958 TREND + 0.088 FUEL - 0.551 INTER - 0.039 AR(1)

t-stat.   (46.27) (-5.84)   (4.19)   (-2.37)   (-0.15)

2-tail sig. [.000]   [.000]   [.001]   [.031]   [.885]

The adjusted R-squared is .95, the Durbin-Watson statistic is 1.94,
and the F-statistic is 95.02. All variables are highly significant and
have the expected signs, including the interactive variable, which
suggests that the decline in air fares increased by .55 percent a year.
When a term to correct for first-order moving average error is included, the explanatory power of the equation is improved slightly.
While the coefficient on INTER falls slightly to -0.51, its significance
level improves substantially to .003.

The general conclusion regarding the impact of deregulation on
air fares is undisturbed when deregulation is represented in the
above equation by a dummy variable. The deregulation dummy suggests that air fares fell by an annual average of 8.8 percent during the
1978 to 1988 period.

27. Dempsey seeks to bolster his claims that airline prices rose (above
what they would have been) under deregulation by charting the air
fare price index computed by the Bureau of the Census relative to
the consumer price index (CPI). He accurately concludes from the
calculations made that relative to consumer prices in general, "real
air fares [as measured by the air fare price index divided by the CPI]
rose some 50 percent after deregulation" [Ibid., p. 33]. However, if
the air fare price index was an accurate assessment of the
complicated structure of air fares (with a broad mix of discounts) in
the post deregulation period, the total airline revenues, given the rise
in passenger boardings, should have risen by 360 percent between
1978 and 1988, whereas they only rose by 175 percent. Obviously, the
index is a flawed measure of the complex structure of air fares.

28. The model developed for this study predicts that in 1979 air fares
across the airline industry would have been 15 percent above what
they were if deregulation had not occurred. In an investigation of air
fares at airports serving small and medium-sized communities, the
General Accounting Office found that average fares per passenger
mile were more than 9 percent lower than they would have been
without deregulation. Even then, average fares at airports serving

small and medium-sized communities averaged 9 percent above the average fares serving larger communities. See General Accounting Office, *Airline Deregulation: Trends in Airfares in Small and Medium-Sized Communities* (Washington, DC: U.S. Government Printing Office, November 8, 1990)].

29. Ibid., p. 45.

30. Ibid.

31. A determination that air fares have risen, and are continuing to rise, because of deregulation is crucial to deregulation critics. Artificially inflated fares are necessary to substantiate additional claims, namely, that the theory of "contestable markets," on which deregulation was founded is intellectually bankrupt and has been empirically falsified, that deregulation has not been socially beneficial because unregulated monopolies have been substituted for regulated monopolies, and that a return of the airline industry to extensive government controls could be socially productive. Indeed, according to Dempsey, a reregulation proponent, consumer welfare may have been reduced since the supposed unregulated monopolies are not required to charge fares that are "just and reasonable." "Neither telephone companies nor electric utilities can charge monopoly rates despite their monopoly position because their rate and service levels are regulated by government agencies. But an unregulated monopoly [airlines in the post-deregulation period] can charge whatever the market will bear" [Ibid., p. 21].

32. Steven A. Morrison and Clifford Winston, "The Dynamics of Airline Pricing and Competition," *American Economic Review*, May 1990, pp. 389–393.

33. Ibid., p, 390.

34. Ibid., p. 390.

35. Ibid.

36. Since deregulation, the airline industry may have become more concentrated as measured by the Herfindahl-Hirschman (H-H) Index, which rises with greater concentration. A rise in the H-H index is supposed to signal greater concentration; and Julius Maldutis, who has calculated the Herfindahl-Hirschman Index for the nation's 50 busiest airports, found that the weighted average index for all airports rose from 2,215 in 1977 to 3,513 in 1987 [as reported in Dempsey, *Flying Blind*, pp. 17–18]. According to other studies, the six largest airlines increased their share of the passenger market from 71.3 percent in 1978 to 79.2 percent in 1987. The largest eight airlines expanded their share from 81 to 92 percent over the 1978–1989 period [as cited in Dempsey, Ibid., p. 13].

37. Stephen Morrison and Clifford Winston estimate that the six major mergers that occurred since deregulation have added $400 million to passenger travel costs due to the elevation of fares above the levels they would have been if the mergers had not taken place. See Peter Passell, "A Plan to Ration Airport Runways," *New York Times*, June 28, 1989.

38. Ibid.

39. The GAO found that the five largest airlines served 69 percent of the nation's air travelers in 1978, 57 percent in 1985, but 74 percent in late 1988. The GAO also found that air fares at 15 major selected concentrated airports were significantly higher than air fares of a comparison sample of 22 unconcentrated airports. See U.S. General Accounting Office, *Airline Competition: Higher Fares and Reduced Concentration at Concentrated Airports* (Washington, DC: U.S. Government Printing Office, July 1990), pp. 12, 19.

40. U.S. General Accounting Office, *Airline Competition: Industry Operation and Marketing Practices Limit Market Entry* (Washington, DC: U.S. Government Printing Office, August 1990).

41. John H. Cushman, Jr., "As Airline Competition Drops, Washington Takes Note," *New York Times*, June 6, 1989.

42. U.S. General Accounting Office, *Deregulation: Increased Competition Is Making Airlines More Efficient and Responsive to Consumers* (Washington, DC: U.S. Government Printing Office, November 6, 1985).

43. Ann Cooper, "Low Income Customers Discover the Down Sides of Phone, Banking Deregulation," *National Journal*, January 26, 1985, p. 204; as reported in Larry N. Gerston, Cynthia Fraleigh, and Robert Schwab, *The Deregulated Society* (Pacific Grove, CA: Brooks/Cole, 1988), p. 100.

44. As reported in Dempsey, *Flying Blind*, p. 11, and attributed to Pelline, "Bumpy Ride under Deregulation," *San Francisco Chronicle*, October 28, 1988.

45. U.S. Congress, Congressional Budget Office, *Policies for the Deregulated Airline Industry*, July 1988, pp. 15–16.

46. U.S. Department of Transportation, *Traffic World*, December 5, 1988, as reported in Dempsey, *Flying Blind*, p. 20 (Chart V).

47. Steven H. Morrison and Clifford Winston, "The Dynamics of Airline Pricing and Competition," *American Economic Review*, May 1990, p. 390.

48. Ibid.

49. Ibid.

50. Alexander Cockburn, "Flying the Unfriendly Skies of Deregulation," *Wall Street Journal*, May 21, 1987.

51. Robert L. Crandall, "Biting the Bullet on Aviation Safety," *Issues in Science and Technology*, Winter 1988, p. 93.

52. Alfred E. Kahn, "Air Travel Needs Peak-Hour Premium Rates," *New York Times* (letter to the editor; September 22, 1987), p. 22. For an analysis of how peak-load pricing could improve the efficiency of airport use, extend the economic benefits of deregulation, and enhance air travel safety, see Richard J. Arnott and Joseph E. Stiglitz, "Congestion Pricing to Improve Air Travel Safety," *Transportation Safety in an Age of Deregulation*, edited by Leon N. Moses and Ian Savage (New York: Oxford University Press, 1989), pp. 167–185.

53. The data exclude accidents attributed to suicide and sabotage.

54. The fatality data do not include deaths on the ground due to airline accidents.

55. The data in figure 10-4 extend from 1961, not 1960, because doing so makes reading the curve easier. The fatality rate in 1960 was unusually high, causing the data for following years to be suppressed close to the horizontal axis, making detection of a break in the downward slope difficult.

56. There was, however, a slight jump in fatality rate in the late 1980s. The average fatalities per billion passenger miles in the 1985–1988 period was 20 percent (.58) above the rate for the entire 1978–1988 period (.48). Given the erratic nature of airline accidents and resulting deaths, such jumps should not be unexpected, especially when the fatality rate approaches so close to zero, as it had by the late 1980s.

57. See McKenzie, *Airline Deregulation and Air-Travel Safety;* and Richard B. McKenzie and N. Keith Womer, "The Impact of Gradual Airline Deregulation in the United States on Air-Travel Safety" (St. Louis: Center for the Study of American Business, Washington University, May 1991).

58. For criticisms of statistical tests based on accidents and fatalities per billion passenger miles flown, see Arnold Barnett and Mary K. Higgins, "Airline Safety: The Last Decade," *Management Science*, January 1989, pp. 1–21.

59. Nancy Rose, "The Financial Influences on Airline Safety," *Transportation in an Age of Deregulation*, pp. 93–114. She uses accidents, not deaths, because she is interested in addressing the question, "What is the probability that a flight selected at random from the pool of available flights will be involved in an accident? One accident that kills all 200 people on board may have different

implications for the safety of the system than 20 accidents with 10 fatalities each" (Ibid., p. 97).

60. Ibid., p. 100. See her several regression equations in table 8.2.

61. Ibid., p. 98.

62. Ibid., p. 100.

63. McKenzie and Womer, "The Impact of Gradual Airline Deregulation."

64. Barnett and Higgins, "Airline Safety: The Last Decade," p. 3.

65. The authors defend their measure of aviation risk on the grounds that "statistics that weight crashes solely by their number of deaths are vulnerable to irrelevant fluctuations in the fraction of seats occupied yet insensitive to salient variations in the fraction of travelers saved" [Barnett and Higgins, "Airline Safety: The Last Decade," p. 4].

66. Ibid., p. 4.

67. Proponents of reregulation point to the possibility that new entrants to airline markets would lack experience and would, accordingly, dilute the industry's safety record in the post-deregulation period. The evidence on the performance of new entrants is somewhat mixed, as might be expected when the studies consider different samples of "new entrants." Barnett and Higgins found that their measure of death risk was 1 in 870,000 flights for the nineteen new jet airlines after deregulation, a risk level that is almost twelve times the level of the trunk-lines [Ibid., p. 14]. That finding caused them to conclude that—on balance, considering the combined safety records of the trunk-lines and the new "jet children of deregulation"— "between 1979 and 1986, deregulation *raised by roughly 60%* the average risk per flight for domestic jet travel" [Ibid., p. 16].

However, such a conclusion may be highly venturesome because, as the authors recognize, their risk assessment for the new jet services is based on a very small number of airlines and accidents: three airlines out of a total of nineteen studied (from a list of 200 total new entrants) that were involved in one fatal incident with at least one person killed and two "disasters" (meaning a majority of the passengers died). @NT2P = Obviously, sixteen of the nineteen new entrants had unblemished safety records throughout the 1979 to 1986 period, a fact that forced the authors to concede the existence of substantial imprecision and uncertainty in their data analysis. Barnett and Higgins write, "[W]e have *not* confirmed that the new entrants—all but three of which had perfect safety records in 1979–86—were uniformly inferior to the trunk-lines in safety. Even the sparse data available contain hints of heterogeneity in risk levels" [Ibid., p. 15].

68. Adib Kanafani and Theodore E. Keeler, "New Entrants and Safety," *Transportation Safety in an Age of Deregulation*, pp. 115–128.

69. Ibid., p. 128.

70. Clinton V. Oster and C. Kurt Zonn, "Is It Still Safe to Fly?", in *Transportation Safety in an Age of Deregulation*, edited by Leon Moses and Ian Savage (New York: Oxford University Press, 1989), p. 151.

71. Ibid. The impact of airline deregulation on air safety should not be isolated from its impact on the safety of other modes of travel, most notably highway travel. Airline deregulation and the lower fares and more convenient flights spawned by deregulation could have caused a substitution of air travel for highway travel. Any small shift in travel from cars to planes could significantly reduce overall travel accidents, injuries, and deaths. Air travel, measured in deaths per million miles, is more than thirty times safer than passenger-car travel. Clemson University economist John Warner and I assessed the impact of airline deregulation on highway safety [Richard B. McKenzie and John T. Warner, *The Impact of Airline Deregulation on Highway Safety*, OP68 (St. Louis: Center for the Study of American Business, Washington University, December 1987)]. From regression analysis, we estimate that between 1979 and 1986 airline deregulation (separate from a number of other factors affecting travel) increased air travel by an annual average of 11.4 percent and reduced passenger-car travel by an annual average of 3.9 percent. Similarly, the FAA found that an increase in government regulation of airlines could raise air fares and increase travel by families [Operations Regulatory Analysis Branch, Office of Aviation Policy and Plans, Federal Aviation Administration, *An Impact Analysis of Requiring Child Safety Seats in Air Transportation* (Washington, DC: Federal Aviation Administration, draft, June 4, 1990)]. Both studies concluded that automobile accidents, injuries, and deaths are directly related to airline regulation. McKenzie and Warner concluded that airline deregulation has, to a nontrivial degree, improved the safety of highway travel without materially worsening the safety of air travel. The FAA concluded that additional government regulation (specifically, a proposal that would require families to buy airline tickets for their infants) would increase the number of deaths and injuries on the nation's highways.

72. Steven A. Morrison and Clifford Winston, "Air Safety, Deregulation, and Public Policy," *Brookings Review*, Winter 1988, p. 14.

73. Andrew Chalk, "Market Forces and Aircraft Safety: The Case of the DC-10," *Economic Inquiry*, January 1986, pp. 43–60.

74. Andrew J. Chalk, "Market Forces and Commercial Aircraft," *Journal of Industrial Economics*, September 1987, pp. 61–81. When the

implicated manufacturer no longer had the aircraft in production, an equity loss was not detected. In general, Chalk found that the depreciation of stock values was, as might be expected, positively correlated with the number of fatalities involved in the accidents.

75. Thomas Gale Moore, "The Myth of Deregulation's Negative Effect on Safety," in *Transportation Safety in an Age of Deregulation*, p. 10.

76. Severin Borenstein and Martin B. Zimmerman, "Losses in Airline Demand and Value Following Accidents," *Transportation Safety in an Age of Deregulation, p. 52, reprinted from "Market Incentives for Safe Commercial Airline Operation," American Economic Review*, December 1988.

77. Ibid., p. 52. The authors found that the impact of the crash was absorbed in the stock price almost totally on the day after the crash.

78. Don M. Chance and Stephen P. Ferris, "The Effect of Aviation Disasters on the Air Transport Industry," *Journal of Transport Economics and Policy*, May 1987, pp. 151–165.

79. Mark L. Mitchell and Michael T. Maloney, "Crisis in the Cockpit? The Role of Market Forces in Promoting Air Travel Safety," *Journal of Law and Economics*, October 1989, pp. 329–356. Insurance premiums were 34 percent higher the year after the crash, 19 percent higher the following year, and 17 percent higher two years after the crash (Ibid., p. 349).

80. Ibid., p. 346.

81. Rowen, "Bring Back Regulation," p. 5.

82. Dempsey, *Flying Blind*.

83. Ibid., p. 44.

84. Robert W. Poole, Jr., "Building a Safer and More Effective Air Traffic Control System," *Policy Insight* (Santa Monica, CA: Reason Foundation, February 1991), p. 4.

85. Robert W. Poole, Jr., "For Safer Skies, Privatize," *Wall Street Journal*, February 11, 1991.

86. Federal Aviation Administration, U.S. Department of Transportation, *Selected Statistics Concerning Pilot-Reported Near Midair Collisions (1985-1988)*, (Washington, DC: U.S. Government Printing Office, March 1990), p. iii.

87. A near miss judged to be critical is a "situation where collision avoidance was due to chance rather than an act on the part of the pilot. Less than 100 feet of aircraft separation would be considered critical." A near miss judged to be no hazard is a situation "when direction and altitude would have made a midair collision improbable regardless of evasive action taken" [Office of Aviation

Safety, Federal Aviation Administration, *Safety Statistical Handbook* (Washington, DC: U.S Government Printing Office, December 1990), p. 67].

88. From conversations with Anna Johnson and David Briales, Office of Safety Analysis, Federal Aviation Administration (January and May, 1991).

89. As reported by Anna Johnson, Office of Safety Analysis, Federal Aviation Administration, May 23, 1991, who maintains the FAA's near-miss data files and reports.

90. "Transponder with Automatic Altitude Reporting Capability Requirement," *Federal Register*, June 21, 1988, p. 23356.

91. Air carriers are far more likely to report near misses than private pilots because the air carrier planes are almost always under surveillance by air traffic control. Private pilots do not, accordingly, suffer the same threat of penalties for failure to report near misses.

92. "Transponder with Automatic Altitude Reporting Capability and Controlled Airspace Common Floor," *Federal Register*, February 12, 1988, pp. 4306–4312.

93. The estimated total benefits were $310 million, based on an assumption that the new rule would prevent at least two fatal midair collisions ["Transponder with Automatic Altitude Reporting Capability Requirement," *Federal Register*, June 21, 1988, pp. 23365–23367].

94. Near-miss reports for January through April, 1991 totaled 88, 48 percent of the total, 183, for the same period of 1990.

95. There was, it should be noted, a slight up-tick in the airline accident rate in the late 1980s that does not, at this writing, appear to be an important divergence from the overall trend toward improved air-travel safety by major airlines. For a review of the available econometric studies, see Richard B. McKenzie, *Airline Deregulation and Air-Travel Safety: The American Experience* (St. Louis: Center for the Study of American Business, Washington University, June 1991). If anything, airline deregulation may have marginally improved the safety records of major airlines during the 1980s. See Richard B. McKenzie and Keith Womer, "The Impact of the Airline Deregulation Process on Air-Travel Safety on Major Airlines," working paper (St. Louis: Center for the Study of American Business, Washington University, June 1991).

96. As reported in Kenneth Labich, "Airport 2000—A Horror Story?" *Fortune* (June 18, 1990), p. 104.

97. U.S. General Accounting Office, *Airline Competition: Passenger Facility*

Charges Represent a New Funding Source for Airports (Washington, DC: U.S. Government Printing Office, December 1990), p. 12.

98. Robert W. Poole, Jr., "Building a Safer and More Effective Air Traffic Control System," *Policy Insight* (Santa Monica, CA: Reason Foundation, February 1991), p. 8.

99. Poole, "For Safer Skies, Privatize," points out that the airport was operating at the time with a twenty-year-old ground radar system that was filled with outdated vacuum tubes and that it had been out of service for eighteen hours prior to the accident. These air-control shortcomings literally meant the air controllers in the tower did not know exactly where the commuter plane was on the runway. Furthermore, the airport's surveillance system was operating so poorly that day that the controller could not accurately locate the incoming 737 jet. And to make matters worse, the controllers were short-handed at the time of the accident.

100. Ibid.

101. Runway incursions totaled 179 in 1988, 223 in 1989, and 267 in 1990. A runway incursion is defined as "any occurrence at an airport involving an aircraft, vehicle, person, or object on the ground that creates a collision hazard or results in loss of separation with an aircraft taking off, intending to take off, landing or intending to land." Office of Aviation Safety, Federal Aviation Administration, *Safety Statistical Handbook: December 1990* (Washington, DC: Federal Aviation Administration), p. 69.

102. The GAO points out, "The [Aviation Safety and Capacity Expansion] act provides broad criteria for the types of projects that airports could finance with PFC [passenger facility charge] funds: capacity, safety, and security projects eligible for funding under the Airport Improvement Program; projects for airport planning and noise reduction; and projects for constructions of gates and related facilities" (U.S. General Accounting Office, *Airline Competition: Passenger Facility Charges Represent a New Funding Source for Airports*, p. 4). However, the Secretary of Transportation has considerable discretion over which projects are approved, which means that the new funding source will be encumbered by approval delays.

103. This proposal was first made in Robert W. Poole, Jr., "Privatizing the Air Traffic Control System," (Santa Monica, CA: Reason Foundation, November 14, 1986); and extended in Poole, "Building a Safer and More Effective Air Traffic Control System," pp. 15–18.

11

THE 1990s: PROSPECTS FOR PROSPERITY

In his campaign for the presidency, Bill Clinton ran against George Bush and the supposedly dismal economic record that Bush and Ronald Reagan built in the 1980s. Shortly after the turn of the decade, Clinton and other critics of the 1980s declared the 1990s to be D.O.A.—Dead on Arrival. The recession that began in 1990 and the extraordinarily sluggish recovery that began in early 1991 did nothing but fortify critics' worst fears that the years ahead may turn out to be a dismal decade for Americans. Should we accept these pessimistic projections? I think not.

Reasons for Optimism

There are several very good reasons for heady optimism for the coming decade. There are even reasons to believe that the 1990s will be far more prosperous than is widely expected. In fact, the 1990s may even prove to be a dynamic decade.

Distortions of the Economic Record

As I have shown, fears about the economic fate of the country in the 1990s are based on a misguided and grossly distorted assessment of the 1980s. We have been repeatedly told that the country wasted away economically in the 1980s. On the contrary, overall economic activity in the American economy expanded by nearly a third in the 1980s. In spite of strong competition from abroad and a reduction in the manufacturing work force, the country's domestic manufacturing output expanded by more than a third. On balance, U.S. gross domestic product at the end of the 1980s represented about the same share of world production than it did at the start of the decade. The main reason many U.S. businesses were able to hold back the foreign competition is that they increased their productivity at record rates.

Real incomes of the overwhelming majority of Americans continued to grow during the 1980s, albeit generally at a slower pace than in the 1950s and 1960s. Although the spread in incomes continued to expand in the 1980s, as it had from the late 1960s, the average incomes of the richest and poorest American households steadily increased—during a decade in which economic retreat was supposed to be widespread. On the other hand, households expenditures of different income groups did not diverge materially during the decade. In short, most Americans lived better at the start of the 1990s than they did ten years earlier.

People took on more debt during the 1980s, but their wealth expanded also, which goes a long way toward explaining why they could go further into debt. People may have been greedier during the 1980s than in earlier times (a highly dubious claim), but America's greed did not show up in contributions to charitable causes. Americans expanded their giving at record rates in the 1980s.

The tax burden was not shifted from the rich to the poor during the eighties. On the contrary, the rich paid a larger share of all federal taxes in 1990 than in 1980, and they did that in spite of (or perhaps because of) reductions in their marginal tax rates enacted during the decade. Moreover, while the growth in government expenditures relative to the size of the U.S. economy was checked, substantially more real dollars were spent on social programs favoring children and families (even excluding Social Security) in 1990 than in 1980. The growth in government regulations was also throttled for most of the decade, but still regulations grew.

If the country's prosperity is related to past performance, which it no doubt is, then the 1990s should be reasonably good years. The American economy did not perform as well as it could have, but neither did it perform anywhere near as miserably as the critics have claimed. The fact that the economy performed better than advertised should give hope that the pessimistic fears are unwarranted projections from misunderstandings about what really happened during the 1980s. But, there are other reasons for expecting the 1990s to be better than "reasonably good years."

Demographic Forces at Work on Wages

The aging of the baby boomers should continue to contribute to income growth. The wages of workers, especially skilled workers, may rise at a relatively faster pace in the 1990s because the "baby-bust"—Americans born in the 1970s when the country's birth rate fell to historically low levels—will begin entering the labor force in the 1990s. The relatively more rapid growth in demand for labor will likely boost wages.

The Benefits of Competitive Challenges

During the 1980s, many Americans confronted severe competitive challenges from domestic and foreign producers, but there were hidden blessings in those challenges that were faced, often, admittedly, with some hardship. Most of those affected—managers and workers alike—learned from their experience. The most important lesson learned is that Americans can no longer ignore the rest of the world. Americans can no longer seek to meet domestic production standards; they must seek to match the best standards in the world. Competition has become global, and Americans (as well as Japanese, Australians, Koreans, Germans, and Italians) have progressively become caught up in mutually beneficial global economic webs that are likely to become more, not less, entangled—to the benefit of practically everyone.

The fact that Americans have revised their thinking, shifting from a narrow local perspective to a global perspective in the conduct of their businesses, means that we no longer have to waste resources defending old patterns of thinking and behaving. America can spend more time, energy, and talent actually meeting the competition head to head. Those Americans who have not yet made "Quality Job 1" can be expected to be brought, perhaps, at times, kicking and screaming, into the new world economic order that demands that they do so. American workers and consumers will gain from a "leaner and meaner" predisposition toward doing business.

Rethinking American Education

During the 1980s, many American workers with limited education and few skills fell behind. Many have learned that it pays more than ever to stay in school and to make their time count when there, and American school boards have learned that they must offer American students an education that comes closer to meeting the education given workers in other countries. These lessons have been learned grudgingly, but they have been learned nonetheless. Productive reform in American education can be expected in the 1990s, again enhancing the competitiveness of the American work force. Parents will likely continue to be given more choice in their children's education as schools respond to competition from other school boards that permit parental choice and because teachers, strapped for state resources, will need to enlist the cooperation and energy of parents in the education process.

Technological Development

At the beginning of the 1980s, personal computers, copiers, and fax machines (and a host of other electronic devices) were expensive novelties. By the beginning of the 1990s, they had all become inexpensive but ever-more-productive necessities for a majority of businesses. Americans have gotten over the nontrivial hurdle of retraining themselves to work electronically. In the process, many, if not most, Americans have changed their conception of work. Work is now more of a mental than a physical exercise. The microchip has eased the physical burden and greatly expanded the ability of individuals to think, to handle information, and to solve problems. Americans now understand that production in the future will, to a greater extent than ever before, constitute the creation of *new ideas* rather than the reproduction of things. Much will be produced over the next decade, but a lesson learned from the experience of the eighties is that the rewards will be in the ideas, not in the things that flow from the ideas. Certainly, computer technology will continue to improve, much as it did in the 1980s. Some experts think that people will be able to carry the computing power of supercomputers in their laptops by the end of the 1990s, and no one should be surprised if these predictions come true.

In 1990, Americans could look around and marvel at the technological "gizmos"—from Dick Tracey-watch beepers to cellular phones to CD players to CAD/CAM computer software—that in 1980 many did not dream would ever exist. When the year 2000 comes around, Americans will be equally surprised at what they have that they could not envision ten years before. The short of the matter is that not all good ideas were exhausted during the 1980s; a lot of good ideas will be developed in the years ahead.

For several decades, researchers have recognized the continuing productivity growth in manufacturing. They have also found disconcerting the lack of productivity growth in services, despite substantial investment in computers and other office devices designed to increase output. The current downsizing of many service firms, including banks and insurance companies, appears to be heralding the long-awaited productivity growth in services. Any productivity growth in services will free American workers to produce more goods and services.

In the 1990s, Americans will simply have a better fix on what counts and, consequently, on what must be done. Americans fretted as they encountered the adjustments that had to be made during the 1980s—seeking, when possible, to blame the high wage Japanese and Germans or low wage Mexicans and Koreans for the country's troubles and trying to obtain government-backed protection from competition. The fretting was a waste; those who did not take the time to fret (no matter what their nationality) had time to move ahead. Many, but hardly all, Americans have come to realize that the capacity of government to protect them from competition has been waning and will continue to wane in the 1990s. Such protection inevitably chokes off profitable business opportunities abroad.

Loosening Resource Constraints

Economists have long argued that world economies are beset with a fundamental problem: the scarcity of resources. Apparently, the scarcity problem has become less pressing, making Julian Simon, a business professor at the University of Maryland, a slightly richer person. In 1980, environmental activist Paul Ehrlich bet Simon $1,000 that in the 1980s the prices of five basic resources—copper, chrome, nickel, tin, and tungsten (which Ehrlich, not Simon, chose)—would rise. Ehrlich had to fork over the money, because the prices of all five fell. He lost the bet not because he chose poorly but because the prices of most basic raw resources fell during the decade. Stephen Moore, an economist with the Washington-based Cato Institute, studied the price behavior of thirty-eight natural resources and found that "thirty-three experienced a real decline in price between 1980 and 1990; three had no change in price since; and only two, manganese and zinc, had a higher real price in 1990 than in 1980."[1]

From 1980 to 1990, the price of lumber fell by 30 percent (relative to the consumer price index) while the price of paper fell by 10 percent. Also, cement fell by 40 percent; glass, by 35 percent; and a composite index of all metals, by 15 percent. While the price of a barrel of oil in 1990 exceeded (temporarily) its 1981 price by 10 percent, attributable to Iraq's invasion of Kuwait, the real price of a barrel of oil in 1991 was down to one-third of its peak price in 1981.[2]

Technology has had the effect of extending the availability of so-called scarce resources, the effect of which has been lower real prices for them. The lesson to be learned from the experience is that fears that the world will run out of resources are not well-founded. There is no reason to believe that the upward supply and downward price trends for natural resources will be reversed. Indeed, they will be extended as other common resources (sand) and non-natural (mental) resources become more important in production. Hence, economic progress in the 1990s will be less constrained by natural limitations. Progress has always involved hurdling one natural resource limitation after another.[3]

Moreover, economic growth in the U.S. in the 1980s does not appear to have occurred at the expense of the environment. Indeed, the fact that incomes grew may have spurred greater public interest in environmental improvement.[4] Stiff environmental laws, the most important of which was passed in 1972, also had a positive impact.[5] Between 1979 and 1988, the Environmental Protection Agency reported substantial reductions in the concentration of key impurities in the atmosphere: lead, down 89 percent; sulphur dioxide, down 30 percent; carbon monoxide, down 28 percent, particulates (dirt, dust, and soot), down 20 percent; and nitrogen dioxide, down 7 percent.[6]

Global Integration

The integration of the global economy, which will continue to proceed apace in the 1990s, will fuel economic improvement for Americans. The competition will spur Americans to produce more cost effectively. It will also give Americans additional opportunities to draw on the talents and resources of the rest of the world, enabling us to come up with things that benefit everyone in ways not yet imagined. Americans can now easily understand how integrated circuits can have synergetic effects on the productivity of computers precisely because they link up the power of individual chips that, in themselves, are powerless. They have not fully understood that the integrated global economy is having the same effect on a human scale. The ongoing integration is fortifying the linkages among hundreds of millions of human brains around the world, similarly yielding the potential for truly astounding positive synergetic effects for economic development in all countries.

The Fall of the Berlin Wall

Whatever else happened in America during the 1980s, one thing went right, in part because of policies followed then and before: Almost the entire communist world turned toward market economies as the Soviet Union and Eastern Bloc countries broke apart, freeing their people to do as they, not the state, felt they should. By the close of the 1980s, something on the order of half a billion people in those formerly communist countries had been freed from the clutches of their respective state economic plans. Another billion or so people in China had been given partial economic (as distinct from political) freedom as progressively greater reliance on markets became official policy in that country. The 1990s might just be a dynamite decade partially because hundreds of millions of world citizens will begin to contribute more to world production, a nontrivial part of which will be bought by Americans at more favorable prices in exchange for goods produced by Americans at more favorable prices. At some point, once the difficulties of transition to market economies have been solved (a task of herculean proportions never before contemplated in the history of the world), many of the freed people who are highly educated and skilled will join the linkages already established in the highly integrated world economy. What former communists probably need to learn most is how to take initiative without state direction and how to compete on a global basis.

Americans spent several trillion dollars on their military since the end of World War II, just to see the Berlin Wall come crumbling down and the Iron Curtain lift. Those expenditures were an immense drag on the economy. The so-called peace dividends that have already begun to flow, and will continue to flow, from the permitted military build-down will contribute to growth and prosperity in the coming decade.

The 1990s will be more prosperous than the 1980s simply because there will be more resources, human and physical, to produce more of what people want.

The Country's True Problems

Did anything go wrong in America during the 1980s? I have unabashedly focused on what went right—or what did not go wrong to the degree claimed. My intent has been to balance the public policy debate—to show that varied dismal claims about the 1980s do not hold up well under careful scrutiny.

This is not an apology for Republicans, for Ronald Reagan, or for anyone else. I have attempted to correct the record about a decade. If not corrected, the 1980s may unjustifiably go down in economic infamy, as did the 1920s. Reporters and policymakers continue to glibly write about the "excesses of the 1980s"[7] as if such casual references no longer need justification or substantiation—this is hardly the case. The overriding lesson is that if excesses were afoot in the country during the decade, they were in the claims about the "excesses of the 1980s."

Slowed Income Growth

But, back to the question: Did anything go wrong? The short answer is, of course, just as many things have gone wrong during every decade. The complete list of wrongs is not short, but any such list would likely start with the fact that income growth slowed more or less abruptly in the early to mid-1970s, and the slowdown in income growth was not completely reversed during the 1980s, for reasons that are not fully understood. However, it seems obvious at this point that technological developments, growing international competition, and shifting supply and demand forces did place some jobs in jeopardy. And some Americans, especially the poorly educated, suffering wage declines.[8] One of the wrongs of the decade is that not enough Americans saw these forces at work and not enough Americans who recognized the forces at work took corrective action on their own.

Faltering Education

Clearly, the faltering of the American public education system was partly to blame for the slowdown in income growth. During the 1980s, education in America became something of an international embarrassment, with falling test scores relative to other nations the most notable measure of decline.

But the public education system cannot be blamed totally. During the past decade, many public schools have had to spread their limited resources over a dizzying and growing array of social objectives—from providing basic nutrition and nurturing not found at home, to fighting the wars on gangs and drugs, to showing students how to wear condoms to prevent the spread of AIDS. Surely, the three Rs got lost in the political shuffle over what schools in America should and must be. On the other hand, American public schools produce many highly competent graduates, and many of the nation's universities are world class. Public schools in themselves were not the problem, but many public schools contributed to the problem.

Critics of American education seem to believe that the core of the problem lies with government policy. Changes in government policy will, no doubt, be helpful. However, far more Americans need to realize that education is not a good, such as a potted plant, that can be produced and then handed over to someone else. Education must be produced by the active participation of the one being educated. Perhaps as much as 90 percent of the cost of education (mainly in terms of forgone activities) must be incurred by the person who is "hitting the books." All the talk about reforming school systems and of governments spending more dollars on schools pales in comparison with the need of more Americans to hit the books more often and for longer periods of time.

The S&L Debacle

The failure of hundreds of saving and loan banks was a major debacle of the decade that threatened continued expansion at the start of the 1990s. The full range of reasons for the S&L breakdown have not yet been uncovered. However, it is obvious at this point that the growing inflation rates of the 1960s, 1970s, and early 1980s (which were unanticipated by the S&Ls) meant that many banks were being drained of their capital as they were caught having to borrow money at high interest rates at the same time that they had outstanding long-term loans at low rates. Deregulation of the banking industry was, in itself, probably not a bad idea. American banks needed more freedom to expand the range of their investments and to attract deposits by paying market interest rates. Where deregulation went wrong was in being incomplete, allowing banks to greatly increase the riskiness of their portfolios without increasing their deposit insurance premiums to reflect the greater risk. Indeed, Congress expanded the coverage of the deposit insurance at the same time banks were encouraged to take on more risk. Banks were simply encouraged to behave recklessly, which many did. From this perspective, a central flaw in bank deregulation was that deposit insurance should have likewise been deregulated.

The costs of the S&L debacle were, however, incurred by the country in the 1980s as banks financed investments that did not pay off. Those investments involved expenditures such as laying out housing tracks that may never be used in, for example, Arizona. They represent resources that were diverted from other productive uses to be sunk in what amounted to "dry holes." The 1990s can be a more prosperous decade than the 1980s partly because Americans, hopefully, will not repeat those mistakes; the country can have more resources available for doing truly productive things.

Low Saving and Investment Rates

Saving and investment was also a continuing problem in America during the 1980s. Americans probably did too little of both, although the low levels did not give rise to the economic crisis that critics of the 1980s feared. Put another way, if Americans had saved and invested more, the country would, without question, have been more prosperous by 1990 than it actually was—and the decade of the 1990s would hold greater promise than it does.

Part of the low saving and investment levels can be explained by federal government policies. Social Security and other transfer payments obviously crowded out federal expenditures on the country's physical infrastructure and on research, both of which are critical to the future prosperity of the country. The federal payments received by many Americans were probably used for consumption—not saving and investment, as backers of expanded payments intended.

The cuts in marginal tax rates probably helped to spur economic growth, but not as much as they could have. The real tax on the economy comes from the expenditure side of the federal budget, and that tax rate—computed in federal expenditures as a percentage of national production—stopped growing and remained more or less stable throughout the decade. The important point is that the tax rate did not fall appreciably in the 1980s.

Perhaps more important, the potential benefits of the tax rate cuts were probably reduced by the constant shifting of the tax burden. First, personal and corporate tax rates were reduced in 1981. Then, individual tax payments were raised in 1982 and 1984; actions that were followed in 1986 by additional personal marginal tax rate reductions accompanied by an expansion of the tax base. Corporate rate tax rates were lowered in 1981 by passage of the investment tax credit and accelerated depreciation; these features were withdrawn in 1986 when the tax burden was shifted from individuals to corporations.

Throughout the decade, Congress continued to show a willingness to raise taxes. The threat of higher taxes proposed throughout the decade by well-positioned members of Congress no doubt dampened the willingness of Americans to save and invest in response to the marginally lower tax rates they faced. The mounting federal deficit that began to run into the hundreds of millions of dollars no doubt fortified fears that the value of savings and invest-ments would, in the not-too-distant future, be undercut by higher tax rates or by inflation (designed to reduce the real burden of the federal debt and reintroduce "bracket creep").

A part of the reduction in saving and investment rates may also be traced to demographic forces. The 78 million members of the baby-boom generation were saddled with the consumption de-mands of children at home in the 1980s, which probably reduced the overall saving and investment rates. Growth in the 1990s will likely be spurred, albeit marginally, when the baby boomers get their children through high school and college and start planning in earnest for their retirement years. "Boomers" may also increase their saving and investment rates when they realize that they may not have the same Social Security benefits that their parents had.

In short, Washington policymakers could have done better, much better, but that is a statement of the obvious.

Nevertheless, no matter how the data are viewed, it is apparent that at least some Americans lived through the 1980s as if there would be no 1990s, and beyond. Their consumption in the 1980s will continue to hold back the country in the 1990s because fewer funds than otherwise are available for investment in future production. However, Americans who saved little did not hold the country back by as much as they would have had they curbed their saving and investment decades ago. The American economy is not as dependent as it once was on saving and investment from domestic residents. Financial markets have become global. The low saving and invest-ment rates by some Americans simply left open profitable domestic opportunities for savers and investors from around the world. This does not mean that the American economy, as such, will be poorer. The American economy as a whole will continue to grow. It does, however, mean that those Americans who do save and invest and join their economic resources with the resources held by foreigners will prosper while those Americans who resist saving and investing and continue to consume as if there were no tomorrow, will fall behind.

The Fractured Moral Infrastructure

In fundamental ways, it is simply wrongheaded to suggest, imply, or infer that America failed during the 1980s. Having said that, however, it must be conceded that some Americans obviously failed, a fact that stands out in daily news reports concerned with the breakup of families, in the growth of teenage pregnancy rates, in the frequency and ferocity of street crimes, in the growth in nonwork among the down and out, and in the escalating bankruptcy rate—to mention just a few real problems that were exacerbated during the 1980s.

Jonathan Rauch, a young but shrewd observer of the country's economic and political life has observed that Americans (including Bill Clinton) have for too long focused policy discussions on the country's physical infrastructure as if there were no other "infrastructure" worthy of concern, whereas in fact there is something that can be dubbed the "moral infrastructure" of America.[9] There may be differences among Americans over what constitutes the country's moral infrastructure, but most Americans would agree that Rauch is onto something important by identifying five attributes that are crucial to human and economic progress:

➤ Lawfulness and Honesty,

➤ Education,

➤ Thrift,

➤ Diligence, and

➤ Strong Family.

"In the longer term, a society, or an individual, that gets all five right cannot be stopped, absent bad luck. A society, or an individual, that gets them wrong cannot be saved, absent good fortune."[10]

It is clear from the record of the 1980s that America did not get these attributes wrong, but it is equally clear that some Americans got them wrong. A nontrivial number of Americans gave up some of their honor, refused to study hard (or even refrain from obstructing others from studying), spent more than their incomes, forwent the usual level of diligence at work, and reneged on family obligations. These Americans constitute the part of America that went wrong in the 1980s, and they have suffered as a consequence. In the process, they held the rest of the country back and fueled suspicions that all of America was failing and falling backwards, which was never the case.

The real difficulty we all must recognize in acknowledging that the country's problems may be centered on weaknesses in its moral infrastructure is that government may be largely irrelevant to the solutions to these problems. What can a government do to solve the teenage pregnancy problem or the abuse problem or the divorce problem or any of the other problems Rauch mentions? How can people in Washington, or even the local social services offices, be expected to play parental surrogates and remind other Americans—those who have shucked social mores—that personal responsibility for actions taken is a key to their own and the country's economic success? The answer is discomforting: Government cannot do it very well. And we should not be surprised that not a whole lot has been accomplished with the best of intentions by Congressional and administrative action. Economic development has historically been a "bottom up" phenomenon, and the 1990s will probably not break from the pattern.

Certainly, government may be able to make adjustments in its policies that may make a marginal difference, but should more be expected? After all, the resources of government are limited and may become even more tightly constrained in the 1990s. The capabilities of the people who run government are equally limited. Might it not be reasonable to expect that in the 1990s the people affected directly by the failures Rauch identifies will have to find their own solutions, which will likely require that they change their behavior or suffer a greater burden of the consequences.

One of the most important lessons learned from the policy experience of the 1960s, 1970s, and 1980s is that it is all too easy for someone to claim that observed problems are "society's fault" and "society's responsibility to solve" only to find that social and economic problems are extremely difficult to solve if the major burden for corrective action is not placed on the people who are misbehaving. Regrettably, attributing identified social and economic problems to society dilutes responsibility by spreading it over so many people that the attribution is tantamount to assigning responsibility for corrective action to no one.

Threats to the American Economy in the 1990s

The future looks bright for the overwhelming majority of Americans. America can stand witness in the 1990s to one of the most prosperous decades of the century. At the same time, a lot can happen, including changes in policy. Criticisms of the dire economic record of the 1980s are invariably followed by recommendations that the policy course of increasing reliance on markets, supposedly followed by the Reagan administration, be reversed. Americans have been told that corrective action requires that the economy be more centrally managed by government—namely, the federal government armed with a variety of policy tools controlled by a number of new and expanded federal agencies.

National Industrial Management

In the early 1980s, many policymakers and scholars wanted the country to adopt a "national industrial policy" (NIP) under which the industrial structure of the country would be managed by a collection of national and regional tripartite boards including representatives of management, labor, and the community.[11] These boards would identify promising emerging (or sunrise) industries, whose development would be encouraged by an array of government incentives. These boards would also ease the pain of contracting or faltering (or sunset) industries. They would, in the vernacular of the time, "pick winners" and "ease the pain of the losers."

Such proposals were quelled by attacks from conservative and liberal economists, most notably Charles Schultze, who was Jimmy

Carter's chief economic adviser and is a Brookings Institution fellow but who in the midst of the industrial policy debate acknowledged,

The United States does have some old-line heavy industries with deep-seated structural problems, especially steel and automobile industries. But they are not typical of American industry generally. There is no evidence that in periods of reasonably normal prosperity American labor and capital are incapable of making the gradual; transitions that are always required in a dynamic economy, as demand and output shift from older industries to new ones at the forefront of technological advances.[12]

The proposals were all but banished from public discussion by the overwhelming defeat in 1984 of presidential candidate Walter Mondale, who had made NIP a central component of his economic platform. However, while the rubric of national industrial policy is rarely employed, the concept has reemerged in the 1990s as a policy theme in academic and political circles.[13] The proponents want to "manage trade," "manage economic development," and "develop a national economic strategy." They want to develop "cooperative partnerships" between industry and government. They no longer want to pick winners and losers; they simply want to encourage promising industries, and they want to create "U.S.A, Inc." to go head-to-head with "Japan, Inc." with the goal of "leveling the playing field." Herbert Stein, American Enterprise Institute fellow, reasons that

they want government, meaning a government agency, to search more aggressively for industrial projects that will make major contributions to national productivity but that will not, for one reason or another, be undertaken by private firms. Having found projects that meet the test, the government would promote them in various ways. The premise is that such projects exist in substantial numbers and that a government agency would be able to find them.[14]

The supporters of such an industrial strategy paint a picture of a corroding market economy that will continue to decline unless government-sponsored boards come to the rescue. They then talk glibly about how the board will seek the common goals of the country through representative democracy that will give everyone a voice in the country's future. They give the impression that the disarray of the competitive market process will be supplanted by a new saneness that will develop naturally from the cooperative political process.

The picture so painted is a snare. The underlying assumptions are not likely to hold. First, backers of such a policy course assume that markets are led by a brainless "invisible hand," meaning it is all too often unguided and misguided. They assume that a greater amount of intelligence will be brought to bear to solve the country's economic problems if their proposals are adopted—the exact opposite will likely be the case. A relatively small number of people on the boards will make most of the important structural decisions for the economy, such as how capital will be allocated across regions and industries. These boards will replace the intelligence of the millions of people who operate in markets and contribute, through market signals, to the structural development of the country. The boards will not be able to handle all the information handled by the millions of market participants and will, accordingly, simplify their problems by ignoring much relevant information on what is best for the country and its regions. They will doubtlessly seek to simplify their decisions in the old fashion way, by looking to political signals that may be no less guided by dollar signs than market signals.

Second, and more important, the critics assume that unfettered markets are all too extensively guided (or misguided) by destructive competition. They also assume that politics is more of a cooperative and less of a competitive process. Casual evidence from the workaday world of the nation's capital suggests that political processes are no less competitive than markets. Various interest groups can be expected to compete in political circles to be members of the governing boards and to warp the country's industrial strategy to serve their own private ends.

When George Bush took a planeload of business executives to Tokyo in December of 1991 to talk with the Japanese about mutually beneficial economic policies, the country got a indication of how politics might represent America's business interests: It would allocate the chairs around the table to existing business firms that have considerable political clout, for example, the automobile industry led by Lee Iacocca, then CEO of Chrysler. Representatives of small business, from which much economic development will spring in the 1990s, were not on board; and the nonexisting businesses of the future could not be on board because they have not yet been identified. When Bill Clinton held his economic summit prior to his inauguration, a disproportionate number of the invitees were from established companies, many of whom unabashedly engaged in special interest pleading when they had a chance to speak. Knowing of Clinton's interest in greater expenditures on infrastructure, a representative from the home-building industry pleaded to have "shelter" as a part of the nation's infrastructure that would be promoted. Another participant wanted to define infrastructure so broadly that "paid parental leave" could be included.

In short, many advocates of such a new policy course seek not an improved economic game but a rigged one. One of the greatest threats to the economic prosperity of the country in the 1990s is that the critics will get their way and market signals will be replaced with political ones.

The Return of "Jobilism"

"Jobilism" is back. Jobilism is the modern day public policy philosophy that mistakenly makes the number of jobs the key measure of a country's economic success or failure. Its return represents another ominous political policy course for the 1990s.

This idea gained political stature in the early 1980s as the Democrats repeatedly sought to spur economic recovery with massive federal jobs programs, all designed to increase government largess under the guise of jobs. Jobilism's political position was fortified when the Reagan administration began measuring the success of its domestic policies by the growth in jobs. Jobilism faded from public policy discussions as the recovery continued into 1990.

The return of jobilism was heralded by President Bush when he characterized his domestic economic program as having three pillars: Jobs, jobs, jobs. Bush intended to create jobs—lots of them—although he was vague on exactly how, given political and budgetary constraints. Republican presidential challenger Pat Buchanan proposed in his 1991–1992 campaign to save jobs by closing the nation's ports to imports.

In the heat of the 1992 presidential campaign, Clinton proposed to redistribute jobs along with incomes. Almost all the Democratic hopefuls that election year wanted to protect "good," middle-class jobs, curiously, by enhancing union powers to drive up American labor costs. The jobs at stake in their proposals were almost always those that represented political clout. Once elected, Clinton took up the Bush chant: Jobs, jobs, jobs—all of which must be high paying.

The continuing policy debate under the banner of jobilism is as misguided as was its intellectual precursor, mercantilism, popular three centuries ago. Under mercantilism, the key measure of national wealth was gold. The bigger the national gold horde, the greater the national power and pride, or so the public was taught. Mercantilism was found to be intellectually bankrupt when it was discovered that gold was an artificial national icon, representing valuable productive resources that could have been used to expand national production had they not been traded away for glitter that had to be buried in a vault and protected.

Jobs are not a form of national gold that should be saved and protected. Indeed, some of them should be destroyed as rapidly as possible because they represent constraints on what else the economy can do to expand income and wealth.

Economic progress and job destruction necessarily go hand in hand. Jobs are destroyed when a better mousetrap or computer program is developed or when work is made obsolete with the advent of a more efficient or cheaper means of production. No country can afford an idle population. By the same token, no country can afford to treat jobs as so many ounces of gold that must be counted, stored, and protected from obsolescence.

Job creation (and protection) is a favored goal of political leaders because it appeals to existing political interests and is seductively misleading and counterproductive. It is also one of the easiest goals to achieve. To create or protect jobs in the 1990s, all Congress has to do is obstruct progress—kill off or retard opportunities for renewal of American competitiveness and entrepreneurial spirit. And Congress might just do that if protectionist and NIP proponents get their way.

Job destruction is shunned as a national policy goal not only because it appears openly hard-hearted (which, paradoxically, it is not) but also because job destruction is so very difficult to achieve. Job destruction requires ingenuity, creativity, and the guts to take a few risks that others will not take. It requires intensive study, hard work, and detailed knowledge of the multitude of economic circumstances that can only be known by real people in the workaday hinterlands, not Washington, D.C. In short, it requires the types of skills and understanding that are generally absent in political circles but are abundant in the private sector.

Over the past several years, our political leaders and policy pundits have called for a renewal of American competitiveness. They don't seem to get the underlying message implicit in America's failures in domestic and international markets: *America has been destroying too few jobs.* Moreover, they have not yet realized that renewed competitiveness must be built on a commitment to progress, which, in general terms, means relying on people to use to their best advantage the knowledge of circumstances that is known only to them.

Revitalized competitiveness mandates a willingness to replace much that is old with much that is new. It requires widespread (not wanton) job destruction, nothing more nor less. And it necessitates that we begin to view the loss of hundreds of thousands of jobs, for example, in the textile industry over the past two decades, as a measure of the success of the industry in dramatically improving productivity and maintaining its status as world class. Similarly, the current wave of job destruction in the service industry must be seen as mirroring the long-awaited productivity gains from computerization of many services. If the 1990s is to be as prosperous as I expect it to be, America is in for a rude awakening. Prosperity will come in the wake of renewed job destruction.

When renowned Harvard economist Joseph Schumpeter lauded the market as a system of "creative destruction" fifty-some years ago, he meant *every* word.[15] Destruction—specifically, job destruction—is endemic to any economic system that is creative. What we need in this country in the 1990s and beyond is more job destruction, not less—because we need more, not less, creativity.

The communist states of Eastern Europe and the former Soviet Union were good at job creation. Not surprisingly, they ended up with more jobs to do than they had people to fill them. In the process of creating so many jobs, they destroyed not only economic progress but also the morale of the people who work for a living and who needed to get on with the arduous task of making the jobs they have obsolete.

There is a valuable lesson to be learned from the fate of those countries and the jobs policies their leaders followed for too long. We can only hope our own political leaders will soon level with the American electorate on what meaningful progress requires.

The Politics of Envy, Again

Bill Clinton based much of his presidential campaign on the claim that only the rich got richer during the 1980s and that almost all middle-class Americans who worked hard and "played by the rules" gained precious little. I have shown how, as a factual matter, that claim was way off base. Nevertheless, Clinton masterfully played the "politics of envy" and promised most Americans a political and economic rose garden if they would agree to soaking the rich through a variety of higher taxes. Early in his administration, Clinton proposed a new top marginal tax rate of 36 percent for taxpaying singles earning more than $115,000 and for those taxpaying couples earning more than $140,000. He then proposed to add a 10 percent surtax on the top rate of those taxpayers earning more than $250,000 and abolish the upper limit on the taxes paid by the rich for Medicare, which would add an additional 2.9 percent to the taxes of the rich. The net effect of all these tax changes, which were passed by Congress in the summer of 1993, is to return the top federal marginal tax rate to 42.5 percent. With state income taxes added, the top marginal income tax rate was slated to return to the 50 percent range for many Americans in 1993.

The tragedy of the proposed tax policy changes is that they represent a return to the days in which hard work, frugality, risk taking, and success were heavily penalized and discouraged—exactly the opposite of what the country needs to take advantage of the opportunities that the 1990s will offer. The tax changes will no doubt encourage tax avoidance and induce American and foreign capitalists alike to invest their capital elsewhere in the world. Unfortunately, Mr. Clinton and his advisers seem to be unaware of the data reported here that show that the tax rate cuts in the 1980s actually substantially increased the taxable income reported by the rich and increased their share of federal taxes paid.

Harvard economist Robert Barro recently reported in the *Wall Street Journal* that during the 1970s the percentage of total federal income taxes covered by the top one-half percent of the income distribution oscillated between 13 and 15 percent and was close to 13 percent in 1981. By 1988, after the top marginal tax rate had been substantially lowered, the share of federal income taxes paid by the top one-half percent of the income distribution had jumped to 22 percent—not bad for a group of taxpayers that Mr. Clinton constantly tagged as "greedy."[16] After the top rate was increased in 1990, the share of federal income taxes covered by this top group plummeted to 19 percent in 1991 (the latest year of available data). Barro also reported that after passage of the 1990 tax bill, which was designed to soak the rich, the total income tax payments of the top 850,000 taxpayers dropped from $106.1 billion to $99.6 billion; the total tax payments of everyone else rose from $345.3 billion in 1990 to $348.6 billion in 1991.[17] These findings understandably caused Professor Barro to conclude that the receipts generated by the 1993 tax rate increases "probably will be close to zero and may actually be negative."[18]

Mr. Clinton appears to have proposed his tax package simply because it was the politically savvy thing to do. He could offer his broad base of middle-class supporters a variety of government benefits as the proverbial "free lunch" by having the rich pay for them. He also appeared convinced that federal expenditures expand economic activity while federal taxes on the rich and poor alike have no apparent impact on anything, aside for fairness in the income distribution.

How can that be? On the one hand, Mr. Clinton's macroeconomic theory appears to be predicated on the simple, if not naive and misguided, faith that economic efficiency, income, and wealth are promoted more when Washington spends people's money than when people spend their own money. Experience will probably prove him wrong, just as it has proved other presidents wrong.

On the other hand, and somewhat more sophisticatedly, he understandably wants to lower the federal deficit, and he reasons that lower deficits will translate into a reduced demand for loanable funds in the nation's money markets and then to lower interest rates. Lower interest rates will inspire more home purchases and more automobile and appliance sales.

That theory is again half-baked and therein lies another threat to the potential for prosperity in the 1990s. What the economic gurus surrounding the oval office don't say is that the claim that lower deficits spell lower interest rates is not supported by the evidence (as noted in chapter 9). Moreover, when deficits are reduced by higher taxes, interest rates should not be expected to fall. Why? The higher taxes—especially when they are levied almost exclusively on the rich, who do almost all of the saving in the country—will drain away the supply of loanable funds in two ways: first, by absorbing loanable funds (savings) directly, and then indirectly by decreasing people's incentive to produce and earn the incomes from which loanable funds can be drawn. The decrease in government demand for loanable funds will at least be offset by a reduced supply.

Actually, Mr. Clinton's macroeconomic policies can be expected to raise interest rates for important political (as distinguished from economic) reasons. This is because he has front-loaded the tax increases and back-loaded the expenditure reductions, which means that the probability that the supply of loanable funds will be choked off is far higher than the probability that the government's demand for loanable funds will be abated.

If past efforts to cure the deficit by raising taxes are any guide, the more heavily taxed rich will do what they have done in the past: Take evasive action, which means that the actual increase in tax collections will be disappointingly small (if there is any increase at all). In addition, Congress and the administration will eventually become faint of heart and not carry through with the proposed expenditure cuts, as they did in 1982, 1984, and 1990. Even if revenues are raised, the additional revenue will likely tempt Washington politicians in search of votes from the multitude of Washington-based interest groups to increase federal expenditures as elections near.

The prospects of higher deficits as a consequence of tax rate increases is one that only the politically naive would not take seriously. Representative Dick Armey's (R-TX) staff at the Joint Economic Committee has found that every $1 increase in federal tax revenues in the 1980s and 1990 caused federal expenditures to increase by more than $1.

If this fiscal history is repeated, federal deficits will obviously rise with any increase in revenues. The demand for loanable funds will fall as the supply of loanable funds declines—meaning interest rates will rise. The economy will then suffer under the burden of added taxes, higher interest rates, and constrained growth—precisely the opposite of what Mr. Clinton seeks. Interest rates may then fall, and Mr. Clinton may claim credit, but the credit should be blame, for interest rates will have fallen because of impaired economic vitality in the country.

The 1990s harbor the prospects of being a prosperous decade for Americans. Mr. Clinton may just muck up the works. For the decade to live up to its potential, the Clinton administration will need to devise a macroeconomic policy course that makes sense and is more substance than show. He actually should look to the tax theory of his mentor, John Kennedy, who proposed to lower tax rates for the same reason Ronald Reagan did: High tax rates represent a drag on the economy.

Concluding Comments

This book has one message that in various forms has been repeated in practically all of the chapters: The 1980s were not the best of times; the decade could have been better. But, neither were they the worst of times. On balance, the decade was a pretty good one.

My message fuels optimism for the future. There are few reasons to believe that dismal projections for the future will come true. As I have argued here, there are important reasons for believing that economic prosperity in the 1990s will build upon the economic and political improvements of the 1980s. The world, both public and private sectors, is likely to continue to become more competitive, leading to a greater availability of new and improved goods and services at prices that reflect the declining costs of material resources. These goods and services and the incomes they generate might even be taxed at lower rates.

The end of the Cold War, including the collapse of communism, should prove liberating to Americans who have had to shoulder an undue defense burden. The overriding threat is that government policymakers and the voters they represent will buy into claims that the 1980s were some of the toughest of times. This could not be further from the truth.

Notes

1. Stephen Moore, "So Much for Scarce Resources," *The Public Interest,* Winter 1992, p. 98. For more details, see Stephen Moore, *Doomsday Delayed: America's Surprisingly Bright Natural Resource Future* (Lewisville, TX: Institute for Policy Innovation, August 1992).

2. Ibid., pp. 103–106.

3. For an account of continuing fears that progress would be abated by resource limitations, see Charles Maurice and Charles W. Smithson, *The Doomsday Myth: 10,000 Years of Economic Crises* (Palo Alto, CA: Hoover Institution Press, 1984).

4. For a discussion of the connection between economic development and environmental quality, see Richard B. McKenzie, *The Sense and Nonsense of Energy Conservation* (St. Louis: Center for the Study of American Business, Washington University, October 1991).

5. See John Goodman, *Progressive Environmentalism: A Pro-Human, Pro-Free Enterprise Agenda for Change* (Dallas, TX: National Center for Policy Analysis, 1991).

6. As reported in Goodman, *Progressive Environmentalism,* p. 9.

7. One recent use of the expression can be found in Hobart Rowan, "The Politics of Recovering," *Washington Post National Weekly,* August 3–9, 1992, p. 5.

8. See Lynn A. Karoly, *The Trends in Inequality among Families, Individuals, and Workers in the United States: A Twenty-Five Year Perspective* (Santa Monica, CA: Rand Corporation, 1992); and Lawrence F. Katz and Kevin M. Murphy, *Changes in Relative Wages, 1963–1987: Supply and Demand Factors* (Cambridge, MA: National Bureau of Economic Research, working paper no. 3927, December 1991).

9. Jonathan Rauch, "America's Crack-Up: Government Can Wage War, Build Roads and Desegregate Schools, But It Can't Save Us from Ourselves," *Los Angeles Times Magazine,* July 26, 1992, pp. 22–23, 31–32.

10. Ibid., p. 22.

11. Variations of national industrial policy agendas were outlined in Barry Bluestone and Bennett Harrison, *The Deindustrialization of America* (New York: Basic Books, 1982); and Robert Reich, *The New American Frontier* (New York: Times Books, 1983). For counter arguments, see Richard B. McKenzie, "NIP in the Air: Fashionable Myths in Industrial Policy," *Policy Review* (September 1983), pp. 75–87; and Richard B. McKenzie, *The Great National Industrial Policy*

Hoax (Notre Dame, IN: Manville American Enterprise Lecture Series, College of Business Administration, University of Notre Dame, 1983).

12. Charles Schultze, "Industrial Policy: A Dissent," *Brookings Review* (October 1983).

13. See Robert Kuttner, "Facing Up to Industrial Policy," *New York Times Magazine*, April 19, 1992, p. 22.

14. Herbert Stein, "Recycling Industrial Policy," *The American Enterprise*, July/August 1992, p. 6.

15. Joseph Schumpeter, *Capitalism, Socialism, and Democracy*, 3rd ed. (New York: Harper & Row, 1950).

16. Robert J. Barro, "Higher Taxes, Lower Revenues," *Wall Street Journal*, July 9, 1993.

17. Paul A. Gigot, "Oops, Weren't We Going to Soak the Rich?", *Wall Street Journal*, July 9, 1993.

18. Barro, "Higher Taxes, Lower Revenues."

Index